W9-CHV-013

The College Board Admissions Testing Program:
A technical report on research and development activities
relating to the Scholastic Aptitude Test
and Achievement Tests

William H. Angoff
Editor

COLLEGE ENTRANCE EXAMINATION BOARD, NEW YORK, 1971

Copies of this book may be ordered from:
Publications Order Office
College Entrance Examination Board
Box 592, Princeton, New Jersey 08540

The price is $5 per copy, with a discount of 20 percent
for orders of five or more copies.

This book was prepared and produced for the College
Board by Educational Testing Service.

Copyright © 1971 by College Entrance Examination
Board. All rights reserved. Library of Congress Catalog
Number 75-150163. Printed in the United States of
America.

Contents

Chapter I. The Admissions Testing Program
WILLIAM H. ANGOFF and HENRY S. DYER

Chapter II. The Scholastic Aptitude Test
THOMAS F. DONLON and WILLIAM H. ANGOFF

Chapter II (CONTINUED)

Chapter III. The Achievement Tests
WILLIAM E. COFFMAN

*Chapter IV. Descriptive Statistics on College Board Candidates
and Other Reference Groups*
W. B. SCHRADER and E. ELIZABETH STEWART

Chapter V. The Predictive Validity of College Board Admissions Tests

W. B. SCHRADER

Chapter VI. Special Studies

JOHN FREMER and MARJORIE O. CHANDLER

Figures and Tables

Chapter II (CONTINUED)

Chapter III

Chapter IV

Chapter VI

xi

Foreword

The College Entrance Examination Board has long since ceased to be engaged solely with examinations, and the examinations it now sponsors are not all concerned with college entrance. It is not surprising, however, that in the minds of many, the College Board is associated with "the College Boards"—the Scholastic Aptitude Test and the Achievement Tests—which constitute the Board's Admissions Testing Program.

This program, the largest by far of the Board's testing programs, has entered the lives of over a million students in each recent year, affecting the decisions made by hundreds of colleges and the counseling services offered in thousands of schools. It is natural that a program involving so many interests should have given rise to many questions about its nature and value. The Board is indebted to Educational Testing Service (ETS), which administers the Admissions Testing Program, for providing in this book information that will answer questions about the more technical aspects of the program.

It is a genuine pleasure for me, on behalf of the College Board, to thank my colleagues on the staff of ETS who worked so hard and well to assemble and report these facts about the Scholastic Aptitude Test and Achievement Tests. I am keenly aware of the special burdens that William Angoff has borne as editor, and share with all who were involved in the project admiration and appreciation for the grace and skill with which he brought the project to completion.

The publication appears at a time when changes in the Board's testing programs are in the wind, some of them stimulated by the work and report of the Commission on Tests, appointed in 1967 by Richard Pearson, former President of the Board, "to review all of the Board's existing examinations, gather evidence of the need for change, and consider what tests may be needed a decade hence." This book shows that significant changes have taken place time after time in the Board's college entrance tests, and it is fair to assume that further changes may well be necessary if the program is to continue to fit the needs of colleges, schools, and students. The resourcefulness and talent underlying the techniques described in this book offer promise that the best possible efforts will be brought to bear on the development of whatever new tests and techniques the needs of the future demand.

John A. Valentine
College Entrance Examination Board
September 1970

Preface

This report was prepared for the specialist who needs technical information about the Admissions Testing Program of the College Entrance Examination Board. It brings together the findings of a considerable number of studies of the Scholastic Aptitude Test (SAT) and the Achievement Tests. It assumes a reader fairly well acquainted with the concepts and statistics of educational measurement.

Three publications might be considered the book's predecessors: *College Board Scores, Their Use and Interpretation, No. 1*, published in 1953; *College Board Scores, Their Use and Interpretation, No. 2*, published in 1955; and *1957 Supplement to College Board Scores, No. 2*. These publications are a compendium of available information on the College Board Admissions Testing Program up to 1957. The present book occasionally refers to the earlier documents, but focuses mainly on more recent data.

The emphasis of this book is also somewhat different from that of its predecessors. The earlier publications were, in a sense, "how to do it" books. Their purpose was to describe how the tests might properly be used in admissions and guidance and to provide data needed for interpreting the test scores. To a considerable extent, this function has been taken over by *College Board Score Reports: A Guide for Counselors and Admissions Officers*, which is revised annually and widely distributed. Mention should also be made of the computation manual, *Predicting College Grades*, published in 1961, and the *Manual of Freshman Class Profiles*, which was published until 1969, when it was incorporated in *The College Handbook*.

These progeny of the old use-and-interpretation books retain some of the "how to do it" emphasis of their ancestors, but tend to be more interpretive than explicative. They do not, however, provide all the data needed for a comprehensive technical evaluation of the tests. The aim of this book is to fill that gap.

The Board's Admissions Testing Program must respond effectively to a variety of unique and complex demands. In order to indicate the setting within which the program operates, the first chapter describes the program as a whole—its history, how it is organized, the unique demands it faces, and technical matters involved in its operation that arise from the demands.

The second chapter discusses the SAT, the third is about the Achievement Tests. The fourth chapter interprets summary statistics for various subgroups of students, and the fifth reports on some of the extensive validity studies of the admissions tests. The sixth and final chapter summarizes the major findings of special studies that have been made in connection with the SAT and the Achievement Tests.

Although there is, quite properly, an interrelationship among the topics covered in the various chapters, the chapters were written independently with the intent that each would stand as an integral unit, containing all the material relevant to it. However, since some material, especially that having to do with technical procedures, has relevance to more than one chapter, there is inevitably some repetition across chapters.

The authors were chosen for their special competence in the subject of their chapters, but the book as a whole is the product of many other persons, most of whom are connected in one way or another with the Admissions Testing Program. In fact, the contributors include a substantial number of the staff members of the College Board and Educational Testing Service, and for this reason it would be practically impossible to list them in this preface for the credit they richly merit.

Especially helpful were those individuals who served with me on the review committee, some of whom were also chapter authors: William E. Coffman, John M. Duggan, Henry S. Dyer, William B. Schrader, Robert J. Solomon, and John A. Valentine.

Additionally, the following members of the College Board Committee of Examiners in Aptitude Testing were of great aid in reviewing chapters in manuscript form: Carl Bereiter, Frederick B. Davis, John R. Hills, Julian C. Stanley (Chairman), Warren S. Torgerson, and Dean K. Whitla. A special debt of gratitude is owed to David E. Loye for his able editorial assistance and to the staff of the ETS publications division for coordinating publication of the book.

The Admissions Testing Program is revised continually to meet changing conditions. Thus, it can be expected that this book, which describes the program, will be revised as necessary to report new developments in the program and to reflect the results of research on new as well as old problems.

William H. Angoff
Educational Testing Service
September 1970

CHAPTER I

The Admissions Testing Program

WILLIAM H. ANGOFF and HENRY S. DYER

Historical background

The College Entrance Examination Board was organized during a meeting held at Columbia University in New York on November 17, 1900. The move culminated efforts over several years in this direction by the Association of Colleges and Preparatory Schools of the Middle States and Maryland, and a number of educators in the East, notably Nicholas Murray Butler of Columbia and Charles W. Eliot of Harvard. The event was, according to the Board's first historian, the first organized "attempt to introduce law and order into an educational anarchy which toward the close of the nineteenth century had become exasperating, indeed intolerable, to schoolmasters." (Fuess, 1950, p. 3.) *

At this time there was, in the opinion of the founders of the Board, appallingly little agreement among the colleges about the types of subject-matter preparation and standards of proficiency required of the applicants. One headmaster, for example, complained that out of 40 or so boys preparing for college in his school, he had, in reality, more than 20 different classes. The effect of this diversity on the secondary schools was to make the task of preparing their students for college an extremely difficult one, and made the task of the student who was not sure which college he hoped to attend difficult and confusing as well.

In its attempt, then, to accomplish its purpose and introduce an order into the transition from school to college, the College Board established the beginnings of a system of syllabi or "course requirements" on which schools and colleges could agree, and which might form the basis of a system of examinations offering the uniformity that was so badly needed. That is to say, the examinations would be uniform in subject matter and uniformly administered at uniform times, but held in many places to meet the convenience of the students, and they would be uniformly graded. It was expected

---

*The authors wish to acknowledge assistance provided by the outline, and, in many instances, the particular phrasing used in Dr. Fuess' excellent overview of the Board's history. They also wish to acknowledge the invaluable source of information provided by the College Board's Annual Reports.

that a system of examinations of this sort would effect marked savings of time, money, and effort in administering college admissions, that it would greatly aid the work of the secondary schools by reducing confusion and easing the strain on students, and that it would represent a cooperative effort of a group of colleges and secondary schools to achieve a set of common goals without asking the colleges to surrender their prerogatives as to the particular examinations they required of their applicants or the manner in which they might wish to select their students.

It is important to recognize that the examinations were secondary to the main purpose of the Board, which was to provide a channel of communication between the schools and colleges and to encourage a degree of uniformity in the secondary school curriculum. On the other hand, it is more than likely that these purposes would never have been achieved without the instrumentality of the examination system which, upon acceptance by the colleges as a way of setting standards, effectively paved the way for the introduction of uniform curriculums in the schools.

In its first year of operation the College Board held essay examinations in nine subjects: English, French, German, Latin, Greek, history, mathematics, chemistry, and physics. The definition of the requirements in each subject was taken from the recommendation of the professional association in each subject-matter area. The substance of each examination was then determined by a carefully selected committee of examiners, consisting of well-known teachers and scholars in the leading colleges and secondary schools in the East, who met to confer on the general content and structure of the examinations and to decide on the specific questions to be asked. After extensive preparation, the first examinations were finally administered during the week of June 17, 1901, to 973 candidates at 69 testing centers. Thus, although the Board was as yet far from being a national institution—758 of the 973 candidates were seeking admission to either Columbia or Barnard—it was at least a going operation with the beginnings of a mechanism for continuation.

As with the committees of examiners, committees of readers were also chosen with care. These committees, one in each subject, were assembled in the Columbia University Library and graded the papers in accordance with a procedure that had been worked out and agreed on in advance. A total of 7,889 examination papers, averaging over eight papers per candidate, were read and graded on a percentage-type scale, in which the designations Excellent, Good, Doubtful, Poor, and Very Poor were attached respectively to the ratings 90-100, 75-89, 60-74, 40-59, and below 40. Special attention was given to papers that were originally given grades below 60. These were always reread and often discussed at length.

In the second year, Spanish, botany, geography, and drawing were added to the list of examination subjects. In 1902 the number of candidates rose to 1,362, a 40 percent increase over the preceding year. Thereafter growth was regular and continuous. In the course of the first decade additional colleges became members of the Board, and by 1910, as a consequence of the growth in membership, the number of candidates had increased to 3,731.

An important early development was the creation of a Committee of Review for the College Board as a whole. Its main function was to examine the requirements in each subject and arrange with the committees of examiners for modifying the requirements whenever this seemed desirable. It soon became clear that the very fact of the committee's existence had become an important factor in the development of the secondary school curriculum, for it had the effect of moving the schools and colleges toward a badly needed system of uniform standards. However, like the establishment of the Board itself, this change was not universally regarded as an unmixed blessing; many of the secondary schools and colleges regarded the movement toward uniform standards as a dangerous encroachment on their autonomy. In 1910, therefore, partly in response to this type of pressure, the evaluative designations for percentage grades that had been introduced in the first year of the Board's operations were dropped, and schools and colleges were left free to attach whatever evaluations they considered appropriate to the various numerical grades.

During the second decade of the Board's existence the philosophy of examinations itself, especially for admission to college, began to change, gravitating toward the idea of "comprehensive examinations," in which students would not be asked to repeat the facts that they had learned in school but to demonstrate an understanding of the relation of discrete facts to one another, to generalize the facts into working principles, and to apply them to new and unexpected situations. This development—the "New Plan," as it was called— provoked violent objections from the conservatives who insisted that it would be impossible to prepare students for the examinations, that it would be difficult to grade the examinations, and that examinations of this sort would place a premium on superficial cleverness at the expense of scholarship. At the same time the

"New Plan" also tended to discourage attempts to out-guess the examinations and to predict the particular test questions that would appear in them.

By 1925 the College Board was ready to enter a new era. Stimulated by the World War I Committee for Classification of Personnel in the Army and its work in the testing of "general intelligence," the Board established a Commission to investigate the relevance of these new psychological tests to the problem of college admissions, and on its recommendation appointed an Advisory Committee of experts, including Carl C. Brigham, Henry T. Moore, and Robert M. Yerkes, to formulate a suitable test development approach. In April 1925 the Board accepted the recommendation that the psychological tests be administered in 1926 and appointed a committee of five with Professor Brigham at its head to prepare and score the tests. Within a short time the Brigham Committee produced a manual on what they called the "Scholastic Aptitude Test," explicitly distinguishing it from tests of achievement in school subjects but disclaiming any intention to measure "general intelligence" or "general mental alertness." In their preface to the manual they introduced a paragraph which expressed a point of view that is still regarded today as highly relevant to the use of test scores:

"The present state of all efforts of men to measure or in any way estimate the worth of other men, or to evaluate the results of their nurture, or to reckon their potential possibilities does not warrant any certainty of prediction . . . This additional test now made available through the instrumentality of the College Entrance Examination Board may help to resolve a few perplexing problems, but it should be regarded merely as a supplementary record. To place too great emphasis on test scores is as dangerous as the failure properly to evaluate any score or rank in conjunction with other measures and estimates which it supplements." (Brigham, 1926, pp. 44-45.)

The first College Board Scholastic Aptitude Test (SAT), a multiple-choice examination for the most part, was added to the College Board Program and administered on June 23, 1926, to 8,040 candidates. During the first two years, it consisted of nine subtests: Definitions, Arithmetical Problems, Classification, Artificial Language, Antonyms, Number Series, Analogies, Logical Inference, and Paragraph Reading. In 1928 these were reduced to seven and a year later to six. In 1929 Dr. Brigham decided that it had become necessary to divide the SAT into two separate sections, one measuring verbal aptitude and the other measuring mathematical aptitude. The decision to report two separate scores was made in order to give differential weight to verbal and mathematical aptitudes in accordance with the nature of the college to which the candidate was applying, and in some instances, in accordance with the nature of the curriculum within the college.

The early 1930s brought additional changes. The Board moved still further toward developing comprehensive examinations in each subject that would call upon a candidate's ability to integrate material that he had learned from various sources in solving examination problems, rather than merely to recall and reproduce isolated bits of information. The Board also began to express more active interest in experimentation and tryout. They also concentrated on gaining more consistency in their operation. It had been observed, for example, that the number of candidates earning passing grades was fluctuating much too widely from one year to another. Since it seemed reasonable to assume that the candidate populations were more stable than were the difficulties of the tests, it was decided to fix the proportion passing each test and not allow it to vary from year to year as it had in the past.

The period of the middle 1930s was a trying one for the Board. The volume of June candidates had dropped over 35 percent in the six years from 1931 to 1936, and the Board was under serious criticism by the secondary schools that were chafing under the restrictions imposed on their curriculums. In response to pressures from the schools, the new requirements were broadened to stress general principles and large aspects of the curriculum rather than the detailed subject-matter material.

Technical aspects of test construction also received increasing emphasis. For example, it was felt that the examinations should not represent a mere accident of the selection of questions, but a wide variety of areas within each subject, yielding a score that would adequately reflect the candidate's ability and training. It was also felt that attention needed to be given to the reliability of the reading process as well as to the methods of formulating the questions without sacrificing attention to the production of a set of examinations that would continue to have a wholesome influence on the schools.

In 1937, for the first time, an additional administration was instituted—to be held in April, principally for scholarship applicants. For the first time also, wholly objective Achievement Tests were introduced at this administration—a move that accelerated the scoring and reporting process, improved test reliability, and permitted the examination of a greater variety of test content. In 1938 the April administration was extended to include applicants for admission to college who were not scholarship applicants. From then on the April administration gained in prominence until in 1940 the number of students taking the SAT in April was larger than the number taking it in June. Because of this increase in the relative size (and importance) of the April administration it was felt necessary to provide a means of comparing SAT scores on the April and June tests directly. Beginning in June 1941, then, the scores on every form of the SAT were equated directly to the scores on some preceding form of the SAT, and ultimately and indirectly to the April 1941 form. The group tested in April 1941 thus became the standardization group, defining the continuing scale in terms of which scores on all future forms of the SAT would be expressed.

In 1937 the Achievement Tests were first reported on a scale with a mean of 500 and standard deviation of 100 (like the scale which had been in use for the SAT since its introduction in 1926) and rescaled each year on the new candidate group. Two years later, beginning with the April administration, adjustments were made in the scales for each of the Achievement Tests in accordance with the level and dispersion of the group choosing to take that test, as reflected by the relevant (verbal or mathematical) section of the SAT.

With the outbreak of World War II, Harvard, Yale, and Princeton decided as an emergency action to accelerate their program of studies and begin their college year in June or July. This shift made it necessary for their 1942 candidates to take the April Achievement Tests, which were now all objective, instead of sitting for the six-day June Achievement Test program, which in 1941 still consisted of essay examinations. It soon became evident that in order to accommodate itself to these sudden changes, the Board would have to confirm a decision that had been under consideration even before the outbreak of hostilities and commit itself broadly to the plan that Harvard, Yale, and Princeton had adopted on an emergency basis. This development, which was originally intended as a temporary measure in response to the nation's entry into the war, actually marked the end of the June essay-type examinations after continuous use for 41 years.

At the same time, the Board adapted itself in other ways to the needs of the nation at war. The Board developed the V-12 Testing Program for use in the selection of high school graduates for officer candidate training. It developed tests for the U.S. Armed Forces Institute and the Army Specialized Training Program, and involved itself in other operational and advisory capacities to the Government. Toward the end of the war, in anticipation of the large numbers of veterans returning from the war who would be seeking post-secondary school education, it prepared tests designed for use in college admission of veteran applicants. It furnished tests for scholarship awards sponsored by the Westinghouse Company and constructed special tests for the Pepsi-Cola Scholarship Program. And it also assisted in the preparation of qualifying examinations for the Foreign Service, the Military Academy, the Naval Academy, the Coast Guard Academy, and the Bureau of Naval Personnel.

In 1947, with the formation of Educational Testing Service (ETS) and a greater focusing of the Board's interests and activities on the transition from secondary school to college, special testing programs were turned over to ETS for management according to the Board's specifications. In subsequent years some of these programs, like the program for the military and naval academies, were incorporated within the general Admissions Testing Program of the College Board. (At the present time, all of the service academies are members of the College Board and require its tests of their applicants.) Special scholarship programs, similar to those previously offered by Westinghouse and Pepsi-Cola, also make use of the College Board tests and are managed in behalf of the Board by the College Scholarship Service staff at ETS.

By now, some 70 years after its formation, the College Board has become a truly national organization. It has also broadened its perspective in an effort to respond to the greater variety of demands on the educational facilities of the country. In addition to the SAT and Achievement Tests, which are the principal tests of its Admissions Testing Program, the Board also offers the Preliminary Scholastic Aptitude Test, the Advanced Placement Examination Program, the College Placement Tests Program, the Comparative Guidance and Placement Program, and the College-Level Examination Program—CLEP, as it is known. The last is a program of credit by examination for unaffiliated students, and can also be used for evaluating students who want to transfer from the lower to the upper division of a college, or from one college to another.

The College Board has also developed a program of aptitude and achievement tests in Spanish for Spanish-speaking students who may be applying for admission to universities in Puerto Rico or in the continental United States. It has developed an English-language aptitude test for African students applying for scholarships in American universities (the ASPAU program). It offers, with the joint sponsorship of ETS, the Test of English as a Foreign Language (TOEFL), which measures the proficiency of foreign students in the English language. The Board also operates the College Scholarship Service, which provides a service for determining the need of students applying for financial aid and assists in the administration of scholarship programs. Finally, the Board has a program of guidance services, a program of seminars for admissions officers and another for guidance counselors, and a validity studies computation service.

At the present time, as opportunities for post-secondary education are being widely extended to youths who in the past would not have been college-bound, the Board through its Commission on Tests is re-examining its test offerings to see if they may be modified and extended to assess a wider range of talent.

Administrative considerations

The size and complexity of the Admissions Testing Program and the variety of the demands upon it generate a great range of administrative and psychometric problems, each requiring special solutions. This section of the chapter will describe the general nature of the program, the problems and conditions of its area of operation, and its administrative solutions. Similarly, the next section will describe its technical solutions for the administrative and technical demands of the program and will set the stage for more detailed discussions in subsequent chapters.

Nature of the program

The College Board Admissions Testing Program, as of the 1968-69 year, consisted of a Scholastic Aptitude Test (the SAT) and 15 Achievement Tests covering English (Composition and Literature), six foreign languages (French, German, Hebrew, Latin, Russian, and Spanish), two branches of the social studies (American History and Social Studies, and European History and World Cultures), two levels of mathematics (Level I and Level II), and three sciences (Biology, Chemistry, and Physics). The SAT is a three-hour test that yields a verbal score and a mathematical score. The Achievement Tests are each one hour in length. They are given in a single three-hour test session, during which a candidate may take any one, two, or three tests at one sitting. Each test yields a single score.

During the 1968-69 academic year, the program's tests were administered as follows: The SAT was given in the morning on six Saturdays during the academic year—in November, December, January, March, May, and July; the Achievement Tests were offered in the afternoon of each of these dates, except the one in November. Sunday sessions were also provided after each of the six Saturday test dates to accommodate candidates who observe the Sabbath on Saturday. Depending upon college admission requirements, a candidate could take the SAT on one date and the Achievement Tests on another date, although both types of tests may be taken on the five dates when both are offered and many candidates do take them both on the same date. Virtually all candidates take the SAT, and in the 1968-69 year about 40 percent of them took the Achievement Tests as well.

As an adjunct to the Admissions Testing Program, a series of Supplementary Achievement Tests was given on a single date in February in any secondary school that wished to administer the tests to its own students. The series consisted of five 30-minute listening comprehension tests in five foreign languages (French, German, Italian, Russian, and Spanish), a 90-minute free-response test in Greek, and a 60-minute objective test in Italian. They were available to candidates who registered for the regular Achievement Tests during the testing year.*

---

*Beginning in the 1970-71 year, new listening-reading Achievement Tests in French, German, Italian, Russian, and Spanish were introduced into the regular Admissions Testing Program. The only Supplementary Achievement Test offered in 1970-71 is the Greek Test. For detailed information on the scope and content of the Admissions Testing Program, see the latest editions of the following: *Bulletin of Information, Scholastic Aptitude Test, Achievement Tests; A Description of the College Board Scholastic Aptitude Test;* and *A Description of the College Board Achievement Tests.* These may be obtained free of charge by writing to: College Entrance Examination Board, Box 592, Princeton, N. J. 08540.

As of the 1968-69 academic year, 834 colleges were members of the College Board, and practically all of them required their applicants to take at least the Scholastic Aptitude Test. About 350 of the then member colleges required some or all of their applicants to submit Achievement Test scores as well, either for use in admissions decisions or for course placement, or for both purposes. Some colleges specified the particular Achievement Tests to be taken, but most permitted the applicant some freedom of choice. Although there was considerable variation among colleges as to the latest test date for which they would accept test scores, there was an increasing trend toward acceptance of earlier (junior-year) SAT and Achievement Test scores for use in admissions decisions, whether or not the student was applying under an early decision plan. Many students also took the Admissions Tests in March or May of their junior year for guidance and practice and repeated them in December or January of their senior year. Many, perhaps most, of these students would also have taken the Preliminary Scholastic Aptitude Test (PSAT), which is offered in the fall as a semisecure test, principally for secondary school juniors for purposes of guidance and familiarization with the SAT type of test.

Typically, close to 40 percent of the candidates taking the SAT in December or January in their senior year have taken the test once before in March or May of their junior year. One result of this fact is that the students and their parents, as well as the schools and colleges receiving score reports, have an opportunity to observe a wide variation in score changes (gains as well as losses) from the first to the second testing, and many write to the Board and to ETS asking for an explanation. These queries have become more frequent because of the increasingly popular practice of taking the tests twice and because of a general downward trend in average score gains in recent years. The task of explaining the problem of score change is not easy because the explanation rests so heavily on considerations of error of measurement—a concept which is neither well understood nor easily accepted by the nonstatistically oriented. However, special efforts have been made to clarify the problem of score change by conducting theoretical and empirical studies, and then describing the findings to test users in special score interpretation booklets. (See Chapter II of this book.) The results of these studies of score change are reported in Chapter VI of this book.

Although test scores frequently play an active role in college admissions, their use varies considerably from one college to another. In some colleges formal prediction equations are calculated, utilizing the secondary school record, SAT scores, and sometimes Achievement Test scores as predictors. The prediction equations are then used in conjunction with recommendations, prizes and awards, nonacademic information about the applicants, and results of interviews. Other colleges use College Board scores in a less formal way. Some use the scores to decide only about marginal candidates, and some (principally certain of the state universities) use them only for out-of-state candidates. Finally, some colleges use the test scores, not for admission at all, but for purposes of counseling and guidance and for placement.

Because of the number of times a candidate may, if he wishes, repeat the tests, it is necessary that the number of active secure forms be sufficiently large to permit relatively infrequent reuse of a given form. To keep the pool of active forms large enough to meet this degree of flexibility, several new forms of the SAT and of each Achievement Test are introduced into the program each year.

All told, the number of candidates participating in the program during 1968-69 was about 1,950,000. They took the tests in over 4,500 centers, of which about 300 were located in some 100 foreign countries on all six continents.

Administration of the tests

Administrative problems are generally of three principal kinds: (1) those involved in bringing together the candidates and the tests at the proper time, (2) those involved in giving the tests under standard conditions that guarantee maximum protection against dishonesty and breaches of test security, and (3) those involved in scoring the tests accurately and reporting the results correctly and in sufficient time for appropriate use by the colleges and schools.

Candidates are informed about the program through a series of publications. The basic document explaining the procedures to follow is the *Bulletin of Information*, which is updated annually and distributed in appropriate quantities to secondary schools before the beginning of the school year. It contains information on the test offerings, the times and places where the tests are given, and methods for registering for the tests. It also refers candidates to *The College Handbook*, published by the Board, the 1969 edition of which contains statements compiled by 832 colleges that are members of the Board. The statements include both general facts about the colleges and descriptions of specific college characteristics, such as their admission and examination requirements, cost of attendance, financial aid programs, and, in some cases, information and statistics about the academic qualifications of enrolled students. Booklets describing the SAT and the Achievement Tests are also distributed in bulk to all secondary schools so that every candidate can obtain a preview of what will be expected of him in the testing.

The candidate registers for the tests by filling out a registration form with the necessary information about himself and indicates the tests he plans to take and the scheduled date on which he will take them. If he plans to take Achievement Tests, he need not specify the particular tests until he actually takes them.* From lists in the *Bulletin of Information*, the candidate selects the center where he will take the tests and the colleges to which he wants his scores sent, and enters this information on the registration form. Once registered, the candidate receives an admission ticket to the test center. The ticket carries, along with other information, the registration number he is to use on the test answer sheets.

Test centers for each administration are usually established a year in advance at secondary schools and colleges, and if possible are located within 75 miles of any candidate. The supervisor of a test center is usually an official of the institution where it is located. Seven to ten days in advance of a test date the supervisor receives the necessary tests and supplies. One week in advance he receives a roster of the names of candidates assigned to the center for the test. The conjunction of tickets and rosters provides a final check on whether the right candidates are taking the right tests at the right time in the right center.

The effort to insure that tests are administered properly begins with the appointment and instruction of the test center supervisors. Each supervisor is given a *Supervisor's Handbook* and a *Supervisor's Manual*, and as a member of the temporary staff of Educational Testing Service he is expected to master both documents and follow the directions in them. The *Supervisor's Handbook* sets forth the general requirements of test center management: for example, type of facilities and staff needed, handling of test materials, seating of candidates, timing, and maintaining test security. The *Supervisor's Manual* is specific to the tests to be administered on a given date. It contains detailed rules for conducting the test sessions, verbatim directions to candidates, and forms for reporting on several aspects of the administration including any irregularities that may occur.

Operations of the test centers are continually reviewed by staff members of Educational Testing Service. If testing conditions at a center are found to be inadequate, appropriate adjustments are made (including replacing the supervisor if necessary).

The number of candidates involved in any single administration of the tests has so far run as high as 632,000. Within four to five weeks after an administration the test scores are sent to the colleges. During this interim period, the task of translating the marks on test answer sheets into interpretable score reports is accomplished largely by high-speed scoring and data processing equipment. The task is complicated by the fact that a candidate may have taken any one of many possible combinations of Achievement Tests—for example, French, American History, and Physics, or English, Chemistry, and Mathematics Level I. It is further complicated by the fact that the English Composition Test may contain an essay section that must be graded by readers. The fact that the score reports are now cumulative over a two-year period adds still another dimension of complexity to the task of score reporting.

To insure the greatest possible accuracy in this scoring and reporting operation a series of checks is built into the data processing system. The system is programmed to reject cases for which the information needed for identifying the candidate or the tests he has taken is inadequate or questionable, or for which the markings on any answer sheet are such as to throw doubt on the score. These rejected cases—some seven percent of the total—are scored by hand. In addition, a continuous quality control procedure, based on a 0.3 percent random sample of all the cases, provides a constant outside check on the total system. Studies of scoring accuracy show that over 99 percent of the SAT and Achievement Test answer sheets are scored with no errors and that errors that do occur are almost uniformly one-point errors in raw score (six to ten points on the standard scale). All answer sheets are kept on file for one year should any question arise concerning the accuracy of a score.

Test scores are accumulated from grade 10 through grade 12 for high school students, and for one year for candidates not in high school. To insure that a candidate's scores will be collated with those he may have earned at earlier administrations, identification is required of the candidate each time he takes the tests—name (expressed precisely the same on all occasions), sex, and birth date, for example, and social security number when available. Failures to secure precisely uniform information of this sort from repeating candidates occur in about 5 percent of the cases in any given series. In such cases only the candidate's current scores will appear on his report. Except for the special case of twins who do not have social security numbers, the additional controls on the data are sufficiently rigorous so that the probability that one candidate's scores will be mismatched with those of another candidate is practically zero.

Influence on curriculum

Because of its involvement in the important process of transition from high school to college, the College Board, through its Admissions Testing Program, is in an unusually strategic position to exert a significant influence on American secondary school education—because many of the secondary schools tend to gear their curriculum to what they expect will appear in the next forms of the tests. This academic fact of life leads to a key problem for Board policy and planning. If, on the one hand, Board tests fail to keep abreast of new

---

*In the 1970-71 year, a student who plans to take one of the new listening-reading foreign language Achievement Tests will have to specify on his Registration Form which languages he wants to be tested in.

trends in curriculum, then the Board is considered derelict in its responsibility to represent what some will consider to be the best in American secondary education. If, on the other hand, the Board tests respond too quickly to the pressures exerted by overly enthusiastic exponents of educational philosophies still in the process of development, then the Board is considered guilty of leading American secondary education along ill-advised, unproved, and dangerous pathways. Consequently, the following philosophy has guided the Board, particularly since the early 1940s, in the selection of content for its tests: that its tests are constructed, not with a single syllabus in mind, but with a blueprint based on sampling widely and fairly the variety of courses represented in the prominent and well-subscribed curriculums throughout the country.

Coaching

It is for this reason—the philosophy just described—that the publications of the Board have maintained that special coaching for the examinations is neither needed nor advised, and that little is gained by trying to outguess and predict the content of the examinations.

The efforts of the Board in regard to coaching have been directed not only to the students who would seek quick and easy answers to the substantive test questions on the Achievement Tests, but also, and more particularly, to those who hope to improve their scores on the far less curriculum-oriented test questions that form the basis of the SAT. During the 1960s, with rapid increases in the numbers of students seeking admission to college and the adoption of increasingly stringent selection procedures by many of the colleges, the College Board tests have come to be regarded by many students as barriers to college that must, at all costs, be overcome. In response to what appeared to be an eager and growing demand, a number of publishers have marketed collections of test items purportedly representative of—and, in some instances, apparently taken directly out of—actual forms of the SAT. A parallel development has been the rise of coaching or cramming schools that guarantee high score benefits to students who enroll in their short-term courses.

Appalled by the subversive effect of these commercial enterprises on the goals of education, the Board has prepared a special booklet (College Board, 1968) describing the effects of coaching. The booklet outlines the findings of seven studies conducted in this area—four by the College Board-ETS staff and three by independent researchers—which showed at best only small and insignificant gains on the SAT resulting from short-term intensive coaching. As a result of these studies the College Board trustees have prepared a statement, which is reproduced in the booklet, that urges students and their parents not to waste their time and money on this kind of coaching.

Security

Since scores on College Board Admissions Tests play an important role in many colleges' admissions decisions, it is not surprising that a few candidates try to improve their scores by cheating. To prevent cheating, Educational Testing Service has stringent security requirements for every phase of a test administration.

Tests are printed by carefully selected printers and shipped by traceable means. Every test book is sequentially numbered, sealed, and inserted in units of five or ten in transparent plastic bags which the test supervisor is instructed not to open until testing is about to begin. No one is permitted to examine the test contents before or after the administration. Only the candidates see the test questions, and then only during the actual administration. All test books, used and unused, must be returned immediately after the testing to ETS, where the books are counted to insure that all have been returned.

Educational Testing Service also gives test supervisors specific instructions for the admission of candidates to test centers and their assignment to seats at specified distances from other candidates. Constant proctoring is required throughout the test session. However, despite these precautions, a test supervisor occasionally observes cheating. More often, evidence of cheating is found later when an institution has questioned a candidate's scores because of inconsistency with the rest of his academic record.

In all investigations of individuals' scores, the sole concern of the Board and ETS is to establish whether the scores in question were or were not earned by the candidate without unauthorized assistance. A candidate who is suspected of having cheated is offered a retest without prejudice—that is, without reporting to the institutions designated by the candidate to receive his subsequent scores that the investigation has been made. The results of the retest are used to confirm—or to invalidate—the scores reported for the original test.

It is evident that all the above-mentioned influences—the attempts to shape the curriculum to reflect the content of the tests, to coach and cram for tests, and finally, to find extralegal or otherwise unethical means of inflating the test scores—derive from an unrealistic and exaggerated view of the importance of test scores on the part of students and test users. Hence, the Board in its various publications and its frequent personal contacts with test users has repeatedly tried to put test scores in their proper perspective. It advises the colleges that the tests should not be overemphasized and that the test results should not constitute the sole basis for evaluating the probable future success of a candidate, but should be considered along with other relevant factors such as the school record, the recommendations of teachers, the record of special prizes and awards, extracurricular activities, and frequently the observations resulting from interviews.

7

Psychometric considerations

The psychometric problems of the Admissions Testing Program are similar to those found in the production and interpretation of any battery of tests having multiple forms. The complicated nature of the program and the many populations and purposes it must serve, however, demand solutions that are somewhat out of the ordinary. The following paragraphs will briefly define the situation with respect to: 1) the validity of the tests, 2) their reliability, 3) parallelism among the forms of any given test, 4) the development and maintenance of a score scale, 5) the development of norms, and 6) miscellaneous factors that must be taken into account in interpreting scores.

Validity

From the standpoint of many of the colleges that require their candidates to take one or more of the tests, the main purpose of the tests is to help select a freshman class that is academically qualified. A secondary purpose, but one that is increasingly important, is to help in the guidance and course placement of admitted freshmen.

The validity of the tests for purposes of selection is indicated by answers to two kinds of questions: 1) To what extent can the test scores increase the accuracy of predicting the candidate's academic standing in college? 2) How well do the test scores reflect the quality of the candidate's academic performance in secondary school? A third question bearing upon the validity of the tests is also occasionally asked, namely, how well do the test scores help to forecast the quality of an individual's eventual contribution to society?

The answers to all three questions determine the emphasis a college places on test scores in deciding whether or not to admit a particular candidate. In this connection much depends upon the admissions policy of the college, upon its translation of policy into rational action, and upon the quality of the candidates it attracts—all of which suggests that no single set of operations can define the validity of the Admissions Tests for purposes of candidate selection. Some colleges are mainly interested in the prediction of academic standing. Others may disregard prediction altogether and settle for describing the candidate not in terms of what he may become but in terms of what he is. Still others may be less concerned with the candidate's present academic status, or with his chances of making good grades, than with identifying those qualities that are presumed to be basic to a satisfying and fruitful career in the post-college world. The relative merits of these several approaches to selection, or any combinations of them, are not here under discussion. The validity question is to what extent the Admissions Testing Program can provide measures that are relevant to these approaches.

The validity of the tests for purposes of *course placement* has received relatively little systematic study. There are, however, two basic models for such studies. In one case the scores on appropriate tests, taken at entrance to college, are correlated with final grades in particular freshman courses to see how accurately they predict performance in these courses. In the other case, the tests are given to enrolled students upon completion of each of several courses in a sequence (for example, first semester French, second semester French, third semester French, etc.) to determine, first, how closely the test scores approximate the level of performance in each course as measured by concurrent criteria such as final examination grades, and secondly, how well the tests measure the progress of students from each course to the next above it. Here again, the validity of the tests for placement will vary from one type of course to another within a given college, as well as from college to college, in accordance with the way freshman instruction in any given field may be organized and in accordance with the level and content of the subject matter.

Studies bearing on these questions are examined in detail in Chapter V. At this point, it is worth noting that the meaning of validity in the context of the Admissions Testing Program is not confined solely to *predictive* validity. Validity can mean an appropriate content balance as well. The content of the College Board tests has from the very beginning been governed by committees of examiners who are chosen from the faculties of secondary schools and colleges representing a wide geographic distribution and a variety of content interests and educational emphases. These committees meet to decide on numbers of each type of item to be included in the tests, the distribution of item content, the degree to which the items represent various current curricular emphases, and the nature of the rational or psychological processes required by the item. Care is taken, in their specifications for the test, not only to maintain an appropriate content balance, but also a balance in the difficulty of the concepts that are being examined.

Reliability

The reliability of each form of each test in the Admissions Testing Program is routinely estimated after its first formal administration, ordinarily by means of the Kuder-Richardson formula #20, adapted for use with formula (R-kW) scores. Each such estimate is ordinarily based on a specially selected sample of at least 900 cases when available, and sometimes numbering as many as 2,000 cases. From the standpoint of the test user, however, the reliability coefficient and error of measurement associated with any particular form of a test in the program can be of little more than academic interest. In a situation where the specific form of test a candidate may take is essentially unpredictable, the important question is whether the general level of reliability is sufficiently high and reasonably uniform to permit the test user to operate on the scores from *any* unspecified form with an even amount of confidence. As subsequent tables in this book will show, the level of reliability as estimated by K-R #20 across the active forms of any particular test is reasonably uniform.

Parallelism of forms

For all their consistency, the estimates of reliability do not, of course, provide sufficient information in themselves concerning the amount of error variance that must be allowed for in interpreting scores. It is necessary to assume, in addition, that the forms of any particular test are parallel in respect both to content and difficulty (Lord, 1964). To the extent that this assumption is not met, the actual standard error of measurement for a score irrespective of form will be slightly larger than that reported for a score on any one form. The fact of the matter is that the assumption of parallelism does not in all probability hold exactly from form to form, and the degree to which it does hold probably varies from one test in the Admissions Testing Program to another. Thus, because of the gradual changes that are introduced into the Achievement Tests in response to changes in curriculum emphasis, successive forms of the Chemistry Test, for example, cannot be regarded as having the same degree of parallelism as do successive forms of the SAT. Accordingly, the difference between the actual and the reported standard error of measurement for the Chemistry Test is very likely to be slightly larger than the difference between the actual and the reported standard errors of measurement for either score on the SAT.

The effort to achieve parallelism among the forms centers on the definition of the test specifications and on the development of test forms that adhere to the specifications. The specifications for any given test in the program consist of three principal elements: 1) the distribution of item difficulty, 2) the distribution of item-test correlations, and perhaps most important, 3) the distribution of item content.

Indexes of item difficulty and coefficients of item-test correlation are routinely prepared and yield information about parallelism in successive forms of a test in respect to their overall difficulty and homogeneity. However, these statistics provide no information about the parallelism of item content. This aspect of the specifications is necessarily less rigorous for two reasons. First, it depends upon verbally defined categories of topics and processes that leave room for ambiguities of interpretation on the part of the item writers. Secondly, with the accumulation of new data on the changing nature of the candidate population, the secondary school curriculums, and the intellectual demands of the colleges, there is a continuous need to change the con-

tent of the tests. In short, strict parallelism in test content, even if it were attainable, would tend over time to bring about a *reduction* of validity. This problem is met by a conscious compromise in the content specifications: changes in content are introduced slowly so that the active forms in use over any five-year period are *approximately* interchangeable as far as content is concerned. The rate of change in the content of the SAT is less rapid than that of most of the Achievement Tests. For this reason, although the SAT itself is constantly evolving, the process is sufficiently slow to permit it to be regarded in a very real sense as the principal stabilizing force in a changing and developing Admissions Testing Program as it develops over the years.

Item analysis

By means of a detailed program for pretesting and item analysis it has been possible to assess the difficulty and discriminating power of the items, to select items of appropriate statistical characteristics, to diagnose sources of ambiguity and detect reasons for failure to provide adequate discrimination, and in general to exert a significant degree of control over the statistical properties of the test forms.

Although the analyses of pretest items yield a variety of information, the principal statistics are the indexes of item difficulty and item discrimination. The index of item difficulty, referred to as "delta," is a function of the percent passing the item. It is the normal deviate of the point above which lies the proportion of the area under the curve equal to the proportion of correct responses to the item. It is expressed in terms of a scale whose mean is 13 and whose standard deviation is 4.

Since pretest samples, especially those used for the achievement pretests, may differ in level of ability from the standard reference group that was originally used to scale the tests, it is necessary to render the raw, or *observed*, deltas obtained from successive pretestings comparable to one another by an equating procedure. This procedure requires that the pretest material consisting of new items be administered together with a number of previously used items whose standard, or *equated*, deltas (indexes of difficulty estimated in terms of the performance of the standard reference population) are known. For each such item an observed delta is calculated based on the pretest sample. When these new observed delta values are plotted against the equated delta values on arithmetic graph paper, the resulting scatterplot typically falls in an elongated, narrow ellipse represented by a high correlation coefficient, frequently in the upper .90's. The line defined by this plot, calculated from the means and standard deviations of the observed and equated deltas, is used to convert the item difficulties for the pretest samples (observed deltas) to item difficulties as estimated for the standard reference population (equated deltas). Although the observed deltas lack comparability—

since they are dependent on the abilities of the various groups to whom the items have been administered—the equated deltas are all defined in terms of the same standard reference group and are therefore directly comparable (Thurstone, 1947).

In the assembly of each new form of a test, care is taken to bring the mean and standard deviation of the equated deltas as close as possible to those of previous forms—except, of course, when the population shifts and it is deemed necessary to adjust the difficulty of the new form to make it appropriate to the new population.

A second statistic that is regularly calculated for every item is the biserial coefficient of correlation between the item and an appropriate criterion, usually the total score on the test. These biserial correlations are used for three purposes: first, to flag items that may be ambiguous; second, to assess the worth of items as discriminators; and third, to provide a basis for checking on the degree of homogeneity among the items of the test. It is this last consideration that has a bearing on the parellelism among test forms. Since a certain degree of heterogeneity is regarded as desirable in any test in the program, and is in part predetermined by the content specifications of the test, some items with relatively low biserials as well as some items with relatively high biserials may be included whenever a new form is being put together. Consequently, the degree to which the means and standard deviations of the biserials over forms agree becomes an important consideration in estimating the parallelism among the several forms.

The data routinely produced in the item analysis yield additional information regarding the behavior of the item, and are particularly useful in making revisions. These include the number of people choosing each option of the item, the percent passing the item, the number of people omitting the item, the number not reaching the item (presumably because of insufficient time), the mean total score on the test for those choosing each option (as well as for those omitting it and for those not reaching it), and the number of people in each of five ability groups (as defined by the total score on the test) choosing each option. From these frequencies and means it is possible to determine, for example, whether the item is appropriately difficult for the group taking it and whether it is appropriately placed in the sequence of items in the test. It is also possible to determine whether an incorrect option is sufficiently attractive to the less able examinees to be helpful, and whether it draws so many of the more able examinees that it may indicate the presence of an ambiguity. This information also makes it possible to determine just where on the continuum of ability the item is making its maximum discrimination and, in an approximate way, whether the characteristic curve for each of the item options, including the correct option, is monotonic as it should be.

Test analysis

After the first formal administration of each test form a specially selected sample of answer sheets (at least 900, as was pointed out earlier, and sometimes as many as 2,000) is assembled and a report of a detailed analysis of the test is made. Reliabilities and standard errors of measurement of the separately timed parts of the test are calculated, as well as intercorrelations among the parts and the total score. Assessments of speededness in terms of percent completing the test are made, and distributions of the total formula score are presented, not only for the special sample but for all students taking that form. In addition, distributions, means, and standard deviations are given of the number of items answered correctly, the number answered incorrectly, the number omitted, and the number not reached. As an additional check on speededness, a bivariate plot is given of score versus number of items attempted. Finally, distributions, means, and standard deviations are given of item deltas and biserial correlations for each separately timed section of the test. All of these data are summarized and evaluated in an introductory text to each test analysis, which is then used in guiding the development of future forms of the test.

The score scale

The results of all the tests in the Admissions Testing Program are reported on a score scale running from 200 to 800. The nature of the program imposes on this score scale a number of requirements, most of which, at the present state of the art, can be met only approximately. These requirements are as follows:

1. The number designating any position on the scale must represent the same level of competence for any form of a given test. Thus, a score of 563 on the verbal sections of the SAT should represent the same degree of competence in the functions measured by the test regardless of whether the candidate takes Form A or Form D or Form G of that test. If, for instance, the mean difficulty of the items in Form A happens to be somewhat greater than the mean difficulty of the items in Form D, this difference in average item difficulty should have no effect whatever on the scaled score a candidate is likely to receive. Thus, no candidate should be put at a special advantage (or disadvantage) because of the fortuitous administration of an easy (or difficult) test form. The probability of his obtaining a scaled score of 563 on Form A should be the same as the probability of his obtaining a scaled score of 563 on Form D (or any other current form of the test).

2. The number designating any position on the scale must represent the same level of competence for any individual or group of individuals taking the test. The same conversion from raw to scaled scores on a form of a test is used, whether the candidate is a male or a

female, whether he comes from the North or the South, whether he comes from a public, independent, or church-related school, or whether he plans to major in fine arts or engineering. The scaled score is simply a reflection of his raw score—that is, the number of items he answered correctly minus a fraction of the number he answered incorrectly. It does not reflect the background characteristics of the candidate except insofar as they may have affected his performance on the test and caused him directly or indirectly to earn a higher or lower score on the test.

Similarly, so long as we are operating with a system of parallel forms, the conversion from raw to scaled scores is independent of the background characteristics of the samples of individuals, indeed, independent of the specific ability characteristics of the samples used in deriving the conversion. Within broad limits the same conversion equation relating raw to scaled scores would result whether the individuals in the samples are male or female, adequately or inadequately trained, homogeneous or dispersed. On the other hand, when we are dealing with tests of *dissimilar* function, say French and Spanish, the conversion equation depends quite crucially on the characteristics of the samples.

3. The number designating any position on the scale must represent the same level of competence for any test administration. That is, a score of 627 on the Chemistry Test should represent the same degree of measured competence in chemistry whether the test is taken in December or March or July. The corollary of this is that if a candidate takes a given test twice, and if there has been any measurable change in his competence between the two testings, the difference between his two scaled scores on the test should, within the limits of sampling error, reflect that change, even if he has taken a different form of the test on the two occasions.

4. The number designating any position on the scale for one test (e.g., Chemistry) is *comparable* to the same number on the scale for another test (e.g., French) in the sense that the two numbers represent the same relative positions in the same reference population. Thus, a score of 563 on the Chemistry Test and a score of 563 on the French Test both represent performances 0.63 standard deviations above the mean of the same reference group, assuming that all members of that group have had adequate preparation for the tests in both Chemistry and French.

One of the most persistent misconceptions of the 200-800 scale used for reporting the results of College Board tests is that it is a standard score scale on which 500 represents the mean score of all College Board candidates and 100 represents the standard deviation of their scores. Another misconception is that 500 and 100 represent the mean and standard deviation of all college freshmen. Still another is that 500 and 100 represent the mean and standard deviation of all secondary school seniors. The fact is that the numbers 500 and 100 simply refer to the mean and standard deviation of the group of 10,654 candidates who happened to assemble to take the tests in April 1941 and who were used to define the scale system for the College Board. Since that group is of interest only from a historical point of view—in the sense that it simply marks the origin of the present College Board scale—and has no normative significance or usefulness in interpreting College Board scores, the 500-point similarly has no special significance other than that it is midway between the end points 200 and 800. The real significance of College Board scores lies in the continuity of the scales in the face of changing test forms and changing populations and the fact that the scores have different normative or evaluative meanings depending on the choice of the normative group. The scaled score of 200 does not stand for a raw score of zero; it is simply the lowest score reported. The scaled score of 800 does not stand for a perfect raw score; it is the highest score reported. This is not to say that a score of 200 and a score of 800 will be possible on every form of every test. Some tests or test forms will be relatively difficult, with the result that the minimum possible score on the test will be above 200, and scores of 200 will not be possible. Similarly, some tests or test forms will be relatively easy, with the result that the maximum possible score on the test will be below 800, and scores of 800 will not be possible. Some of this variation is the natural consequence of random fluctuation in the construction of alternate forms. Some of it, however (especially the failure to reach 200), is the natural consequence of constructing tests that are especially designed to be appropriate to highly select and able groups of candidates—for example, those who elect to take the Physics Test or the Mathematics Level II Test.

Unlike other scales in common use that have built-in normative meaning, there is no inherent meaning claimed for the College Board scale system. When normative interpretations are required, test users are urged to collect their own local norms. In some instances special norms studies are conducted by the Board. The meaning of the College Board scale is the meaning that is given to it by the test user himself. As he uses the scores, he comes over the course of time to attach certain known levels of competence to the scores on the scale. That is to say, he learns to understand and appreciate the "meaning" of a score of 563 in the same sense that he has learned to understand and appreciate the "meaning" of 14 inches, a process which is possible only if the units remain constant. It is for this reason that the College Board devotes its effort to the job of preserving the constancy of that meaning, and it does so by an intricate system of form-to-form equating. That system will be described in the next two chapters.

The norms

The function of norms for college admission tests is to provide high school guidance counselors and college admissions officers with a means of comparing a candidate's test performance with that of certain well-defined groups of students. These groups are of three principal kinds: those made up of individuals drawn at random from the nation's secondary school seniors, those made up of individuals who are applying for college admission, and those made up of individuals who have enrolled in college. By comparing a candidate's scores with those earned by a group of the first type, it is possible to evaluate his performance relative to the entire cohort—that is, all the individuals in the country who are potentially competitive with him. By comparing a candidate's test scores with those earned by a group of the second type, the candidate and his counselor should be able to get some notion of where the candidate stands academically within the population of students who hope to go to college. By comparing his scores with those made by a group of the third type, some information should be forthcoming as to where the candidate will stand with respect to the academic demands that will be placed upon him after he gets there.

There are, of course, many meaningful groupings of students headed for college and enrolled in colleges. The most useful normative data are those that tell the candidate, his counselor, and the college admissions officer how the candidate compares with the group that is applying to a particular college in which he may be interested and also with the group that will enroll at that college.

Such individual college norms are available for many of the 520 College Board member colleges in the 1967-69 edition of the *Manual of Freshman Class Profiles.** In most instances these individual college norms apply only to SAT scores, since the majority requires only this test. However, some colleges require specific Achievement Tests and publish norms for these as well.

The test norms appearing in the *Manual of Freshman Class Profiles* do not take the customary form of tables of percentile ranks. Typically, a college reports three series of statistics on each test, SAT-verbal, and mathematical, sometimes on one or more of the Achievement Tests, and sometimes on class rank. The three series are: 1) a frequency distribution of the scores of its applicants in the year just previous to publication, 2) the number accepted at each of the score intervals, and 3) a frequency distribution of the accepted students who actually enrolled. Where appropriate, separate norms of this sort are given for men and women.

Since only a fraction of the Board member colleges supply the data for the individual college norms, national norms, based on candidates in most instances,

are also provided in the booklet, *College Board Score Reports: A Guide for Counselors and Admissions Officers.* These are presented in the form of percentile ranks. The groups of students on which they are based vary from test to test, but in general, include all candidates tested over the course of the year, beginning with the May administration and ending with the March administration. Within the candidate group homogeneous subgroups are found by amount of training in the subject, where this kind of subdivision is appropriate, and, where appropriate, by secondary school class and sex.

The central problem in furnishing norms for the College Board Admissions Tests grows out of the fact that it is difficult to define appropriate populations or subpopulations to be sampled. The characteristics of the population applying to colleges in the Board membership may change from year to year. These changes are the result of a number of factors: the general and continuing increase in the proportion of secondary school students going on to college; the increase in the number and kinds of colleges requiring the College Board Admissions Tests; variability over time and over colleges in the degree to which colleges are selective in the admissions process; changes in the test requirements of the colleges; variability in the time of year at which candidates take the tests; the changing patterns in secondary school curriculums; the mobility of secondary school students. To develop overall norms distributions under these conditions, it is necessary to assume, first, that the changes in any candidate population over a limited period—say, two to five years—are not sufficient to make for anything more than negligible changes in the characteristics of the score distribution for that population, and second, that the total group of candidates taking a test for any particular college or for the Board member colleges as a whole in any given year constitutes a representative sample of all the candidates in one or the other category who will be taking the test in the following two-to-five-year period. The extent to which these assumptions hold can be estimated by extrapolation from the amount of stability to be found in the score distributions over past years. Detailed data on this point will appear in subsequent chapters.

Scoring methods

At the present time all the tests in the College Board Admissions Testing Program are scored by the formula, No. Right *minus* (No. Wrong)/n, where n = one less than the number of choices per item.* (The number of choices varies somewhat from test to test, but is usually five.)

The decision to score by formula rather than to score

---

*See Chapter IV, pages 84-88, for additional information about the *Manual of Freshman Class Profiles*, which was superseded in the fall of 1969 when information previously included in the *Manual* was incorporated into the 1969 edition of *The College Handbook.*

---

*This statement is only approximately true for the English Composition Test, of which some forms are part essay. In these forms the essays are graded by readers. The objective sections are scored by formula, as described.

for rights only—simply a count of the number of items answered correctly—was arrived at by the following line of reasoning: In a rights-scored test the best strategy for the candidate would clearly be to attempt every item. However, it has been argued that it is educationally unsound and even morally improper to encourage students to guess at items about which they have little or no knowledge. On the other hand, it can also be argued that for various reasons it is similarly improper to give the candidates directions that are less than completely structured and informative. Most persuasive is the argument that, aside from the difficulty of preparing appropriate and candid directions for a rights-scored test, permissive or unstructured directions will allow candidates who are more inclined to guess to earn higher scores on a rights-scored test and will give them an unfair advantage over candidates who are not so inclined. This argument is supported by the results of a study conducted by Swineford and Miller (1953), which was designed to investigate the effect of different guessing directions on actual guessing behavior. It led to the conclusion that, in respect to the problem of guessing, formula scoring is to be preferred over rights scoring, even under conditions of rights directions, and especially to be preferred when the accompanying directions are so phrased as to discourage random guessing.

In tests or testing programs where the premium placed on high scores is not great, differences in scores that result from differential tendencies to guess might conceivably be tolerable. However, in the case of the College Board Program it was felt that the reward of college acceptance was perceived to be too great, and the competition among candidates for that reward too keen, for the Board to tolerate score advantages of this sort, however small or rare they may be, especially when the test scores constitute a significant part of the candidate's record. Thus, to reduce the effect of guessing the decision was made to score the SAT and Achievement Tests by formula, and to prepare directions for taking the tests that would discourage the candidates from strictly random guessing. It was also agreed that for the sake of consistency the PSAT should also be scored by formula, even though it is not ordinarily used as a selection instrument.

The decision to adopt formula scoring brought with it a need to make additional decisions, for example, with regard to the treatment of negative scores, which will occur when the number of wrongs in a test with five-choice items is more than four times the number of rights. This particular decision was supported by the results of a study by Boldt (1968), in which it was found that there was valid discrimination in the region of negative formula scores. In an effort to discriminate among candidates with different degrees of misinformation, differentiations on the scaled score scale are made and reported for candidates with different negative scores. Although in theory this procedure allows discriminations as low as -22 on SAT-verbal, for example, and as low as -15 on SAT-mathematical, virtually no candidates earn scores lower than -10. The available range of negative scores is more than adequate to make the discriminations needed in that part of the score continuum.

The foregoing psychometric considerations find their applications in the context of the SAT and the Achievement Tests, which are dealt with in the chapters that follow.

REFERENCES

Boldt, R. F., "Study of Linearity and Homoscedasticity of Test Scores in the Chance Range." *Educational and Psychological Measurement*, 1968, 28, pp. 47-60.

Brigham, C. C., and others, "The Scholastic Aptitude Test of the College Entrance Examination Board," in T. S. Fiske, ed., *The Work of the College Entrance Examination Board, 1901-1925.* New York: Ginn and Company, 1926.

College Entrance Examination Board, *Effects of Coaching on Scholastic Aptitude Test Scores.* New York: College Entrance Examination Board, 1968.

Fuess, C. M., *The College Board: Its First Fifty Years.* New York: College Entrance Examination Board, 1950.

Lord, F. M., "Nominally and Rigorously Parallel Test Forms." *Psychometrika*, 1964, 29, pp. 335-345.

Swineford, F., and Miller, P. M., "Effects of Directions Regarding Guessing on Item Statistics of a Multiple-choice Vocabulary Test." *Journal of Educational Psychology*, 1953, 44, pp. 129-139.

Thurstone, L. L., "The Calibration of Test Items." *American Psychologist*, 1947, 2, pp. 103-104.

CHAPTER II

The Scholastic Aptitude Test

THOMAS F. DONLON and WILLIAM H. ANGOFF

The purpose of the SAT

The Scholastic Aptitude Test (SAT) is a measure of basic reasoning abilities in two areas: verbal and mathematical. It provides a separate score for each of these areas, and is intended to supplement the school record and other information about the student in assessing his competence for college work. It is a broad-gauge instrument, providing effective discrimination over most of the range of academic ability of college-bound students. It is aimed not only at serving the decisions of institutions that have high-scoring candidates but also at describing levels of ability among lower-scoring candidates for admission to college.

The utility of this kind of supplementary measure arises in part from the fact that it can provide unique information about the student, and in part from its ability to confirm or to question the assessment based on subject-matter achievement. It is, therefore, a supplement that will normally help establish candidate ability when it is consistent with other information, but that will be perhaps most useful when it is in disagreement with other data. When properly used in the context of other information with which it is inconsistent, it effectively sounds a warning bell and leads to the search for more data to clarify the assessment in question.

The inherently supplemental nature of the SAT is worth some emphasis, for it is frequently ignored in the popular conception of the test and, more regrettably, in some admissions practices. The SAT was, in a sense, intended to provide some redress for possible errors and inconsistencies in secondary school records and in the old essay examinations that were tailored to specific curriculums. By stressing the direct measurement of basic abilities, the rationale was that it would offer an opportunity for a more balanced assessment of the student who had failed to achieve subject-matter mastery in keeping with his development of these basic abilities. Similarly, it would help to identify the occasional case where the achievements in subject-matter areas were gained only through unusual expenditures of effort, or where the secondary school record was more a reflection of a pleasing personality than of learning.

In practice, however, the SAT-verbal score and the SAT-mathematical score are often made part of a formal regression equation that may include information from the high school record, from the results of the College Board Achievement Tests, and sometimes additional predictors of the college's own choosing. In such equations the test has clearly demonstrated that it makes a unique contribution to the prediction of college success. Indeed, the test showed this ability to contribute something of its own from the very beginning. The *Second Annual Report of the College Board* contains the following quotation (College Board, 1927, p. 202):

"The fact that the Scholastic Aptitude Test does contribute something to the prediction of college grades . . . justifies its inclusion as a member of a team, and the findings to date indicate that it is a useful supplementary measure. Its inclusion helps the prediction of college grades."

The essential supplementary nature of the SAT is further attested to by the manner in which its effectiveness is ordinarily evaluated. Its simple (zero-order) correlation with college performance is by itself not a sufficient indicator of its usefulness in selection. Far more interest attaches to its *incremental* effectiveness, that is, to the degree to which it can improve the prediction of college grades when combined with high school records and Achievement Test scores. The SAT, therefore, is valued to the extent that it can add something unique to the other measures.

In addition to its supplemental and incremental value, the SAT has a value of its own in confirming the grades from different schools. Since the high school record is a reflection of locally controlled curriculum and local grading practices (which themselves are dependent on the nature of the student body and on the objectives of the school), there are variations from school to school in the meaning of the grades. This fact inevitably works to the advantage of some college applicants and to the disadvantage of others. The SAT, on the other hand, represents a standardized measure of the same mental tasks that is expressed on a common scale for all students. Thus, it operates as a "leveling agent," cutting across differences in local customs and conditions and affording the admissions officer a single metric for considering the records of all applicants. Especially in the case of students coming from little-known schools, the SAT provides information about the student that would otherwise be unavailable, or at best, difficult to obtain.

The development of the SAT has generally been both planned and purposive. From the beginning, it has followed a basic rationale as to the nature and role of an aptitude test. The field of measurement, of course, does not offer any single, universally accepted definition of an aptitude test. Of several which have been offered, perhaps the sharpest contrast is afforded by the following. According to Cronbach (1960, p. 31), "An *aptitude test* is one used to predict success in some occupation or training course . . . In form, these tests are not distinctly different from other types . . . The test is referred to as an achievement test when it is used primarily to examine a person's success in past study, and as an aptitude test when it is used to forecast his success in some future course or assignment." However, Ryans and Frederiksen (1951, p. 456) find that "An *aptitude test* is commonly thought of as a device for measuring the capacity or potentiality of an individual for a particular kind of behavior. In the measurement of aptitude, previous experiences or training on the part of the individual is assumed either to be lacking or to be constant for all individuals comprising the population considered."

The Cronbach view, of course, is extremely functional. While the SAT obviously meets this functional criterion, its development over the years since 1926 has also been guided largely by a conception similar to the Ryans and Frederiksen definition, that "previous experience or training . . . is assumed . . . to be constant for all individuals." The test is intended to measure aspects of developed ability. It makes use of basic verbal and mathematical skills that apparently grow slowly over the years through interaction with the student's total environment. They are assumed to be part of every student's equipment, and relatively independent of what he is currently learning in the formal classroom curriculum. It is also recognized that differences in background and in interests will influence the amount and kinds of information acquired by the student as he grows, and test content is carefully balanced to avoid as much as possible inequities to any subclass of the intended population.

For example, while SAT candidates vary in the number of years of mathematics studied in high school, the mathematical section of the test requires as background only the mathematics of grades 1 through 9—that is, only those skills and concepts that are presumed to be attained by all candidates. While many of the mathematical questions may well be more readily solved by a candidate who is equipped with more advanced methods learned in higher level courses, a candidate equipped only with basic algebra and some intuitive notions of geometry and the theory of numbers would be able to complete all problems satisfactorily and in the allotted time.

There is certainly no reason why the SAT could not include measures of other domains in addition to the verbal and mathematical. There has in fact been a considerable and continuing research effort to identify other domains that might be relevant to the prediction of college success, and research into new methods of measurement is also an enduring concern. However, over the 40 years of the SAT's existence, no other measures have demonstrated such a broadly useful relationship to the criterion of college achievement as have the verbal and mathematical tests.

The requirement that the SAT be useful for many colleges and candidates sets a distinct limit on its scope, for in order for the test to be efficient it should contain only test materials that are suitable for measuring the abilities of the majority of students who are asked to take it. This makes sense, for it would not be efficient to widen the scope of its content when this increased scope can only be attained at the expense of requiring most students to be examined on material that has little relevance to their particular college admission situation. No formula governs the inclusion of additional material or measures—a potential additional item type would not have to demonstrate any fixed standard of effectiveness in terms of some minimum proportion of candidates for whom it is relevant. Nonetheless, the test is seldom altered to reflect special conditions that may exist in a minority of the colleges that require it. Adaptability of the test is chiefly provided by varying the relative weights given to SAT-verbal and SAT-mathematical, appropriate to different types of college criteria, and also by the possibility of adding the scores on one or more of the Achievement Tests to the predictors that are already available in the high school record and the SAT.

Over the years the test has shown some evolution in the measurements of verbal and mathematical abilities. In contrast to its principally literary focus during the twenties, thirties, and forties, today the orientation of the verbal test is eclectic, drawing from the social, political, and scientific areas as well as from the literary, artistic, and philosophical. In mathematical material the test has moved away from the curriculum-oriented type of item to items that depend more heavily on logical reasoning and on the perception of mathematical relationships. Additional changes, which have been more in the nature of refinements than radical innovations, have been introduced to eliminate irrelevant speed factors and also to reduce the coachability of the test. The latter has been accomplished by eliminating item types (like artificial language and number series) which appear to be more susceptible to coaching, and by moving away from items that appear to be dependent on the student's current curriculum.

Another constraint upon the test is the requirement of form-to-form comparability, which limits the rapidity with which changes can be made in the test. The college admissions officer is confronted by large numbers of

SAT scores based on different forms of the test taken at different times of the year and even in different academic years. In order to remove the variations from one form to another in the meaning of a given raw score, scores on all forms of the test are equated and converted to the 200-800 standard score scale for the tests of the College Board Admissions Testing Program.* Obviously, however, no equating process can cope with differences in the factorial structure of the test forms, and so the task of changing the SAT is one of a controlled introduction of new content and new types of test items in reasonably small amounts over a long period of time.

While the main purpose of the SAT has not changed greatly since 1926, there have been some changes of importance. There has been an enormous growth in the numbers of students taking the SAT—from 8,040 in 1926 to about 1,625,000 in the 1968-69 academic year—and there has been a concomitant change in the reliance placed upon the scores by the college admissions offices. How has the test responded to this growth? In the sections that follow the current test is described, the salient features of its historical development are outlined, and the present methods of its assembly are described. These are followed in turn by some summaries of statistical data on parallelism, speed, reliability, and similar technical matters, and, finally, by discussions of the PSAT and the SAT for the handicapped.

A description of the current test

The verbal sections of the SAT currently consist of 90 items, including antonym items, sentence completion items, analogies items, and reading comprehension items. These are typically divided into separately timed sections, each section containing some of each item type.

The mathematical sections of the SAT consist of 60 items in which there are only two formally distinct item types: general mathematics items common in form to many other tests, and data sufficiency items.

Within the test each block of items of a similar type is arranged in order of increasing difficulty from easiest to hardest, and as much as possible the mean difficulty of each block is made equal to that of the test as a whole. That is, the difficult items are not all antonyms, the easy items all sentence completion. Rather, there is an effort to achieve the same level and range of difficulty for each item type, a goal which is, of course, only approximated in practice. The difficulty arrangement of the test may be indicated by the idealized diagram (top of the next column) of a typical verbal section.

This degree of regularity is only approximated. However, the actual pattern is essentially similar. All items in any block of items are presented in order of difficulty

*See the section in this chapter, "Origin and maintenance of the SAT score scale." Also, for a less technical discussion of the SAT score scale, see Angoff (1968).

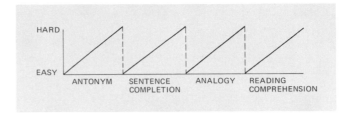

if possible. The exceptions to this rule are the reading comprehension questions, which are presented in the order in which the passage is explored by the reader and essentially the order in which they were printed for the pretesting (the administration for item tryout) prior to their appearance in the final operational forms.

Extensive samples of each item type—including a short practice test—are provided in the candidate's booklet, *A Description of the College Board Scholastic Aptitude Test.* This booklet gives advice on preparing for the examination, describes the question types, and provides a sample test. In all, the booklet presents over 50 pages of preparatory material.

All items in the test are five-choice items. The test is "formula scored" (that is, the Number Right *minus* one-fourth of the Number Wrong). A rather large body of instruction surrounds the actual test items. As mentioned earlier, the candidate's booklet provides extensive discussion. At the administration, but prior to the test, the candidate is asked to read instructions (see Figure 2.1) that are presented on the outside back cover of the test book. The instructions within the test book include statements at the beginning of each section as to the number of items in that section and the total time allowed for working on it. As each new item type is introduced, a completely worked example is provided. As the general level of familiarity with multiple-choice tests in American schools has increased over the years, the net effect of this elaborate system of examples has probably declined. Nonetheless, the test is taken by people from other countries and American children studying abroad. The presentation of the examples is a natural extension of a tradition that goes back to the first days of the test, as will be seen in the discussion of its history below.

The actual booklet which a candidate receives contains more items than those on which his reported scores are based. The extra items are "variant" items, so called because they vary from candidate to candidate (and from booklet to booklet) among 25 different sets of items. Some of these variant sets of items are used to gather the information necessary to equate forms of the test, while others are used to pretest items for future use in the test, or for research studies. To insure that the candidate's approach to these items will parallel his approach to the operational items—a condition that is clearly necessary to guarantee unbiased results—the variant items are made, insofar as possible, indistinguishable from the operational items.

Although the set of variant nonoperational items

Figure 2.1

SCHOLASTIC APTITUDE TEST

You will be given three hours to work on this test, which is divided into five sections. The time limit for each section is printed at the beginning of the section and at the bottom of this page. During the time allowed for one section you are to work only on it. The supervisor will tell you when to begin and end each one. If you finish a section before time is called, you may check your work on it, but you are not to work on any other.

Do not worry if you are unable to finish the test or if there are some questions you cannot answer. Many students leave questions unanswered and no one is expected to get everything right. You should work as rapidly as you can without sacrificing accuracy. Do not waste time puzzling over a question which seems too difficult for you.

Many students wonder whether or not to guess the answers to questions about which they are not certain. In this test a percentage of the wrong answers will be subtracted from the number of right answers as a correction for haphazard guessing. It is improbable, therefore, that mere guessing will improve your score significantly; it may even lower your score, and it does take time. If, however, you are not sure of the correct answer but have some knowledge of the question and are able to eliminate one or more of the answer choices as wrong, your chance of getting the right answer is improved, and it will be to your advantage to answer such a question.

YOU ARE TO INDICATE ALL OF YOUR ANSWERS ON THE SEPARATE ANSWER SHEET ENCLOSED. You may use the margins of the test book for scratchwork, but no credit will be given for anything written in the test book. Be sure that all your answer marks are black and that they completely fill the space; do not make any stray marks on your answer sheet. If you erase, do so completely; an incomplete erasure may be considered as an intended response. MARK ONLY ONE ANSWER TO EACH QUESTION.

Section I	30 minutes
Section II	45 minutes
Section III	30 minutes
Section IV	45 minutes
Section V	30 minutes
Total Time	180 minutes

DO NOT BREAK THE SEAL UNTIL YOU ARE TOLD TO DO SO.

that is taken by each examinee is different from the sets of his immediate neighbors in the testing room, the operational items (the items on which his reported scores are based) are the same for all examinees in the testing room—and indeed, the same for all examinees taking the SAT on that date, both within the continental limits of the United States and abroad. Of the total net testing time of three hours, which is divided into three 30-minute separately timed periods and two 45-minute periods, the operational items require 2½ hours, equally divided between verbal and mathematical sections. This leaves one-half hour for the nonoperational variant items, which, for any given examinee, may be *either* verbal *or* mathematical.

The arrangement of the booklets with the different variant sets of items is called "spiralling." Assuming 25 variant sets of items, the stacks of test books after printing are arranged in sequence so that booklets 1 to 25 consist, respectively, of variants 1 to 25; booklets 26 to 50 repeat, respectively, variants 1 to 25, and so forth. The result is that any sizable block of booklets selected for shipment to a center will contain the 25 variants in very nearly equal proportions.

The intent of the spiralling plan is to effect a system of systematic, or spaced, samples, one such sample for each group of candidates taking a different variant section. Since the supervisors are instructed to hand out the booklets in the sequence in which they are received, the candidates who work on a given set of variant items do, as planned, constitute a representative sample of the total group tested at this administration, and random samples drawn within them may be expected to retain this property.

The foregoing brief description of the principal facts about the SAT has covered its physical characteristics: the items, time allowances, format, and descriptive or instructional material. This discussion leads naturally to a consideration of the history of the SAT, for over the years it has changed significantly in all of these characteristics.

History and evolution of the SAT

The section on the purpose of the SAT concluded with the assertion that this purpose had not changed greatly in its history. Strictly speaking, this is true only in the broad context of general descriptions and in the sense that the early forms of the test, if administered to SAT candidates today, would contain many recognizable item types and would yield scores which correlated highly with the present forms. As the program has developed, however, there have been important external changes—that is, changes in the candidate population, their preliminary preparation and instruction, and the educational context within which the test is offered. In response to these changes, there have also been important internal changes in the test and in the testing process—for example, changes in the time limits, test

length, content, item types, scoring, equating, method of assembly specifications, and manner of administration. It is beyond the scope of this brief discussion to do more than suggest a few such changes. In general, many of these changes have been the result of concern about the speededness of the test, and about the extent to which item types might foster attempts at coaching. Other changes have been brought about as a result of research in new item types, or because of practical considerations about the machine scoring of the tests. Thus, the abandonment of "six-choice" antonyms was influenced by the nature of the IBM 850 scoring machine and answer sheet, as was the 1958 minor adjustment in test length. Additional information is provided by such sources as Brigham (1932), Coffman (1963, 1964), Fuess (1950), and Loret (1961).

The principal facts about time and test length over the years are provided by Tables 2.1 and 2.2, adapted from Loret. A related table, Table 2.3, describes the various item types that have been used over the years. In general, the trend has been toward less speeded tests insofar as time-per-item is an indicator, and (as was pointed out above) toward item types that are difficult to "coach" and that bear least resemblance to the types used in the schools. In the beginning the test offered only a single score, lumping both mathematical and verbal material into one sum, but in 1930 the presence of two factors was detected and thereafter the mathematical material was separately scored. However, during two periods there were no mathematical items: The tests of 1928 and 1929 did not have any, apparently because it was felt that there was insufficient time to be divided between two factors, and in the years 1936 to 1940, during an experiment with an independent Mathematics Attainment Test, the SAT contained no mathematical section.

From 1926 until 1944 each candidate received in the mail prior to the test administration a practice booklet that he was required to present, completed, at the door of the testing center. In view of the careful mailing during this period, the internal instructions for taking the test were kept to a minimal terseness. Today, the mailing has been abandoned, but the internal instructions are longer and there is a model of an answer to each item type except the reading comprehension and the basic mathematical questions. In 1926, of course, the SAT with its objective item types was an innovation; today it must be a rare candidate who has not become quite familiar with multiple-choice tests by the time he comes to take the SAT. Nevertheless, as was described earlier, this familiarity is not taken for granted. Extensive descriptive literature concerning the SAT, accompanied by a complete practice test, is made available to all candidates well in advance of the formal operational administration.

Formula scoring of the test was introduced in December 1953, accompanied by a concerted effort to retain the comparability and previous meaning of the scaled scores. From the available evidence, this effort was

Table 2.1

Data relating to speededness: SAT-*verbal sections*

Historical record of the time allowances and numbers of items: 1926-69

Years	Total time (in min.)	Number of items	Time per item (in sec.)
1926	82	245	20
1927	75	265	17
1928-1929	115	350	20
1930-1935	75	220	20
1936-1939	115	300	23
1940-1941	125	250	30
1942-1943	100	200	30
1944-1946	80	160	30
1947	100	170	35
1948	90	140	39
1949-1950	90	135	40
1951-1957	90	107	50
1958-1969	75	90	50

Table 2.2

Data relating to speededness: SAT-*mathematical sections*

Historical record of the time allowances and numbers of items: 1926-69

(Years)	Total time (in min.)	Number of items	Time per item (in sec.)
1926	15	65	14
1927	20	45	27
1928-1929	No mathematical sections offered		
1930-1932	75	100	45
1933-1935	80	100	48
1936-1941	No mathematical sections offered		
1942	60	61	59
1943-1946	60	64	56
1947	60	60	60
1948-1957	60	50	72
1958-1969	75	60	75

successful; the introduction of the formula scores did not produce any distortion in the Board scale. There is now a section of advice to candidates regarding behavior appropriate to the formula-scored test both on the back of the test book and in the descriptive booklet. The scaled score equivalents of negative raw scores are reported if these are greater than 200 on the Board scale.

From 1926 to 1941 the SAT was essentially the creation of Carl Brigham, Associate Secretary for the College Board, who, with Cecil R. Brolyer, put the SAT on a firm psychometric footing. Since 1948 the actual assembly of the test has been the responsibility of Educational Testing Service. The work at ETS is reviewed both by the College Board staff and by the Committee of Examiners in Aptitude Testing. This committee, consisting of six and sometimes seven prominent specialists in educational and psychological measurement, oversees the general development of the test.[*]

The techniques for the assembly of the SAT, which are described below, have grown increasingly formal and prescriptive over the years. In the late 1950s, the ETS staff, under the guidance of the Committee of Examiners in Aptitude Testing, developed detailed specifications for the content of the test and for the statistical characteristics of the items. These specifications, with small adjustments, remain the basis for the present development techniques. Control charts, specified frequencies, and many reviews constitute the basic framework of the present process, and many of the items which Brigham used to make the early tests would be unacceptable by today's item-writing standards. The need for this tightened control is evident: Many more persons are now involved in the assembly of the test, and many more forms are assembled within a given year. Further, today's system of form-to-form equating makes heavy demands on the parallelism of succeeding forms, heavier than in Brigham's day, when each year's form was independently scaled to a mean of 500 and standard deviation of 100. Then too, staffing changes, which are more frequent now than in Brigham's time (Brigham's own tenure lasted about 18 years), mean that the direct responsibility for the test currently passes through successive hands in a relatively short time. All of these reasons militate for the view that the specifications for the assembly process need to be detailed, demanding, and objectively stated.

The powerful simplicity and usefulness of the device of the variant items, which was first introduced by

---

[*]The members of the committee for 1967-68 were:

Julian C. Stanley, Johns Hopkins University, *Chairman*
Carl Bereiter, Ontario Institute for Studies in Education
Frederick B. Davis, University of Pennsylvania
John R. Hills, Florida State University
Warren S. Torgerson, Johns Hopkins University
Dean K. Whitla, Harvard University

Table 2.3

Item types used in SAT-*verbal and* SAT-*mathematical sections, 1926-69**

Item type	1926	1927	1928	1929	1930	1931	1932	1933	1934	1935	1936	1937	1938	1939	1940	1941	1942	1943	1944	1945	1946	1947	1948	1949	1950	1951	1952	1953	1954	1955	1956	1957	1958	1959	1960
Verbal																																			
Antonyms:																																			
6-choice	x	x	x	x	x	x	x	x	x	x	x	x	x	x	x	x	x	x	x	x	x	x	x	x	x	x									
5-choice																											x	x	x	x	x	x	x	x	x
Part of speech				x																															
Analogies:																																			
Select 4th term	x	x																																	
Select 2 terms	x	x									x	x	x	x	x	x	x																		
Select 2nd pair																		x	x	x	x	x	x	x	x	x	x	x	x	x	x	x	x	x	x
Paragraph reading	x	x	x	x	x	x	x	x	x	x	x	x	x	x	x	x	x	x	x	x	x														
Reading comprehension																						x	x	x	x	x	x	x	x	x	x	x	x	x	x
Double definition	x	x	x	x	x	x	x	x	x	x	x	x	x	x	x																				
Sentence completion																						x	x	x	x	x	x	x	x	x	x	x	x	x	x
Definitions	x	x																																	
Classification	x	x	x																																
Artificial language	x	x																																	
Logical inference	x	x																																	
Synonyms (2-choice)			x	x																															
Mathematical																																			
Problems: fill-in					x	x	x	x	x																										
Problems: 6-choice																x																			
Problems: 5-choice																	x	x	x	x	x	x	x	x	x	x	x	x	x	x	x	x	x	x	x
Arithmetic word problem	x	x																																	
Data sufficiency																																		x	x
Number series completion	x	x																																	

*Test format unchanged from 1960 to 1969

Brigham, probably cannot be overstated. This notion of "extra" items containing material not used in summing the candidate's basic raw score has made possible the pretesting of SAT materials under virtually ideal conditions. In addition, it permits the equating of the test with ease and flexibility, and it permits the introduction of experimental material for preliminary trial. If the quality of the test is due to any one factor, it is probably this constant replenishment of item stocks with fresh material about which the most useful statistical information is known with a high degree of reliability.

Assembly of the SAT-*verbal sections*

The specifications for the SAT are more elaborate than the tables of item arrangement suggest. Thus, the items are classified not only by item type and by difficulty, but along other dimensions as well, which vary somewhat from item type to item type. The development of test specifications is, of course, a familiar process in educational measurement. It is perhaps most familiar in the case of the Achievement Tests, where the development of grids for classifying items as to content or process or other subject-matter dimensions is a common procedure. The descriptions that follow, both for the verbal and mathematical sections, will be seen to resemble the more familiar achievement grids, underscoring what is perhaps a truism: the SAT is an achievement test in the sense that it measures developed ability. The important difference, however, between the SAT and the usual achievement test is that there is minimal dependence on school curriculum. Whereas achievement tests typically seek to reflect some fairly well-defined and recent educational program, the SAT is intended to go into the broadest sources of education, beyond any academic curriculum. A specific curriculum is considered only in an effort to give it proportionate weight among all the basic learnings. Much of the explicit subject-matter content of secondary school education, therefore, is excluded.

In addition to content specifications, there are a number of other dimensions which are considered. Process variables are specifically described in the case of SAT-M. For SAT-V they are not explicitly mentioned, but are implicit in the differences among the four item types. Finally, a number of minor dimensions have been formulated to insure consistency in the appearance of the test—the number of words omitted in sentence completion items, for example. These classification dimensions may be summarized as follows in Table 2.4:

Table 2.4

Classification scheme for SAT-*verbal items*

Item type	Classification dimensions
Sentence completion	(a) Content
	(b) Number of blanks
Antonym	(a) Content
	(b) Generality of distinction required
	(c) Number of words in options
	(d) Part of speech used
Analogy	(a) Content
	(b) Abstraction of terms
	(c) Independence of stem and options
Reading comprehension	(a) Content (determined by passage)
	(b) Functional skill tested

The sentence completion, antonym, and analogy items are called discrete items because they are complete in themselves, rather than being associated in common with a passage as are reading comprehension questions. The discrete items are drawn from the aesthetic and philosophical areas, the world of practical affairs, science, and human relationships.

The content classification scheme suggests a precision in classification that is in fact unattainable. In actuality, with complex stimuli such as the analogies or the sentence completion items, it is frequently quite difficult to assign a question clearly to one or the other of the categories. Nor are the categories ideally named, for they suggest a correspondence with school subject categories that does not exist. Thus, aesthetic-philosophical includes not only such obvious stems for antonym items as EXQUISITENESS and INIQUITOUS, but also LATENT and LUCID. Science antonyms might embrace ERUPT as well as COAGULATE. In view of this latitude, some unreliability in classification is not surprising. Nevertheless, in spite of the less than perfect reliability of the classifications, the items are forced into categories whenever possible and the proportion of items considered "general" is quite small.

The content of the reading comprehension items is actually determined by the content of the passage upon which they are based. There are currently seven passages, each with five associated questions, in the typical SAT. These passages consist of one each from the following seven content categories: narrative, biological science, physical science, synthesis, argumentative, humanities, and social studies.

The narrative passage is fiction, the argumentative passage is typically propaganda or polemic material, and the synthesis passage is that type of writing which explores basically philosophical questions (the nature of man, of mind, or of the universe) from the background of the sciences. The other passages are reasonable examples of writings in the various areas which might appeal to a literate college graduate who is not a specialist in the area. It is intended that all passages be limited to topics that are not normally covered in the scope of secondary school curriculums.

The other classification dimensions (besides content) are different for the various "discrete" item types. Three of these dimensions concern purely formal characteristics of the items they govern and are intended more as guides to item writers than as desirable characteristics of the test, although it may be argued that they relieve the test of a certain blandness. These three are the "number of blanks" dimension under the sentence completion item type, the "number of words in options" dimension for antonyms, and the "part of speech" dimension, also for antonyms. The remaining dimensions, however, are felt to govern more important characteristics of the items in question and to permit the measurement of ability by means of an assortment of complex tasks. These are the "general definition-fine distinction" dimensions in the antonyms, the "concrete-abstract" and "independent-overlapping" dimensions in the analogies, and the six-category dimension for classing the reading comprehension questions according to the functional skill tested.

A "general definition" item requires only a general knowledge of the word in the stem, for only one possible contender is presented among the options. In a "fine distinction" item, however, there is more homogeneity among the options and the item may require considerable reflection.

Among the analogies a concrete relationship would be HOUSE:ROOF, an abstract one, ELECTORATE:DEMOCRACY, while a mixed analogy might contain a relationship such as SHERIFF:JUSTICE. An analogy is said to be independent if the relationship in the stem would not normally suggest the relationship in the answer. Thus, FIRE:ASHES—EVENT:MEMORIES demonstrates independence, while FAMINE:FOOD—DROUGHT:WATER shows overlapping. The six categories for assigning items according to the reading skill tested are:

1. the comprehension of the main idea as explicitly stated
2. the comprehension of a supporting idea, explicitly stated
3. the completion of an intended inference
4. the application of a generalization found in the passage to a particular instance
5. the evaluation of the logic of the language in the passage
6. the perception of the style and tone of the passage.

The first two categories are basic comprehension questions. The next three categories stress logical reasoning, while the sixth category calls for a sensitivity to emotional aspects of language. There are some natural correlations between these categories and the content of the passages with which they are associated. Thus, Type VI questions tend to be asked of narrative passages, and there are only rare instances in which a "style and tone" question is appropriate for a science passage.

All of these dimensions are used to describe SAT-V in terms of the frequency with which its items are specified to fall into the various categories, and there is a genuine effort to meet these specification frequencies. Perhaps the most significant benefit to come of the system of specifications is the likely control one gains toward a greater parallelism of content among the test forms and the relative assurance that the performances of students taking the different forms will be evaluated on essentially the same dimensions.

The test assembler must construct a test which meets not only the specifications for the content and other classification dimensions, but certain statistical criteria as well, including criteria for item difficulty and discrimination. As described in Chapter I, the index of difficulty is delta, which is that value on the baseline of a normal curve with mean 13.0 and standard deviation 4 above which the area under the curve is equal to the proportion passing the item among those who reach it. Any students who mark a later item are deemed to have attempted (that is, to have reached and considered) the item in question, even if in fact they fail to give any response to it. The delta values that are observed in the pretest administration are used to estimate "equated delta values," deltas which would have been obtained, had the items been administered to the standard reference population (see Chapter I).

All specifications as to item difficulty are developed in terms of these "equated deltas," which, if estimated without error, would be entirely independent of the ability characteristics of the sample of students to whom they were administered at time of pretest, and therefore capable of being compared with one another without further adjustment.

The index of item discrimination is the biserial correlation for the item, calculated on data collected at the pretest administration. It expresses the correlation between the item and the total score on the operational form of the test. Observed biserials of the items, when the items appear in operational final forms, are, in general, slightly higher, since the item itself is included in the criterion against which it is correlated.

Specifications for SAT-verbal (and SAT-mathematical) call for a particular mean and standard deviation of equated deltas and a minimum and mean biserial r. To insure the desired mean and dispersion of deltas, a detailed distribution of deltas is specified. The distribution is somewhat platykurtic and dispersed in order to provide discrimination over the desired range of talent.

Specifications for SAT-verbal at the time of this writing call for a mean equated delta of 11.7, a standard deviation of equated deltas of 2.9, and biserial correlations of at least .30 and averaging .42, or as close to .42 as possible. These specifications were introduced in forms after July 1967 for reasons that are discussed in a later section concerning "800-scores" and the desired range of scaled scores, where some of the practical relationships between item statistics and test statistics will be considered.

Table 2.5 illustrates the extent to which the test specifications for SAT-verbal have been met in practice. The specified distributions of equated deltas and the specified mean biserial for SAT-verbal forms beginning with the December 1967 form are given at the left of the table. On the right are the distributions of deltas and summary statistics of item data (at the time of assembly) for eight test forms that were prepared for administration after July 1967. As may be observed in Table 2.5, the consistency of the item data is marked. The test assemblers rarely deviate from the prescribed numbers, and then only when forced to by the limits of the item pool.

Assembly of the SAT-*mathematical sections*

As stated earlier, there are only two formally recognized item types in the SAT-mathematical sections, general math and data sufficiency. Each of these is classified as to the content, setting, and solution process involved. In addition, general math items are classified as to the solution process, a dimension that is less applicable within the format of data sufficiency items. There are three categories for the content dimension: arithmetic-algebra, geometry, and "other." The arithmetic-algebra category includes items whose subject matter should have been covered in grade school arithmetic and the first year of high school algebra. Arithmetic and algebra are combined for two reasons: (1) the basic rules of combination for arithmetic and algebra are the same, and (2) in many cases items can be solved by either arithmetic or algebraic methods. The geometry category includes items requiring some knowledge of geometry. Only topics that should have been encountered informally and independent of any formal study of deductive Euclidean geometry should be included in the SAT. An item that involves geometry and either arithmetic or algebra should be classed as geometry. The "other" category includes problems dealing with inequalities, logic, intuitive topology, unusual symbols, operations, and definitions. The "other" category is essentially open-ended.

The setting may be familiar or nonfamiliar. A setting is familiar if it is similar to a setting which a typical candidate is likely to have encountered several times previously, either in actual experience or in a classroom exercise. The test for familiarity is the question, "Is the candidate likely to accept the setting of this problem without puzzlement?" If the setting is familiar, the well-prepared candidate can proceed immediately to the solution of the problem without asking himself what the setting means.

The solution process is classified as straightforward or not, depending on the extent to which it involves a routine process that has normally been well-drilled in the classroom. The straightforward process requires little original thought, although some variation from the usual classroom procedure may be involved.

Related to the foregoing setting-process dimensions is the concept of the "insightful reasoning" item. This item type was introduced into the test as a result of a validity study by French (1964). An "insightful reasoning" item goes beyond the limits of the normal non-straightforward process item in that it offers two possible solution processes, one a tedious and time-consuming method, the other an insightful and rapid technique. An example of an "insightful reasoning" item would be as follows:

(123 x 456) + (877 x 544) + (877 x 456) + (123 x 544) = (A) 579,000 (B) 667,000 (C) 1,000,000 (D) 1,333,000 (E) 1,421,000

Table 2.5

Distributions of SAT-verbal items by difficulty level:

Specified item statistics versus actual statistics in eight final test forms

EQUATED DELTA	SPECIFIED DISTRIBUTION	ACTUAL DISTRIBUTIONS AT TIME OF TEST ASSEMBLY: 1967-69							
		Dec	*Jan*	*Mar*	*May*	*Dec*	*Jan*	*Mar*	*May*
18			1	1	1				
17	2	2	1	1	1	2	2	2	2
16	4	4	4	4	4	4	4	4	4
15	8	8	8	8	8	8	8	8	8
14	10	10	10	10	10	10	10	10	10
13	10	10	10	10	10	10	10	10	10
12	10	10	10	10	10	10	10	10	10
11	10	10	10	10	10	10	10	10	10
10	10	10	10	10	10	10	10	10	10
9	8	8	8	8	8	8	8	8	8
8	7	7	7	7	7	7	7	7	7
7	6	6	6	6	6	6	6	6	6
6	3	3	3	3	3	3	3	3	3
5	2	2	2	2	2	2	2	2	2
Total number	90	90	90	90	90	90	90	90	90
$M_\triangle$	11.7±0.2	11.7	11.7	11.7	11.7	11.7	11.7	11.7	11.7
$SD_\triangle$	2.9±0.2	2.9	2.9	2.9	2.9	2.8	2.9	2.9	2.9
$M_{r_{bis}}$	.420±.004	.42	.42	.42	.42	.42	.42	.42	.42

While a more consuming method would be to do all the multiplications and additions as indicated, an insightful approach would be to recognize these products as representing the form,

$$ac + bd + bc + ad,$$

which would be factored to yield

$$(a + b)(c + d) = (123 + 877)(456 + 544) = (1,000)(1,000) = 1,000,000.$$

The classification of the items as to the type of thinking required sorts them into four categories, one for "computation," one for "numerical judgment," one for "relational thinking," and finally one for "miscellaneous." These specifications prevent the form from becoming predominantly one of these item types or another.

Table 2.6 presents data on the extent to which the statistical specifications for SAT-mathematical items are followed in the actual assembly, and as such is comparable to Table 2.5 for the verbal items.

General comments on the assembly

Although the need for parallelism provides the major basis for a system of controls, it cannot justify the specific numbers of items in each category. Why, for example, is it important to have one passage from each of seven major areas? Why not some other configuration? The answer may be self-evident. In keeping with the underlying philosophy of equity—that is, to avoid favoring one type of candidate over another—the materials are controlled so as to provide a variety of content situations. The specific frequencies, of course, are merely judgmental ones; there is no formula by which one can assert that a test in which the 19 analogy items are divided into subgroups of 5-5-5-4 among the four broad content categories is optimally suited to be most equitable. The existing set of specified frequencies is not unreasonable, however, and there is some empirical evidence that it contributes to a better balance for

Table 2.6

Distributions of SAT-*mathematical items by difficulty level:*

Specified item statistics versus actual statistics in eight final test forms

EQUATED DELTA	SPECIFIED DISTRIBUTION	ACTUAL DISTRIBUTIONS AT TIME OF TEST ASSEMBLY: 1967-69							
		Dec	*Jan*	*Mar*	*May*	*Dec*	*Jan*	*Mar*	*May*
20					1				
19	1	1	1	1	0			1	1
18	2	2	2	2	2	3	3	2	1
17	4	4	4	3	4	4	5	4	5
16	4	4	4	5	4	4	4	4	4
15	4	4	4	4	4	4	4	4	3
14	5	5	5	6	4	5	4	5	6
13	5	5	5	5	6	5	4	5	5
12	5	6	5	4	5	5	6	5	5
11	8	6	8	7	8	8	8	8	8
10	8	9	8	9	8	8	8	8	8
9	7	7	7	7	7	7	7	7	7
8	4	4	4	4	4	4	4	4	4
7	2	2	2	2	2	2	2	2	2
6	1	1	1	1	1	1	1	1	1
Total number	60	60	60	60	60	60	60	60	60
$M_\triangle$	12.5±.05	12.5	12.5	12.5	12.5	12.5	12.5	12.5	12.5
$SD_\triangle$	3.2±0.1	3.2	3.2	3.2	3.2	3.2	3.2	3.2	3.1
$M_{r_{bis}}$	.470±.04	.47	.47	.47	.46	.47	.47	.47	.47

the scores between the sexes. Thus, Coffman (1965) reports data that support the notion that the world of practical affairs category and the science category are typically easier for boys, while the aesthetic-philosophical and human relationships categories are easier for girls. Just as the frequencies are specified by judgment rather than by an explicit rationale, so the very nature of the categories themselves cannot be defended as the only rational approach to controlling the desired content properties of the test. Nonetheless, the definition of major content categories and the establishing of balanced frequencies across them seems to accomplish its purpose. Some of the minor categories, such as one-blank versus two-blank sentence completion, or the part-of-speech category in the antonyms, are, as mentioned earlier, more useful as guides to item writers than as determiners of formal test properties.

The foregoing discussion of the different dimensions of SAT-verbal and SAT-mathematical items would not be complete without some mention of the assumptions that are made about the correlations among these dimensions. As was suggested in describing the internal organization of the SAT, the various blocks of items of a given type are supposed to be roughly equivalent in difficulty in the test as a whole. That is, the difficulty dimension is supposed to be independent of the item type dimension. In general, this property of independent dimensions is assumed throughout. There are some logically necessary correlations, as in the case of "style and tone" reading items being more often associated with narrative passages, and there are some correlations due to the inherent properties of the items, as in the case of difficulty and item type: antonym items seem, on the average, to be more difficult than sentence completion items. Lastly, there is an arbitrary relationship imposed in SAT-mathematical items between setting (familiar-nonfamiliar) and process (straightforward-nonstraightforward). The correlation between item type and difficulty would seem to result from the disparity in the context that they offer to a solution: the sentence completion item asks about a word that might fit in a context of several other words; the antonym stem sits starkly by itself without any assisting context. Thus, the sentence completion blank is probably somewhat inherently easier.

The work of the test assembler is complicated by the requirement of independence when the item pool within which he is working by and large exhibits certain natural correlations among the dimensions. The assembler must use his knowledge of these correlations, in a sense to foil them. He begins his selection not randomly, but in the area where he knows there is rarity due to the correlation. Thus, he strives to locate a difficult sentence completion or an easy antonym in order to minimize the influence of the pool's limitations on his assembly. When one considers the many dimensions among which the assembly is balanced and the many possible combinations of items that might satisfy the specifications, and further, when one appreciates the essentially clerical nature of the work once the items themselves have been coded to reflect category membership, then it is not surprising to learn that there are major efforts under way to produce a computer assembly of these tests. Phototype assemblies of tests by computer were begun in the academic year 1965-66 and the work has continued.

The pretest program

In the early days, the Scholastic Aptitude Test program required but one form of the test each year. A conversion from raw to scaled scores was effected for that form by arbitrarily setting its mean scaled score and standard deviation of the scaled scores at 500 and 100 respectively. Today each form is formally equated to its predecessor forms and there are five new forms assembled regularly for use in each academic year. These forms must be closely parallel to permit the application of linear equating techniques. As described above, the specifications for the SAT have been established in great detail, and are followed in the assembly as scrupulously as the item pool allows. This central role for the item pool inevitably focuses attention upon the pretest program, for it is only through a successful pretesting program that the annual drain on the item pool through the assembly of new final forms and equating items can be replaced. It is one thing to establish specifications on the basis of a rationale which deduces test properties from item properties. It is perhaps another thing to insure that the hypothetically ideal set of items can in fact be achieved through the inputs of the pretesting program into the pool. Table 2.7 presents data on the number of items pretested for both verbal and mathematical sections during the academic year 1965-66. These items are broken down to show the distribution of difficulties that they exhibit and further, the number of "satisfactory" items that were achieved within each difficulty level and for the total pretest program.

The most salient characteristics of this table are the general tendency for the pretest efforts both in verbal and in mathematical items to produce markedly fewer items at the extremes of difficulty, both hard and easy, and for the proportion of satisfactory items to be associated with the level of difficulty. Thus, the work of the item writer is such that it is not likely that very many easy or difficult items will be written; the difficult (high delta) items face an even greater hazard in that when written they frequently fail to yield satisfactory biserial correlations. The existence of a relationship between difficulty level and the biserial coefficient may surprise readers who recall that this coefficient, unlike the point biserial, is not limited by item difficulty, but retains the full range of possible values from -1.00 to $+1.00$ regardless of item difficulty. However, it is not easy to write unambiguous difficult items, and many items fall by the wayside because of their failure to discrim-

Table 2.7

Distribution of equated deltas for SAT-*verbal and*
SAT-*mathematical items at time of pretest: 1965-66*

	SAT-VERBAL			SAT-MATHEMATICAL		
	Frequency of:		Proportion of satisfactory items*	Frequency of:		Proportion of satisfactory items*
Equated delta	All items	Satisfactory items*		All items	Satisfactory items*	
18+	2	0	.00	13	3	.23
17	13	4	.31	25	13	.52
16	39	13	.33	53	25	.47
15	69	36	.52	77	45	.58
14	87	54	.62	110	78	.71
13	143	99	.69	114	93	.82
12	147	115	.78	124	96	.77
11	163	131	.80	106	94	.89
10	129	116	.90	64	55	.86
9	114	100	.88	44	40	.91
8	80	72	.90	27	22	.81
7	36	34	.94	16	12	.75
6	32	28	.88	12	11	.92
5	13	10	.77	4	4	1.00
Not computed	8			11		
Total	1075	812	.76	800	591	.74

*An item is arbitrarily defined as satisfactory if it has a biserial of .30 or greater.

inate appropriately. The effects of "chance" success may also help to explain this phenomenon. Items of equated delta-level 15 or greater are usually answered correctly by relatively small proportions of the total group—some below the 20 percent chance level for five-choice items. Thus, the mean ability level of the correct response may be dramatically lowered by the chance success of the less able group.

The general failure of the item writers to produce items at the extreme levels of difficulty is a perennial problem in test construction. The ability of judges to determine absolute difficulty level prior to pretesting is only limited. This finding is, of course, not unique. An article by Tinkelman (1947) and a similar one by Lorge and Kruglov (1952) have reported on their work in assessing the accuracy of these judgments.

The data in Table 2.7 may be related to the total volume of items that were required by the SAT program in the course of the 1965-66 academic year: 520 verbal items and 340 mathematics items. This means that there are about 2.1 items being pretested for each verbal item that is required and about 2.4 items being pretested for each mathematics item required. After the rejection of items with unsatisfactory biserials, the

pretest program still supplies somewhat more items than are drawn out for routine assembly: about 1.7 items supplied by math pretests, and about 1.6 items supplied by the verbal. This moderate excess is essential, since the distribution of difficulties developed by the pretest program is not exactly in line with the distribution called for in the specifications. In order to compensate for item writers' failures to reach extreme difficulty levels, a greater number of items must be pretested. The "excess" is even smaller than indicated, for additional demands are also placed upon this pool to assist in such other College Board activities as the assembly of the Preliminary Scholastic Aptitude Test, of a test that is supplied to an African population, and of special tests for various College Board research projects.

All active SAT forms are completely independent of one another, no item being used in more than one of these forms. The number of such forms in use is typically between 15 and 20, for there are old forms of the test being used in such special situations as Sunday administrations, institutional validity studies, and so forth. Currently, two forms are required each year to provide the basis for the assembly of PSAT forms.

Parallelism and reliability of the SAT

All of the work of assembly, all of the specifications and careful coding of items is intended to produce consistently reliable tests with a high degree of parallelism. This section will present some evidence of the extent to which the processes succeed.

Table 2.8 gives the internal consistency reliabilities and standard errors of measurement for the 12 forms introduced during the academic years 1966-67, 1967-68, and 1968-69. This table is supplemented by the parallel-forms reliabilities presented in Table 2.9, which are based on recent forms as indicated. It is apparent that SAT forms regularly exhibit an acceptable reliability.

Some notion of the parallelism of the forms may be gathered from the similarity in the results of equating the various forms. That is, the equation converting raw scores to the 200-800 scale summarizes the relationship between the raw scores and the scale. If the tests are built to be parallel, there should be only minimal variation in these equations from form to form, since, under these conditions, the equating process is independent of the group on which it is carried out. Table 2.10, which presents the scaled score equivalents for three selected raw score points for each form, provides this summary for forms developed between December 1967 and May 1969, during which time the difficulty specifications for the test remained constant. The test construction processes yield forms so parallel that given raw score

points on any form may be anticipated to have approximately the same scaled score equivalent. The maximum scaled score differences between the forms shown in Table 2.10 represent less than five raw score points at the SAT-verbal midscore (45) and less than three raw score points at the SAT-mathematical midscore (30). This finding is, of course, a welcome one in a program devoted to test parallelism, but it has, as well, the decided benefit that successive forms of the SAT are pitched at very nearly the same level and range of difficulty and therefore represent the "same" test for all candidates no matter which form they take.

Validity

The long history of the SAT has produced a wealth of validity coefficients, many of which are summarized in Chapter V. Earlier documentation on validity is set forth in *College Board Scores No. 2* (Dyer and King, 1955) and in the *1957 Supplement to College Board Scores* (Fishman, 1957). While there is no routine formal validity study for each new form of the SAT, colleges that use the SAT undertake validity studies of their own, based on their own criteria of college success, and conducted with the aid of the College Board Validity Study Service. The results of these studies are supplemented by special research studies carried out by ETS in behalf of the College Board, which contrast new item types with those appearing in current operational forms

Table 2.8

Internal-consistency reliability estimates and standard errors of measurement
for 12 recent SAT forms

Form: Date of first administration	SAT-VERBAL		SAT-MATHEMATICAL	
	Reliability*	Standard error of measurement	Reliability*	Standard error of measurement
Dec 1966	.898	32.8	.893	35.1
Jan 1967	.906	32.3	.908	34.9
Mar 1967	.912	32.2	.912	33.5
May 1967	.917	32.7	.900	35.1
Dec 1967	.910	32.7	.897	36.3
Jan 1968	.902	33.3	.912	33.6
Mar 1968	.913	30.9	.912	33.9
May 1968	.907	33.3	.898	35.8
Dec 1968	.912	31.7	.911	34.6
Jan 1969	.915	31.5	.913	32.4
Mar 1969	.912	30.9	.900	32.8
May 1969	.903	31.9	.888	36.3

*These reliability estimates are based on Dressel's (1940) adaptation of Kuder-Richardson formula (20) (1937).

Table 2.9

Estimates of parallel-form reliability for SAT *scores**

Academic year	SAT-VERBAL				SAT-MATHEMATICAL			
	Mar-Dec	Mar-Jan	May-Dec	May-Jan	Mar-Dec	Mar-Jan	May-Dec	May-Jan
1962-63 to 1963-64	.89	.88	.89	.89	.87	.85	.89	.87
1963-64 to 1964-65	.90	.89	.89	.89	.89	.88	.88	.88
1964-65 to 1965-66	.89	.89	.88	.89	.87	.86	.87	.88
1965-66 to 1966-67	.89	.91	.88	.89	.87	.89	.86	.87
1966-67 to 1967-68	.90	.90	.88	.89	.88	.89	.86	.88
1967-68 to 1968-69	.89	.90	.88	.90	.88	.89	.86	.88
1968-69 to 1969-70	.90	.90	.89	.90	.88	.89	.87	.88

*These correlations are based on regular candidates who elect to take the SAT in the spring of their junior year in secondary school and repeat the test in the winter of their senior year. Numbers of cases range from 2,949 (March 1969 to January 1970) to 207,094 (May 1967 to December 1967).

of the SAT. In these studies it is apparent that the SAT provides substantial correlation against grade-point criteria, and at a variety of institutions representing a wide range of ability levels among their undergraduate populations.

Speededness

The SAT is intended to be basically a power measure, and its evolution over the years has called for increasing amounts of time per item for both SAT-V and SAT-M as indicated by the chart presented earlier in this chapter. As in any timed test, however, speed is inevitably a factor, however small. In the factor analysis studies of Coffman (1966) and Pruzek and Coffman (1966), both SAT-V and SAT-M were found to contain clear speed factors which seemed to account for about 9 percent and 4 percent of the total variance, respectively. Some indication of the extent of speededness is made possible by the Tables 2.11, 2.12, and 2.13. These three tables present different aspects of the speed problem: the percent completing the sections of the test, the percent completing three quarters of a section, and the mean and standard deviation of the number of items "not reached."

Table 2.11 shows that the 45-minute mathematics sections are least speeded, while the 30-minute mathematics sections are the most speeded, in terms of the percent of the group completing them. The 45-minute verbal sections are somewhat more speeded than their 30-minute counterparts. The explanations for these differences probably lie in the types of item content

associated with these sections. The 45-minute mathematics sections contain the block of data sufficiency items, an item type that typically is answered extremely rapidly by knowledgeable candidates. The 45-minute verbal sections contain somewhat more reading comprehension material than their 30-minute counterparts, which explains why they require somewhat more time per item. Table 2.12, which compares the various

Table 2.10

Scaled score equivalents to selected raw scores for eight SAT *forms — December 1967 to May 1969*

Form: Date of first administration	SAT-VERBAL			SAT-MATHEMATICAL		
	20	45	70	10	30	50
Dec 1967	363	534	706	367	559	752
Jan 1968	373	545	718	360	536	712
Mar 1968	368	528	688	362	542	723
May 1968	355	528	701	367	556	746
Dec 1968	361	525	690	371	554	737
Jan 1969	367	530	693	366	537	708*
Mar 1969	353	513	674	362	532	703*
May 1969	364	526	688	356	548	739

*Special linear methods were used to equate these forms operationally at the upper end of the scale. The results of the operational equating yielded scaled scores, corresponding to the raw score of 50, of 722 for the January 1969 form and 703 (unchanged at this point on the scale) for the March 1969 form.

sections with respect to the percent completing three-fourths of the test, shows that there are very few basic differences from this point of view. The variations between the two sections of SAT-verbal and between the two sections of SAT-mathematical are consistent with those in Table 2.11. Table 2.13 presents the same basic pattern, but in terms of the mean and standard deviation of the number of items "not reached" in each of the sections. It may be seen that for most candidates the number of such failures to reach items is quite small.

The foregoing discussions contrast the various sections of the test. The variation among tests themselves is best seen in Table 2.13, since the "percent completing" in Table 2.11 fails to distinguish between those who reach the last item but omit it and those who never reach it, and since Table 2.12 is concerned with the portion of the test that is within the reach of all candidates and yields figures that are all very close to 100 percent. Table 2.13 shows that the SAT forms are quite consistent with respect to the average time per item that they require. If one assumes that candidates work at constant rates of speed, these data suggest that one could remove all variation in the "not reached" figures by a time adjustment of no more than one minute for any given form for both the 30- and 45-minute verbal sections and for the 45-minute math sections. An adjustment of approximately two and one-half minutes would be required for the 30-minute mathematical sections to remove the greatest observed difference in speededness. Since no formal statistic of the time required for each item is calculated, the foregoing

Table 2.11

Percent completing the test for
12 SAT forms — December 1966 to May 1969

Form: Date of first administration	SAT-VERBAL		SAT-MATHEMATICAL	
	30-minute sections	45-minute sections	30-minute sections	45-minute sections
Dec 1966	80.4	63.7	40.2	73.6
Jan 1967	68.1	56.1	39.0	89.1
Mar 1967	67.7	71.6	69.3	87.0
May 1967	73.1	62.9	48.9	82.3
Dec 1967	68.0	68.3	67.0	86.6
Jan 1968	73.2	60.1	62.3	79.9
Mar 1968	83.4	71.4	69.2	79.1
May 1968	78.1	74.6	43.4	85.4
Dec 1968	70.9	69.8	57.3	82.2
Jan 1969	66.1	61.8	40.2	84.3
Mar 1969	77.6	81.6	44.9	85.4
May 1969	79.3	76.3	68.3	89.4
	40 items	50 items	25 items	35 items

Table 2.12

Percent completing three quarters of the test for
12 SAT forms — December 1966 to May 1969

Form: Date of first administration	SAT-VERBAL		SAT-MATHEMATICAL	
	30-minute sections	45-minute sections	30-minute sections	45-minute sections
Dec 1966	99.9	99.2	98.7	99.3
Jan 1967	98.6	98.0	94.9	97.3
Mar 1967	99.9	99.3	95.8	98.3
May 1967	99.1	99.2	95.8	98.7
Dec 1967	100.0	99.8	93.7	98.6
Jan 1968	99.7	97.7	96.3	98.1
Mar 1968	99.8	98.9	93.5	98.0
May 1968	99.9	99.1	97.6	98.7
Dec 1968	99.4	99.2	96.1	98.6
Jan 1969	99.4	97.3	87.4	97.3
Mar 1969	99.7	99.7	98.6	98.4
May 1969	99.9	99.4	97.2	97.7
	40 items	50 items	25 items	35 items

regularity must be attributed to the validity of item writer's judgments of the amount of time needed to answer the items.

The 45-minute mathematics sections are the least speeded, probably because they are the sections that contain the data sufficiency items. Recent reports from the test proctors have indicated that however well the sections may satisfy the psychometric criteria of a power test, they may, possibly because of that, leave something to be desired as a practical work sample to be administered under real time limits. Proctors sometimes complain that during these sections of the test inordinate numbers of candidates finish early and sit for the remaining interval, creating a difficult proctoring situation.

Correlation between SAT-*verbal and* SAT-*mathematical scores*

The usefulness of the two separately recorded scores for the SAT is, of course, strongly influenced by the extent of the correlation between them. Table 2.14 shows the recent experience with these correlations for the 12 forms that have been reported here. The average correlation for these forms is .67. There is some variation in the magnitude of the correlation from form to form, but in general the pattern is markedly similar.

Correlations of the type demonstrated in Table 2.14 have been increasing in magnitude since the 1940s. In

Table 2.13

*Mean and standard deviation of the number not reached for
12 SAT forms — December 1966 to May 1969*

Form: Date of first administration	SAT-VERBAL				SAT-MATHEMATICAL			
	30-minute sections		45-minute sections		30-minute sections		45-minute sections	
	M	S.D.	M	S.D.	M	S.D.	M	S.D.
Dec 1966	0.64	1.62	1.91	3.20	1.39	1.68	0.66	1.67
Jan 1967	1.16	2.35	2.51	3.74	1.87	2.21	0.69	2.46
Mar 1967	0.96	1.85	1.42	2.82	1.16	2.22	0.66	2.45
May 1967	1.13	2.54	1.56	3.11	1.74	2.32	0.62	1.97
Dec 1967	1.12	1.97	1.45	2.67	1.37	2.59	0.58	1.98
Jan 1968	1.01	2.06	2.62	4.05	1.14	2.05	0.74	2.26
Mar 1968	0.62	1.67	1.24	2.70	1.42	2.63	0.82	2.60
May 1968	0.80	1.85	1.32	2.81	1.45	1.89	0.58	1.98
Dec 1968	0.98	1.99	1.44	2.86	1.38	2.19	0.62	1.90
Jan 1969	1.38	2.44	2.49	3.99	2.54	3.19	0.83	2.68
Mar 1969	0.79	1.83	0.83	2.17	1.11	1.66	0.61	2.05
May 1969	0.90	2.09	1.12	2.86	1.17	2.09	0.58	2.24
	40 items		50 items		25 items		35 items	

Table 2.14

*Correlation between SAT-verbal and SAT-mathematical scores
for 12 forms — December 1966 to May 1969*

Form: Date of first administration	r_{vm}
Dec 1966	.651
Jan 1967	.668
Mar 1967	.738
May 1967	.656
Dec 1967	.706
Jan 1968	.642
Mar 1968	.684
May 1968	.648
Dec 1968	.690
Jan 1969	.645
Mar 1969	.690
May 1969	.647

Table 2.15

*Trend in the correlation
between SAT-verbal scores and SAT-mathematical scores*

Time period	No. of test forms	Average correlation
1950-53	6	.54
1953-56	6	.56
1956-59	9	.62
1959-62	14	.64
1962-65	12	.66
1965-69	16	.67

1945 the correlation was in the range of .40 to .45. By 1950, the correlation had begun to rise. Table 2.15 shows the trend in the correlation between SAT-verbal and SAT-mathematical scores from 1950 to 1969.

As will be seen from the table, the correlation between SAT-verbal and SAT-mathematical scores for the six forms from 1950 through 1953 were, on the average, some 12 points higher than in 1945. No adequate explanation has been advanced for the increasing correlation. It has been attributed to increasing variability in the population, as more and more varied candidates approach college; it has been attributed to changes in item content, most frequently to the introduction of data sufficiency items; and it has been attributed to changes in educational processes, most frequently to the improved mathematics education available to girls. No one of these arguments has received adequate empirical support, and all are subject to the criticism that they do not coincide in the pattern of the introduction of their influence to the steady rise of the various coefficients. In any case, the level of correlation between SAT-verbal scores and SAT-mathematical scores has caused concern for their independent usefulness.

Factor analyses of the SAT

Coffman has made the point that knowledge about SAT factor structure should be useful in at least two ways. "First, it should provide a guide to the building of parallel forms of the test. At present, test specifications are stated in terms of content categories based on rational analyses and statistical indices derived from item analysis. It has been recognized since the early days that a score on the SAT-verbal sections represents a composite . . . and that it is important to balance the several factors in each new test form if each is to make its intended contribution to the reported score. A factor analysis ought to provide information about the number of factors entering into the reported score and the relative weight of each. A second advantage of studying the factor structure of SAT-verbal sections is that factors might be identified which might have significant validity but which have little influence on the reported score because there are very few items on the test which load on the factor. By changing the relative weight of the several factors in the test, or by building separate subtests and reporting separate scores, it might be possible to increase the validity of the SAT." (Coffman, 1966, pp. 1-2.)

Two factor studies of SAT items have been undertaken recently (Coffman, 1966; Pruzek and Coffman, 1966). Both of these were aimed primarily at ways of generating the SAT factor pattern rather than at obtaining immediate and definitive answers about the SAT's structure. Basic data for these analyses were item responses for 1,479 candidates who took the December 1959 SAT.

The analysis of the verbal sections of the SAT (Coffman, 1966) involved principal axis factoring followed by three different rotations. In the SAT-mathematical analysis (Pruzek and Coffman, 1966) two factoring methods and four rotational methods were used. Since the analyses were primarily methodological and exploratory in aim, it is not surprising that they did not generate definite conclusions regarding the factor structure of the SAT although 6 mathematical factors and 10 verbal factors were tentatively named. As Coffman points out, "This exploratory study has raised more questions than it has answered. On the other hand, it has demonstrated that factor analysis procedures can throw light on the nature of the SAT-v." (Coffman, 1966, p.11.) Three directions for further research are proposed on the basis of these exploratory studies: first, that somewhat different factor analytic approaches should be tried; second, that more than one form of the SAT should be studied; and, third, that there should be separate studies on clearly defined subgroups (e.g., groups classified by socioeconomic status or by college curriculum). Studies using groups of different ability levels might also be instructive.

Origin and maintenance of the SAT score scale

The present system of scales for the SAT began with the April 1941 administration of the test. Prior to that time the SAT was reported on a 200-800 scale that was redefined at each administration by a linear conversion of the raw scores which set the mean at 500 and the standard deviation at 100. This repeated redefinition of the scale was carried out under the assumption that actual changes in the abilities of the candidate groups from one administration to another were relatively small and insignificant. Although this was probably a reasonable assumption at the time, the outcome left something to be desired. Since the means and standard deviations of successive candidate groups were set equal to the same scaled-score numbers year after year, it was obviously not possible to make precise comparisons between candidates tested in one administration and candidates tested at another administration.

Consequently, in April 1941 the stage was set for a new score reporting system. As before, the scale for the new form was defined anew. The mean and standard deviation of raw scores on the verbal sections of the SAT were set equal to 500 and 100 for the entire group of 10,654 candidates tested at that administration. What was new about the system was the provision for equating the scores on all subsequent forms of the test to the scale established for this April 1941 reference group. The purpose of the equating process was (and still is) to insure that the score system would have the same meaning from year to year—that is, that any given scaled score would represent the same level of ability regardless of the difficulty characteristics of the form of the test on which it was earned, the nature of the group taking the test, or the time of the year when the test was administered.

In order to carry out this equating, a set of items in the form administered in April 1941 was carried over and administered as part of the June 1941 form of the test. Differences in mean and standard deviations on the "carried-over" (or "common") items were observed for the groups taking the test in April and June and were then used to adjust the statistics on the entire test forms for those groups. With these adjustments completed, it was then possible to set the adjusted raw score means and standard deviations on the new form equal to scaled score means and standard deviations on the old form, thereby providing a linear conversion from raw to scaled scores for the new form.

In April 1942 the same process of equating was carried out. A section of the form administered in June 1941 was carried over and administered as part of the April

1942 form of the test. Again, differences in the statistics on the common section observed in June 1941 and April 1942 were used to make adjustments in the statistics for the entire test forms, making it possible, as before, to provide a linear conversion from raw to scaled scores for the April 1942 form.

The foregoing method of equating was applied in the beginning only to SAT-verbal. The scale for SAT-mathematical traces its origin to April 1942 when the raw score mean and standard deviation were set equal, respectively, to the scaled score mean and standard deviation of SAT-verbal.

From 1942 until the present time new SAT-verbal forms have been equated to predecessor forms by linear conversion. Similarly, new SAT-mathematical forms have been equated to predecessor forms by linear conversion, and quite independently of the equating of the SAT-verbal forms. During this period, the specific methods of equating have been revised in accordance with new insights for improving the reliability of the system. However, the basic model of linear equating has been retained, as has the procedure of adjusting for group differences in the process of equating (that is, the procedure of administering with each new form a collection of test items that had previously been administered with an old form).

During the early 1950s the question of the reliability of the equating system was subjected to intensive and continuing study. Obviously the process of equating, like any other statistical process, is subject to random error which, if left unchecked, could eventually become quite considerable. It became clear that if successive forms were each equated to their immediate predecessors in chain fashion, then the variance error of equated scores for the most recent form in relation to the original form in the chain of forms would be $n\sigma_e^2$ (where σ_e^2 = the average variance error of any one equating process, and n = the number of equating links in the chain). That is to say, the variance error in the entire system would increase directly as a function of the number of links, or equatings, involved, just as the variance error of any total process is the sum of the variance errors of the individual (independent) parts of the process. On the other hand, if the equating system were allowed to develop, not as a simple chain, but without any plan, then it was entirely possible that separate strains or "families" of scales could develop. The likely result would be that two forms, contiguous with respect to the time of their appearance, could be quite distantly related in terms of the number of equating links between them, and as a result of equating error alone could yield far different scaled scores for a given level of ability than if they were schematically closer together.

While it has been impossible to develop a precise estimate of the standard error of equated test scores, it appears that it is in the neighborhood of five points on the College Board scale, that is, about five percent of a typical standard deviation. Although this is small indeed, when compared to the standard error of measurement of SAT-verbal or mathematical of 30 or 35 percent of a standard deviation, the cumulative error of equating in a chain of 25 links of test forms is about one-fourth of a standard deviation, or 25 points on the score scale. This amount of error is *not* small, and it throws doubt on any equating system that involves successively the equating of each new form of a test to the form immediately preceding it. Moreover, since the error of equating appears in the conversion equation itself, it is transmitted to every score to which the equation is applied and affects the summary statistics of scores in the manner of a bias. In this respect it is unlike other kinds of statistical error, as for example the error of measurement in a mean, which tends to vanish as the sample size is increased. Equating error can be controlled by controlling the size of the sample from which the conversion is derived; but once the conversion is derived, its error is just as large whether the sample to which it is applied consists of 10 cases or 10,000 cases. Thus, while the error of equating is small in relation to the error of measurement of a single test score, it can loom quite large in relation to the error of measurement in a mean and can seriously affect comparisons of group performance.

Accordingly, a system has been introduced in which each form is equated not to one, but to *two* previous forms, and the results averaged. In its inception the "double part-score equating" plan was not as formal and elaborate as it was later to become. Originally it required only that the new form of the test be equated to two forms—one that was introduced only a year previously, and one that was introduced three or four years previously. By 1959, as a result of informal examinations of equating results and as a result of a more formal study by Angoff and Waite (1961), it became clear that the system of equating was in fairly good control. However, there was still room for improvement, and Wilks (1961) made a series of detailed recommendations for the future conduct of the College Board scaling and equating operations. One of these recommendations was that the linkages among the test forms be organized in a systematic "braiding" fashion, by which it was hoped to shorten the equating distance between every form and every other form and to knit the system more tightly together. If properly executed, this plan (McGee, 1961) would not only enhance the reliability of equating any new form, but also—and in consequence of this greater reliability—would enhance the comparability among forms.

Figure 2.2 presents the "genealogical chart" for SAT-verbal, a diagram of the "parental" and "ancestral" linkages for each of the forms of SAT-verbal from 1969 back to 1941, when the scale for the SAT-verbal was first established. Each line in the diagram that connects two forms of the test indicates that the more recent form has been equated to the older form and, through it, to the basic reference scale for the SAT. As may be seen in the chart, each of the forms of the SAT-verbal since

Figure 2.2
Genealogical chart for SAT-verbal

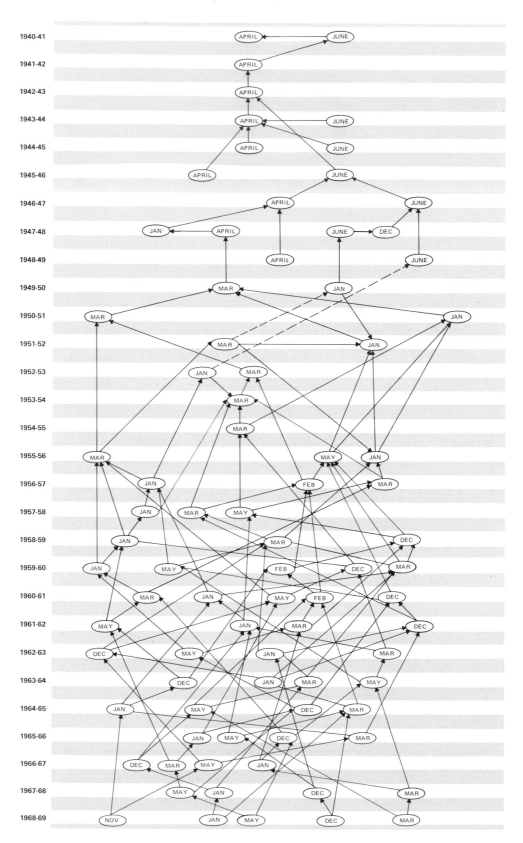

about 1954 has undergone two equatings, one to each of two old forms. These two equatings are carried out independently and averaged before the scores for any of the candidates are released. The chart also describes the system by which the linkages among the forms are braided and interwoven to yield an internally consistent and homogeneous network. Figure 2.3 gives the corresponding genealogical chart for SAT-mathematical.

Current procedures and their results

The methods that have been adopted for equating the successive operational forms of the SAT have been mainly dictated by certain practical considerations. One consideration is that, for reasons of security, no form of the SAT is ever administered prior to its first operational use. Another is that *all* candidates taking the test at a regular administration earn operational scores—that is, scores that are reported to the colleges they apply to—that are based on precisely the same test items. These restrictions make it imperative that all equating be done between the time that a new form is first administered and the time that score reports are issued for the candidates who first take that form. These restrictions also place a considerable strain on the design of the equating, since randomization of forms is not permitted either in a prior experimental administration or in the operational administrations for which score reports are to be issued. The significance of these restrictions is that the equating of the SAT has to be conducted with groups (one taking the current form and the other taking the old form) that can easily differ appreciably with respect to mean and variance.

In order to control for the effect of group differences on the conversion equation, a plan instituted in the early 1940s of using common test items for equating is followed. In the administration of the SAT all students, as pointed out above, take the same operational form of the test. However, in addition to the operational items, the students also take a variable set of special items that do not contribute toward their reported scores. These variable items may be used for equating. Whenever an operational form of the SAT is administered for the first time, three sets of verbal equating items are administered (but never more than one set to a candidate): one that has previously been administered along with a form that was first introduced about three years ago, one that has previously been administered along with a form that was first introduced about one year ago, and one "planted" for future equating. The same plan is followed with respect to mathematical equating items. We shall refer to such items hereafter as "equating sections." During the balance of this discussion we will consider equating procedures in some detail.

The plan of administration and the data used for the equating may be described as follows in terms of the notation that will be used below: "Equating Section" u is a set of verbal equating items, yielding a single total

score, that is administered along with Form w, the current operational form of SAT-verbal, to Group α, a random subgroup of the candidates who have taken the SAT at this time. The identical set of verbal equating items, Equating Section u, was also administered along with Form x, an operational form of SAT-verbal that was given at a previous administration, to Group β, a random subgroup of the candidates who had taken the SAT at that time.

In parallel to the foregoing plan there is a second set of verbal equating items, Equating Section z, that is also administered with Form w, the current operational form of SAT-verbal, but to Group γ, a *different* random subgroup of the candidates who have taken the SAT at this time. The same set of verbal equating items, Equating Section z, was also administered with Form y, an operational form of SAT-verbal that was given at a different previous administration, to Group δ, a random subgroup of the candidates who had taken the SAT at that time.

(Correspondingly, there is a set of mathematical equating items material that are common to the current form and also to one old form of the SAT-mathematical, and a second set of mathematical equating items that are common to the current form and to another old form of the SAT-mathematical.)

A summary of the notation is given below:

Variables

w, x, y = Raw scores on test forms to be equated. Form w is new; Forms x and y are the old forms to which Form w is to be equated.

u, z = Raw scores on the sets of equating items. Equating Section u is common to the administration of both Forms w and x. Equating Section z is common to the administration of both Forms w and y.

S = Standard score scale.

Groups

α = Group taking Form w and Equating Section u

β = Group taking Form x and Equating Section u

t = α + β

γ = Group taking Form w and Equating Section z

δ = Group taking Form y and Equating Section z

c = γ + δ

Data for equating each new form, say of SAT-verbal, to two previous forms of SAT-verbal are assembled by drawing a sample of 5,000 candidates* who have taken

---

*This number has not always been 5,000. Over the course of the last 15 years or so, because of the increase in the numbers of candidates taking the SAT, and also because of the availability of high-speed data processing equipment, the numbers of cases used for equating the SAT forms have gradually been increased from 500 to 5,000. It is entirely possible that with the continued growth of the College Board candidate group and with the continued improvement in data processing facilities, this number will be increased still further in the future.

Figure 2.3

Genealogical chart for SAT-*mathematical*

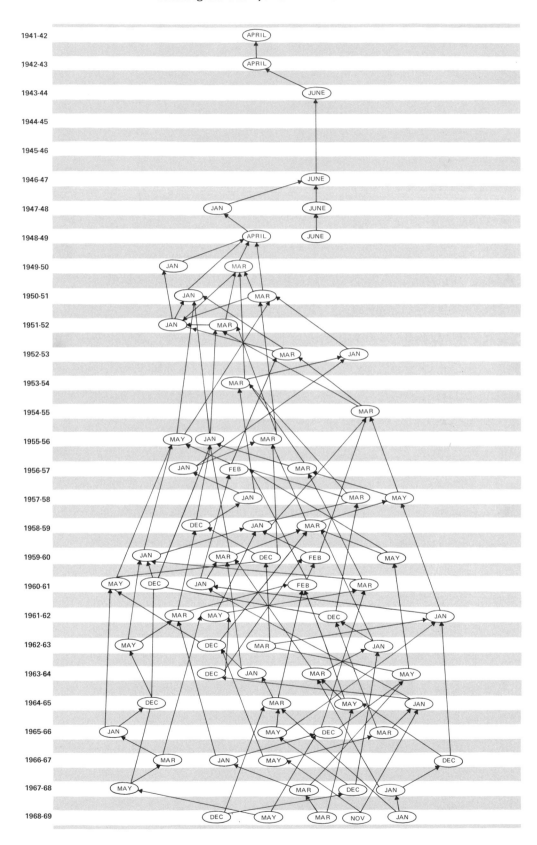

Form w and Equating Section u, and using this sample in conjunction with a sample of 5,000 cases who have taken the old Form x and the same Equating Section u. The equating of Form w to Form x is accomplished by: 1) estimating the mean and standard deviation of raw scores on Form w for the combined group (t), those taking Form w (Group α) plus those taking Form x (Group β); 2) estimating the mean and standard deviation of raw scores on Form x for the combined Group (t); 3) setting the estimated mean and standard deviation on Form w equal, respectively, to the estimated mean and standard deviation on Form x, thus forming a linear equation relating the raw score scale of Form w to the raw score scale of Form x; and 4) substituting this equation into the existing raw-to-scaled conversion for the old form, Form x, to yield a raw-to-scaled conversion for Form w.

The equations for estimating the mean and variance on Forms w and x for the total Group, t, are derived from selection theory, in which it is assumed that the variance errors of estimate, the slopes, and the intercepts of Form w, for example, predicted from Equating Section u, are the same for Group t and Group α (Angoff, 1961). That is to say, it is assumed that:

$$s^2_{w_t}(1 - r^2_{wu_t}) = s^2_{w_a}(1 - r^2_{wu_a}); \quad b_{wu_t} = b_{wu_a};$$

$$\text{and} \quad M_{w_t} - b_{wu_t}M_{u_t} = M_{w_a} - b_{wu_a}M_{u_a}.$$

Parallel assumptions are made for the relationship between Form x and Equating Section u for Groups t and β. The resulting estimation equations are given as follows:

1) $\hat{M}_{w_t} = M_{w_a} + b_{wu_a}(M_{u_t} - M_{u_a}),$

2) $\hat{M}_{x_t} = M_{x_\beta} + b_{xu_\beta}(M_{u_t} - M_{u_\beta}),$

3) $\hat{s}^2_{w_t} = s^2_{w_a} + b^2_{wu_a}(s^2_{u_t} - s^2_{u_a}),$ and

4) $\hat{s}^2_{x_t} = s^2_{x_\beta} + b^2_{xu_\beta}(s^2_{u_t} - s^2_{u_\beta}).$

The equation relating raw scores on Form w to raw scores on Form x is derived by setting equal the estimated standard score deviates on the two tests for the combined Group, t:

$$\frac{X - \hat{M}_{x_t}}{\hat{s}_{x_t}} = \frac{W - \hat{M}_{w_t}}{\hat{s}_{w_t}},$$

thus yielding the equation,

5) $X = A_{xw} W + B_{xw},$

where $A_{xw} = \hat{s}_{x_t}/\hat{s}_{w_t}$ and $B_{xw} = \hat{M}_{x_t} - A_{xw} \hat{M}_{w_t}.$

A_{xw} and B_{xw} are the slope and intercept, respectively, of the line converting scores on Form w to the scale of Form x.

Then, substituting in the existing equation relating the Form x raw scores to the standard scale,

6) $\quad\quad S = A_{sx} X + B_{sx},$

the equation relating Form w scores to the scale is obtained:

7) $\quad\quad S = A'_{sw} W + B'_{sw},$

where $A'_{sw} = A_{sx}A_{xw}$ and $B'_{sw} = A_{sx}B_{xw} + B_{sx}.$

A parallel and independent procedure is carried out for equating the new Form w to the old Form y. The mean and variance of raw scores on Form w and also on Form y are estimated for the combined group (c) taking Form w (Group γ) and Form y (Group δ). In making these estimations the "common test," Equating Section z, the set of equating items which have been administered to both groups γ and δ, is used for making adjustments for differences between those groups.

8) $\hat{M}_{w_c} = M_{w_\gamma} + b_{wz_\gamma}(M_{z_c} - M_{z_\gamma}),$

9) $\hat{M}_{y_c} = M_{y_\delta} + b_{yz_\delta}(M_{z_c} - M_{z_\delta}),$

10) $\hat{s}^2_{w_c} = s^2_{w_\gamma} + b^2_{wz_\gamma}(s^2_{z_c} - s^2_{z_\gamma}),$ and

11) $\hat{s}^2_{y_c} = s^2_{y_\delta} + b^2_{yz_\delta}(s^2_{z_c} - s^2_{z_\delta}).$

As in the equating of Forms w and x, the equation relating raw scores on Form w to raw scores on Form y is derived by setting equal the estimated standard score deviates on the two tests for the combined Group, c:

$$\frac{Y - \hat{M}_{y_c}}{\hat{s}_{y_c}} = \frac{W - \hat{M}_{w_c}}{\hat{s}_{w_c}},$$

thus yielding the equation for converting scores on Form w to the scale of Form y:

12) $\quad\quad Y = A_{yw} W + B_{yw},$

where A_{yw} (slope) $= \hat{s}_{y_c}/\hat{s}_{w_c}$

and B_{yw} (intercept) $= \hat{M}_{y_c} - A_{yw} \hat{M}_{w_c}.$

Substituting into the existing equation relating Form y raw scores to the standard scale,

13) $\quad\quad S = A_{sy} Y + B_{sy},$

the equation relating Form w scores to the scale is obtained:

14) $\quad\quad S = A''_{sw} W + B''_{sw},$

where $A''_{sw} = A_{sy} A_{yw}$ and $B''_{sw} = A_{sy} B_{yw} + B_{sy}.$

There are now two independently derived equations, (7) and (14), both providing conversions from raw scores on Form w to the standard score scale. If they disagree by no more than 25 scaled score points at any point on the raw score continuum, the angle between them is bisected to yield a final conversion equation which becomes the official and operational conversion for reporting scores for candidates who have taken Form w. If the conversion lines disagree beyond acceptable tolerances, then further study is undertaken to determine whether computational errors, or errors of other kinds (e.g., errors in scoring keys, inaccurate reproduction of equating items, etc.), have not caused the disagreement.

Figure 2.4 and Figure 2.5 each describes a pair of conversion lines for SAT-verbal scores. In each figure the "current" or new form of the test, given on the abscissa, is converted to the standard score scale as a result of the equating to two old forms, as described above. Clearly, the pair of conversion lines shown in Figure 2.4 are in good agreement. The lines in Figure 2.5, on the other hand, although marginally acceptable, nevertheless, disagree beyond desirable limits. If, as was

true of the lines in Figure 2.5, no errors are uncovered in the equating process or in the system of form-to-form equatings, then the errors are taken to be random, though larger than ideal, and the lines are averaged, as is done for forms that agree closely, to yield a single official conversion line.

The formulas that have been presented above for equating the new and old forms (equations (1) to (4) and equations (8) to (11) above) were originally derived by L. R Tucker (Angoff, 1961) under assumptions appropriate to observed scores, and are found to operate quite effectively when the groups taking the new and old forms (Groups α and β, in the equating of Forms w and x; Groups γ and δ, in the equating of Forms w and y) do not differ too sharply. In those instances, however, when the groups differ by a substantial amount —for example, when the difference between means on Equating Section u or on Equating Section z is greater than a quarter of a standard deviation, or when the

Figure 2.4

Illustration of highly consistent equating results

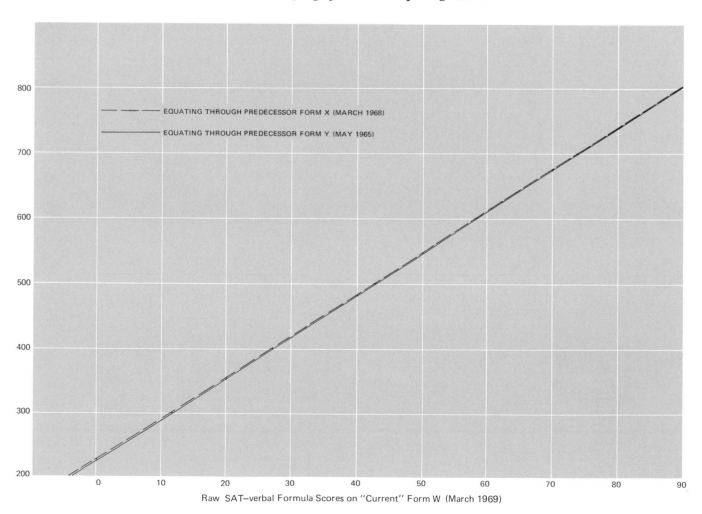

Raw SAT—verbal Formula Scores on "Current" Form W (March 1969)

variances on Equating Section u or on Equating Section z differ by more than 25 percent—a set of formulas derived by R. S. Levine (1955) is used that depends on assumptions appropriate to true scores. However, these formulas require the assumption that the operational forms (w, x, and y) be parallel to the sets of equating items (u and z), that is, that the items may all be considered as having been drawn at random from the same item pool. For this reason the Levine formulas are used only when the groups differ by amounts greater than those specified above.

This method of maintaining the College Board scale, which involves a system of form-to-form equating, derives from the point of view that there is a unique conversion from the raw scores of a particular form to the standard score reporting scale, a conversion that is dependent only on the general level and dispersion of difficulty of the items that constitute the test form and on the intercorrelations among the items. Implicit in

this point of view is the notion that the test forms in the system are all measures of the same ability or set of abilities; for if they were not, they could not be depended on to yield a unique conversion that would apply with equal validity to different subgroups of the candidate population. It is obvious that this requirement cannot be maintained if the content of the SAT is permitted to change, as indeed it has. However, it is judged that if the content changes are moderate and gradual—as they have been—then the comparability across test forms will be reasonably accurate over a limited span of years. A recent study of this problem by Stewart (1966) has shown that the score scale for the SAT-verbal has been highly stable from 1963, when the study was initiated, as far back as 1953, and appears to be in relatively good control even as far back as 1948.

The model that is used for equating successive forms of the SAT is the linear model, by which it is assumed that differences in the shapes of the distributions of

Figure 2.5

Illustration of marginally acceptable equating results

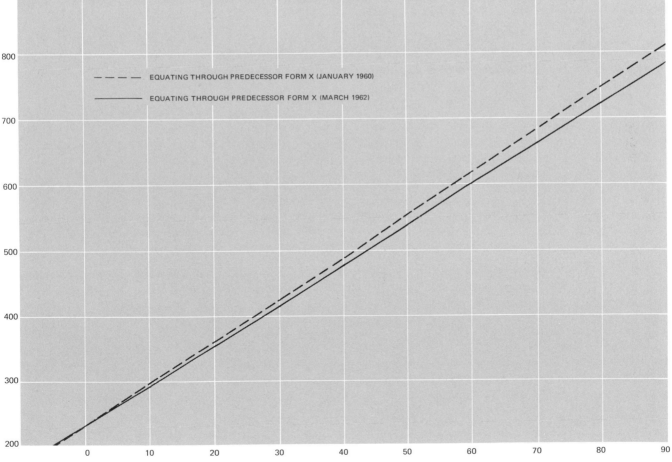

EQUATING THROUGH PREDECESSOR FORM X (JANUARY 1960)

EQUATING THROUGH PREDECESSOR FORM X (MARCH 1962)

Raw SAT—verbal Formula Scores on "Current" Form W (May 1963)

scores on successive test forms are either nonexistent or too small to require equating by area transformation methods (methods that would be used to standardize all the moments of a score distribution for a particular group of candidates). The linear transformation allows the raw score distribution to retain its original shape, and effects a change only in the mean and standard deviation of scores. That is, it effects a change only in the separation of scale units (which, because of the linear transformation, are all of the same size for a given form) and in the overall placement of the scale of the test form within the limits 200 and 800, which are arbitrarily imposed on the scaled scores of all the tests of the College Board Admissions Testing Program. In the large majority of instances the linear model has been more than adequate to meet the needs of the Program. Newly produced test forms have been pitched so nearly appropriately in terms of the level and spread of difficulty of their component items that they have in fact yielded distributions very nearly identical in shape. Nevertheless, the results of curvilinear equating are regularly compared with the linear equations in order to check on the similarity of the distribution shapes. In those few instances in which successive forms have yielded slightly different distribution shapes and a test form has failed to yield the maximum allowable score of 800, curvilinear (area transformation) methods of equating have been used to define the conversion of raw to scaled scores, particularly in the score range 700 to 800. Thus, although the system for defining the conversions is essentially linear, provision is nevertheless made to insure that when a deviation from the standard procedure is warranted, appropriate action is taken.

The 800-score

Because 800 is the highest score that is reported on the College Board scale, it has acquired a special salience, or "visibility," and the concept of "perfect" test performance has come to be popularly, albeit inappropriately, attached to it. The fact is that an upper limit of 800 is arbitrarily imposed on all scaled scores in the College Board Admissions Testing Program. This is done mainly to control for the fact there is inevitably some variation in difficulty from form to form of the test, and consequently some variation in the maximum scores earned by highly able candidates who are taking different test forms. The 800-limit operates in such a way that if, for example, the maximum raw score of 90 on SAT-verbal sections is established by linear equating as 812 on the scale, the reported score is nonetheless 800. (The same, but opposite, restriction is imposed at the lower end of the scale by the 200-scores, which are the lowest scores reported. Ordinarily, the curtailment of raw scores at zero does not permit the reporting of scaled scores as low as 200. However, since valid differentiation is possible among formula scores lower than zero (Boldt, 1968), the use of these scores does make it

possible to extend the scale to the desired limit.)

Difficulties arise, however, when the test form is slightly easier than ideal, and the maximum raw score converts to something less than 800, with the result that no student, however capable, is enabled to achieve the score of 800. Difficulties of another sort, somewhat less troubling, arise when the test is too difficult and the maximum raw score converts to a scaled score too far above 800—in which case the 800-score limit causes the loss of too many differentiable raw score units near the end of the test. Accordingly, the statistical specifications for the SAT reflect careful attention to this problem. Since the control system is necessarily probabilistic, the average scaled score equivalent to a perfect raw score is ideally set at a value near 820, with some confidence that if this can be accomplished, the obtained maximums will fall between 800 and 840.

The establishment of the value 820 and the determination of the range 800-840 are not susceptible to rigorous formulation. To achieve the ideal maximum for the test—without sacrificing the requirements for good discrimination throughout the rest of the desired scaled score range—one relates the mean and standard deviation of equated deltas and the mean of the item biserials to the scaled score properties of the test. Then one uses these relations, as well as the empirical relations established by Swineford (1959), in setting future specifications for the tests. Table 2.16 presents some past experience with maximum raw score values, an experience that led to adjusted specifications.

In view of the fact that three verbal and five mathematical forms failed to achieve the 800 maximum, a minor adjustment was made in the item specifications beginning with the December 1966 form of the SAT. This adjustment may be seen in the change from the

Table 2.16

Maximum scaled scores obtained with linear equating for eight SAT forms—December 1964 to May 1966

	Verbal	Mathematical
Dec 1964	800	791
Jan 1965	792	765 *
Mar 1965	793	824
May 1965	808	782 *
Dec 1965	806	797
Jan 1966	799	812
Mar 1966	820	792
May 1966	805	812

*Nonlinear methods were used to equate these forms operationally. The results of the operational equating yielded maximum scores of 792 for the January 1965 form and 793 for the May 1965 form.

Table 2.17

Specified distributions of item difficulties and mean biserials for the SAT

Equated delta	SAT-VERBAL			SAT-MATHEMATICAL		
	Before Dec 1966	Dec 1966 through May 1967	Dec 1967 through May 1969	Before Dec 1966	Dec 1966 through May 1967	Dec 1967 through May 1969
19					1	1
18					2	2
17	1	2	2	1	4	4
16	4	4	4	3	4	4
15	4	9	8	4	4	4
14	13	12	10	10	5	5
13	8	10	10	7	5	5
12	9	8	10	5	5	5
11	9	9	10	5	8	8
10	14	9	10	7	8	8
9	10	8	8	10	7	7
8	6	7	7	4	4	4
7	7	7	6	3	2	2
6	3	3	3	1	1	1
5	2	2	2			
Total Number	90	90	90	60	60	60
$M_\triangle$	11.4	11.8	11.7	12.0	12.5	12.5
$SD_\triangle$	2.8	3.0	2.9	2.7	3.2	3.2
$M_{r_{bis}}$	.42	.42	.42	.46	.47	.47

specifications that were in effect prior to December 1966 to those that were in effect from December 1966 through May 1967 (Table 2.17).

Some indication of the effectiveness of the new specifications is provided by the results achieved in the four forms developed for use in the academic year 1966-67 (Table 2.18).

Table 2.18

Maximum scaled scores obtained
with linear equating for
four SAT forms — December 1966 to May 1967

Form: Date of first administration	Verbal	Mathematical
Dec 1966	846	831
Jan 1967	830	830
Mar 1967	839	817
May 1967	841	837

Clearly, the modifications worked and these more recent forms enjoyed greater margins of safety. However, in view of the likelihood that the item specifications, and consequently, the tests, may have been overadjusted somewhat, the specifications for the verbal sections were cut back slightly, as shown in Table 2.17. Table 2.19 demonstrates that this additional modification had the intended effect of reducing the maximum scaled scores, but not to the levels that prevailed prior to December 1966.

Score change

Although most of the students taking the SAT take it only once, about 40 percent currently take it more than once, not only within a single academic year, but also, and more often, between academic years. The most frequent pattern of repetition involves a first testing in the spring (most often in May) of the junior year and a second testing in the winter (most often in December)

Table 2.19

Maximum scaled scores obtained
with linear equating for
eight SAT forms — December 1967 to May 1969

Form: Date of first administration	Verbal	Mathematical
Dec 1967	843	838
Jan 1968	856	800
Mar 1968	817	813
May 1968	839	841
Dec 1968	821	829
Jan 1969	823	794 *
Mar 1969	802	789 *
May 1969	818	834

*Special operational methods were used to equate these forms operationally at the upper end of the scale. The results of the operational equating yielded maximum scaled scores of 821 for the January 1969 form and 800 for the March 1969 form.

of the senior year. About a third of the 605,000 candidates tested in December 1967, for example, had taken the SAT in the preceding May. Generally speaking, the repeaters are abler than the nonrepeaters, scoring about 40-50 points higher on both the verbal and mathematical sections.

The fact that two measurements are available for so many of these students makes the matter of score change a source of great interest to the students, who seek to improve their scores on a second testing, and to the high schools and colleges, which regard the score change as a measure of growth. However, because of the nature of the abilities measured by the SAT and the short period of time typically intervening between the first and second measurement (about seven months) only small gains are observed on the average, about 15-20 points in recent years. This average score gain, coupled with a large standard deviation of gains (about 50 points) implies that relatively large proportions of students (35-40 percent) will drop in score from first to second testing, and some by substantial amounts. It also means, of course, that some will gain by substantial amounts.

During recent years inquiries have increased from students, parents, schools, and colleges who were puzzled by the fact that the numbers of students losing score points were greater than ever before. The Board and ETS initiated a series of studies in 1967 to investigate this matter of score changes on the SAT, and interpretive documents were issued to schools and colleges in the winter of 1967-68 in an attempt to explain the score change phenomenon. In the summer of 1967, the *College*

Board Review also carried an article by Kendrick (1967) in which some of the reasons that scores change as they do were discussed. The following points were made by these sources:

1. In general, there is a small increase in score from junior to senior year, attributable in part to intellectual growth and in part to the effect of practice on the SAT for those who have had little experience with this type of test.

2. On the basis of the typical average score change and the typical variability of score changes that have been observed recently, it can be predicted that about one student in 20 will gain 100 points or more and that about one student in 100 will lose 100 points or more.

3. There has been a slight downward trend in the average gains observed in recent years. (See Tables 2.20 and 2.21 for a summary of recent score change data.) However, the reason for the overall gain, as well as the downward trend in the gain, is not that the tests are more or less difficult in the spring than in the winter. The tests are built to precise specifications, and any minor differences that remain are adjusted for in the equating. Although the reasons for the decrease in the average score gain for the entire candidate group are not clear, two hypotheses suggest themselves: the continuing decrease in the number of students for whom practice effect on multiple-choice tests like the SAT represents a significant factor; and the decreasing tendency for only those students to repeat the test who felt that their initial score was erroneously low. This latter hypothesis suggests that students now tend to repeat the test regardless of their initial score.

4. Inter-individual differences in score gain are partly the result of individual differences in real intellectual growth and experience with the test, but they are *principally* the result of random error in the test, error which is inherent in all tests, and, indeed, in all kinds of measurement. Score change, involving two scores, is subject to both sources of error. (The standard error of measurement of a single SAT score is about 30 points; the standard error of measurement of a score change is about 42 points.) These random errors, which can cause a score to be *too high* as well as too low, are one of the principal reasons for the large score losses, just as they are one of the principal reasons for the large score gains.

5. Theoretical and empirical studies of score gains indicate that it is extremely unlikely that any third variable (in addition to initial and final score) will correlate very highly with them. Empirical validities of score gains (against grade point average in college) are very nearly zero. Other studies show no reliable differences in mean score gains between highly selective independent schools and randomly chosen unselective schools. Still other studies have shown that although there appear to be significant differences between schools with respect to their mean score gains in any one year, there is no reason to expect similar mean gains from one year to the next; mean score gains experienced by the same schools (for different students) in another

Table 2.20

Seven-year summary of change in SAT-verbal scores from March or May of the junior year to December or January of the senior year

	MARCH TO DECEMBER							MARCH TO JANUARY						
	1962	1963	1964	1965	1966	1967	1968	1962-63	1963-64	1964-65	1965-66	1966-67	1967-68	1968-69
N	44,930	63,447	82,595	72,754	71,925	67,153	39,248	5,891	6,946	9,089	4,460	4,565	3,938	3,836
Senior scores														
M	536	525	522	519	514	515	509	498	510	507	500	496	502	492
SD	107	105	104	104	107	107	106	101	104	105	111	113	115	113
Junior scores														
M	494	497	496	500	498	495	486	458	472	468	476	481	477	466
SD	101	101	105	104	105	107	102	97	100	107	109	113	111	107
Senior minus junior scores														
M	42.1	27.8	26.0	18.5	16.0	19.9	23.0	40.1	38.0	38.9	23.7	14.6	25.0	26.7
SD	47.7	48.6	47.5	47.3	49.4	48.5	48.0	49.0	49.7	48.0	47.5	48.5	49.9	48.7
Percent showing decreases	18	29	28	34	37	33	31	20	21	21	31	37	30	28

	MAY TO DECEMBER							MAY TO JANUARY						
	1962	1963	1964	1965	1966	1967	1968	1962-63	1963-64	1964-65	1965-66	1966-67	1967-68	1968-69
N	96,474	142,628	172,933	176,607	192,620	207,094	131,827	16,634	18,709	20,359	12,233	13,255	13,008	14,289
Senior scores														
M	512	502	498	495	487	487	484	490	498	494	491	482	485	474
SD	104	103	103	100	101	102	101	100	103	103	107	106	109	110
Junior scores														
M	488	486	477	476	474	473	470	467	471	463	465	469	466	455
SD	103	101	101	103	99	104	104	102	102	100	108	106	110	110
Senior minus junior scores														
M	24.1	15.8	21.2	18.9	13.0	14.0	14.0	22.9	27.0	31.4	25.7	12.6	19.3	18.0
SD	49.6	47.0	48.4	48.7	49.6	50.1	49.5	49.2	47.5	47.9	48.8	49.0	50.2	49.4
Percent showing decreases	31	37	34	36	39	38	38	32	28	25	29	39	35	35

Table 2.21

Seven-year summary of change in SAT-*mathematical scores from March or May of the junior year to December or January of the senior year*

	MARCH TO DECEMBER							MARCH TO JANUARY						
	1962	1963	1964	1965	1966	1967	1968	1962-63	1963-64	1964-65	1965-66	1966-67	1967-68	1968-69
N	44,930	63,447	82,595	72,754	71,925	67,153	39,248	5,891	6,946	9,089	4,460	4,565	3,938	3,836
Senior scores														
M	555	551	547	540	536	542	539	530	543	529	528	534	526	521
SD	108	111	111	107	107	109	110	106	107	108	114	113	111	111
Junior scores														
M	522	527	515	527	523	524	518	492	504	492	506	507	507	499
SD	104	102	104	106	106	107	105	101	101	106	111	113	114	112
Senior minus junior scores														
M	33.2	24.9	32.4	12.1	12.8	18.0	21.0	38.0	38.7	37.0	22.5	27.3	19.0	22.3
SD	53.3	54.3	50.8	53.8	53.4	52.5	53.5	55.4	56.6	51.2	54.7	53.4	52.4	52.3
Percent showing decreases	26	32	26	41	41	36	33	24	23	23	34	30	35	33

	MAY TO DECEMBER							MAY TO JANUARY						
	1962	1963	1964	1965	1966	1967	1968	1962-63	1963-64	1964-65	1965-66	1966-67	1967-68	1968-69
N	96,474	142,628	172,933	176,607	192,620	207,094	131,827	16,634	18,709	20,359	12,233	13,255	13,008	14,289
Senior scores														
M	536	530	525	521	513	517	519	522	531	517	521	522	513	506
SD	105	108	105	103	102	106	107	105	106	105	110	110	108	110
Junior scores														
M	513	513	497	502	504	504	505	493	500	485	492	499	499	494
SD	108	106	108	103	102	103	104	107	106	109	111	110	110	111
Senior minus junior scores														
M	23.3	17.6	27.3	18.5	9.0	13.5	13.8	28.8	30.8	32.3	29.0	22.5	14.0	12.6
SD	52.9	51.1	52.6	52.7	53.4	54.7	55.0	55.2	53.4	52.7	53.1	55.4	52.5	53.3
Percent showing decreases	32	36	29	36	43	40	39	29	28	27	29	34	40	40

academic year are only negligibly correlated (about .07 for verbal scores and .16 for mathematical scores).

6. The correlation between initial score and gain is about −.25. Thus students with low initial scores can expect relatively high gains; students with high initial scores can expect relatively small gains and proportionately more frequent and greater losses.

7. Because of the fact that error of measurement is virtually absent in the average score gain for the hundreds of thousands of students who repeat the SAT, variations in score gain from one year to the next must be attributed to some other source, probably to equating error. The standard error of equating is probably in the neighborhood of 5 scaled score points for any one form, 7 points for a score gain, and about 10 points for the difference between two score gains. Although an error of 10 points is normally regarded as something very small in the context of individual scores, it tends to loom quite large in the context of mean gains, which themselves are small. Nevertheless, however it is regarded, the error of equating is still small, and for the purposes for which the scores should be used, still negligible.

8. In spite of the fact that the SAT itself is highly reliable (about .90) and very useful to admissions officers in predicting college success, the SAT score *change* —that is, the simple difference between the junior and senior SAT scores—is extremely unreliable (about .20) and, with few exceptions, tells us virtually nothing about the student's intellectual abilities, or about the school he comes from. The score change bears little or no relation to the quality of work that he has done in the past or the quality of work that he may be expected to do in the future.

9. The foregoing information implies—and experience has demonstrated—that SAT scores earned in the junior year generally provide as good an indication of the abilities measured by the SAT as scores earned in the senior year, unless, of course, a student felt handicapped by illness or other such personal conditions during his first taking of the SAT.

Very likely, as long as candidates take the SAT on more than one occasion and as long as the differences in their scores are available, questions will continue to be raised, asking why a particular student has experienced a drop in score, why the score change for a given school is smaller one year than another, and why so many students from that school have lost score points. However, nothing can be done to reduce the variability of score changes substantially without increasing substantially the correlation between the junior-year and senior-year SAT beyond the present correlation of about .88. But if this happens, then the need for taking the SAT a second time will tend to vanish, since the second testing is so easily predicted from the first. The result is that candidates will not be as likely in the future to repeat the test. Under these circumstances, the entire problem of score gains—their level and variability—also vanishes.

Coaching

Because the SAT is so often regarded as a significant hurdle—even a barrier—to be passed by secondary school students who aspire to college, a number of commercial coaching schools have appeared on the scene, claiming that they can improve the student's verbal and mathematical skills and essentially promising them higher scores on the SAT (see Chapter I). In response to these claims and in response to the students and parents who feel that the "coachability" of the SAT disadvantages students who cannot attend these schools, the College Board issued a booklet, *Effects of Coaching on Scholastic Aptitude Test Scores* (1965). The booklet summarizes the results of several studies of coaching, all of which point to the negligible effects of coaching (see Chapter VI), and quotes a formal statement by the College Board trustees, calling attention to the inherently slow and stubborn growth of the abilities measured by the SAT and their relative insensitivity to the efforts to cram a young lifetime of learning into a space of a few weeks. The statement goes on to deplore the activities of the commercial coaching schools and their corruptive effects on the process of education, and urges students and their parents not to be tempted by their false and misleading claims.

Preliminary Scholastic Aptitude Test (PSAT)

The Preliminary Scholastic Aptitude Test is a somewhat shorter version of the Scholastic Aptitude Test, constructed from old forms of the SAT as they are retired. It is administered under semisecure conditions (destruction of test copies is the responsibility of the cooperating schools) to a population of high school juniors and seniors. The purpose of the test is to assist in guidance decisions relevant to college attendance.

The PSAT is made to content specifications that parallel those of the parent SAT. In difficulty, it is somewhat easier, in order to provide a more effective measurement for the more heterogeneous and somewhat lower-scoring population. Normative information is developed that relates PSAT scores to college success. Virtually every point concerning the test development for the SAT is relevant to the development of the PSAT. The attention to parallelism of forms, the consideration of the problems of the maximum obtainable scaled score, and the sense of a test that derives from a tradition of some 45 years of work in test construction, is as evident for the PSAT as for the SAT. The verbal section consists of 70 items (as compared with 90 for the verbal sections of the SAT), while the mathematical section consists of 50 items (as compared with 60 for the mathematical sections of the SAT). The time allowed for verbal and for math is one hour in each case. There are only these two sections, without the breakdown into smaller sections, as is the pattern for SAT, and because the PSAT program does not require its own pretesting, such additional materials as are required are provided for through the routine pretesting for the SAT. All in all, the PSAT may be considered to be a parallel form of the SAT, somewhat easier, but affording all the parallelism, reliability, and validity that the SAT provides.

Arrangements for handicapped students

Special arrangements are available for handicapped students who wish to take the SAT. For students with nonvisual handicaps, these arrangements may include permission to take the test without its regular time limit at a special session, or to take the test in the usual manner but with the aid of a typewriter or an amanuensis to record the responses.

Students with visual handicaps may also take the test without adhering to its regular time limits. They may use either a large-type edition or a braille edition in their work. Such special printings of the SAT have been available for two forms of the test since 1939. One form is intended for juniors, one for seniors. The braille editions include records providing aural versions of the reading comprehension material.

The practices of relaxing the time limits and of providing special materials make possible the testing of students with a variety of handicaps. The test scores are reported on the same 200-800 scale that is used for nonhandicapped students. The use of the scale, however, is not intended to imply that SAT scores earned by handicapped students under special testing conditions have exactly the same meaning as the scores of nonhandicapped students. The very nature of the problem —for example, the large variety of the types and degrees of severity of physical handicap—makes it extremely difficult to evaluate the validity of "handicapped" scores and to design an adequate equating experiment for determining equivalent "nonhandicapped" scores. Moreover, the population of handicapped students is so small and their college attendance spread over so many institutions that rigorous validity studies cannot be undertaken. Finally, the question of the extent to which the possession of a handicap influences grades and other college criteria would rule out a decisive answer in any case.

The meager data presently available, while indicating that the SAT does predict the college grades of handicapped students about as well as it does those of nonhandicapped students, can nevertheless do no more than support the following injunction to users of the handicapped editions, which appears in the descriptive booklet for the program (College Board, 1968, p. 11): "The usual caution that test scores be considered as only one part of the student's record assumes particular importance in the evaluation of a handicapped student's test scores." Accordingly, it would be expected that formal test scores would assume less weight as an index of the future academic performance for handicapped students than they would for nonhandicapped students and that the previous academic record would correspondingly take on more than its usual importance. Clearly, there is no substitute for judicious use of test results, particularly when somewhat less than full reliance can be placed on the scores.

REFERENCES

Angoff, W. H., "Basic Equations in Scaling and Equating," in Wilks, S. S., ed., *Scaling and Equating College Board Tests*. Princeton, N.J.: Educational Testing Service, 1961, pp. 120-129.

Angoff, W. H., and Waite, A., "A Study of Double Part-score Equating for the Scholastic Aptitude Test," in Wilks, S. S., ed., *Scaling and Equating College Board Tests*. Princeton, N.J.: Educational Testing Service, 1961, pp. 73-85.

Angoff, W. H., "How We Calibrate College Board Scores." *College Board Review* No. 68, 1968, pp. 11-14.

Boldt, R. F., "Study of Linearity and Homoscedasticity of Test Scores in the Chance Range." *Educational and Psychological Measurement*, 1968, 28, pp. 47-60.

Brigham, C. C., *A Study of Error*. New York: College Entrance Examination Board, 1932. 384 pp.

Coffman, W. E., *The Scholastic Aptitude Test: 1926-1962*. Test Development Report 63-2. Princeton, N.J.: Educational Testing Service, 1963.

Coffman, W. E., *The Scholastic Aptitude Test of 1963-64*. Research Memorandum 64-1. Princeton, N.J.: Educational Testing Service, 1964.

Coffman, W. E., "Principles of Developing Tests for the Culturally Different." *Proceedings of the 1964 Invitational Conference on Testing Problems*. Princeton, N.J.: Educational Testing Service, 1965, pp. 82-92.

Coffman, W. E., *A Factor Analysis of the Verbal Sections of the Scholastic Aptitude Test*. College Entrance Examination Board Research and Development Report 65-6, No. 17, and Research Bulletin 66-30. Princeton, N.J.: Educational Testing Service, 1966.

College Board Tests for Handicapped Students. New York. College Entrance Examination Board, 1968. 15 pp.

College Entrance Examination Board, *Effects of Coaching on Scholastic Aptitude Test Scores*. New York: College Entrance Examination Board, 1965.

College Entrance Examination Board, *Twenty-seventh Annual Report of the Secretary*. New York: College Entrance Examination Board, 1927. 211 pp.

Cronbach, L. J., *Essentials of Psychological Testing*. Second edition. New York: Harper & Row, 1960. 650 pp.

Dressell, P. L., "Some Remarks on the Kuder-Richardson Reliability Coefficient." *Psychometrika*, 1940, 5, pp. 305-310.

Dyer, H. S., and King, R. G., *College Board Scores (No. 2): Their Use and Interpretation*. New York: College Entrance Examination Board, 1955.

Fishman, J. A., *1957 Supplement to College Board Scores No. 2*. New York: College Entrance Examination Board, 1957.

French, J. W., "New Tests for Predicting the Performance of College Students with High-level Aptitude." *Journal of Educational Psychology*, 1964, 55, pp. 185-194.

Fuess, C. M., *The College Board: Its First Fifty Years*. New York: College Entrance Examination Board, 1950. 222 pp.

Kendrick, S. A., "When Scores Go Down." *College Board Review* No. 64, 1967, pp. 5-11.

Kuder, G. F., and Richardson, M. W., "The Theory and Estimation of Test Reliability." *Psychometrika*, 1937, 2, pp. 151-160.

Levine, R. S., *Equating the Score Scales of Alternate Forms Administered to Samples of Different Ability*. Research Bulletin 55-23. Princeton, N.J.: Educational Testing Service, 1955.

Lorge, I., and Kruglov, L., "A Suggested Technique for the Improvement of Difficulty Prediction of Test Items." *Educational and Psychological Measurement*, 1952, 12, pp. 554-561.

Loret, P. G., "A History of the Content of the Scholastic Aptitude Test," in Wilks, S. S., ed., *Scaling and Equating College Board Tests*. Princeton, N.J.: Educational Testing Service, 1961, pp. 97-119.

McGee, V. E., "Towards a Maximally Efficient System of Braiding for Scholastic Aptitude Test Equating," in Wilks, S. S., ed., *Scaling and Equating College Board Tests*. Princeton, N.J.: Educational Testing Service, 1961, pp. 86-96.

Pruzek, R. M., and Coffman, W. E., *A Factor Analysis of the Mathematical Sections of the Scholastic Aptitude Test*. College Entrance Examination Board Research and Development Report 65-6, No. 10, and Research Bulletin 66-12. Princeton, N.J.: Educational Testing Service, 1966.

Ryans, D. G., and Frederiksen, N., "Performance Tests of Educational Achievement," in Lindquist, E. F., ed., *Educational Measurement*. Washington, D.C.: American Council on Education, 1951, pp. 455-494.

Stewart, E. E., *The Stability of the SAT Score Scale*. College Entrance Examination Board Research and Development Report 66-7, No. 3, and Research Bulletin 66-37. Princeton, N.J.: Educational Testing Service, 1966.

Swineford, F., "Some Relations between Test Scores and Item Statistics." *Journal of Educational Psychology*, 1959, 50, pp. 26-30.

Tinkelman, S., "Difficulty Prediction of Test Items," in *Teachers College Contributions to Education. No. 941*. New York: Bureau of Publications, Teachers College, Columbia University, 1947. 55 pp.

Wilks, S. S., *Scaling and Equating College Board Tests*. Princeton, N.J.: Educational Testing Service, 1961. 195 pp.

CHAPTER III

The Achievement Tests

WILLIAM E. COFFMAN

Introduction

The Scholastic Aptitude Test was designed with a specific purpose in mind—to identify those individuals who, regardless of the subjects they might have studied in secondary school, possess the general academic skills necessary for successful college work. In contrast, the College Board Achievement Tests come from a distinctly different tradition, and it is not possible to understand their function in the Admissions Testing Program without first examining the historical context out of which they evolved. During the years since the formation of the College Board in 1900, they have served many purposes. In this chapter three main purposes of the Achievement Tests will be identified and their development traced.

Purposes

Colleges may require that candidates for admission submit scores on certain Achievement Tests for one or more of the following reasons: (1) to aid in certifying that a candidate has or has not achieved a level of competence in a subject-matter field considered prerequisite to admission to the college; (2) to assist in placing students in a college sequence at different levels depending on their prior achievement; and (3) to make predictions of performance in college in combination with other information, such as SAT scores and secondary school grades. The particular way each purpose is viewed will depend on the individual college and the program within the college.

To certify competence—Many colleges and universities develop their curriculums on the assumption that students entering the curriculums bring with them a particular level of competence and are ready to study the subject at that level. For example, an engineering college may begin the study of mathematics at the level of a combined course in analytical geometry and calculus. It is assumed that the students have already developed the understanding of algebraic and trigonometric concepts and the mathematical skills that will permit them to master the concepts and processes being presented in this course. But the level of achievement in secondary school mathematics is not necessarily reflected in a passing grade in a secondary school course in algebra or trigonometry. The requirements for a passing grade may vary from school to school. The Achievement Tests in mathematics, by providing a common sample of problems for all candidates, can provide evidence of the extent to which applicants from different schools—and with different types of exposure to the subject matter—have reached a common level of achievement. Similarly, the English Composition Test may be used to certify that an acceptable level of skill in the basic elements of composition has been already achieved in secondary school—particularly if, as in certain selective colleges, there is no intention to devote time during the freshman year to the development of such skills.

Of course, such a use of the tests is indirectly concerned with prediction since individuals without the prerequisite skills will be unable to succeed in the college work. It is unlikely, however, that faculty committees responsible for making decisions about the use of College Board Achievement Tests often think of prediction in the concrete terms of increments to a multiple correlation coefficient. Otherwise, how might one explain the popularity of the English Composition Test, which seems to have relatively little unique contribution to make to the prediction of college performance. The fact is that college faculty members recognize that the ability to write clear and correct English is a legitimate requirement for admission to a selective college and that high scores on the English Composition Test reflect, or at least imply, that ability.

The use of the test score to certify competence is illustrated with particular force in the case of tests in foreign languages. Some colleges have a requirement that any graduate of the liberal arts program be able to read a foreign language. Students are required to demonstrate their ability to do so before they may receive a degree. In certain instances, it has been determined that students who have the required level of skill are able to perform at a particular level on College Board tests in a foreign language; therefore, students who perform at this level at the time they apply for admission to the college are certified as meeting the foreign language requirement.

To provide placement information—Even though selective institutions may require certain minimum levels of achievement for entering certain courses, there is still recognition that students may vary widely in the level of their achievement and competence at the time they enter college. To provide for such individual differences, many colleges, particularly those that are not highly selective, offer a variety of freshman courses and place students in these courses on the basis of their level of achievement at the time of admission. There may be several levels of freshman English, mathematics, or foreign language. Because of the wide variation in secondary school courses and in grading standards, such colleges often use placement examinations to assess the level of entering students. The College Board Achievement Tests, since they can be administered prior to admission to the college, provide a convenient way of sorting students so that schedules may be developed and classes assigned in time to begin course work promptly.

In order to use College Board scores effectively for placement it is necessary that each college determine the appropriate score level to use in a particular placement situation. If, for example, it is desired to determine the score level on the French Test that would certify ability to enter a third semester college French course, one approach would be to administer the test to students completing the second semester course at the college and to require any entering student wishing to register for the third semester course to earn a score in the range achieved by these students. For example, the required score might be the average score achieved by students who received a C in the college course. More precise methods may be adopted as data permit.

To improve prediction—In the admissions situation, any information that will improve the prediction of the performance to be expected from an applicant is welcomed by the admissions officer, particularly if competition for admission is heavy. From time to time, studies have been made of the effectiveness of the Achievement Tests for predicting freshman grade-point average. A common procedure is to compute the average of whatever Achievement Tests the student elects to take. The justification for this procedure is that if the student is free to choose the examinations he will take (within the restrictions imposed by colleges to which he is applying) he will choose those for which he thinks he is best prepared. His performance, then, will reflect the level of achievement of which he is capable when he is studying a subject for which he has some definite ability or interest. Since students more often than not elect in college those subjects in which they have a special ability or interest, the Achievement Test performance is likely to be even more appropriate for predicting future performance than would a common battery that might include subjects in which the

student has neither special ability nor interest. This particular reasoning might seem faulty since in many cases college freshmen have to study required courses regardless of their interest; however, since colleges often require one or two Achievement Tests related to such required courses (e.g., English composition or mathematics), the examinations a student chooses to take tend to reflect a combination of college requirement and student election.

Formal assessment of the predictive validity of the Achievement Tests has usually been carried out on samples for which secondary school grades and SAT scores were also available (see Chapter V). Such studies have shown that in most instances the addition of the Achievement Tests leads to only modest increases in the multiple correlations. What is not generally recognized is that in certain colleges the combination of Achievement Tests is more highly related to college achievement than the combination of SAT-V and SAT-M and that if the Achievement Tests were entered first into the multiple correlation the SAT might not increase the multiple correlation to the same extent as the Achievement Tests do when the SAT is entered first. For example, Olsen (1957) found that in 10 of the 13 groups she studied a combination of Achievement Test scores produced a higher correlation with college freshman grade-point average than a combination of SAT-verbal and SAT-mathematical scores, and that in every case the Achievement Tests carried a larger sum of beta weights in the multiple regression equation.

It should be recognized, however, that the relative usefulness of the SAT and the Achievement Tests cannot be evaluated overall simply on the basis of their relative contributions to a multiple correlation. Scholastic Aptitude Test scores are generally available earlier than Achievement Test scores and on a more flexible schedule. Furthermore, high scores on the Achievement Tests depend to a considerable extent on the opportunities offered in secondary school for learning the particular concepts and skills measured by the tests. Therefore, a college may wish to give primary emphasis to the SAT in order to be sure to identify those candidates whose abilities may be inadequately reflected in their scores on the Achievement Tests (ETS, 1961, pp. 23-24).

Historical background

The College Board Achievement Tests of the 1960s can be best understood as the results of a series of modifications and adaptations in a program that has been in continuous existence since the first examinations were administered in 1901. A general review of the history of the College Board was presented in Chapter I, but it will be well to review the history again here, specifically from the point of view of the Achievement Tests. The College Board, it is recalled, was established for the purpose of bringing together schools and colleges with a common concern for establishing sound practices in the transition from school to college. One of the first actions of the Board was to establish a common set of college entrance examinations to replace the many different sets of examinations required by individual colleges.

Evolution of the Achievement Testing Program—Originally, the "College Boards," as the examinations came to be called, consisted of a series of essay questions, one for each of the commonly taught college preparatory courses. The examinations were seen as providing evidence that students had mastered course content at an acceptable level. Typically, examinations were given at the end of the school year in which courses were taken, and it was assumed that passing grades indicated that necessary credits had been attained. The examinations, which in some instances took as long as a week, were administered in June, graded in July and August, and the results were reported to colleges prior to the opening of the fall session.

Responsibility for setting the examinations was placed with committees of examiners appointed by the College Board, one for each of the examinations. Originally "the definition of the requirement in each was taken from the recommendations of national committees: for example, the requirements in Latin were based on the recommendations of the American Philological Association; those in French met the demands of the Committee of Twelve of the Modern Language Association; and the requirement in history followed closely the outline submitted by the Committee of Seven of the American Historical Association." (Fuess, 1950, p. 41.) Early in its history, the Board adopted the practice of appointing special commissions to consider developments in secondary school curriculums and their implications for examinations, a practice that has continued to the present day. For example, about the time of World War I, the practice of setting course examinations based on specific syllabi was called into question, and an alternate series of tests covering broad curricular areas rather than specific courses was introduced into the program. In recent years, commissions on English and mathematics have exerted considerable influence on secondary school practices and on content specifications for the examinations.

It has been recognized, however, that major responsibility for the quality of the examinations must rest with the examiners—that the success of the Board's examination program depends, finally, not on the statements of national committees about what the examinations should be, but rather on the extent to which qualified committee members are able to produce examinations that are recognized by the membership of the Board and the academic community at large as relevant, fair, and effective. Every effort has therefore been made to induce leading educators to accept appointment as examiners and to provide sound technical support. The list of examiners over the years is testimony to the success of the effort. The stream of research and statistical reports issued by the Board is testimony to the soundness of the technical support.

Among the early studies were those conducted prior to 1920 that indicated that tests were not strictly equivalent from year to year and that a student's examination grade might depend to a considerable extent on the year in which the examination was written, and on the person who happened to read the paper and assigned the grade, rather than simply on the quality of the student's answers. In response to these findings, systematic efforts were exerted to improve the reliability of reading of examinations and to reduce the variability in test difficulty from year to year. In 1937, in an effort to provide tests for scholarship purposes, the College Board contracted with the Cooperative Test Service of the American Council on Education in New York to provide a series of one-hour multiple-choice achievement examinations that could be administered along with the SAT on a single day in April and scored in time to make scholarship awards in May. In the following years responsibility for constructing the objective scholarship examinations was gradually shifted from the Cooperative Test Service to the regular College Board committees of examiners, who also prepared the June essay examinations.

With the onset of World War II, colleges began operating on a full-year schedule, admitting students to a summer quarter directly from high school. Because of this change and also because there were now fewer teachers available to read the essay examinations, the objective Achievement Tests were substituted temporarily for the June essay examinations. Within a short time it became clear that the Achievement Tests were giving admissions officers the information necessary for making their decisions at a much earlier time than had been possible with the June essay examination program, and, as a result, the subject-matter Achievement Tests, which had been introduced initially as scholarship tests only, were continued indefinitely.

At the end of World War II, the Admissions Testing Program consisted of the Scholastic Aptitude Test (verbal) and a Mathematical Attainment Test administered in a morning session, plus 10 Achievement Tests —English Composition, Social Studies, French, German, Latin, Spanish, Chemistry, Physics, Biology, and Comprehensive Mathematics—and an aptitude test, Spatial Relations, administered in an afternoon session. The candidate elected one, two, or three of the one-hour tests according to the requirements of colleges to which he was applying and according to his own abilities and interests.

Each Achievement Test consisted of questions selected from files or newly written by the Committee of Examiners appointed by the College Board to set the examination. Responsibility for coordination and technical work on the tests rested with the College Board technical staff, which had grown up in Princeton around the group of specialists who were in charge of the SAT, but all policy decisions and final approval of each

Achievement Test question remained with the respective committees. The technical staff in Princeton formed part of the staff of Educational Testing Service when that organization was formed in 1947.

The formation of Educational Testing Service did not change in any fundamental way the established relationships between technical staff and committees of examiners. Examiners continued to have responsibility for the content specifications for the Achievement Tests and for approving test questions to be included in each new test; the technical staff continued to provide coordinating and editorial services and to prepare and interpret statistical analyses indicating how well each test had met expectations.

Since 1945, the Achievement Tests have continued to evolve. In 1947 the Mathematics Attainment Test, which had been a three-level examination from which each candidate elected one level, was dropped from the program. In its place was offered a single mathematical aptitude test, as one part of the morning SAT program, and two one-hour Achievement Tests—an Intermediate Test, appropriate for candidates with 2½ or 3 years of mathematics, and an Advanced Test, appropriate for candidates who are studying a fourth year of mathematics.

During the 1950s there began a revolution in mathematics education that led to changes in the Mathematics Achievement Tests in the 1960s. The Committee of Examiners in Mathematics contributed to this revolution by requesting that the Board set up a special commission to study the mathematics curriculum of the secondary schools and make recommendations for the future. In 1959 the two-volume *Report of the Commission on Mathematics* was published. Included in the report are outlines of recommended subject matter for grades 9 through 12, suggestions for the training of elementary and secondary school teachers, and proposed changes in college mathematics. In the appendixes to the report, the Commission provided information, instruction, and materials for teachers. Some of the appendixes introduced new ideas and facts; others set forth new methods for approaching old topics.

The report received widespread attention among mathematics educators. By 1963, so many changes in educational practices had taken place in the secondary schools that it became necessary to change the pattern of the tests again. The Level I (Standard) Mathematics Achievement Test, appropriate for students following the typical secondary school program, and the Level II (Intensive) Mathematics Achievement Test, appropriate for students in more advanced programs, are now offered instead of the Intermediate and Advanced Tests.

The Spatial Relations Test, which had originally been included for its value in predicting performance in engineering schools, gradually lost its usefulness during the early part of the 1950s as engineering programs evolved in response to new demands. Originally required by most of the College Board member institutions offering engineering programs, it had by 1958 been dropped as a requirement by most of them. It was therefore dropped from the program.

In 1963 the Social Studies Test was replaced by two separate tests, American History and Social Studies and Modern European History and World Cultures. For a brief period beginning in 1960 a special examination in physics was offered for students who had studied a new secondary school course prepared by the Physical Science Study Committee (PSSC), but by May 1962 it had been demonstrated that it was possible for the Committee of Examiners to develop a test appropriate for both the traditional and the PSSC course. New developments in biology and in chemistry have been reflected in successive forms of the tests over the years, but the basic pattern established prior to 1945 is still in evidence.

The period since the end of World War II has seen a number of modifications in the Achievement Test in English Composition. The first form of the test consisted of a single essay written on an assigned topic. When it proved impossible to read this examination with an acceptable degree of reliability, modifications were tried in subsequent forms. However, neither an examination made up of three 20-minute essays nor one made up of four 15-minute essays proved more satisfactory than the single essay; therefore, efforts were made to develop substitute procedures. Between 1945 and 1960 a number of objective and semiobjective types of questions were developed and validated. All produced scores of acceptable reliability and most were demonstrated to have acceptable degrees of relationship to grades in English composition courses or ratings of writing ability. Of particular interest was the *interlinear exercise*, a semiobjective type of test that required the candidates to edit (between the printed lines) an expository passage into which had been introduced certain types of errors. The candidates were placed in much the same situation as they would be when trying to edit first drafts of their own writing. Raters were able to grade such papers with a high degree of reliability.

During the 1950s the typical English Composition Test consisted of three completely objective sections or of two objective sections and an interlinear section. Meanwhile, however, in response to the urging of those who felt that such indirect approaches to the measurement of writing ability were unacceptable, the College Board continued its efforts to develop acceptable essay examinations. An experimental General Composition Test was administered for three years beginning in 1954, but it proved no more satisfactory than the essay examinations of the 1940s. By 1960 a Writing Sample, copies of which were transmitted directly to the college without central grading, was competing with the English Composition Test for the candidates' time. The Writing Sample continued in the program until 1968.

In the early 1960s Godshalk, Swineford, and Coffman (1966) demonstrated that an English Composition Test made up of a single short essay, read independently by three different raters, and two objective sections would produce scores that were both reliable and valid. At the same time, they produced evidence that the one-hour examination consisting of only objective items or of combined objective and interlinear sections provided essentially the same information to users of the scores on the English Composition Test. Current forms of the English Composition Test are guided by their findings.

In 1959 the Board set up a Commission on English. The Commission recognized that its first task was to secure a consensus among its members on the nature of the problems in English instruction and on steps that might be taken to solve these problems. This proved to be extraordinarily difficult. By 1960, however, the Commission had prepared a "position paper" that identified three components in the teaching of English: literature, language, and composition. At this level, which was admittedly a general one, it was possible for the Commission members to agree on a position with respect to subject matter. The task of defining the content of instruction proved more difficult. The Commission did not issue its final report until 1965. The report, *Freedom and Discipline in English* (College Board, 1965), analyzes the conditions and practices of English teaching in America's secondary schools; makes specific recommendations for the improvement of English instruction in the areas of teacher preparation, teaching conditions, curriculum, language, literature, and composition; and advises English teachers, curriculum planners, and supervisors on the basic approaches and methods necessary to accomplish the best possible teaching.

A report of such wide scope must inevitably have an influence on the testing program of the Board if only indirectly through its influence on teaching practices. At the May 1968 administration of the Achievement Tests, a test in English Literature was offered for the first time since 1941, and exploratory work has already begun to determine the feasibility of offering a test in English Language.

In no area has there been greater ferment than in modern foreign languages, and the ferment has been reflected in the College Board Achievement Tests. In 1957, recognizing the need to examine listening skills as well as reading skills in the modern foreign languages, the Board authorized a supplementary program that permitted schools to offer their students 30-minute listening comprehension tests in French, German, and Spanish. Examinations of listening comprehension in Russian and in Italian and a reading test in Italian were subsequently offered in the Supplementary Achievement Test Program.

As of the academic year 1968-69, 15 Achievement Tests were offered as part of the regular College Board Admissions Testing Program: English Composition, Literature; American History and Social Studies, European History and World Cultures; French, German, Latin, Spanish, Hebrew, Russian; Biology, Chemistry, Physics; Mathematics Level I (Standard), Mathematics Level II (Intensive).

Testing dates—One of the major elements in the evolution of the Achievement Tests has been the shift from a program that emphasized the testing of achievement at the end of a program of study to a flexible program with a number of testing dates distributed over the year. The introduction of alternate testing dates developed originally as a means of accommodating candidates who presented special problems of one sort or another. For example, the end-of-course essay examinations were originally administered in June, but makeup examinations were offered in September. Later, a December administration was introduced to accommodate candidates seeking admission to college in midyear. It was expected, however, that unless the candidate was taking the examinations for practice he would have completed the course work on which the examinations were based.

The testing date for the scholarship examinations introduced in 1937 was placed in April in order to facilitate early decision regarding awards, but it was assumed that there would be little handicap attributable to testing at this late a point in the school year. Although the April date became the major administration for the one-hour objective tests of achievement, which replaced the essay examinations in 1942, opportunities to take the examinations were also offered in June, September, and December.

Increasing pressures for earlier decisions by admissions offices gradually led to changes in testing dates and to changes in the relationship between testing dates and instructional schedules. By the 1949-50 academic year the tests were offered in March, May, and August instead of April, June, and September. The December administration continued to be offered, but a January administration had also been added to the schedule. The March administration was the most popular, the typical candidate being a senior who might be taking an examination in a subject he was currently studying. By the 1960s many colleges were recommending that the Achievement Tests be taken in December or January by candidates applying for admission the following September.

These changes in the testing dates forced a careful examination of the specifications for the examinations. In the case of the examinations in English composition, mathematics, and foreign languages, the changes in testing dates have been accommodated with relative ease. These examinations focus on developed skills and broad understandings, and students typically study the subject for two or more years in secondary school. A student's score is unlikely to be affected markedly by the particular sequence in which content has been presented, and the testing date can be considered in making interpretations. Some of the examinations, however, are designed to measure achievement in subjects that are typically taught for a single year. If a candidate is studying physics during his senior year, for example, it may seem reasonable to test him in April, or even March, although such a practice tempts the teacher to try to "cover the book" rapidly rather than thoroughly. But when the test is to be administered in December or January, serious questions arise as to his readiness to take the test.

Committees of examiners have spent much time thinking about the implications of variable test dates for the Achievement Tests in Biology, Physics, Chemistry, European History, and American History. Ordinarily, these subjects are taught for only one year, and the typical December or January candidate will either have completed his course in the subject in a previous year or find himself in the middle of the course at the time of the examination. In recent years, the decision has been made to construct each examination in a "one-year" subject as if the examination were to be taken near the end of the year of study, and to encourage colleges to differentiate between one-year terminal subjects and continuing subjects, and to encourage candidates to register for examinations in terminal subjects near the end of their period of study or after they have completed the course. The result has been an increasing popularity of the May examination date for examinations in terminal subjects.

Construction procedures

The fact that the present Achievement Testing Program has evolved over a long period makes it difficult to describe systematically how a particular test is constructed. Each new form of a test to some extent reflects the whole history of the program, and as one observes the operations, it is often difficult to understand the pattern. Everything seems to be going on at one time. The fact is that at any particular time work may be progressing on the evaluation of a previous test form, on the construction of the form to be used at the next regularly scheduled administration, and on the development of new questions for a test form scheduled for some years in the future. It is possible, for purposes of simplification, to separate the steps in the development of a single form of an Achievement Test, but an accurate description must include the complex interactions that accompany a program of this duration and complexity.

The committee system—Central to the College Board Achievement Testing Program is the committee system. The system rests on the assumption that a representative committee of competent school and college teachers can construct a single examination in a subject-matter field that will be appropriate for assessing the level of achievement of candidates who may have been taught courses based on different textbooks and with somewhat different emphases. Committee members are appointed by and responsible to the President of the College Board. They work closely with members of the

staff of Educational Testing Service in developing and reviewing new forms of the Achievement Tests.

The first criterion in choosing committee members is competence. The potential committee member must have demonstrated, by achieving status among his colleagues, that he has a sound subject-matter background, a deep commitment to teaching, and an interest in contributing to the development of the field. The second criterion is representativeness with respect to the problem of transition from school to college. This means that committee members will ordinarily be those who are teaching either secondary school seniors or college freshmen and who are therefore aware of current practices at these levels. It means also that an effort will be made to have all significant viewpoints within a subject-matter field represented on the committee. Finally, it means that in a country as large as the United States, an effort will be made to have the different geographical regions of the country and the different types of educational institutions represented. In recent years, most of the committees have been enlarged from five to seven members in order to achieve greater representativeness.

In an attempt to balance all of the various considerations, it is usually necessary to compromise. Seldom is it possible to achieve the "ideal" committee composition. However, the type of balance that is the goal may be indicated by setting forth specifications for a hypothetical "ideal," but not unrealistic, committee of examiners in the field of physics. One member is a college professor of some years' experience with the required freshman course in physical science in a men's college in the Northeast who has also devoted much time to developing techniques for teaching the basic concepts of the physical sciences to students who do not intend to major in the subject. A second member is a professor of physics at a large midwestern university who devotes most of his time to research and the teaching of graduate students, but who has demonstrated his concern for undergraduate teaching by participating in a panel responsible for the beginning course for freshmen in a newly organized honors college. A third member, from a women's college on the West Coast, is one of the authors of a widely adopted secondary school textbook in physics. A fourth is chairman of the beginning physics course at an institute of technology in the Southeast. A fifth, a teacher of physics in a large public high school in the Southwest, has been an active member of the group responsible for developing the PSSC Physics course and conducted one of the early field trials of the draft program. The sixth member of the committee is on the staff of an independent school in New England and has spent the previous summer on the staff of a summer workshop for secondary school physics teachers. The seventh member, a teacher in a rural consolidated school in North Carolina, has just completed a term on the executive committee of the National Science Teachers Association.

The members of this committee will have had differing amounts of experience on the committee. The chairman will be someone with several years' prior experience as a committee member who has demonstrated leadership ability and broad understanding of the responsibilities of the committee. Two may be newly appointed to fill vacancies resulting from resignation, or they may have been appointed in accordance with the Board's policy of rotating the membership of the committee to insure a flow of new ideas and at the same time sufficient continuity to provide stability and experienced guidance for new members.

Working closely with the committee and assuming responsibility for coordinating the work between meetings of the committee is a test development associate from the staff of Educational Testing Service. The associate who works with the physics committee will have been trained both in physics and in educational measurement and will have received an advanced degree either in physics or in science education. Drawing on the resources of ETS, he is able to design and monitor research studies for the committee and to bring to bear on the committee's work relevant findings of research in the fields of measurement and science education.

Test planning—Each committee of examiners works within certain limits imposed by the requirements of the testing program. Since candidates must be able to take three Achievement Tests in a half-day testing session, only a single hour is available for each test. (It is possible to take more than three Achievement Tests only by registering for more than one administration.) Furthermore, scores on a particular test will be reported in a context that assumes that the subject matter and the score scale for one form of the test bear a close correspondence with the subject matter and the score scale for other active forms of that test. Thus, the scores on the Chemistry Test in January of this year should mean very much the same thing as the scores on the Chemistry Test of May of last year or of March of next year.

On the other hand, each committee of examiners is charged with the responsibility of keeping the test closely related to the curriculums of the schools. As curriculums change, the content of the test should reflect the changes. Thus, while tests in successive years follow very much the same specifications, over a period of years there may be marked changes.

Marked changes, however, require the approval of the Board membership. The basic framework of the testing program has developed over the years through the operation of an elaborate system of checks and balances involving the Board staff, the standing committees that advise the President, and the commissions that are appointed from time to time to study particular questions and submit recommendations. It is to this system that requests for changes in the subjects to be examined or for changes in the testing time available must be directed. Recommendations for changes in specifications that would require a marked increase in costs must also be referred even though the changes would not violate the one-hour limit on testing time. For example, the decisions to include an essay as part of the English Composition Test and to include tests of listening comprehension in the regular tests in modern foreign language could not be made by the committees of examiners. Rather, recommendations were made by the committees and then processed through the Board's policymaking system.

Each committee of examiners in a content field, then, begins its work within a framework established by the College Board. The test to be constructed must fit into the allotted testing time, it must be reasonably parallel in structure as well as content to immediately preceding forms, and it must conform to general budgetary requirements. The committee of examiners may initiate a request for changes in the framework. In fact, it is encouraged to do so if it feels that changes are desirable; but until changes in the framework are approved, the committee must carry out its work within the framework.

Logically, the work of a committee begins with the establishment of specifications for its test. What categories of content should be sampled and what categories of operations should students be required to apply to the content? And what proportion of each test should be devoted to each cell in the grid generated by the categories of content and of operations? These questions need to be answered by each committee before its test can be assembled.

In the process of establishing the specifications, categories of the grid are often defined and clarified by referring to test items that experts agree are worth asking. Thus, the process of building specifications is carried on continuously as committee members examine the results of tests already administered, as they examine items they have just written, and as they relate what they have come to know about curricular practices in the field with what they know about testing techniques and procedures.

Each committee maintains at all times a more or less detailed set of specifications for its test. A typical example is the outline for the Social Studies Test of some years ago, which is presented in Table 3.1. The outline calls for a test of 108 items distributed over 19 categories of content and 11 categories of process. The fact that some marginal cells in the outline are vacant reflects the fact that the Committee of Examiners was further along in its conceptualization than in its implementation. Each year the committee examines the content specifications in relation to what is known of evolving curriculums in the schools and makes whatever modifications appear necessary to keep the test representative. If, as sometimes happens, there are revolutionary changes occurring in school curriculums, a committee may conclude that a major change in specifications is warranted. If so, it may recommend that a new test be introduced. It was through such a process that the Level I and Level II Mathematics Tests were introduced in 1964 as replacements for the tests in

Intermediate and Advanced Mathematics.

The specifications for a test include more than a plan for sampling content. In addition, there are statistical specifications that insure that the test will be appropriate in difficulty for measuring the candidates who are to take the test.* Specifications also include provisions for including equating items so that scores on the new form of the test may be made equivalent to scores on previous forms. It is the responsibility of the ETS associate working with the committee to recommend statistical specifications that will insure that the test fits into the total program.

In addition to setting specifications, the committee of examiners is responsible for writing and reviewing test items, for revising items on the basis of information provided by a special experimental administration of the items (pretesting), and for approving items that are to appear in each new form of the test. At a typical meeting, all of these functions will receive attention. In addition, committee members will devote many hours between committee meetings to writing and reviewing items.

The meeting is likely to begin with an examination of the analysis of a previous form that has been pre-

---

*Further discussion of statistical specifications appears later in this chapter.

Table 3.1

Example of a test outline for an Achievement Test (Social Studies)*

Content categories	A	B	C	D	E	F	G	H-1	H-2	H-3	H-4	Total by content
U.S. history—												
1900 - 1952		6	2		①		3		1	4④		16⑤
1865 - 1900	2	1	1③		1	1	1			2		9③
1860 - 1865			2				1					3
1790 - 1860		7①	1		1		5					14①
1775 - 1790		4										4
Colonial		1			1							2
American gov't.	2①	3①	2				①		8	4		19③
U. S. geography		2										2
World history	①	⑤	①	1	①	①				①		1⑩
Ancient history		1		1	1	1						4
Medieval history			1		1①		1			1		4①
English history	1	①			1①							2②
Mod. Eur. hist.	1	4③	2	②		1						8⑤
Comparative gov't.	②		②			1						1④
Economics	1		2③		1		1					5③
Economic history			6									6
Cont. world affairs	1①		①			①			2	3		6③
World geography		1										1
General social studies concepts									2			2
Total by mental process	8	30	19	2	7	4	12	0	13	14	0	109

*Entries in the cells indicate how many items were classified by each mental process and each content category. Circled entries indicate the number of items receiving a secondary classification in a cell in addition to a primary classification in another cell.

**Process Categories: (A) Understanding of fundamental terms and concepts; (B) Acquaintance with basic facts; (C) Ability to relate concepts to facts; (D) Understanding of basic trends; (E) Understanding of cause and effect relationships; (F) Understanding of means-ends relationships; (G) Understanding of attitudes and motivations; (H-1) Ability to comprehend direct communication; (H-2) Ability to analyze, interpret, and extrapolate; (H-3) Ability to apply appropriate outside information; (H-4) Ability to evaluate in terms of external criteria.

pared by the Statistical Analysis Division of ETS. The test analysis provides information regarding the extent to which the test actually met the statistical specifications. Such items as the following can be answered by referring to the data provided in the analysis: To what extent were candidates able to complete the test in the time allotted? Did the test meet the established standards of reliability? Was the test appropriate in difficulty? Did it produce scaled scores within the desired range? Did each item contribute appropriately in terms of difficulty and discrimination to meeting the statistical specifications of the test? If the answer to any of these questions is "no," was the fault in the test specifications or in the attempt to fill them?

Sometimes the examination of the test analysis leads to a modification of the specifications. At other times it leads to new insights into the ways of meeting the specifications. Sometimes the committee concludes that there is need for a greater number of items of a certain type to permit greater flexibility in meeting specifications. This means that additional items have to be included in item writing assignments. In many instances an examination of the test analysis reveals that everything is in order and that the committee may proceed with the knowledge that previous specifications were adequate and have been met.

A typical committee meeting will also include the selection of items for a new form of the test. Usually, the ETS associate will have brought to the meeting a collection of pretested items assembled to test specifications. It is the responsibility of the committee to examine and approve each question. In some cases, the item analysis data from the pretesting indicates that items may be improved by judicious editing. In other cases, a committee member may raise questions about the content of an item, particularly if in reviewing it he has been attracted to one of the options intended to be incorrect.

The process of reviewing and approving items for a new form of the test may require a longer or shorter period of time depending on the subject-matter area, the experience of the particular committee (new committee members may require time to become familiar with the reviewing process), and the extent to which the pool of available items has made possible the assembly of a high quality draft form. In any case, this task must be completed to meet publication deadlines of an ongoing test program, and many times committees work long into the night to complete their task.

At the committee meeting, time will also be given to reviewing items that have not yet been pretested. During the period since the preceding meeting, each committee member will have written a number of test items. Writing assignments are typically made in relation to three considerations—the area of specialization of the committee member, the categories of test items already accumulated as a result of the work of the committee in previous years, and the extent to which the committee is in the process of experimenting with new types of items. The newly written questions may have been distributed in advance so that committee members may review them before coming to the meeting. At the committee meeting the judgments and suggestions for editing are pooled and a final decision is made regarding each item. It may be discarded as inappropriate for the test. It may be approved, either in its original form or as edited, for inclusion in a pretest. Or it may be referred back to the writer for detailed revision.

The range and depth of the discussion of individual items cannot be adequately described in a book of this nature. The reader is referred to the film, *One in a Hundred*, produced in 1966 by the College Board and ETS, which describes the history of a single question through two committee meetings. It provides a demonstration of the central position of committee judgment in the item development process. At the same time it indicates how the pretesting provides an independent check on the judgment of the committee.

Curriculum bias in the Achievement Tests*

A particularly difficult challenge for the College Board's program of Achievement Tests is the variety of content and curriculums in American secondary schools today. This variety, which has always characterized American education and is a natural consequence of a traditional philosophy of local autonomy and control, was further spurred by the launching of Sputnik in 1957—an event that accelerated changes in mathematics, physics, chemistry, and biology curriculums, and also in the humanities, but not to the same degree.

It became clear that to accommodate students in any of the new curriculums, the Achievement Tests would have to change to reflect curricular innovations as well as the broader understandings appropriate to all curriculums. At first it was thought that a separate test would have to be built for each course—in the new PSSC Physics as well as in traditional physics; in the CHEMS and CBA curriculums as well as in traditional chemistry; in the Blue, Green, and Yellow versions of the BSCS curriculum as well as in traditional biology; and so on. Separate tests were in fact constructed for students of PSSC Physics and were offered in March of 1959, 1960, and 1961.

However, the existence of two tests in physics proved to be confusing—some students took the wrong test, and mistakes could not be readily detected. It was soon recognized that it would be possible to construct one test for each field that would be "fair" to students of all the widely used and identifiable curriculums in that field. One possible approach was to define a "common core" of knowledge and abilities basic to all curriculums and to restrict the test to this common core. However, this approach would tend to neglect the content in each

---

*This section on curriculum bias in the Achievement Tests was written by William H. Angoff.

curriculum that made it distinctive and that, its proponents maintained, rendered it superior to other courses in that subject.

An alternative and decidedly preferable approach—one that has been discussed by Fornoff (1962) and adopted in the Board's tests—is to include in the tests items drawn not only from a common core but also the content specific to the various curriculums. The intent was to avoid giving an advantage to students of any one curriculum. Specifically, this means that each test should contain items representing each of the different curriculums, pitched at various levels of difficulty, so that students of equal ability but enrolled in different types of courses will earn the same scores on the test. ("Equal ability" is taken operationally to mean equal scores on SAT-verbal and mathematical sections *and* on a set of items that are judged and found to be equally appropriate to students of all the different courses.)

In the test development process, a committee of examiners familiar with the different courses in a given subject evaluates the proposed items in terms of their appropriateness for different courses. Sometimes pretest data indicating how students of different courses can be expected to perform on an item are available. Items are then chosen for inclusion in the test with the goal of effecting an overall balance among the courses. After the formal administration of the test, about 10 teachers of each of the major courses in the field of the test judge the appropriateness of each item for the course they teach. A core of items judged highly appropriate by the teachers of all the courses involved is then identified. Samples of students, each representing one of the courses, are selected*, and four scores are recorded for each student: SAT-verbal score, SAT-mathematical score, the score on the total test, and the score on the core of items judged to be equally appropriate to all courses. A covariance analysis is then performed on total score, controlling on SAT-V, SAT-M, and the common core items. In those instances where the differences in the adjusted means are found to exceed a specified maximum number of points (for example, 15 scaled score points), special interpretive material is prepared for test users announcing this fact and suggesting that these differences be taken into consideration in dealing with the scores. The results of the analysis also provide feedback information for the test developers so that they can improve the next forms of the test.

As time went on and it became clear that the tests were not seriously biased against students in the various curriculums, the judgment was made that the formal analyses described here need not be conducted on each new test form. More recently the practice has been to carry out the analyses about once every two years to

---

*These samples are defined on the basis of the student's own report, at the time of testing, of the type of course in which he is enrolled. Studies of the accuracy of the students' self-reports have shown an agreement with the teachers of their courses ranging from 66 percent to 98 percent.

see whether the test development process is still in good control. The results of a study of all the forms of the science tests introduced in 1967 indicate that in no case did the adjusted means for the special (or new) curriculum differ from the traditional curriculum by more than 15 points. In the 12 analyses conducted, 9 showed differences of less than 10 points.

Obviously, the procedure of testing for bias is possible only as long as the different courses in a subject are distinct from one another. As time passes and the teachers in the secondary schools select what they judge to be the best of each curriculum, the boundaries between curriculums tend to blur. Students are no longer able to identify their curriculum and it becomes increasingly difficult to associate particular items with particular curriculums. The consequence is that formal analyses of bias such as the kind described here will become virtually impossible, attesting essentially to a growing maturity in educational practice.

The quality control system

Primary responsibility for determining the content of College Board Achievement Tests rests with the Committees of Examiners who represent the schools and colleges that make up the College Board. As indicated in the preceding section, these committees devote much time to setting test specifications based on an analysis of the field to be covered and what is known about teaching practices throughout the country. However, there is no guarantee that a particular test item written by a committee member or by a special item writer will actually serve the function it is intended to serve. A newly written test item is a proposal to be considered rather than an accomplished fact. The writer of the item—and the committee members who have suggested revisions and finally approved the polished product—have judged (a) that the item is appropriate in difficulty, (b) that it is unambiguous and therefore understandable to any candidate who has mastered the skill or knowledge being tested, and (c) that it represents a legitimate question to ask—that is, that it belongs in the content universe for the subject area. It is the purpose of item analysis procedures to examine the soundness of these judgments.

Each of the tests in the Achievement Test series is a one-hour examination, designed to assess the achievement of large numbers of candidates who differ widely in their levels of achievement and who are applying to colleges that differ markedly in their requirements for admission. Because the tests represent a compromise among the many levels and kinds of uses to which they will be put, one cannot afford the luxury of many items that are so easy that they will be answered correctly by almost all candidates or so difficult that almost none of the candidates mark the correct answer. Such items would be more appropriate for tests designed for restricted purposes—for example, to certify specific levels of achievement for students applying to a single college. The primary purpose of a College Board Achievement Test is to indicate the relative achievement of the candidates—that is, to differentiate among candidates and to indicate which have learned the most and which have learned the least. Very easy or very difficult items do not contribute to this purpose and therefore must be eliminated regardless of their value for other purposes.

It is important to know that the item itself discriminates—that is, that it is answered correctly by candidates who are "good" students of the subject and incorrectly by those who are "poor" students. An item may fail to discriminate either because it is too easy or too difficult, because it is ambiguous or otherwise improperly written, or because it does not belong in the content universe for the test. For example, an item covering an obscure point treated in a single, recently published textbook might be missed by a majority of good students and answered correctly by relatively poor students who happened to study the particular textbook. Or an item might be so worded that good students with knowledge of a particular complex concept might find fault with the intended answer and hesitate to mark it while students with a superficial knowledge of the concept might have no reason to be critical of the intended answer and so have a greater chance to select it.

To determine the difficulty and discrimination of items proposed for the Achievement Tests, items are pretested by administering them to students similar to those who will be candidates in the Admissions Testing Program. Ideally, items should be tried out on random samples of the candidate group; however, in a program as complex as this it is difficult to define the candidate group, much less to sample within it. The group changes from year to year as new institutions begin requiring the tests. Furthermore, there are difficult logistics problems. It has proved convenient and feasible, however, to define a *standard reference population* and to refer pretest statistics to the standard population by a process of item equating. Pretest samples are obtained by enlisting the cooperation of schools and colleges that teach courses at the level covered by the examinations and the results are related to the standard reference population by including in each pretest a group of test items that have been used in the program and for which indexes of difficulty (deltas) for the standard population are already known. A scatterplot relating the delta values observed in the pretest sample to the delta values for the standard reference population is then used to generate an "equating line," and this line is used to estimate standard indexes of difficulty ("equated deltas") for the new items being pretested (see Chapters I and II).

The item statistics obtained through pretesting are used to evaluate and select items of a certain level of difficulty and discrimination to insure that this form of the test will be reasonably parallel to previous forms

of the test. Following the use of a new test form, a quality control check is made by preparing a *test analysis*, described in Chapter I. This procedure includes, among other things, an item analysis, the results of which may be compared with the estimates based on pretest data at the time the test was assembled.

An example of the item analysis form is presented in Table 3.2, which is a copy of the computer output for two different analyses of item number 71 in the May 1963 Physics Test. One analysis was based on a sample of 370 candidates who had completed a secondary school physics course using one of the generally available "traditional" textbooks. The other analysis was based on a sample of 370 candidates who had studied the texts prepared by the Physical Science Study Committee (PSSC). (It should be mentioned here that at the time of this writing, item and test analysis samples are considerably larger than in the early 1960s. Currently they vary in size from a minimum of about 900 cases to a maximum of about 2,000 cases.)

In each case, the analysis was carried out as follows:

1. Test papers were scored using the key certified by the Committee of Examiners and total ("criterion") scores on the test were translated to a standard score scale with a mean of 13.0 and a standard deviation of 4.0.

2. The papers were divided into five equal groups based on the total score, and the number in each group giving each response was determined.

3. The average standard ("criterion") score of candidates marking each response was computed.

4. An index of discrimination and two indexes of difficulty were determined.

5. An index of difficulty for the "standard" group (the "equated delta") was estimated.

The results of such an analysis may be clarified by examining Table 3.2. The frequencies of response for each option for each of the five groups are reported in the table occupying the central portion of the reporting sheet. For example, for the sample of 370 "traditional" candidates, there were 74 in each fifth of the distribution. In the low fifth, 11 students omitted the item— that is, they did not mark an answer but did mark an answer to one or more subsequent items in the test. Ten marked option A; seven, B; five, C; ten, D; and ten, E. This accounted for 53 of the 74 candidates in the lower fifth. The remaining 21 are classified as "not reached." Since they marked neither this item nor any subsequent item, it is assumed that they did not have time to read and consider the item. Similarly, in the high fifth, 5 omitted the item; 1 marked A; 45, B; 1, C; 3, D; and 4, E. Fifteen were classified as "not reached." There is a sharp rise in frequency of right answers from 7 in the low fifth to 45 in the high fifth, and in general the frequency of wrong answers decreases from low to high fifth.

The two-row strip at the bottom of the sheet con-

Table 3.2

Examples of item analysis computer output
(Item 71 of College Board Physics Test, May 1963)

Based on candidates studying "traditional" physics

ITEM NO: 71 CARD NO: 2 SERIES: 515 TEST: PHYSICS FORM: MAY 1963 BASE N: 370 DATE TABULATED: 10 07 63

EDUCATIONAL TESTING SERVICE — ITEM ANALYSIS (650 OUTPUT)

RESPONSE CODE	LOW N_1	N_2	N_3	N_4	HIGH N_5
OMIT	11	7	9	4	5
A	10	8	5	2	1
B	7	11	13	22	45
C	5	7	4	3	1
D	10	1	4	1	3
E	10	16	10	15	4
TOTAL	53	50	45	47	59

*DENOTES CORRECT RESPONSE

FORM	BASE N	OMIT	A	B	C	D	E	M_{TOTAL}	Δ_E SCALE	Δ_E	CRITERION
MAY 63	370	36	26	98*	20	19	55	13.2		16.9	
TEST CODE	**ITEM NO.**	M_O	M_A	M_B	M_C	M_D	M_E	P TOTAL	P+	Δ_O	r_{bis}
TRAD	71	12.0	10.6	15.6	11.4	10.3	12.4	.69	.39	14.3	.62

Based on candidates studying PSSC physics

ITEM NO: 71 CARD NO: 2 SERIES: 514 TEST: PHYSICS FORM: MAY 1963 BASE N: 370 DATE TABULATED: 10 02 63

EDUCATIONAL TESTING SERVICE — ITEM ANALYSIS (650 OUTPUT)

RESPONSE CODE	LOW N_1	N_2	N_3	N_4	HIGH N_5
OMIT	10	14	11	7	4
A	17	8	5	4	1
B	4	8	18	22	45
C	5	2	5		
D	3	8	1		1
E	14	8	11	16	10
TOTAL	53	48	51	49	61

*DENOTES CORRECT RESPONSE

FORM	BASE N	OMIT	A	B	C	D	E	M_{TOTAL}	Δ_E SCALE	Δ_E	CRITERION
MAY 63	370	46	35	97*	12	13	59	13.2			
TEST CODE	**ITEM NO.**	M_O	M_A	M_B	M_C	M_D	M_E	P TOTAL	P+	Δ_O	r_{bis}
PSSC	71	11.7	10.1	16.0	9.8	10.9	12.8	.71	.37	14.5	.68

tains summary data. The correct answer, B, was marked by 98 candidates with an average "criterion" score of 15.6. In contrast, the average "criterion" score (total test score converted to a standard score scale with mean = 13 and standard deviation = 4) of those marking wrong answers or omitting the item range from 10.3 to 12.4. The mean "criterion" score (M_{TOTAL}) of those reaching the item was 13.2. Sixty-nine percent of the candidates were in this group (P_{TOTAL}). The remaining 31 percent did not reach the item. Thirty-nine percent of the group marked the right answer (P+), which provides one index of difficulty.

The second index of difficulty is the observed delta (Δ_O), an index expressed in terms of the standard score criterion scale. It represents the normal deviate on this scale at which the ordinate separates the percentage (P+) marking the item correct from the percentage missing the item, after an adjustment has been applied to take care of any discrepancy between the ability of the group trying the item and the group not reaching it. The scale for delta is inversely related to the scale for P+. That is to say, the *more difficult* the item, the *higher* the value of delta. If all candidates in the sample try an item, a delta of 13.0, for example, is equivalent to 50 percent marking the correct answer; a delta of 9.0 is equivalent to 84 percent marking the correct answer; and a delta of 17.0 is equivalent to 16 percent marking the correct response. In the case of item 71 of the Physics Test, 39 percent of the group reaching the item marked the correct response. The delta corresponding to 39 percent is 14.1. The reported delta, 14.3, represents an adjustment for the fact that the group reaching the item had a mean criterion score of 13.2, slightly higher than the mean criterion score of 13.0 for the total sample. The fact that the delta is higher after adjustment reflects likelihood that the item would have been more difficult for the total group than for the group that reached it.

The estimated delta for the College Board standard group ("equated" delta) is entered just above the delta computed from the data. It is 16.9. This means that the item would have been more difficult for the standard reference group than for the item analysis sample and reflects the fact that the item analysis sample was more able.

The index of discrimination, the biserial coefficient of correlation (r_{bis}), is entered at the extreme right. It is .62. There is a space above the biserial correlation for identifying the criterion. If there is no entry, it is assumed that the criterion was the total score on the test.

The item analysis based on the PSSC group does not differ appreciably from that based on the "traditional" group. There are small differences in the figures, but they are not different from those one comes to expect when similar samples are compared. It is therefore concluded that this particular item is equally difficult for both regular and PSSC candidates.

It can be seen from Table 3.2 that the item analysis provides the test writer with considerable information about students' responses to the items he has written. This particular analysis strongly suggests that the item is suitable for the test. It is difficult, but not extremely so. All options are functioning properly, and there is no evidence of ambiguity. The item discriminates sharply between high-scoring and low-scoring candidates, not only within the "traditional" physics group but also within the PSSC group.

The use of the total score on a test as the criterion for item analysis has often been criticized. It is argued that the use of such a criterion could lead to a kind of inbreeding through which gradually a narrower and narrower aspect of an area is measured. Ideally, it is argued, each question should make an independent contribution to the measurement of the total; therefore, the best item is one which has a low correlation with other questions in the test while measuring some important aspect of the criterion performance.

This possibility is recognized in the ETS item analysis procedure and from time to time criteria other than the total scores on a test may be used. However, it should be noted that in the construction of College Board Achievement Tests the item analysis procedure is used as a supplement to, rather than as a substitute for, the judgment that the item is an appropriate and useful one. Generally, the question being asked by the test writer is: "Is the biserial correlation for this item high enough to preclude the possibility that it is ambiguous or irrelevant?" This is quite a different question from: "Of all the items that have been written, which have the highest biserial correlations?" Item analysis is used to eliminate from the item pool or mark for revision defective items, not necessarily to determine which items shall be selected for a test.

Carl Brigham, who with Cecil Brolyer was responsible for devising the item analysis procedures applied to College Board tests, recognized that the item-test correlation is a useful index of the item's discriminating power. He had constructed the SAT-verbal aptitude test for the purpose of predicting performance in liberal arts colleges, particularly in English classes. He therefore carried out an item analysis in which he correlated the antonym items in Form C of the SAT with grades obtained in English six months after the administration of the test. The results were compared with those obtained from the analysis against the total score on the test. His conclusions read:

> More important than the range of biserial r's, however, is the fact that these items derive their validity from exactly the same traps or from the same characteristic item pattern which indicated their validity when the total score in the scholastic aptitude test was used as a criterion. Changing the criterion did not alter the pattern of the item charts materially. (Brigham, 1932, p. 355.)

If one is attempting, by a purely empirical procedure, to construct a test that will predict performance of a complex and not very well understood criterion, a process of item analysis based on correlations with an external and independent measure of that criterion may be the only justifiable approach. But when one is evaluating test items that have been judged appropriate in terms of their content for inclusion in a test designed to assess achievement in an academic field, the total score on a representative sample of such questions is likely to be a highly satisfactory criterion. It is assumed, of course, that systematic studies will be made of the relationship of the total score criterion to whatever other criterion measures may be available. Usually, the information obtained from studies relating reasonably reliable test scores to other performance criteria is more definitive than that obtained by carrying out item analyses against performance criteria, particularly when there are, as in the college admissions situation, as many criteria as there are colleges and schools within the colleges.

This position is strongly supported by data from a study that compared various methods of item selection for the Law School Admission Test (Olsen and Schrader, 1953). The test in its original form consisted of a number of different subtests, each created on the basis of rational judgment and then refined through item analysis procedures using the total score on the subtest as the criterion. The total testing time was approximately six hours, and it was decided to attempt to shorten the test by selecting from the total pool of questions those most predictive of performance in law schools. In this situation, the external criterion for item analysis did not prove to be superior for this purpose to the internal criterion.

Item analysis, then, is used at two points in the test development process—at the pretest stage to assess the appropriateness of questions for use in a test form and at the final form stage to reveal the extent to which statistical specifications were met and to obtain a final check on the adequacy of the pretest analysis. In addition, certain data are obtained that are useful in evaluating the test as a whole. A score distribution is prepared for the total group of candidates taking the test. Reliability coefficients and standard errors of measurement are computed. If there are part scores, or if it is desired to study the relationships of scores on the particular Achievement Test to other measures, a correlation table is prepared. Finally, certain operations are performed to obtain estimates of the extent to which speed is a factor in determining performance on the test. Test data, together with a summary of the item analysis data, are included in a test analysis distributed to those responsible for the various stages in the test development process.

Examples of the test analysis data for the May 1963 form of the College Board Physics Test are presented in Tables 3.3, 3.4, 3.5, 3.6, and 3.7. Table 3.3 contains the distribution of scores for the candidate group of 9,378. It also contains summary statistics and the conversion parameters for translating raw scores to scaled scores. It can be readily determined that the test was relatively difficult for the candidate group. The mean score on the 75 items was 26.40 (where the scoring formula was $R - W/4$). A test of middle difficulty would be expected to produce a mean score of approximately half of 75 or 37.5. On the other hand, if admissions decisions based on Achievement Tests involve primarily scores in the upper half of the distribution, this positively skewed distribution is an acceptable one. The interpretation of data of this sort depends on knowledge of the context within which the test is to be applied.

It will be recalled that there were two item analysis samples, one for "traditional" candidates and the other for PSSC candidates. The remaining data of the test analysis are based on these samples. Data on reliability and speededness are presented in Table 3.4, additional data on speededness in Tables 3.5 and 3.6, and a summary of the item analysis results in Table 3.7. Data similar to these are reported for each new test form of each Achievement Test and the results studied by committees of examiners as they determine whether or not to change specifications for the tests.

Scaling and equating the Achievement Tests*

Because the Achievement Tests are administered only to those candidates who elect to take them, special problems unlike those of defining the scales for the Scholastic Aptitude Test are encountered. In order to define the scale initially for the SAT, which is taken by virtually all the candidates in the College Board Program, it was only necessary to set the raw score means and standard deviations for the entire candidate group at that time at the same scaled score values for the two parts of the test. However, because of the self-selection that is characteristic of the groups taking the Achievement Tests, it is observed that candidates who take some tests are typically of higher ability, or more dispersed in ability, as measured by the SAT, than are candidates who take the other tests. This being the case, it seemed reasonable to set the scale for each of the Achievement Tests in such a way as to reflect the ability of the group taking the test, at least to the extent that the SAT is relevant to or correlates with that test. The operational method of doing this is to estimate for each test the mean and standard deviation of raw scores that would have been earned on that test by a specially defined subgroup of candidates taking it and then to set the estimated mean and standard deviation at 500 and 100, respectively. This type of scale definition also specifies in the following way the sense in which the scales for the different Achievement Tests are made comparable: Each of the scales for the Achievement Tests is set with a mean of 500 and standard deviation of 100 for the hypothetical sub-

---

*This section on the scaling and equating of the Achievement Tests was written by William H. Angoff.

Table 3.3

*Example of score distributions and conversion data reported
in test analyses of Achievement Tests (Physics Test, May 1963)*

TEST ANALYSIS REPORT FORM

Test <u>College Entrance Examination Board</u>   Subject <u>Achievement</u>   Form _____

Taken by <u>Board May candidates</u>   Date <u>May 1963</u>

Project _____ Job _____

Physics							
Raw Score X	Standard Score Y	f	Percentile Rank of Lower Limit of Interval	Raw Score X	Standard Score Y	f	Percentile Rank of Lower Limit of Interval
72–75	800	2	99.98				
68–71	800	6	99.9				
64–67	800	15	99.8				
60–63	799–800	48	99.2				
56–59	769–791	98	98.2				
52–55	740–762	155	96.5				
48–51	710–732	259	93.8				
44–47	681–703	379	89.7				
40–43	651–673	503	84.4				
36–39	622–644	625	77.7				
32–35	592–615	862	68.5				
28–31	563–585	1054	57.3				
24–27	534–556	1151	45.0				
20–23	504–526	1262	31.6				
16–19	475–497	1100	19.8				
12–15	445–467	894	10.3				
8–11	416–438	559	4.3				
4– 7	386–408	274	1.4				
0– 3	357–379	132	0.0				
		9378					

M_x = <u>26.40</u>

σ_x = <u>12.42</u>

M_y = <u>551</u>

σ_y = <u>91</u>

Md_x = <u>25.13</u>

(75 items)

<u>Conversion Data</u>

Converted to Board standard scale through scores on 25 items in common with an earlier form.

$Y = 7.3637 X + 356.8229$

M_x = _____

σ_x = _____

M_y = _____

σ_y = _____

Md_x = _____

<u>Conversion Data</u>

Table 3.4

Example of data on reliability, intercorrelations of sections, and speededness of sections reported in test analyses of Achievement Tests (Physics Test, May 1963)

Test College Entrance Examination Board   Subject ___Physics___   Form _____

N = 370 each group

Description of Sample:

Spaced samples

Scoring Formulae and Reliability Coefficients for Sections

Section of Test	Scoring Formula	Relia-bility*	SE$_{meas.}$	Section of Test	Scoring Formula	Relia-bility*	SE$_{meas.}$
Sample:							
Traditional	R-W/4	.868	4.52				
PSSC	R-W/4	.889	4.44				

*Adaptation of Kuder-Richardson formula (20).

Intercorrelations of Sections

Section												

Speededness of Sections

Section	Trad.	PSSC									
Per cent completing test..	42.7	51.1									
Per cent completing 75 per cent of test..	94.3	95.1									
Number of items reached by 80 per cent of the candidates	66	67									
Total number of items	75	75									

Table 3.5

*Example of detailed data on speededness reported in test analyses
of Achievement Tests (Physics Test, May 1963, "traditional" sample)*

Test __College Entrance Examination Board__ Subject __Physics__ Form _____

Section __Total__ __Traditional Sample__ Number of Items __75 (5-choice)__

R+W \ Score	6-10	11-15	16-20	21-25	26-30	31-35	36-40	41-45	46-50	51-55	56-60	61-65	66-70	71-75	f
60-63														2	2
56-59													2	5	7
52-55												1	1	6	8
48-51												2	1	2	5
44-47											1	3	7	10	21
40-43									2	1	1	5	4	10	23
36-39										5	4	9	3	10	31
32-35								1	1	2	6	7	14	9	40
28-31								3	4	8	7	10	6	5	43
24-27							1		4	11	5	10	10	7	48
20-23							2	3	1	7	6	8	3	3	33
16-19							4	3	4	8	6	7	4	7	43
12-15				1	1	4	9	3	1	3	4	2	6		34
8-11					1	3	4	3		2	2	2	5		22
4-7	1					1		1				1	1	1	6
0-3					1			1	1					1	4
Total	1			2	2	15	24	24	43	41	69	60	89		370

Score f	R No. of Items	R f	W No. of Items	W f	O No. of Items	O f	NR No. of Items	NR f
2	64-67	2						
7	60-63	7	56-59	2			51-53 ⎱	1
8	56-59	7	52-55	3			⎰	
5	52-55	9	48-51	5	36-38	3		
21	48-51	23	44-47	16	33-35	3		
23	44-47	29	40-43	12	30-32	7	30-32	3
31	40-43	39	36-39	32	27-29	10	27-29	4
40	36-39	47	32-35	31	24-26	7	24-26	4
43	32-35	52	28-31	56	21-23	12	21-23	6
48	28-31	45	24-27	64	18-20	25	18-20	9
33	24-27	48	20-23	55	15-17	24	15-17	9
43	20-23	30	16-19	52	12-14	32	12-14	19
34	16-19	23	12-15	23	9-11	41	9-11	25
22	12-15	5	8-11	15	6-8	50	6-8	30
6	8-11	2	4-7	3	3-5	53	3-5	48
4	4-7	2	0-3	1	0-2	103	0-2	212
370		**370**		**370**		**370**		**370**

Score = R-W/4

Physics, traditional sample

	Score	R	W	O	NR
Mean	27.82	34.34	26.59	9.38	4.69
Standard Deviation	12.43	11.18	9.91	8.71	7.13

group of candidates for whom the means and standard deviations on both SAT-verbal and SAT-mathematical are 500 and 100, respectively, for whom the verbal-mathematical covariance is 4,000, and who are adequately prepared to take the test in that subject. For the foreign language Achievement Tests further restrictions are made in terms of the number of semesters of study in each language, as will be described below. Thus, the scales for all the tests in the Admissions Testing Program—the SAT as well as the Achievement Tests—are comparable in the sense that their means and standard deviations are all fixed at the same values (500 and 100) for the hypothetical subgroup.

The equations that are used for estimating the performance of the hypothetical subgroup on each of the Achievement Tests are quite similar to those that are used for equating. The principal differences are these: first, the scaling equations require only a single estimation of mean and variance for each test, rather than two estimations, as in equating (one for the new form and one for the old form); and second, the scaling equations make use of SAT scores, rather than scores on common item material, in adjusting for differences between groups.

Table 3.6

Example of detailed data on speededness reported in test analyses
of Achievement Tests (Physics Test, May 1963, PSSC sample)

Test __College Entrance Examination Board__   Subject __Physics__   Form _____

Section __Total__   __PSSC Sample__   Number of Items __75 (5-choice)__

R+W Score	28-30	31-33	34-36	37-39	40-42	43-45	46-48	49-51	52-54	55-57	58-60	61-63	64-66	67-69	70-72	73-75	Score f	R No. of Items	R f	W No. of Items	W f	O No. of Items	O f	NR No. of Items	NR f
69-73																1	1	70-74	1			42-44	1		
64-68																2	2	65-69	2	52-55	2	39-41	1		
59-63															1	5	6	60-64	9	48-51	7	36-38	2	26-38	1
54-58													3	1	2	7	13	55-59	22	44-47	6	33-35	1	33-35	4
49-53											1	1	4	7	5	9	27	50-54	35	40-43	18	30-32	6	30-32	2
44-48									1	1	4	5	4	6	3	7	31	45-49	47	36-39	23	27-29	8	27-29	2
39-43									2	3	4	6	9	6	6	9	45	40-44	37	32-35	28	24-26	7	24-26	5
34-38						1	4	1	2	5	3	3	1	4	5	6	35	35-39	61	28-31	47	21-23	14	21-23	2
29-33						1	1	5	2	4	6	4	8	4	2	5	42	30-34	55	24-27	51	18-20	15	18-20	4
24-28				1	1	4	2	3	3	6	7	7	5	5	1	12	57	25-29	54	20-23	49	15-17	21	15-17	10
19-23		1	4	3	3	2	1	3	7	3	9	2	5	4	1	5	53	20-24	31	16-19	55	12-14	25	12-14	13
14-18				1	1	1	2	1	3	1	1	3	3	3	4	4	28	15-19	13	12-15	50	9-11	47	9-11	20
9-13						1	3	3	2	2	3	1	1	1	2	3	22	10-14	2	8-11	27	6-8	55	6-8	40
4-8	2					1		1				1	1		1	1	8	5-9	1	4-7	7	3-5	62	3-5	35
																						0-2	105	0-2	232
Total	2	1	6	6	6	11	12	16	20	25	39	33	43	42	32	76	370		370		370		370		370

Score = R-W/4
Physics, PSSC sample

	Score	R	W	O	NR
Mean	31.95	37.90	24.30	8.64	4.16
Standard Deviation	13.33	11.74	10.31	8.48	7.00

Establishing the initial scale

Notation:

x = Raw scores on an Achievement Test, for which a standard score scale is to be defined. This may be a test of English Composition or American History or Biology or Level I Mathematics, etc.

v, m = Scaled scores on SAT-verbal and -mathematical sections.

S = Standard score scale.

M, s, s_{gh} = Observed statistics for group taking Form x. $s_{gh} = r_{gh} s_g s_h$.

μ, σ, σ_{gh} = Designated statistics for hypothetical sub-group. $\mu_v = \mu_m = 500$; $\sigma_v = \sigma_m = 100$; $\sigma_{vm} = \rho_{vm} \sigma_v \sigma_m = 4,000$.

$b_{gh.ij...}$ = Partial regression coefficient for predicting g from h, holding fixed all variables to the right of the decimal.

Data for scaling a new test (x) are assembled by drawing all, or virtually all, of the population of candidates taking that test at its first administration, calculating the means, variances, and covariances among SAT-verbal, SAT-mathematical, and Test x, and entering the appropriate values in the equations below.

1) $\hat{\mu}_x = M_x + b_{xv.m}(\mu_v - M_v) + b_{xm.v}(\mu_m - M_m)$

2) $\hat{\sigma}_x^2 = s_x^2 + b_{xv.m}^2(\sigma_v^2 - s_v^2) + b_{xm.v}^2(\sigma_m^2 - s_m^2) + 2b_{xv.m} b_{xm.v}(\sigma_{vm} - s_{vm})$.

The equation relating raw scores on Test x to the standard score is then derived by designating the mean and

Table 3.7

Example of item analysis summary data reported in test analyses
of Achievement Tests (Physics Test, May 1963)

Test   College Entrance Examination Board   Subject Physics   Form

Frequency Distributions of Original Deltas
and Biserial Correlations, by Sections

Standard Δ = a(original Δ) + b

Delta	Trad.	PSSC							
19.0 up ..									
18.0-18.9	1								
17.0-17.9	–	1							
16.0-16.9	4	2							
15.0-15.9	7	11							
14.0-14.9	18	13							
13.0-13.9	16	10							
12.0-12.9	11	17							
11.0-11.9	8	6							
10.0-10.9	3	6							
9.0- 9.9	2	2							
8.0- 8.9	2	4							
7.0- 7.9	1	1							
6.0- 6.9	1	2							
Total	74*	75	Equ.						
Mean	13.2	12.8	15.6						
σ	2.1	2.4	2.4						
a	1.13								
b	0.66								

*When drop-out exceeds 50 per cent, Δ and r_{bis} are not reported.

r_{bis}									
.90-.99									
.80-.89									
.70-.79									
.60-.69	3	6							
.50-.59	21	22							
.40-.49	21	25							
.30-.39	16	10							
.20-.29	8	6							
.10-.19	2	3							
.00-.09	3	1							
Negative .		1							
Total	74*	74							
Not Comp.		1							
Mean	.41	.44							
σ	.14	.14							

standard deviation of scaled scores on that test for the hypothetical subgroup as 500 and 100, respectively:

$$\frac{S-500}{100} = \frac{X - \hat{\mu}_x}{\hat{\sigma}_x},$$

which yields the linear equation relating raw scores on Test x to the scale:

3) $\quad S = a_{sx} X + b_{sx}$,

where $a_{sx} = 100/\hat{\sigma}_x$ and $b_{sx} = 500 - a_{sx} \mu_x$.

Clearly, equation (3) applies only to the particular form of Test x for which these calculations were made. When a new form of Test x is produced and administered to a candidate group, that form must be equated to a previous form of the test in order to derive a new conversion equation appropriate for it.

The process just described applies to all the Achievement Tests in the College Board Program except for the language tests. In the latter 1940s, as a result of a study by L. R Tucker (Angoff, 1961) of differences in language Achievement Test scores associated with levels of language training, a third variable, semesters of language training, was added to the SAT-verbal and SAT-mathematical predictors in setting the scales for the tests in French, German, Latin, and Spanish. This new variable was added in an effort to make the scales for the language tests reflect the differences in amount of language training that were—and still are, for the most part—characteristic of students who took the different language tests. The equations for estimating the mean and variance of raw scores on the language tests for the hypothetical subgroup correspond precisely to equations (1) and (2), except that a third predictor variable is added. Thus, if n is used to designate number of semesters of training, equations (1) and (2) become respectively, equations (4) and (5):

4) $\hat{\mu}_x = M_x + b_{xv.mn}(\mu_v - M_v) +$
$\quad b_{xm.vn}(\mu_m - M_m) + b_{xn.vm}(\mu_n - M_n)$

5) $\hat{\sigma}_x^2 = s_x^2 + b_{xv.mn}^2(\sigma_v^2 - s_v^2) +$

$\quad b_{xm.vn}^2(\sigma_m^2 - s_m^2) + b_{xn.vm}^2(\sigma_n^2 - s_n^2)$

$\quad + 2b_{xv.mn} b_{xm.vn}(\sigma_{vm} - s_{vm})$

$\quad + 2b_{xv.mn} b_{xn.vm}(\sigma_{vn} - s_{vn})$

$\quad + 2b_{xm.vn} b_{xn.vm}(\sigma_{mn} - s_{mn}).$

The values of μ_v, μ_m, σ_v, σ_m, and σ_{vm} are, respectively, 500, 500, 100, 100, and 4,000, as before. The values μ_m, σ_n, σ_{vn}, and σ_{mn} are taken from the original data collected by Tucker in his study of language Achievement Test scores, in which the hypothetical values are taken to represent the combined group of candidates taking French, German, Latin, and Spanish.

In general, the system of scaling the Achievement Tests allows the scores on those tests to reflect the level and dispersion of SAT scores for students who typically choose to take them. Specifically, the scheme has the effect of raising the entire scale of scores for a test that

is typically taken by high-ability students (as measured by the SAT) and lowering it for a test that is typically taken by lower-ability students. In the case of the foreign language tests for which the number of years of language study is added to the team of predictors, it also raises the scale for a test in a language that is typically studied for an extended period of time in secondary school and lowers it for a test in a language that is typically studied for a short period of time. It broadens the scales for tests that are taken by heterogeneous groups of students (heterogeneous in terms of SAT scores and/or length of language study) and produces narrow scales for tests taken by homogeneous groups of students.

The purpose underlying this system for scaling the Achievement Tests is to avoid some of the inequities that would result if, for example, each test were set on a 500 (mean)-100 (standard deviation) scale based only on the performance of the candidates taking that test. Such a scale system would make it possible for a candidate to earn high scores simply by taking tests in subject-matter areas that attract students of lower ability. Such a scale would also cause a candidate to earn low scores if the tests he took were in areas commonly studied by high-ability students. This is not to say that the scale system for the Achievement Tests solves all the problems of score interpretation across optional tests in different subject-matter areas. However, it *is* claimed that it helps to avoid some of the problems of the more conventional scale system.

To the extent that the SAT is correlated with the particular Achievement Test, the College Board system provides that the scale for a test be adjusted upward or downward to reflect the level of ability of the candidates who elect to take that test. As a result, the scales for certain tests, notably Mathematics Level II, have a characteristically higher floor and higher ceiling, in terms of the scaled scores, than other tests, for example, Spanish. If there were no further restrictions placed on the scale it would be possible for a candidate to earn far higher scaled scores on Mathematics Level II than on Spanish. For this reason principally, scaled score differentiations are made among negative formula scores, a procedure that effectively extends the lower end of the scale. In addition, special adjustments are made in the scales for tests like Mathematics Level II to insure greater uniformity among the Achievement Tests with respect to their minimum possible scaled scores. Finally, rigid cutoffs are imposed on the scales for all the tests, both at the top and at the bottom. At the upper end of the scale the limit of 800 is imposed on the scales so that no candidate, however able he may be, can earn a score higher than 800 on any Achievement Test. All scores that would be reported as something higher than 800—as a result of the simple application of the conversion equation—are curtailed and reported simply as 800. (Similarly, the lower limit of 200 is imposed at the bottom end of the scale.) However, in the particular case of Mathematics Level II the 800-

score cutoff makes it impossible to discriminate among the very able candidates in mathematics for whom the test was explicitly introduced into the program. Therefore, for those colleges who request it, special score reporting is provided in terms of equated raw scores to permit discriminations for the full range of talent measured by the test.

To illustrate some of the observations made above, Table 3.8 is presented, giving a picture of the summary statistics for the various Achievement Tests in the College Board Program for the academic year 1968-69. These kinds of data are collected annually as part of a continuing effort, initiated on the recommendation of Professor S. S. Wilks (Wilks, 1961), to assess the appropriateness of the scales for the various tests and to compare the scales as they exist at present with the scales as they might appear today if they were defined on the basis of current data. Means and standard deviations are given for each of the Achievement Tests, for SAT-verbal, and for SAT-mathematical. In addition, the correlations among the three tests are given separately for the group taking each Achievement Test. The data just described are given for the tests in English, history, science, and mathematics. Data for the language tests are given in Table 3.9, and include, in addition to those described for Table 3.8, corresponding statistics for years of training in each language and the correlation between years of training with SAT-verbal, SAT-mathe-

matical, and Achievement Test scores.

Unlike the process of equating (in which the collection of items that is used for adjusting for differences in the groups is ordinarily chosen to be a parallel miniature of the test itself), the process of scaling the Achievement Tests involves making adjustments on the basis of observed differences on the SAT and carries with it special problems that derive from the fact that the SAT is not a parallel measure of any of the Achievement Tests. For example, the slope of the growth curve for any Achievement Test is in general much steeper than the growth curve for the SAT. For this reason, it can be expected that the performance of candidates on a given Achievement Test, relative to their performance on the SAT, would be different at different times in the school year. Such differences will be reflected in the results of the scaling. Also, it can be expected that the slope of the growth curve for any Achievement Test, relative to the slope of the growth curve for the SAT, might vary considerably from one type of group to another. For these reasons, it is important in any scaling operation in which data are drawn from a single administration to specify and standardize the particular point in time in the candidates' pursuit of the subject that the testing is to take place and the data be collected for scaling. It is similarly important to specify and standardize in some way the nature of the group for whom scaling data are to be collected. Identical scaling operations based

Table 3.8

Summary statistics for English, Social Studies, Science, and Mathematics Achievement Tests for candidates taking both the SAT and the Achievement Tests in 1968-69*

	English Composition	Literature	American History and Social Studies	European History and World Cultures	Biology	Chemistry	Physics	Math Level I	Math Level II
No. of candidates	4701	7332	4634	7235	4773	4877	5057	4637	4717
Mean									
SAT-verbal	514	538	513	541	511	531	534	507	578
SAT-mathematical	543	511	525	526	520	601	631	554	666
Achievement Test	514	531	496	540	509	564	581	538	673
Standard Deviation									
SAT-verbal	104	111	104	110	106	101	107	103	108
SAT-mathematical	107	104	106	103	102	96	95	101	91
Achievement Test	106	111	104	108	108	104	105	101	95
Correlation									
SAT-V vs. Ach. Test	.81	.82	.72	.74	.71	.59	.61	.56	.61
SAT-M vs. Ach. Test	.57	.58	.57	.54	.66	.68	.69	.83	.82
SAT-V vs. SAT-M	.60	.65	.62	.63	.60	.58	.57	.61	.61

*Based on samples drawn for studying the scales for the Achievement Tests.

on data for candidates tested at different times in their school year will yield different kinds of results, as will identical scaling operations based on data for different compositions of candidate groups.

Equating subsequent forms

As was pointed out earlier, the scaling process is applied to only one form of each Achievement Test and is carried out at the time that the particular Achievement Test is introduced into the program. From that time on, the scale is perpetuated by equating each subsequent form to a predecessor form, and therefore, indirectly to the initial form. Thus, except for read-justments (described below) that are periodically introduced into the scales, the concepts of score equating (score calibration) and the concept of scaling (scale definition) are kept distinct and separate.

The general conception underlying the equating of the Achievement Tests parallels the conception for equating the SAT and is carried out in the manner described in Chapter II. The restrictions that apply to the SAT—that it is administered for the first time in its final form at the operational administration of the test and that it is administered to all candidates on that date—

also apply in the case of the Achievement Tests. The result of these restrictions is that, as with the SAT, successive forms of the Achievement Tests have to be equated with the use of data from groups that may not be equivalent. In order to determine the degree to which these groups are different and to adjust for these differences in the equating process, common test material has to be provided. This material is embedded within the operational test form itself and appears as a set of items interspersed throughout the test, yielding a single total score. The items appear as operational items in both the new form and in the form to which the new form is to be equated and are placed in such a way as to present the same "task" to the candidate. That is, attempts are made to control contextual effects that are caused, for example, by differences in ordinal position in the test, and to control the effects of differences in speededness. The "equating section" yields a single total score taken over all the common items. The equating process takes the form of estimating the mean and variance on each test form for the combined group of candidates who take both test forms and then setting those means and variances equal.

The foregoing process yields a linear equation relating the raw scores on the new form to scaled scores on the old form. As in the case of the SAT, this equation is com-

Table 3.9

Summary statistics for language Achievement Tests
for candidates taking both the SAT and the Achievement Tests in 1968-69*

	French	German	Hebrew**	Latin	Russian	Spanish
No. of candidates	3555	3779	989	5163	883	3610
Mean						
SAT-verbal	549	555	552	550	594	518
SAT-mathematical	555	585	575	565	610	534
Semesters of study	5.86	5.37	....	5.74	5.19	5.44
Achievement Test	510	508	569	531	508	494
Standard Deviation						
SAT-verbal	96	95	110	100	97	96
SAT-mathematical	98	99	110	98	99	97
Semesters of study	1.43	1.50	....	1.44	1.63	1.53
Achievement Test	97	95	97	100	112	100
Correlation						
SAT-V vs. Ach. Test	.57	.48	.35	.58	.40	.51
SAT-M vs. Ach. Test	.45	.38	.33	.47	.33	.38
Sem. of study vs. Ach. Test	.49	.48	....	.49	.34	.52
SAT-V vs. Sem. of study	.25	.13	....	.23	.05	.22
SAT-M vs. Sem. of study	.17	.09	....	.18	.11	.20
SAT-V VS. SAT-M	.59	.54	.65	.57	.57	.57

*Based on samples drawn for studying the scales for the Achievement Tests.

**Data on semesters of study are not available for the Hebrew Test.

bined with the equation converting raw scores on the old form to the standard scale to yield a new linear equation relating scores on the new form to the standard scale.

The equating of the Achievement Tests has been done separately, test by test, in an effort to maintain the scale system for each test as it was originally conceived. More recently, as mentioned above, studies have been undertaken to investigate the following matters: to what extent the scales for the various tests bear the same relation to one another that they did when they were originally defined; and to what extent they have drifted away from this original mooring as a result of accumulated errors of equating, changes in the content of the test, and changes in the composition of the candidate population. The results of the annual scaling studies are averaged with the results of the equating studies in maintaining the score scales for the various tests. The procedures thus recognize the need both for equivalence of scores on different forms of the same test and for comparability of scores on different tests.

Although the need to maintain a rigid scale system is recognized to be as great for the Achievement Tests as it is for the SAT, the restrictions are such that the desired flexibility that would permit optimum equating is not always possible. For example, the inclusion of items in a new form of the test that are carried over from an old form necessarily slows down any attempt to make revisions in the style or content of new forms. The requirements for good equating, on the other hand, dictate that as many items as possible be carried over from old forms, and that these items, as a group, constitute a test that parallels in miniature the test forms in which they appear. Minimum requirements are that 20 items or 20 percent of the test—whichever represents the larger number of items—be repeated in the new form. Consequently, if double part-score equating (described in Chapter II) were made a standard operation for the Achievement Tests as it is for the SAT, it would mean that no more than 60 percent of a new form could be composed of new material—a proportion that is felt to be not nearly enough if the tests are to keep pace with changing philosophies and practices in education. Therefore, in order to effect a reasonable balance between the two opposing considerations—the maintenance of a rigorous equating system and the provision for changing test content—about half of the forms of the Achievement Tests are equated by single part-score methods and half by double part-score methods. The exceptions to the above rule are the Level I and Level II Mathematics tests and the Russian, Hebrew, and Latin tests, which are almost always equated by single part-score methods.

Because of these limitations on the equating system, it would be expected that the scales for the Achievement Tests would not be in control to the same degree as are the SAT scales. Nevertheless, within these limitations, "genealogical" charts are regularly prepared for the Achievement Test scales and are carefully studied during the equating process in an effort to strengthen the scale bonds among all the forms of every test.

As is true of the SAT, the equating and scaling model for the Achievement Tests is also a linear one. However, here, too, when it is felt that the difficulties of the items in a particular test form and the intercorrelations among the items have caused a bias in the linearly-derived scaled scores near 800, curvilinear equating methods are applied in order to achieve a greater consistency and uniformity in the maximum scores from form to form. For the most part, however, the equating is linear and follows precisely the statistical procedure described in the preceding chapter for equating the SAT.

Statistical characteristics of the Achievement Tests

As has been stated, responsibility for the content of each Achievement Test rests with the committee of examiners appointed by the College Board. If, however, each new form of an Achievement Test is to fit into the system of the Admissions Testing Program, it must be equated (as described in the preceding section) so that scores on the new form mean essentially the same thing as scores on forms used in the program in the preceding years. Admissions officers in colleges need to operate from a stable base in making decisions. Otherwise, they cannot profit from their experience.

If the equating procedures are to be successful, it is necessary that successive forms of an Achievement Test have similar statistical characteristics as well as similar content. It is the responsibility of the ETS test development specialist working with the committee of examiners for each Achievement Test to keep an eye on the statistical characteristics.

Each specialist has a set of statistical specifications designed to insure that successive forms are reasonably parallel. The committee is advised with respect to these specifications and, as the test is assembled, a scatterplot of the difficulty and discrimination indexes of each question is recorded in a two-way table like the one in Table 3.10. Specifications are typically stated in terms of mean and standard deviation of deltas and the mean of the biserial correlations, statistics that can be calculated from the information generated in the scatterplot.

From time to time, as the characteristics of the candidate group change, changes become necessary in the statistical specifications of a test. As is true in the case of changes in content specifications, changes in statistical specifications are introduced gradually to insure reasonable stability of meaning for scores on successive forms.

Table 3.11 presents statistical specifications for recent forms of 14 of the tests now offered in the Achievement series together with actual statistical characteristics

Table 3.10

Example of scatterplot form used to record item data for Achievement Tests

Project _____   ITEM DISTRIBUTION SHEET

Test _____ Form _____ Part _____ Administration _____

Δ'	5.9 down	6.0-6.9	7.0-7.9	8.0-8.9	9.0-9.9	10.0-10.9	11.0-11.9	12.0-12.9	13.0-13.9	14.0-14.9	15.0-15.9	16.0-16.9	17.0-17.9	18.0-18.9	19.0-19.9	20.0-up	Distribution of r_{bis}		
Δ																	f	r	r^2
.90-.99																		.9	.81
.80-.89																		.8	.64
.70-.79																		.7	.49
.60-.69																		.6	.36
.50-.59																		.5	.25
.40-.49																		.4	.16
.30-.39																		.3	.09
.20-.29																		.2	.04
.10-.19																		.1	.01
.00-.09																		.0	.00
.01 down																		-.1	.01
Not Comp.																		XX	XX
																	$N_r =$ $\Sigma fr =$ $\Sigma fr^2 =$		
f																	$N_\Delta =$		
Δ	5	6	7	8	9	10	11	12	13	14	15	16	17	18	19	20	$\Sigma f\Delta =$		
Δ^2	25	36	49	64	81	100	121	144	169	196	225	256	289	324	361	400	$\Sigma f\Delta^2 =$		

Difficulty Index Δ (Scale: _____)

$$M_r = \Sigma fr / N_r + .045$$
$$M_r = \quad + .045 =$$

$$\sigma_r^2 = (N_r \Sigma fr^2 - (\Sigma fr)^2)/N_r^2$$
$$\sigma_r = \sqrt{\quad} =$$

$$M_\Delta = \Sigma f\Delta / N_\Delta + .45$$
$$M_\Delta = \quad + .45 =$$

$$\sigma_\Delta^2 = (N_\Delta \Sigma f\Delta^2 - (\Sigma f\Delta)^2)/N_\Delta^2$$
$$\sigma_\Delta = \sqrt{\quad} =$$

Educational Testing Service

Computed by: _____
Checked by: _____

revealed by the item analysis of the forms administered in May 1967 and January 1968. (The test in English Literature was first offered in May 1968.) However, as expected, the actual always falls short of the ideal. In the first place, there is not an unlimited pool of test items from which one can draw in assembling a new form of a test. Items in some categories are more difficult to formulate than in other areas, so that the test assembly stage represents a succession of compromises between content and statistical specifications. Second, statistical characteristics of test items are based on samples of limited sizes that are not always completely representative of the candidates who finally decide to register for a particular test administration. Finally, subtle and not completely understood influences are sometimes introduced when the context within which a test item is presented changes from pretest to final form or from one final form to another. Moreover, changes associated with the passage of time also introduce changes in item difficulties. For example, items dealing with American presidential elections prove to be easier in election years than in the years between. Also, item statistics appear to be more stable for items appearing in the middle portion of a test form than if

Table 3.11

Specified and actual item statistics
for Achievement Tests administered in May 1967 and January 1968

Test	Administration	Specifications			Actual statistics		
		$M_\triangle$	$SD_\triangle$	$M_{r_{bis}}$	$M_\triangle$	$SD_\triangle$	$M_{r_{bis}}$
English Composition	May 1967	11.9	2.4	.45	12.0	2.2	.49
	Jan 1968*				11.7	2.3	.50
American History	May 1967	12.2	2.2	.44	13.3	2.3	.40
	Jan 1968				12.8	2.1	.39
European History	May 1967	12.0	1.8	.47	12.3	1.8	.45
	Jan 1968				12.7	2.5	.46
Biology	May 1967	13.0	2.2	.40	13.0	2.4	.46
	Jan 1968				13.2	2.6	.40
Chemistry	May 1967*	13.0	2.0	.48	13.7	2.2	.44
	Jan 1968*				13.7	1.7	.48
Physics	May 1967	14.0	2.2	.48	14.7	2.3	.46
	Jan 1968*				14.8	2.2	.44
Mathematics Level I	May 1967	13.0	3.0	.50	13.6	2.9	.57
	Jan 1968				13.5	2.8	.52
Mathematics Level II	May 1967*	15.2	2.2	.54	15.0	2.0	.54
	Jan 1968*				15.1	2.1	.54
French	May 1967*	12.7	2.7	.50	12.8	2.7	.55
	Jan 1968*				12.8	2.8	.53
German	May 1967*	12.7	2.5	.54	12.4	2.2	.59
	Jan 1968*				12.5	2.5	.53
Hebrew	Jan 1968	12.5	3.0	.54	12.3	3.3	.60
Latin	May 1967	12.8	2.2	.45	12.8	2.0	.45
	Jan 1968				12.1	2.3	.50
Russian	Jan 1968*	12.5	2.5	.54	12.7	2.3	.53
Spanish	May 1967*	12.6	2.8	.48	12.1	2.7	.56
	Jan 1968*				12.5	3.2	.54

*For these tests, actual statistics do not include data on a minority of items that were answered by fewer than 50 percent of the sample used for the analysis.

items appear either as the first item in a test or toward the end of the test where there may be a significant number of candidates classified as "not reached."

As has been illustrated in Table 3.4, data on reliability appear in each test analysis. The reliability estimate is a modification of the Kuder-Richardson Formula 20 that takes into account the fact that the tests are scored with a correction for guessing. The purpose of this statistic is to indicate the stability of the item sampling and to provide an estimate of the correlation to be expected if two parallel Achievement Test forms were administered in counterbalanced order to random halves of the population at a single sitting. Since reliability coefficients may vary with the variability of the sample, estimates of the standard error of measurement are also recorded. Reliability coefficients and standard errors of measurement for the May 1967 and January 1968 forms of the Achievement Tests are presented in Table 3.12.

Indexes of speededness are computed for each new form of an Achievement Test as indicated in Tables 3.4, 3.5, and 3.6. The aim is to set an examination that is of such a length that there will be optimum measurement of the candidate group as a whole. This means that a certain proportion of the candidates who work very slowly or who are not able to make a reasoned response to all of the items will not complete the examination. In order to minimize the possibility that slow workers might be at a special disadvantage, items in the Achievement Tests are arranged roughly in order of their difficulty.

As an arbitrary guide for evaluating the speededness of a College Board Achievement Test, two criteria have been established that seem to balance the need for allowing time for most candidates to consider all items they are likely to be able to answer and the need to keep most candidates working productively during the testing session. These are: (1) all of the candidates should complete 75 percent of the test, and (2) 80 percent of the candidates should complete the test. The data on speededness are designed to provide a check on these criteria. The more detailed data presented in Tables 3.5 and 3.6 provide additional information should the general statistics of Table 3.4 suggest the possibility of undesirable speededness. On the basis of the data in these three tables, the writer of this test analysis concluded: "Both NR ("not reached") variances tend to be high relative to the score variances. The dropping out may be a function of difficulty, but there is also the possibility that the candidates could have used more time to their advantage."

Data on the speededness of the May 1967 and January 1968 forms of the Achievement Tests are presented in Table 3.12 along with information on reliability and standard errors of measurement. The data indicate that the speededness criteria are not being met. There are various explanations for this finding, depending on the particular test involved. The January 1968 form of the English Composition Test was particularly speeded.

Apparently, one of the item types—construction shift, so-called—requires more time than is the case with item types included in other sections of the test. There were no construction shift items in the May 1967 form, which is relatively unspeeded.

In the case of the tests in foreign languages, candidates have had widely varied backgrounds of study of the language. Some may have completed more than eight semesters of study while others may have completed fewer than four semesters. Those with fewer semesters of study are not expected to complete the final (and more difficult) items. The relatively high dropping out of students toward the end of these tests appears to be a function of the difficulty of the items toward the end of the test for candidates with limited background rather than of insufficient time for candidates to read and consider the items.

For most of the other test forms, the speededness data approach the criteria. More than 97 percent of the candidates are completing 75 percent of the test and 80 percent of the candidates are reaching more than 90 percent of the items. The only exceptions are the May 1967 form of the Chemistry Test and the January 1968 form of the Physics Test. These two forms appear to be somewhat speeded. Committees of examiners for these tests will be studying these findings and drawing implications for the development of future forms of the tests.

One final statistical characteristic of the Achievement Tests that is of considerable interest is the correlation between each of the tests and the two scores on the Scholastic Aptitude Test. Ideally, if a test is to be used along with other measures for making a statistical prediction, it should have a relatively high correlation with the criterion to be predicted and a relatively low correlation with the other measures. On the other hand, whether or not a correlation coefficient will be viewed as "relatively high" or "relatively low" will depend on the context in which it is found. Statistical independence does not inevitably accompany logical independence. If, for example, a group of secondary school students have been taught a course in American history by a teacher who challenges each student to maximum effort, the students' scores on a final examination in the course are likely to be closely related to their scores on a test of general verbal ability administered at the same time. On the other hand, if students are permitted to exert effort on the basis of interest in the subject that they bring to the class at the beginning of a course or if a course is boring to students of high aptitude while rewarding unimaginative memorizing of details by students of low ability, correlations between scores on a verbal aptitude test and scores on a course examination may be quite low. And if, as is the case with College Board Achievement Tests, students are given some freedom of choice in selecting tests, the meaning of correlation coefficients may be difficult to determine. It does not help much to suggest that one administer the Achievement Tests to a representative sample of SAT candidates, some of whom have studied the subject

Table 3.12

Numbers of items (n), reliability estimates (r_{aA}), standard errors of measurement (SE_{meas}), and indexes of speededness (a, b, c) for Achievement Tests administered in May 1967 and January 1968

Test	Administration	n	r_{aA}	SE_{meas}	$a*$	$b*$	$c*$
English Composition	May 1967	100	.925	29	56.7	97.7	93
	Jan 1968	100	.919	30	33.6	75.2	24(35)**
American History	May 1967	100	.905	34	55.0	97.2	93
	Jan 1968	100	.897	33	61.0	97.2	94
European History	May 1967	100	.926	28	68.2	97.8	98
	Jan 1968	100	.927	30	62.1	98.2	96
Biology	May 1967	100	.929	30	69.3	99.7	98
	Jan 1968	100	.904	31	65.7	99.6	97
Chemistry	May 1967	90	.903	34	39.1	95.5	78
	Jan 1968	90	.921	31	29.1	98.1	80
Physics	May 1967	75	.901	32	67.9	97.9	70
	Jan 1968	75	.885	34	32.9	94.1	64
Mathematics Level I	May 1967	50	.903	33	58.7	99.1	48
	Jan 1968	50	.880	34	68.6	99.3	47
Mathematics Level II	May 1967	50	.895	33	46.6	99.4	48
	Jan 1968	50	.890	34	34.1	97.6	47
French	May 1967	94	.950	25	45.6	93.9	78
	Jan 1968	90	.943	24	33.9	94.9	77
German	May 1967	93	.950	23	37.8	99.3	83
	Jan 1968	96	.941	23	37.1	97.1	86
Hebrew	Jan 1968	90	.955	20	50.5	98.2	80
Latin	May 1967	70	.894	33	52.1	96.4	64
	Jan 1968	70	.910	33	58.2	98.5	68
Russian	Jan 1968	84	.939	27	42.5	97.2	74
Spanish	May 1967	87	.949	24	44.8	98.4	78
	Jan 1968	87	.943	24	49.4	97.3	77

*a: Percent of candidate group reaching last item
b: Percent of candidate group completing 75 percent of the items
c: Number of items reached by 80 percent of the candidates

**There were three sections to this test with suggested time of 20 minutes each.
Data are for the most speeded section, which contained 35 items.

matter covered by the test and some of whom have not studied it. In that case, correlations would certainly be low, but the meaning of a coefficient of a particular magnitude would be obscure. In other words, although there is considerable interest in the relationships between Achievement Test scores and aptitude scores, it is difficult to interpret a given degree of relationship.

To some observers, the typical correlations are unusually high. For example, the following appears in the *Sixth Mental Measurements Yearbook* (Buros, 1965, p. 980).

Here are correlations between scores from the main achievement tests and the SAT-V: ECT, .76; Social Studies, .78; French, .60; Chemistry, .65; Physics, .67; Intermediate Mathematics, .53; and Advanced Mathematics, .54. The corresponding correlations for SAT-M are: .55, .64, .46, .72, .69, .80, and .75.... These almost unbelievably high correlations suggest that whatever is measured by the ECT and the social studies test is also measured by the SAT-V, and that whatever is measured by the intermediate and advanced mathematics tests is also measured by the SAT-M.

The correlation coefficients relating Achievement Test scores to SAT scores for samples of candidates who took both tests in 1968 and 1969 are presented in Tables 3.8 and 3.9. In general they are consistent with those re-

Table 3.13

Reliability coefficients, multiple correlation coefficients, and estimates of three different proportions of variance of Achievement Test scores for samples of candidates taking the SAT *and Achievement Tests in 1968-69*

Test	Column*					
	1	2	3	4	5	6
English Composition	.894	.924	.814	.106	.717	.177
Literature	.836	.929	.821	.164	.726	.110
American History	.903	.932	.739	.097	.585	.318
European History	.920	.932	.746	.080	.597	.323
French	.944	.921	.583	.056	.369	.575
German	.939	.921	.498	.061	.270	.669
Hebrew	.961	.947	.373	.039	.147	.814
Latin	.891	.928	.609	.109	.399	.492
Russian	.928	.925	.418	.072	.189	.739
Spanish	.947	.919	.519	.053	.293	.654
Biology	.923	.939	.769	.077	.630	.293
Chemistry	.900	.922	.718	.100	.559	.341
Physics	.916	.924	.738	.084	.590	.326
Mathematics Level I	.887	.899	.831	.113	.768	.119
Mathematics Level II	.902	.891	.834	.098	.780	.122

*Column Headings

1. Estimate of the reliability of the Achievement Test scores. [r_{aA}]

2. Estimate of the reliability of the sum of the two SAT scores, weighted to achieve optimal correlation with the Achievement Test scores. [$r_{(vm)(VM)}$]

3. Multiple correlation between Achievement Test scores and SAT-verbal and -mathematical scores. [$R_{a.vm}$]

4. Estimate of the proportion of the variance of Achievement Test scores attributable to errors of measurement. [$1 - r_{aA}$]

5. Estimate of the proportion of the variance of Achievement Test scores that can be "explained" by the correlation with perfectly reliable SAT scores, optimally weighted. [$R^2_{a.vm}/r_{(vm)(VM)}$]

6. Uniqueness coefficient: Estimate of the proportion of the variance in Achievement Test scores remaining, after taking into account the true-score correlation between the Achievement Test scores and the optimally weighted composite of SAT-V and SAT-M (Flanagan, 1962, p. 218). [$r_{aA} - R^2_{a.vm}/r_{(vm)(VM)}$]

ported in the *Sixth Mental Measurements Yearbook*. When the multiple correlation coefficients using both SAT-V and SAT-M as predictors are computed, it is found that they range between .718 and .834 for all tests except those in foreign languages, which range between .373 and .609. These are indeed high correlations if one expects the Achievement Tests to provide totally new information about the student, information not already provided by the SAT scores.

On the other hand, the multiple correlation coefficients are in almost every case considerably lower than the estimates of reliability for the Achievement Test they are predicting. The Achievement Tests may have a high proportion of variance in common with the SAT, but they are clearly not measuring exactly the same factors. Relevant illustrative information has been summarized in Table 3.13, indicating that estimates of the proportion of the variance in Achievement Test scores remaining, after taking into account the true-score correlation between the Achievement Test scores and the optimally weighted composite of SAT-V and SAT-M, range between .110 for Literature and .814 for Hebrew (see Column 6 of Table 3.13).

In summary, the Achievement Tests of the Admissions Testing Program of the College Entrance Examin-

ation Board are constructed by committees of examiners working with test development specialists on the staff of Educational Testing Service. Each new form of an Achievement Test is planned in the context of the gradually evolving pattern of curricular practices in schools and colleges throughout the country and of the statistical data derived from the field administrations of previous forms of the test. Following a detailed test plan, test items are written, reviewed, pretested, and revised prior to becoming eligible for inclusion in a new form of a test. Included in each new form of many of the tests is a sample of items from previous forms of the test, and scores on these subsets of items are used to equate the forms and establish scaled scores equivalent to those for other forms of the test. Tests that do not include equating items are equated through the use of SAT scores as "quasi-common" equating material. Following the use of a new form of an Achievement Test, a detailed statistical analysis is made to determine the extent to which the test met the specifications to which it was assembled. Finally, special studies are carried out from time to time to determine the relationship of each Achievement Test with the SAT, and periodic adjustments are made in the scaling to bring the scaling system up-to-date.

REFERENCES

Angoff, W. H., "Language Training Study: 1947," in Wilks, S. S., ed., *Scaling and Equating College Board Tests*. Princeton, N.J.: Educational Testing Service, 1961, Appendix X, p. 130.

Brigham, Carl, *A Study of Error*. New York: College Entrance Examination Board, 1932.

Buros, O. K., ed., *Sixth Mental Measurements Yearbook*. Highland Park, N.J.: The Gryphon Press, 1965.

College Entrance Examination Board, *Freedom and Discipline in English, Report of the Commission on English*. New York: College Entrance Examination Board, 1965.

College Entrance Examination Board, *Report of the Commission on Mathematics. Volume 1: Program for College Preparatory Mathematics. Volume 2: Appendices*. New York: College Entrance Examination Board, 1959.

Educational Testing Service, *Annual Report, 1960-61*. Princeton, N.J.: Educational Testing Service, 1961, pp. 23-24.

Educational Testing Service and the College Entrance Examination Board, *One in a Hundred*. 16 mm sound film, 25 minutes. Purchase price $50; also available on a free-loan basis for audio visual centers in most states.

Flanagan, J.C., and others, *Design for a Study of American Youth*. Boston: Houghton Mifflin Company, 1962. 240 pp.

Fornoff, F., "Developing the New Physics Test." *College Board Review* No. 46, 1962, pp. 19-21.

Fuess, C. M., *The College Board: Its First Fifty Years*. New York: Columbia University, 1950.

Godshalk, F. I.; Swineford, F.; and Coffman, W. E., *The Measurement of Writing Ability*. New York: College Entrance Examination Board, 1966.

Olsen, Marjorie, *Summary of Main Findings on the Validity of the College Entrance Examination Board Tests of Developed Ability as Predictors of College Grades*. Statistical Report 57-41. Princeton, N.J.: Educational Testing Service, 1957.

Olsen, M., and Schrader, W. B., *An Empirical Comparison of Five Methods of Shortening a Test*. Research Bulletin 53-5. Princeton, N.J.: Educational Testing Service, 1953.

Wilks, S. S., ed., *Scaling and Equating College Board Tests*. Princeton, N.J: Educational Testing Service, 1961, 195 pp.

CHAPTER IV

Descriptive Statistics on College Board
Candidates and Other Reference Groups

W. B. SCHRADER and E. ELIZABETH STEWART

Introduction

Information about the test performance of different groups of candidates has implications both for score interpretation and for educational planning. This chapter will summarize what is known of the characteristics of candidates who take the various College Board tests.

Among the matters to be covered are the uses of descriptive statistics on test performance, methodological considerations, performance on the SAT, and performance on Achievement Tests. Also discussed in these contexts are such familiar concerns to the test developer and user as score interpretation, group comparisons, SAT norms, and trends in candidate performance on the SAT over the past 13 years. For the Achievement Tests, the discussion focuses on such concerns as the nature of candidates, characteristics of groups, candidate norms, and, again, trends in candidate performance over the past 13 years.

Uses of descriptive statistics on test performance

Score interpretation—The primary reason for tabulating data on the test performance of candidates and other suitable student groups is to aid in score interpretation. Indeed, for most uses of tests, identification of a candidate's relative standing within some appropriate reference group is indispensable. This need is most adequately filled by local norms based on a college's own data. General norms, however, are useful in providing a wider basis of comparison for a particular college or secondary school. They may also be used by a college as a substitute when local norms have not been prepared or by a secondary school or candidate when norms for particular colleges are not available. Using general norms as a substitute for local norms, however, places relatively heavy demands on the judgment of the user, since general norms frequently differ from norms developed locally in ways that are not always well understood. For example, the fact that a student stands in the top 10 percent of College Board candidates on SAT-verbal scores has fairly clear implications for a decision about whether

or not to attend college. To aid in college choice, however, information is needed concerning the level of SAT-verbal scores in various colleges and also concerning how much weight the college gives to these scores in admissions. In any case, general information about the performance of suitable student groups can be a vital element in sound score interpretation.

From the outset, the College Board has published, in one form or another, data on candidate performance. Initially, the data were presented in the annual report. During the 1950s, substantial normative data were provided in Henry S. Dyer's *College Board Scores No. 1* and its two successor editions. Since 1962, current performance data have been provided in *College Board Score Reports*. These data on candidate performance are updated annually. Data on other student groups have also been published, as described later in this chapter.

Group comparisons — A less crucial, but still valuable, contribution of score data is to permit comparison of the test performance of various student groups. In particular, comparisons of boys and girls, of students with various amounts of preparation in the subject tested, and of students tested in successive years may, when cautiously interpreted, contribute to an understanding of what the tests measure and of the nature of the groups tested. As will be stressed in this chapter, however, generalizations based on these comparisons must be very carefully circumscribed, particularly when they are based not on representative samples of the appropriate groups but rather on candidate groups that are probably not representative of the groups being compared.

Methodological considerations

Test norms should describe the test performance of carefully defined, educationally meaningful student groups. Since candidates taking the College Board tests are obviously self-selected, traditional conceptions of norms as stated in the foregoing proposition would imply that descriptive statistics on candidate performance have little value as norms. A careful examination of the strengths and limitations of data on candidate performance, however, makes it clear that these data, when properly used, can contribute substantially to the interpretation of scores and to an understanding of the nature and composition of the candidate group.

For the great majority of College Board candidates, the decision to take the tests is by no means whimsical or fortuitous but is the direct outcome of a decision to apply to a college that requires the tests. In turn, the colleges that require the tests have reached a decision that the tests will help them in achieving their educational objectives and in selecting the kind of student body to which they wish to address themselves. It is true that the number of candidates taking the tests and the number of colleges requiring them have shown a dramatic growth over the years. The proportion of entering college freshmen who have taken College Board tests has shown a similar great increase. Data for the past 13 years shown later in this chapter indicate that a great increase in numbers of candidates has been accompanied by a reasonably stable level of candidate performance. On the face of it, this stability is remarkable. It may be conjectured, however, that the tendency toward lower scores which would be expected as the group is broadened has been offset by a generally rising level of teaching and academic interest.

Some idea of the ability level of College Board candidates who take the SAT can be obtained by comparing program statistics with the results of a study (reported in greater detail later in this chapter) of the twelfth-grade SAT performance of a cross section of all seniors who entered college directly from high school. The following data have been abstracted from Tables 4.1 and 4.4.

Performance on SAT during the
senior year of high school by:

		Candidates tested at regular College Board administrations in 1968-69	Students in the 1960 national norms sample who entered a two- or four-year college in 1961-62
		SAT-*verbal*	
Boys	M	457	440
	SD	110	114
	N	498,462	1,878
Girls	M	464	467
	SD	110	122
	N	415,925	1,659
		SAT-*mathematical*	
Boys	M	510	509
	SD	116	111
	N	498,462	1,878
Girls	M	465	461
	SD	105	105
	N	415,925	1,659

The foregoing data suggest that the level and dispersion of scores earned by students taking the SAT as seniors in the College Board Admissions Testing Program are similar to those of a national cross section of high school seniors who go directly to college. Except for the SAT-verbal mean for boys and the SAT-verbal standard devia-

tion for girls, the agreement is remarkably close. The agreement may be partially explained by the fact that not all students taking the test in the program enter a College Board member college. Although current comparative score data are not available for program candidates classified by type of college entered, this explanation is supported by data from the 1960 norms study, which indicate that the mean SAT scores for seniors who enter College Board member colleges are 50 to 75 points higher than the corresponding means for all seniors who enter any college (Table 4.1). The detailed results of the comparison should not be taken too literally, of course, not only because a period of eight years separates the two sets of data but also because of limitations in the national norms study. These limitations are described on page 82. The similarity in performance of the two groups, moreover, does not imply that College Board senior candidates are similar in other respects to the total group of seniors entering college directly from high school. For example, of prospective college students, a greater proportion of those who are attending secondary school in the Northeast take the SAT than is the case for other regions.

Virtually all College Board candidates take the SAT; each Achievement Test, on the other hand, has its own candidate group. Moreover, it is known that the groups taking the various Achievement Tests differ appreciably with respect to SAT-verbal and SAT-mathematical mean scores. These differences are taken into account in establishing the score scale for each Achievement Test, as described in Chapter III, so that scaled scores for the various tests are, in a defined sense, comparable with each other. The mean score on a particular test thus depends in part on the aptitude level of the candidates whom the test attracts. On the other hand, it should be clear that if scores are expressed as percentile ranks *within* each candidate group, the fact that SAT scores differ for students choosing different Achievement Tests does not affect a student's percentile rank on a particular test.

The interpretation of descriptive statistics on candidate performance is further complicated by the fact that, at one test administration, a candidate can take no more than three Achievement Tests. Since he will ordinarily be prepared academically to take more than three, he must make a decision as to which tests he will take. The *Bulletin of Information for College Board Admissions Tests, 1969-70* offers the following suggestion: "Your choice of tests will depend upon the requirements of the colleges to which you are applying. Some colleges specify the particular tests they wish applicants to take; others expect applicants to take tests in their strongest subjects." Providing a choice makes it possible to examine the candidate in some depth in subjects in which he is (or should be) well prepared. From the viewpoint of descriptive statistics, however, the availability of choice means that the group is presumably composed of students who consider themselves relatively well prepared in the subject or who choose to apply to one or more colleges that require the test.

The candidate groups for the various Achievement Tests are determined, then, by candidate decisions based in part on college requirements and in part on a variety of other considerations. For purposes of score interpretation, this characteristic of the candidate data is advantageous. The candidate whose score is being interpreted has, presumably, also tried to take advantage of the opportunity for choice. His performance can then be compared with that of other students tested within the same general framework. At the same time, it must be recognized that the statistics for Achievement Tests (with the possible exception of English Composition) cannot be assumed to describe the performance of all Achievement Test candidates who have had the necessary subject matter preparation for the test.

Two further features of the College Board program become important when score data for two or more test administrations are combined into a single distribution. First, a candidate may take a particular test more than once. Although he takes a different form of the test on the two (or more) occasions, it is obviously undesirable from a statistical standpoint to count the same student twice. This question will be discussed more fully in connection with results for specific tests. Second, candidates attending different test administrations are at somewhat different stages of their academic programs. For example, a student who studies chemistry in his junior year and who attends the May or July administration will probably take the Chemistry Test then. Another student who also studies chemistry in his junior year may not take the Chemistry Test until January of his senior year. It may be thought that comparing the mean Chemistry scores of all juniors tested in May with the mean Chemistry scores of all seniors tested in January would be useful. As it turns out, however, this group comparison would be influenced to an unknown extent by the self-selection of the two groups. In this chapter, accordingly, results for the various test administrations will be combined into a single overall result, although separate results for junior and senior candidates will be presented in some instances.

On the whole, descriptive statistics based on program data describe the performance of highly motivated candidates tested under realistic conditions. The statistics are relatively easy to keep current and are based on very large samples. They are also useful in describing the characteristics of the candidate group itself. As an aid in score interpretation, they have substantial value when used with an understanding of their limitations. Attempts to draw more general inferences, however, are seldom justified because there is no satisfactory way to assess the effect of self-selection on the results. This same limitation applies, it may be added, to comparisons based on subgroups of candidates. Comparisons of test performance from one high school to another and even from one year to another within the same high school must be interpreted in the light of possible differences in the nature and extent of self-selection.

Performance on the SAT

High school senior and college freshman norms — Because self-selection plays so prominent a role in the formation of the College Board candidate group, this group cannot be considered representative either of high school seniors or of those seniors who are planning to enter college. In order to obtain data for representative samples of high school seniors, two special norms studies have been conducted, one in the fall of 1960 and one in the fall of 1966. The results of these studies are useful not only in interpreting SAT scores with respect to a familiar reference group but also in providing a better understanding of the ability level of the SAT candidate group. National norms based on the 1960 study have been presented in the 1963 through 1967-68 editions of *College Board Score Reports*. A technical report of the study was prepared by Chandler and Schrader (1966). National norms based on the 1966 study appear in the 1968-69 and subsequent editions of *College Board Score Reports*.

The special test administrations on which the two sets of SAT norms are based used the Preliminary Scholastic Aptitude Test (PSAT) rather than the SAT. Although the PSAT is intended for use in secondary school guidance programs and requires only two hours of testing time, it is parallel in form and content to the SAT. The score scales on the two tests are directly related, so that multiplication of a PSAT score by 10 yields the comparable SAT score.

The general design of the two norms studies was similar. However, the 1966 study included 8,581 senior boys and 9,077 senior girls in 166 schools as compared to 4,638 senior boys and 5,107 senior girls in 147 schools in the 1960 study. In part, the difference in number tested is attributable to increased enrollments in 1966 as compared to 1960. The mean scores for the various groups tested were as follows:

	SAT-*verbal*		SAT-*mathematical*	
	Boys	Girls	Boys	Girls
1960 study	372	376	438	385
1966 study	390	393	422	382

The extent to which the differences in means for the two studies are attributable to changes in the ability level of seniors during the six-year period, to changes in self-selection of the schools participating in the two studies, to sampling error, or to other factors cannot be determined precisely.

Because a follow-up study has been completed only for the 1960 sample, the discussion in this section will focus on the results of the earlier study. By following up a subsample of the 1960 norms group, it was possible to obtain data on the distributions of SAT scores earned as high school seniors for representative samples of high school graduates who enrolled as full-time or part-time students in college during the academic year directly following high school graduation, and for representative samples of several other college student groups, to be described below.

In the selection of the 1960 national sample, the secondary school was the sampling unit. By using random sampling within strata, 200 schools were selected from a master list of secondary schools in the United States. Geographical region and type of support were the basis of stratification. Of the 200 schools, each of which was requested to test its entire senior class, 147 schools provided usable data (32 schools did not agree to participate, 12 that did agree to participate were unable to do so, and 9 that did participate were excluded from the analysis because each had tested less than 80 percent of its senior class).

Follow-up studies were based on a 2,423-case subsample of the original 9,745-case sample. Since it was judged that students with higher test scores would be more likely to enter college, the 9,745-case sample was divided into three groups on the basis of a PSAT score composite (2v + M), and different sampling fractions were applied to the three groups. In the analysis of the follow-up results, the observed data were weighted by the reciprocals of the sampling fractions in order to give the proper weight to each of the three strata in determining the results. The differential sampling and subsequent weighting are summarized in the following table:

Score interval PSAT 2v+M	Approximate proportion of total sample in interval	Proportion of cases in interval selected for follow-up (sampling fraction)	Weight applied in analysis
177 or higher	.05	1.00	1
128 - 176	.25	.50	2
127 or lower	.70	.10	10

The follow-up concerned with college attendance and first-year standing was completed in the fall of 1963. As a result of the follow-up, each of the 2,423 students in the follow-up sample was placed in one of three categories: students whose enrollment during the academic year 1961-62 had been verified by a college (N=1,440); students who had reported, or whose secondary schools had reported, that they did not enroll in college during 1961-62 (N=880); and students about whom there was insufficient or inconsistent information (N=103). Thus, firm data were obtained for 96 percent of the sample. For the 1,440 students who entered college, information about end-of-year standing was provided by the colleges.

Before the score data were analyzed, small adjustments were made in the scores in order to allow for increases in ability between October, when the national sample was tested, and January, to allow for the fact that seniors at that time usually took the SAT between December and March. Data from a growth study done by Levine and Angoff (1958) were used as a basis for estimating the adjustment. The adjustment consisted of adding 7.5 scaled score points to the verbal scores of all students, 5.6 scaled score points to the mathematical scores of boys, and 1.9 scaled score points to the mathematical scores of girls.

Certain limitations of the norms and follow-up study should be noted. First, usable data were received from slightly less than three quarters of the schools selected for the norms sample. Incomplete participation is, of course, characteristic of studies of this sort in which schools that have been selected by a mechanical random sampling process are asked to cooperate on a voluntary basis. Although the participating schools were fairly similar to the overall national distribution of secondary schools with respect to proportions of public and nonpublic schools and with respect to the proportions of Southern and non-Southern schools (Chandler and Schrader, 1966), there is no way of ascertaining whether the nonparticipants were atypical of the total sample with respect to other relevant characteristics. A related limitation arises from the fact that adequate follow-up data could not be obtained for some of the students in the follow-up sample. However, since such students constituted only 4 percent of the total sample of students for whom follow-up data were sought, the effect of the data loss should be very minor. Second, the sample results undoubtedly differ to some extent from the corresponding population values as a consequence of random sampling error associated both with the selection of schools and with the selection of students to be included in the follow-up study. Since the school rather than the individual student was the primary sampling unit, the sampling error for the national norms sample is larger than the error that would be associated with a random sample of 9,745 students in which the student represents the sampling unit. In addition, except for the 5 percent of the sample in the highest PSAT score interval, the students in the follow-up study constituted only a subsample of the national norms sample. (In the highest 5 percent, all students were followed up.) As a consequence, the actual numbers of observations on which statistics for certain subgroups are based are relatively small, and the sampling errors are correspondingly large. Third, SAT scores were estimated from PSAT scores by adding to the PSAT scores a growth constant (which had been determined in an independent study) to represent the average increase in scores between the beginning and the middle of the senior year. Since the growth adjustments were small, errors in them would also be small; nonetheless, any such errors would appear as biases in the estimated statistics. Finally, over 90 percent of the students in the norms sample had taken a single edition of the PSAT, so that any random sampling error in the scale placement of that edition is reflected as a bias in the score statistics.

Estimated SAT means and standard deviations are presented in Table 4.1. The results are shown, separately for boys and girls, for all seniors in the national sample, for those seniors who entered college in 1961-62, and for several subsamples of the college-going group. It should be noted that since the various college subsamples are not independent, the extent to which they overlap is relevant to the interpretation of mean score differences.

As shown in Table 4.1, the means for high school seniors based on the students included in the follow-up study were as follows:

	Boys	Girls
SAT-V	370	377
SAT-M	437	387

The follow-up study showed that 41 percent of the boys and 32 percent of the girls entered college directly from high school in 1961-62. The verbal mean for boys and the mathematical means for boys and girls were 70 to 75 points higher for the college entrants than for all seniors. For girls, the difference in verbal means was 90 points. Among the college entrants, 81 percent of the boys and 82 percent of the girls enrolled in four-year colleges. The means for enrollees in four-year colleges were about 15 points higher than the corresponding means for all college entrants. Students who entered two-year colleges had means 50 to 75 points lower than

Table 4.1

Scholastic Aptitude Test means and standard deviations for a national sample of secondary school seniors tested in 1960, by sex and academic status in 1960-61

Group	SAT-V		SAT-M		NUMBER OF CASES	
	Mean	SD	Mean	SD	Weighted	Unweighted
Boys						
All seniors in national sample	370	113	437	115	4,585	*
Seniors who in 1961-62:						
Entered any college	440	114	509	111	1,878	756
Entered a four-year college**	453	114	526	106	1,516	659
Entered a two-year college**	385	96	438	103	358	95
Entered a College Board member college***	511	105	573	94	592	337
Completed the first year of college	448	114	515	112	1,599	678
Completed the first year of college "in good standing"	468	109	530	110	1,263	593
Girls						
All seniors in national sample	377	118	387	103	5,162	*
Seniors who in 1961-62:						
Entered any college	467	122	461	105	1,659	684
Entered a four-year college***	483	119	477	102	1,366	610
Entered a two-year college***	392	109	386	86	293	74
Entered a College Board member college	542	107	512	105	550	321
Completed the first year of college	474	118	466	105	1,506	635
Completed the first year of college "in good standing"	481	117	472	103	1,377	600

*The statistics presented for all seniors in the national sample and for the various subsamples are based on the weighted follow-up sample. The means and standard deviations of the scores actually earned by all seniors in the national sample are as follows:

	SAT-V		SAT-M		Number
	Mean	SD	Mean	SD	of cases
Boys	372	114	438	115	4,638
Girls	376	117	385	103	5,107

**The number of entrants to four-year colleges plus the number of entrants to two-year colleges does not equal the number of entrants to any college because information about the programs in which two boys were enrolled was not provided.

***The statistics presented for these groups differ slightly from those published in Seibel's reports (1965a, 1965b). The differences are due to changes in the way in which a few students were classified, changes effected during a reanalysis conducted as part of a further follow-up study (Pitcher, 1968).

the corresponding means for all college students. For the subgroup of college entrants who were enrolled in colleges which at that time were College Board members (32 percent of the boys and 33 percent of the girls), the means were 50 to 75 points higher than the corresponding means for all college entrants.

The first year of college was completed by 85 percent of the boys and 91 percent of the girls who entered. The students who completed the year scored, on the average, five to eight points higher than all who entered college. Of those who completed the first year of college, 79 percent of the boys and 91 percent of the girls completed it "in good standing," as reported by the colleges. The mean scores of the students who completed the year in good standing ranged from 6 to 20 points higher than the mean scores of all students who completed the year. The percentage of students completing the first year of college may seem relatively high in view of the widespread belief that attrition is high during the freshman year. Flanagan and Cooley (1966), in three separate Project Talent studies, found 79 to 82 percent of males and 76 to 83 percent of females remaining in college at the end of the first year. The extent to which the difference is attributable to sampling error, to methodological differences, or to bias in the samples cannot readily be judged. It should be noted that both the present results and the Project Talent results are based not on a representative sample of all entering freshmen but on those students who entered college during the year after they finished high school.

Seibel (1965a) has provided percentile rank tables for seniors who later entered college and for seniors who later completed the first year of college in good standing. His report also includes detailed analyses of the relationships among PSAT scores, secondary school performance, college attendance, and college performance. Seibel (1965b) has further analyzed the follow-up data for students in the national sample who later entered junior colleges.

Local norms — Data compiled by a college on its own applicants and various groups of enrolled students can be exceedingly valuable in score use. Because of the wide variation among College Board colleges in the test scores of their applicants and entering students, it is important for many colleges to be able to interpret the scores in terms of relative standing within their own student groups. For many placement purposes, current data on a student's relative standing within the group eligible for various placements may provide an adequate basis for placement decisions. It should be emphasized that this approach assumes that the test has satisfactory content validity for the decisions being made. For counseling purposes local percentile distributions are clearly more useful. For a number of years, the College Board has been offering a Validity Study Service to interested colleges. As part of the service, enrolled student norms on each predictor are provided to participating colleges.

Beginning in 1961, the College Board published the *Manual of Freshman Class Profiles* to facilitate the use of college norms in guiding prospective college students. Each edition of the *Manual* was designed to give secondary school counselors, teachers, and administrators relatively detailed information about applicants and entrants to each participating college. It should be emphasized that each college determined what information it wished to give. The basic tables followed a standard form to facilitate their use, but the college decided which tables to present and what further interpretation to provide. Data were usually provided on test scores and secondary school academic performance for one or more of the following groups: applicants for admission, applicants accepted by the college, enrolled freshmen, and applicants who applied for and who received financial aid. In instances in which sex, type of support of secondary school, geographical residence, or intended college curriculum were taken into account in admissions practices, the data could be differentiated on the basis of the relevant variables.

The recommended manner of presentation of data has evolved as experience has suggested ways of increasing the usefulness of the information. In the 1967-69 edition of the *Manual* and its immediate predecessor, the colleges had the option of presenting score data in one of three formats: (1) separate distributions of SAT-verbal scores and SAT-mathematical scores, accompanied by a distribution of class rank or grade-point average in secondary school; (2) cross-classifications of SAT-verbal scores and secondary school standing and of SAT-mathematical scores and secondary school standing; (3) a cross-classification of a composite of SAT-verbal and -mathematical scores and secondary school standing. (In the third format the composite reflects the relative weights assigned by the college to SAT-verbal and -mathematical scores.)

In the fall of 1969, the College Board incorporated the kinds of data that had previously appeared only in the *Manual* into its 1969 edition of *The College Handbook*, which superseded the *Manual of Freshman Class Profiles*. That edition of the *Handbook* introduced a new, more informative optional format for the presentation of SAT scores and secondary school standing. The new format provides a single distribution of a composite score derived by combining the SAT-verbal score, the SAT-mathematical score, and secondary school standing, using weights based upon validity study data for each participating college.

In all, six editions of the *Manual* were produced between 1961 and 1967 (1961, 1962, 1963, 1964, 1965-67, and 1967-69). In each edition, the data presented were based on the year preceding the first year in which the edition was made available for use. Thus, the 1967-69 edition, published for use in counseling students entering college in 1968 and 1969, contained information about the class that enrolled in college in 1966.

Mean SAT scores based on applicants, accepted applicants, and enrolled students can be calculated for a substantial number of colleges. Table 4.2 shows the results obtained for a sample of 18 colleges that provided us-

Table 4.2

SAT-*verbal and* SAT-*mathematical mean scores for applicants,
accepted applicants, and enrolled students reported by 18 colleges
in the* Manual of Freshman Class Profiles *of 1962, 1964, and 1965-67*

College	Year	SAT-verbal mean			SAT-mathematical mean		
		Applicants	Accepted applicants	Enrolled students	Applicants	Accepted applicants	Enrolled students
				Men's colleges			
A	1965-67	619	681	675	715	760	759
	1964	630	689	687	703	751	751
	1962	619	680	678	690	747	749
B	1965-67	627	648	640	660	686	679
	1964	628	659	656	657	690	683
	1962	602	641	635	630	667	663
C	1965-67	591	632	628	627	664	657
	1964	596	638	635	616	657	650
	1962	589	629	626	608	649	642
D	1965-67	572	606	600	639	669	660
	1964	577	607	603	633	662	652
	1962	570	600	590	618	640	625
E	1965-67	543	583	576	612	647	637
	1964	549	584	573	604	634	622
	1962	532	563	563	587	618	612
				Women's colleges			
F	1965-67	657	710	706	633	684	678
	1964	656	699	700	624	672	668
	1962	649	709	709	601	666	665
G	1965-67	615	658	655	546	592	588
	1964	601	643	637	534	588	584
	1962	578	640	636	509	556	548
H	1965-67	596	625	621	575	603	600
	1964	594	622	616	575	601	588
	1962	587	620	610	545	575	566
I	1965-67	566	610	601	554	594	588
	1964	570	597	590	550	580	575
	1962	564	596	585	528	560	553
J	1965-67	554	600	593	540	585	579
	1964	554	593	588	538	577	572
	1962	538	580	570	507	547	542

(*Table 4.2 continued on page 86*)

Table 4.2 (continued)

College	Year	SAT-verbal mean			SAT-mathematical mean		
		Applicants	Accepted applicants	Enrolled students	Applicants	Accepted applicants	Enrolled students
				Coeducational colleges			
K	1965-67	539	574	575	539	575	575
	1964	528	561	560	531	558	554
	1962	535	572	564	529	543	538
L	1965-67	545	574	568	544	569	557
	1964	540	569	560	531	555	546
	1962	512	556	547	501	534	527
M	1965-67	511	546	544	522	556	553
	1964	501	528	525	511	533	532
	1962	485	530	532	492	532	534
N	1965-67	514	545	531	548	578	563
	1964	513	543	525	539	569	554
	1962	489	519	507	510	538	526
O	1965-67	502	527	521	522	555	548
	1964	493	514	501	515	534	527
	1962	484	508	498	511	532	524
P	1965-67	490	512	509	521	539	531
	1964	488	506	503	521	534	528
	1962	466	487	479	489	507	503
Q	1965-67	496	510	503	496	510	496
	1964	495	506	498	494	504	499
	1962	466	474	468	460	467	468
R	1965-67	477	505	503	498	523	520
	1964	468	504	497	484	516	506
	1962	458	476	471	472	490	490

able data for all three groups in the 1962, 1964, and 1965-67 editions of the *Manual*. Because the colleges providing usable data cannot be considered representative of all College Board member colleges or even of colleges providing some data for the *Manual*, only 18 were selected, at random, for presentation. The results for these colleges illustrate the variation from one college to another in score level and permit an examination of trends in performance for the colleges included.

Table 4.2 makes it clear that during the time period studied there was a perceptible upward trend of scores in nearly all of the 18 colleges. The upward trend in applicant scores presumably reflects greater self-selection. The upward trend in accepted applicant and enrolled student scores suggests that selection within the higher-scoring applicant group continued to be based on the kinds of abilities measured by the tests. It is true that an upward trend in scores could arise even if applicants re-

mained at the same level, provided that the number of applicants increased while the number accepted remained the same or provided that more weight were given to the scores in admissions. Thus, although the upward trend in the means for these 18 colleges could be the result of an upward shift in the ability level of high school seniors in general, it could also be the result of increasing selectivity on the part of the colleges—or it could result from some combination of both factors.

Comparisons of applicants, accepted applicants, and enrolled students show, as would be expected, substantially higher scores for the accepted applicants and enrolled students than for the applicants. The fact that the accepted applicants earn somewhat higher scores than the enrolled students probably results from the fact that able applicants may be accepted by several colleges but can attend only one and that some of the more able applicants accepted by the colleges included in the study chose to attend college elsewhere.

Hills (1966) has reported SAT means for students enrolled in 19 colleges and universities belonging to the University System of Georgia. In 1964 these colleges had SAT-verbal means ranging from 260 to 546 and SAT-mathematical means ranging from 294 to 635. The weighted average increase in means for the 1958 to 1964 period was 47 scaled score points for SAT-verbal and 40 scaled score points for SAT-mathematical, and substantial increases in mean scores occurred in nearly all 19 colleges and universities. During the same period, entering freshman classes increased nearly 50 percent in size.

A broader survey of shifts in ability level over time has been reported (Walberg and others, 1966). These data are important in evaluating the feasibility of using the data for a class admitted in a particular year for two or more years after the class is admitted. In this study, the 1963, 1964, and 1965-67 editions of the *Manual* were examined in order to identify, for each pair of editions, all institutions that provided comparable distributions in the two years. The examination was performed separately for men applicants, women applicants, enrolled freshman men, and enrolled freshman women. (In a few instances in which coeducational institutions did not present separate distributions for men and women, the distributions based on men and women combined were categorized as distributions based on men. When an institution provided distributions for subgroups within sex, all distributions for the subgroups were combined.) The within-institution differences between corresponding percentile ranks for scores of 400, 500, and 600 were tabulated for each pair of editions. Some of the results of the comparison of the 1963 and 1965-67 editions are summarized in the following table (derived from Table 4.3), which gives the percentages of institutions in which the percentile rank of the selected SAT scores differed by 10 points or less for the two years. The numbers of colleges on which the percentages are based are: men applicants, 69 colleges; women applicants, 79 colleges; enrolled freshman men, 112 colleges; enrolled freshman women, 127 colleges.

Percent of colleges

| | Men | | | | | |
| | SAT-V | | | SAT-M | | |
	600	500	400	600	500	400
Applicants	99	84	91	84	84	99
Enrolled freshmen	86	73	93	72	85	97
	Women					
	SAT-V			SAT-M		
	600	500	400	600	500	400
Applicants	87	63	95	89	84	94
Enrolled freshmen	70	68	96	69	83	94

Distributions of differences between corresponding percentile ranks published in the 1963 and 1965-67 editions of the *Manual* are shown in more detail in Table 4.3. From this table it can be ascertained that of the 2,322 individual comparisons of percentile ranks, there was no difference between percentile ranks in 270 comparisons. In 90 percent of the remaining 2,052 comparisons, the percent of students scoring below the selected scores was smaller in 1965 than it was in 1963.

The available evidence indicates that the score distributions published in the *Manual* have changed over the two- or three-year periods studied and that the level of the scores at a particular institution has been much more likely to increase than to decrease. In comparison with the differences among the profiles published by different institutions in a single edition, however, the differences among the profiles published by a given institution in several successive editions typically are not great.

Candidate norms, 1967-68 and 1968-69—Performance of College Board candidates for the years 1967-68 and 1968-69 is summarized in Table 4.4. A few points should be noted in interpreting these results. First, many candidates take SAT as juniors for guidance and practice and then take the test again as seniors. In 1968-69, the number of candidates who took SAT in March or May of their junior year and who repeated it in December or January of their senior year was about 190,000. Repetition of the test within a particular year is very much less common. The most recent available data (based on the testing years 1962-63 and 1963-64) showed that about 8 percent of senior SAT scores and about 5 percent of junior SAT scores were earned by students who had already taken the test during the same year. Second, the figures reported combine results for administrations occurring at different times during the year. By far the most popular administration for juniors was May; for seniors, the most popular was December. Third, the figures reported do not represent all candidates tested during the year. In particular, scores for Sunday administrations are excluded and scores are also excluded for a small proportion of candidates who, for various reasons, were not treated as part of the main score reporting group. The exclusion of these scores is unlikely to have any appreciable effect on the results. Finally, the available data have not been analyzed in terms of skewness and kurtosis. Detailed distributions for candidates tested from May 1968 through March 1969 are, however, given in the 1969-70 edition of *College Board Score Reports* both for SAT and for the Achievement Tests.

Certain comparisons based on Table 4.4 justify some comment. First, it is clear that the means and standard deviations for the two years agree fairly closely, although mean scores tend to be slightly lower in the more recent year. Second, juniors earn somewhat higher scores than seniors. Presumably, the juniors are more highly self-selected than the seniors, so that the normal expectation that seniors would earn higher scores is not fulfilled. Third, girls score higher than boys on SAT-verbal sections, but their advantage is only about five scaled score points. Boys, on the other hand, substantially excel girls on SAT-mathematical sections. Their advantage ranges from 39 to 45 points in the four basic groups. It is worthy of mention that candidates who were tested from August 1956 through May 1957 and expected to attend college

Table 4.3

Numbers of colleges in which changes of various amounts occurred in percentile ranks* for selected scaled scores between the 1963 edition and the 1965-67 edition of the Manual of Freshman Class Profiles

Change in percentage of students scoring below designated scaled score	Men** SAT-V score 600	500	400	SAT-M score 600	500	400	Women SAT-V score 600	500	400	SAT-M score 600	500	400
Applicants												
Decrease larger than 20		1		1				2				2
Decrease of 11 to 20	1	10	5	10	11	1	10	27	4	9	14	3
Decrease of 1 to 10	61	51	47	55	46	45	63	47	61	66	62	60
No change***	2	3	7	1	7	16	1	2	11	1	0	10
Increase of 1 to 10	5	4	9	2	5	7	5	1	3	3	3	4
Increase larger than 10			1									
Number of colleges	69	69	69	69	69	69	79	79	79	79	79	79
Enrolled freshmen												
Decrease larger than 20	1	6	1	4	3	1	4	6	1	10	4	2
Decrease of 11 to 20	14	23	7	26	13	2	33	35	4	29	18	5
Decrease of 1 to 10	80	71	59	70	69	47	72	66	63	74	79	74
No change***	5	6	32	2	16	47	6	8	46	4	6	31
Increase of 1 to 10	11	5	13	9	10	15	11	12	13	9	20	15
Increase larger than 10	1	1		1	1		1			1		
Number of colleges	112	112	112	112	112	112	127	127	127	127	127	127

*For convenience of reference, the percentage of cases below a specified score is denoted here as the "percentile rank" of the score.

**Including a few distributions based on men and women combined.

***Some instances of no change, particularly in the percentile rank of 400, occur because no persons presented lower scores in either year.

the following fall (for the most part, senior candidates) showed the following score differences: girls' SAT-verbal scores were eight points higher and boys' SAT-mathematical scores were 64 points higher. Although the comparison of 1956-57 results with recent results is complicated by the fact that not all of the students in the 1956-57 group were seniors in high school (although the very large majority of them *were* seniors), it seems safe to conclude that the superiority of boys over girls on SAT-mathematical sections is somewhat less now than it was in 1956-57.

Trends in candidate performance, 1956-57 to 1968-69 —Because the candidate group has changed in a variety of ways during the designated period, it is desirable to consider certain of these changes before examining trends in performance. Figure 4.1 shows the yearly attendance of twelfth-grade candidates at Scholastic Aptitude Test sessions. It should be noted that the number of test sessions attended is somewhat greater than the number of different persons tested (in 1963-64 about 8 percent of

senior SAT scores were earned by students who had already taken the test at a previous administration during the same year).

In Figure 4.2 the number of SATs taken annually by twelfth-grade candidates has been expressed as a fraction of the number of births 18 years earlier. The data in Figure 4.2 thus incorporate an approximate adjustment for the increase over time in the total number of persons in the appropriate age group.

Figures 4.1 and 4.2 make it clear that there has been a spectacular increase in the number of SAT scores reported during this period and that the increase is still very large when account is taken of variations in the birth rate 18 years earlier.

Along with the increase in activity, certain other changes can be noted. For the period August 1956 through May 1957, 30 percent of the SATs administered were taken by juniors and 64 percent by seniors. For the period July 1968 through May 1969, juniors earned 38 percent of the scores and seniors, 58 percent. During the

Table 4.4

*Means, standard deviations, and numbers of Scholastic Aptitude Test scores,
classified by candidate's sex and educational level, 1967-68 and 1968-69*

Educational level	Testing year	BOYS			GIRLS			TOTAL		
		Mean	SD	N	Mean	SD	N	Mean	SD	N
					SAT-*verbal*					
Juniors	1967-68	468	108	307,493	473	103	282,382	470	105	589,879
	1968-69	465	106	314,223	469	105	293,667	467	105	607,896
Seniors	1967-68	463	111	490,737	464	109	399,977	463	110	890,721
	1968-69	457	110	498,462	464	110	415,925	460	110	914,395
All grades	1967-68	464	110	837,315	467	106	706,511	466	108	1,543,839
	1968-69	460	108	852,105	466	108	733,439	462	108	1,585,560
					SAT-*mathematical*					
Juniors	1967-68	522	110	307,493	483	100	282,382	504	107	589,879
	1968-69	515	110	314,223	474	98	293,667	495	106	607,896
Seniors	1967-68	509	117	490,737	466	107	399,977	490	115	890,721
	1968-69	510	116	498,462	465	105	415,925	490	114	914,395
All grades	1967-68	513	115	837,315	471	105	706,511	494	112	1,543,839
	1968-69	511	114	852,105	468	103	733,439	491	111	1,585,560

same period, there was a marked shift of seniors from the January test to earlier dates. In 1956-1957, 8 percent of the senior scores were earned in December and 54 percent in January. In 1966-67, December accounted for 68 percent and January, for 13 percent. In 1968-69, November accounted for 31 percent; December, for 43 percent; and January, for 12 percent.

Additional trends may be noted by comparing results of special studies of test-taking patterns of College Board candidates. These studies were based on a 5 percent sample of all candidates tested in a two-year period. Because of the great flexibility in the testing program, a great variety of testing patterns are possible with respect to time of testing, tests taken at a particular administration, and repetition of specific tests. Comparisons of test-taking patterns of various groups (boys and girls, juniors and seniors, and students attending secondary schools in various geographical regions) throw additional light on the composition of the candidate group at different administrations. An important feature of these studies is that the unit of analysis is the candidate, defined as any student who took at least one test during the designated two-year period as a junior or senior in secondary school. For comparing groups, the percentage of candidates is a more meaningful figure than the percentage of scores, since the frequency of test repetition may vary among the groups being compared.

Two trends, based on test-taking pattern studies for the testing years 1957-59 and 1962-64 (Pitcher, 1960 and Pitcher, 1966), will be noted here. First, the percentage of girls increased from 40.9 to 44.9 over the period studied. Second, there has been a trend with respect to the region in which the candidate's secondary school is located, as follows:

Geographical location of secondary school	Percent of sample	
	1957-59	1962-64
Northeast	54.0	42.5
South	19.8	23.0
Midwest	14.4	18.1
West	10.2	13.0
Other	1.4	3.6

It is clear that there is a trend toward broader national distribution. The Northeast, which includes the New England and Middle Atlantic census regions, accounts for a markedly smaller proportion of the candidates in the more recent study. That this decrease cannot be explained by a shift in population is indicated by the fact that the high school population did not shift much during this time. The nine states included in the Northeast accounted for 23.8 percent of all public high school graduates in the United States in 1959-60 and 23.4 of such graduates in 1963-64. Data available for the latter year

Figure 4.1

Attendance of twelfth-grade students at SAT *sessions, 1956-57 through 1968-69*

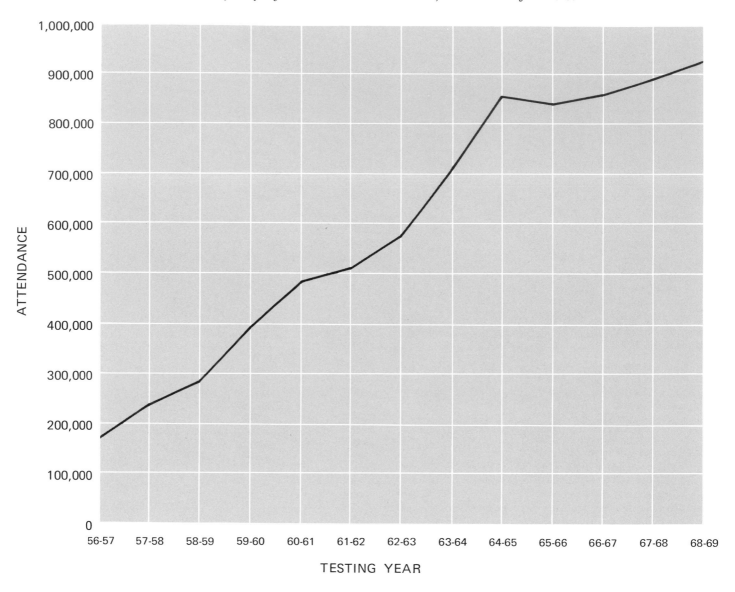

show that the corresponding percentage for all public and nonpublic graduates was 25.5. Data were obtained from the *Digest of Educational Statistics* prepared by the U. S. Office of Education (1962, 1965).

By far the most interesting question, of course, is the nature of the trend with respect to test performance. Since the scores for all new test forms are reported on a continuing score scale, it is possible to compare scores directly for different testing years. Table 4.5 provides the data for such comparison. It is true, of course, that score equating is subject to random errors, and that the opportunity for these random errors to cancel each other out is limited by the fact that there are only five or six separate test forms represented in the statistics for a given testing year.

On the whole, the most striking feature of Table 4.5 is the lack of conspicuous trends. The SAT-verbal median for the 13 years is 473. The highest mean (478) occurred in 1962-63, the lowest (462) occurred in 1968-69. Two possible trends may be noted. The mean declined slightly each year for the last six years, shown in the table, and the standard deviations for the first three years are slightly smaller than those for the last ten. The highest SAT-mathematical mean (502) also occurred in 1962-63, and there is again a slight downward tendency for the last seven years. Conjectures about these relatively subtle trends should not obscure the remarkable fact that over the entire 13-year period, SAT-verbal means ranged only from 462 to 478 and SAT-mathematical means ranged only from 491 to 502.

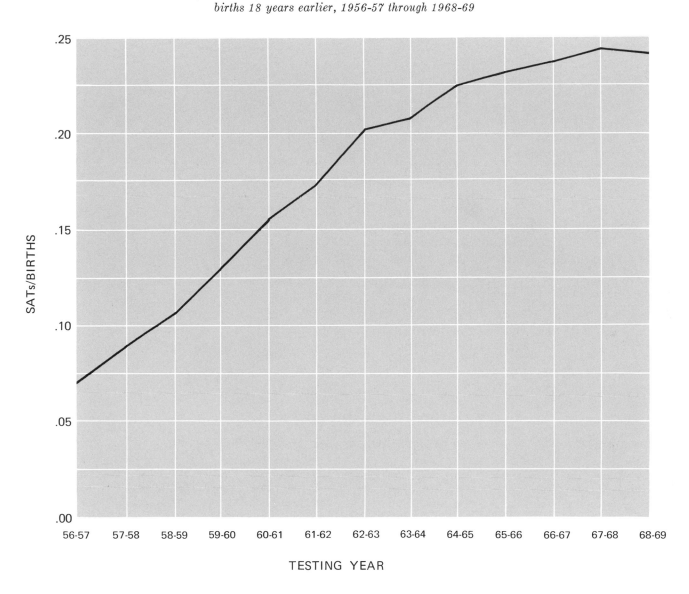

Figure 4.2

Ratio of number of SATs *taken by twelfth-grade students to number of
births 18 years earlier, 1956-57 through 1968-69*

TESTING YEAR

Performance on Achievement Tests

Nature of Achievement Test candidates—For some purposes, it is useful to think of all candidates who take one or more Achievement Tests as forming a group. For example, data on the number of seniors taking one or more Achievement Tests at each administration may be added across administrations to provide an indication of the growth in volume of the Achievement Test program, as shown in Figure 4.3. The growth over the period 1956-57 through 1968-69 is clearly quite large. Figures are given for seniors in order to remove the effect of attendance by the same candidate both as a junior and as a senior. If a candidate attended more than once as a senior, he is, of

course, counted each time he attends. In the study of test-taking patterns based on the 1962-64 testing years (described on pages 89 and 90), it was found that, on the average, each candidate attended 1.13 Achievement Test administrations as a senior. (The comparable figure for SAT attendance is 1.08 administrations.) Part of the increase in Achievement Test attendance shown in Figure 4.3 may be attributed to an increased proportion of candidates attending more than one administration, since these data are based on the total number of attendances, not on the total number of candidates.

The studies of test-taking patterns also provide data on the question of the growth in the number of Achievement Test candidates relative to the growth of the total

Table 4.5

Means, standard deviations, and numbers of cases* (in thousands)
for all candidates taking the SAT, *by year, 1956-57 through 1968-69*

Testing year	SAT-verbal			SAT-mathematical		
	Mean	SD	N	Mean	SD	N
1956-57	473	105	270.6	496	111	270.5
1957-58	472	106	376.9	496	109	376.8
1958-59	475	106	469.7	498	110	469.7
1959-60	477	108	564.3	498	109	564.2
1960-61	474	108	716.4	495	109	716.3
1961-62	473	109	802.6	498	112	802.5
1962-63	478	109	933.2	502	111	933.1
1963-64	475	108	1,164.0	498	113	1,163.9
1964-65	473	108	1,361.4	496	112	1,361.2
1965-66	471	108	1,381.4	496	111	1,381.4
1966-67	467	109	1,422.5	495	110	1,422.5
1967-68	466	108	1,543.8	494	112	1,543.8
1968-69	462	108	1,585.6	491	111	1,585.6

*The term "case" is used here to denote an attendance at an SAT administration. Thus, if a candidate attended two administrations, he is counted as two cases.

candidate group. In these figures, each candidate is counted only once, even if he attends several administrations. The proportion of candidates who took one or more Achievement Tests as juniors or seniors in high school is as follows:

Testing year	Percent taking Achievement Tests	Sample size
1957-59	34.5	14,288
1960-62	40.3	24,618
1962-64	41.7	35,523

An indication of the present scope of the Achievement Tests program is given by the fact that, according to the information given in the publication *1969-70 Admissions Schedules of the Member Colleges,* some 232 College Board member colleges required that all candidates take the Achievement Tests.

Characteristics of groups taking specific tests—Virtually all candidates who take the SAT take both the verbal and mathematical sections. The Achievement Test candidates, by contrast, take a great variety of test combinations. As part of the studies of test-taking patterns (described on pages 89 and 90), information was obtained on the percentage of Achievement Test candidates who took each Achievement Test. For the period 1962-64, the percentage of Achievement candidates taking each test is shown in Table 4.6.

Of the 14 tests studied, only English Composition was taken by nearly all candidates (86 percent). A clear majority of the candidates (56 percent) took the Intermediate Mathematics Test. About 22 percent of the candidates took the Advanced Mathematics Test, but some of them undoubtedly also took the Intermediate Mathematics Test (especially as juniors), so that the percentage of candidates taking a mathematics test cannot be stated precisely. Of the remaining tests, only American History and Social Studies (30 percent), Chemistry (19 percent), French (18 percent), and Biology (11 percent) were taken by more than 10 percent of the candidates. As would be expected, the study also showed that Physics and Advanced Mathematics were appreciably more popular with boys than with girls, while French, Spanish, and Biology were more popular with girls than with boys.

Since virtually all Achievement candidates also take the SAT, it is possible to determine the ability level on SAT of candidates choosing each Achievement Test. As part of the statistical work of maintaining the score scales for the Achievement Tests, data on SAT performance for samples of Achievement candidates have been prepared. Results for 1968-69 testing are shown in Table 4.7. (The footnote to Table 4.7 indicates how the samples were defined.)

Means on SAT-verbal range from 507 for candidates taking Mathematics Level I to 594 for candidates tak-

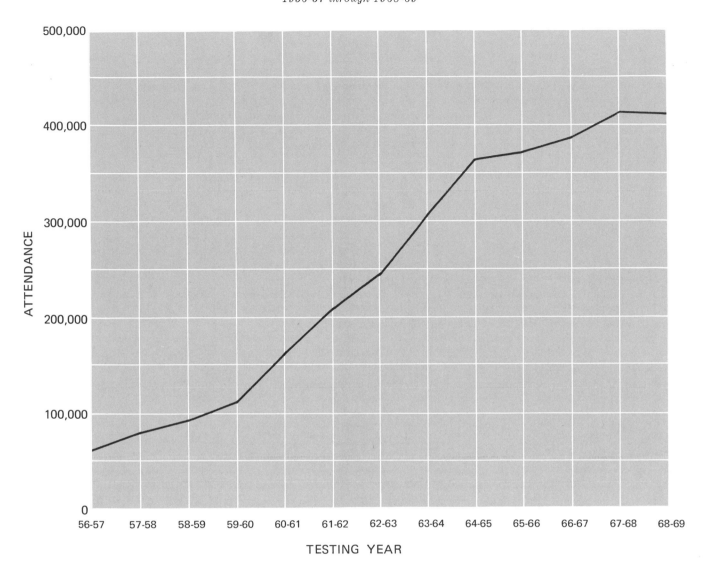

Figure 4.3

*Attendance of twelfth-grade students at Achievement Test sessions,
1956-57 through 1968-69*

ing the Russian Test. On SAT-mathematical the range is from 511 for Literature to 666 for Mathematics Level II*. Scaling procedures for determining the College Board scaled scores for the various Achievement Tests take account of the variation in ability level from test

to test, as described in Chapter III. Table 4.7 makes it clear that the differences from test to test in level of candidate ability are sufficiently large to make the scaling operation worthwhile.

The Achievement Test candidates choosing various tests differ also in the proportion of candidates tested in the junior and senior years. Table 4.8 presents data for students tested in 1962-64. (Results are based on the test-taking pattern studies described on pages 89 and 90.) A substantial proportion of candidates take certain tests in their junior year only, presumably near the end of their course of work in the subject. For European History and World Cultures and for Chemistry, nearly half (48 percent and 47 percent, respectively) of the candidates took the test in their junior year only. Other tests having

---

*Mathematics Level I and Level II replaced the Intermediate and Advanced tests beginning in 1964-65. According to *A Description of the College Board Achievement Tests, 1967-68*, Mathematics Level I is the appropriate test for most candidates who take a mathematics achievement test; Mathematics Level II "stresses those aspects of pre-calculus mathematics which are prerequisites for a good course in calculus and analytic geometry" and is appropriate for a "good student who has completed three and a half to four years of a sequence of courses which approximate the recommendations of the College Board Commission on Mathematics."

Table 4.6

*Percentages of Achievement Test candidates taking the various tests
at least once during the last two years of secondary school**

Achievement Test	Number of candidates	Percent** of total achievement sample
English Composition	12,788	86.3
American History and Social Studies	4,421	29.8
European History and World Cultures	408	2.8
French	2,743	18.5
German	486	3.3
Hebrew	20	0.1
Latin	831	5.6
Russian	47	0.3
Spanish	1,207	8.1
Biology	1,645	11.1
Chemistry	2,758	18.6
Physics	1,387	9.4
Intermediate Mathematics	8,320	56.2
Advanced Mathematics	3,226	21.8
Any Achievement Test	14,817 (base for percents)	100.0

*Based on a 5 percent sample of Achievement Test candidates who were juniors in 1962-63 and seniors in 1963-64.

**The percentages do not add to 100 because each candidate is included in the percentage for each test that he took.

relatively large proportions of junior-year-only candidates were Latin (34 percent), Biology (32 percent), Physics (28 percent), American History and Social Studies (26 percent), and Intermediate Mathematics (25 percent). The tests having the highest percentage of senior-only candidates were Russian (96 percent), Advanced Mathematics (80 percent), Hebrew (80 percent), and German (79 percent). Relatively few candidates took the same subject both as juniors and as seniors; for only four tests, English Composition (20 percent), French (13 percent), Latin (13 percent), and Intermediate Mathematics (13 percent), did more than 10 percent of the candidates follow this pattern in 1962-64. The results suggest that candidates took Achievement Tests during their junior year in order to present scores earned near the end of their course work in a subject and to a noticeably smaller extent for practice or for guidance purposes in a subject that they take again in their senior year. Finally, it may be noted that a considerable percentage (11 percent) of the candidates who took Achievement Tests took them only as juniors. A majority of these candidates *did* take the SAT during the senior year. At some time between the junior and senior administrations, such candidates presumably decided—in some cases reversing an earlier decision—to apply to colleges that did not require Achievement Tests or that were willing to accept junior Achievement Test scores. Of the rest of the candidates who took the Achievement Tests only in their junior year, some undoubtedly skipped their twelfth grade and entered college directly. However, it seems likely that for other candidates, nonattendance at a senior administration was the result of a change in educational plans, either to attend a college that does not require College Board tests or not to attend college at all.

Candidate norms, 1967-68 and 1968-69—Table 4.9 shows the means and standard deviations for boys and girls separately and for juniors and seniors separately for substantially all candidates tested in two recent testing years. In these tables, results for tests administered from November through July are combined. (It should be noted that the Literature Test was introduced in May 1968; in 1968-69, it was administered in January and May.) Comparison of the overall means for the two testing years shows that seven of the shifts in means were less than five scaled points. However, the Physics mean increased by 8 points, while means for Hebrew, European History, and French declined by 16, 12, and 10 points,

Table 4.7

Scholastic Aptitude Test means and standard deviations
for Achievement Test candidates*

Achievement Test	SAT-verbal		SAT-mathematical		Number of candidates
	Mean	SD	Mean	SD	
English Composition	514	104	543	107	4,701
Literature	538	111	511	104	7,332
American History and Social Studies	513	104	525	106	4,634
European History and World Cultures	541	110	526	103	7,235
French	549	96	555	98	3,555
German	555	95	585	99	3,779
Hebrew	552	110	575	110	989
Latin	550	100	565	98	5,163
Russian	594	97	610	99	883
Spanish	518	96	534	97	3,610
Biology	511	106	520	102	4,773
Chemistry	531	101	601	96	4,877
Physics	534	107	631	95	5,057
Mathematics Level I	507	103	554	101	4,637
Mathematics Level II	578	108	666	91	4,717

*Based on samples of candidates who took the designated Achievement Test as seniors in December 1968, January 1969, or March 1969, or who took that test as juniors in May 1968 but did not repeat it at any of the specified senior administrations. (The sample sizes do not reflect the relative total volumes for the various tests.)

respectively. These shifts are relatively small and are no doubt attributable in part to random fluctuations inherent in scaling and equating. It may be noted also that American History, European History, Latin, Russian, Chemistry, and Physics showed decreases in number of candidates tested; the other tests showed an increased candidate volume in 1968-69.

Table 4.9 facilitates comparison of the performance of boys and girls with respect to performance on the Achievement Tests. It may well be emphasized again that generalizations of the results beyond the candidate group itself are not warranted. Within the candidate group itself, however, a fairly clear pattern of sex differences is discernible, as shown in Table 4.10, in which the tests are ordered according to the difference observed for seniors in 1968-69.

As might be expected, boys have an advantage in the sciences, in mathematics, and in history and social science, while girls score higher in English and foreign languages. It is interesting to note that differences for Latin are quite small. On the whole, the pattern of differences is similar for juniors and for seniors. However, the advantage of boys in chemistry is smaller for juniors than for seniors. For tests on which girls have the higher average scores, their advantage is larger for seniors than for juniors in French, Hebrew, and Spanish and is larger for juniors than for seniors in Russian.

It should be noted that the foregoing comparisons do not take into account the existence of sex differences in the amount of preparation in those subjects that are generally sequential and cumulative in secondary school (foreign languages, mathematics). Reference to the more detailed information in Tables 4.12 and 4.14 indicates that the relative advantages of senior girls on the French and German Tests and of senior boys on the Mathematics Level I Test are smaller when boys and girls with the same amount of preparation are compared. However, these results are probably attributable in part to differential self-selection.

Table 4.9 makes it possible to compare mean scores for junior and senior candidates. The differences between junior and senior means, separately for boys and girls, are presented in Table 4.11. On the whole, the observed differences may be attributed primarily to greater self-selection of juniors than of seniors. It is worthy of note that there are appreciable differences from one field to another in the size of the differences. French, German, Latin, Spanish, and Physics show relatively large differences.

Table 4.12 presents results for each of five languages for candidates classified by number of semesters of preparation, by sex, and by testing year. Because instruction

Table 4.8

Percentages of Achievement Test candidates tested in the junior year, senior year, or both years, by specific Achievement Test*

Achievement Test	Number of candidates (base for percents)	Percent of candidates tested in the:		
		Junior year only	Senior year only	Junior and senior years
English Composition	12,788	11.8	68.4	19.8
American History and Social Studies	4,421	25.7	68.2	6.1
European History and World Cultures	408	47.5	50.0	2.5
French	2,743	18.9	67.8	13.3
German	486	11.9	79.0	9.1
Hebrew	20	15.0	80.0	5.0
Latin	831	33.9	53.5	12.6
Russian	47	2.1	95.7	2.2
Spanish	1,207	16.4	73.8	9.8
Biology	1,645	32.1	62.7	5.2
Chemistry	2,758	46.9	48.4	4.7
Physics	1,387	27.8	65.2	7.0
Intermediate Mathematics	8,320	25.2	62.1	12.7
Advanced Mathematics	3,226	10.1	80.5	9.4
Any Achievement Test	14,817	11.3	64.4	24.3

*Based on a 5 percent sample of Achievement Test candidates who were juniors in 1962-63 and seniors in 1963-64.

in Hebrew does not necessarily follow closely the pattern of other languages with respect to semesters of preparation, it has not been included in this table. Data for Hebrew, separated by sex and testing year, are given in Table 4.9.

Table 4.13 summarizes information about the mean score differences associated with successive levels of preparation for juniors and seniors separately. (Only the four languages that are taken by relatively large numbers of candidates have been summarized.) It should be noted that in reporting the number of semesters studied, the candidate is asked to count the semester during which he takes the test, if he is currently studying the language, and to count semesters beginning with grade 9. The grouping of semesters in Tables 4.12 and 4.13 introduces a complication in interpretation because most seniors are tested near the middle of the academic year and most juniors are tested near the end of the year. It is clear that when students at the same educational level are compared, those having had five or six semesters earn substantially higher scores than those having had three or four semesters. For seniors, the median difference for the four languages is 67 points; for juniors, it is 70 points. The increment between students having had five or six semesters and those having had seven or eight semesters is substantial for seniors in French and

Spanish, ranging from 75 to 79 points. For German and Latin it is somewhat smaller, ranging from 56 to 64 points. Interestingly enough, the increments for juniors are relatively small, ranging from 27 to 53, with a median of 44. It is possible that the smaller gain for juniors at this level is an artifact, especially since a junior would have to follow some sort of special program in order to complete more than six semesters of a language by the end of his junior year. Finally, it should be noted that the observed score differences, based as they are on cross-sectional data, may arise from self-selection as well as from the additional training. The observed differences might be somewhat larger than corresponding differences obtained by a longitudinal study of the same student group.

A similar analysis for the two mathematics tests is shown in Table 4.14. The score differences for successive levels of training for Mathematics Level I are summarized in Table 4.15. These results no doubt reflect the interaction of the effects of training and of self-selection. For both seniors and juniors the increase from six semesters to seven or eight semesters is larger than the increase shown by the other two steps in the categories used for amount of training. The fact that juniors reporting "more than 8 semesters" scored lower than those reporting "7

(*Continued on page 100*)

Table 4.9

Means, standard deviations, and numbers of Achievement Test scores, classified by test and by candidate's sex and educational level, 1967-68 and 1968-69

Educational level	Testing year	BOYS			GIRLS			TOTAL*		
		Mean	SD	N	Mean	SD	N	Mean	SD	N
English Composition										
Juniors	1967-68	517	107	49,678	540	105	50,984	529	106	100,662
	1968-69	517	107	55,439	539	102	54,927	528	105	110,367
Seniors	1967-68	498	104	191,283	529	104	148,140	511	105	339,426
	1968-69	498	105	194,857	527	103	152,540	511	105	347,397
All grades	1967-68	501	105	251,656	531	104	204,245	514	106	455,906
	1968-69	501	106	260,936	530	103	212,893	514	106	473,832
Literature										
Juniors	1967-68	521	111	2,184	545	106	3,252	535	109	5,436
	1968-69	516	110	2,992	536	111	4,246	528	111	7,238
Seniors	1967-68	496	109	984	522	112	1,758	513	111	2,742
	1968-69	511	116	5,309	526	111	8,792	521	113	14,101
All grades	1967-68	511	111	3,348	536	109	5,227	526	110	8,575
	1968-69	512	114	8,747	529	111	13,527	522	112	22,274
American History and Social Studies										
Juniors	1967-68	530	114	23,202	497	104	17,749	516	111	40,951
	1968-69	535	110	22,030	495	102	16,699	518	109	38,730
Seniors	1967-68	505	106	56,294	468	96	37,522	490	103	93,817
	1968-69	502	105	55,613	461	94	37,409	486	103	93,022
All grades	1967-68	511	109	81,829	476	100	56,576	497	107	138,406
	1968-69	510	108	80,250	471	98	55,643	494	106	135,894
European History and World Cultures										
Juniors	1967-68	563	111	2,469	521	95	1,319	548	107	3,788
	1968-69	555	112	2,468	508	99	1,341	538	109	3,809
Seniors	1967-68	552	113	3,412	497	95	2,290	530	109	5,703
	1968-69	530	112	3,870	494	97	2,062	518	108	5,932
All grades	1967-68	553	112	6,610	504	96	4,060	534	109	10,671
	1968-69	536	113	6,876	497	98	3,780	522	109	10,656
French										
Juniors	1967-68	556	107	9,717	562	100	18,806	560	103	28,523
	1968-69	553	110	10,244	559	104	20,427	557	106	30,671
Seniors	1967-68	506	110	22,122	532	105	44,301	523	107	66,423
	1968-69	493	104	23,872	519	102	47,350	510	103	71,222
All grades	1967-68	522	112	33,264	541	105	64,889	535	108	98,153
	1968-69	512	111	35,491	531	105	69,549	525	107	105,040

*Includes candidates who did not indicate sex.

(Table 4.9 continued on page 98)

Table 4.9 (continued)

Educational level	Testing year	BOYS			GIRLS			TOTAL*		
		Mean	SD	N	Mean	SD	N	Mean	SD	N
German										
Juniors	1967-68	557	112	1,777	573	113	1,243	563	113	3,020
	1968-69	538	109	1,966	557	106	1,412	546	108	3,378
Seniors	1967-68	504	109	8,834	529	111	5,656	514	110	14,490
	1968-69	500	106	8,884	525	106	5,936	510	107	14,820
All grades	1967-68	515	113	10,989	539	114	7,134	524	114	18,123
	1968-69	508	109	11,243	532	108	7,537	518	109	18,780
Hebrew										
Juniors	1967-68	613	87	47	605	87	47	609	87	94
	1968-69	587	104	71	603	89	65	595	98	136
Seniors	1967-68	575	98	604	596	97	372	583	98	977
	1968-69	556	97	606	583	98	414	567	98	1,020
All grades	1967-68	578	99	665	597	96	424	586	98	1,090
	1968-69	558	98	688	587	97	491	570	99	1,179
Latin										
Juniors	1967-68	561	96	2,652	557	92	2,992	559	94	5,644
	1968-69	557	97	2,359	560	93	2,503	558	95	4,862
Seniors	1967-68	512	104	6,128	519	101	5,538	516	103	11,666
	1968-69	505	104	5,442	515	100	4,801	510	102	10,243
All grades	1967-68	529	104	9,400	533	100	9,062	531	102	18,462
	1968-69	522	105	8,280	530	100	7,640	526	102	15,920
Russian										
Juniors	1967-68	524	119	61	600	124	43	556	127	104
	1968-69	560	130	65	601	127	28	573	130	93
Seniors	1967-68	531	132	707	534	124	549	532	129	1,256
	1968-69	521	136	661	539	126	562	529	132	1,223
All grades	1967-68	532	132	783	542	126	603	536	130	1,386
	1968-69	524	137	744	543	128	599	532	133	1,343
Spanish										
Juniors	1967-68	543	123	4,446	548	112	6,220	546	117	10,666
	1968-69	538	123	5,201	548	112	7,184	544	117	12,385
Seniors	1967-68	488	125	16,178	510	116	22,823	501	120	39,001
	1968-69	489	121	18,581	515	115	25,998	504	118	44,579
All grades	1967-68	501	128	21,542	518	117	29,859	511	122	51,401
	1968-69	501	125	24,889	522	115	34,119	513	120	59,008

*Includes candidates who did not indicate sex.

Table 4.9 (continued)

Educational level	Testing year	BOYS			GIRLS			TOTAL*		
		Mean	SD	N	Mean	SD	N	Mean	SD	N
Biology										
Juniors	1967-68	546	112	6,954	515	105	8,155	529	109	15,109
	1968-69	534	113	7,120	506	104	8,238	519	110	15,358
Seniors	1967-68	507	112	15,484	476	100	17,996	490	107	33,481
	1968-69	514	112	16,207	484	102	18,361	498	108	34,568
All grades	1967-68	531	116	28,696	497	106	33,283	513	112	61,980
	1968-69	530	117	29,647	500	107	33,915	514	113	63,562
Chemistry										
Juniors	1967-68	588	101	22,961	552	91	7,142	580	100	30,103
	1968-69	582	104	20,626	542	96	6,934	572	104	27,560
Seniors	1967-68	561	107	24,745	499	91	7,575	546	106	32,322
	1968-69	558	109	24,002	498	97	7,429	544	109	31,431
All grades	1967-68	577	106	52,148	529	96	16,250	565	105	68,400
	1968-69	573	109	48,177	523	100	15,523	561	109	63,701
Physics										
Juniors	1967-68	612	102	6,710	556	90	619	607	102	7,329
	1968-69	631	101	6,031	567	96	587	625	102	6,618
Seniors	1967-68	571	100	18,631	524	87	1,111	568	100	19,744
	1968-69	578	104	18,526	520	93	1,123	575	104	19,649
All grades	1967-68	581	103	27,220	536	89	1,843	579	102	29,066
	1968-69	591	106	26,266	537	97	1,820	587	106	28,087
Mathematics Level I										
Juniors	1967-68	576	106	50,559	545	97	36,222	563	103	86,781
	1968-69	574	97	52,035	543	89	39,034	561	95	91,070
Seniors	1967-68	549	100	150,047	516	95	85,864	537	100	235,913
	1968-69	542	98	149,839	508	92	91,588	529	98	241,427
All grades	1967-68	556	103	210,349	524	97	124,885	544	102	335,238
	1968-69	550	100	211,232	518	93	133,649	538	99	344,883
Mathematics Level II										
Juniors	1967-68	700	86	3,785	673	85	1,071	694	87	4,856
	1968-69	697	95	4,239	668	94	1,055	691	96	5,294
Seniors	1967-68	676	93	16,884	654	95	3,685	672	94	20,571
	1968-69	668	97	18,536	647	96	4,214	664	97	22,750
All grades	1967-68	679	93	21,927	658	94	4,857	675	93	26,786
	1968-69	672	98	24,110	651	96	5,380	668	98	29,491

*Includes candidates who did not indicate sex.

Table 4.10

*Mean differences in Achievement Test scores earned by
boys and girls, 1967-68 and 1968-69*

(Based on data given in Table 4.9)

| | MEAN DIFFERENCES | | | |
| Achievement Test | Juniors | | Seniors | |
	1967-68	1968-69	1967-68	1968-69
	Boys higher			
Chemistry	36	40	62	60
Physics	56	64	47	58
American History and Social Studies	33	40	37	41
European History and World Cultures	42	47	55	36
Mathematics Level I	31	31	33	34
Biology	31	28	31	30
Mathematics Level II	27	29	22	21
Hebrew	8*	....	....	....
Latin	4	....	....	....
	Girls higher			
English Composition	23	22	31	29
Hebrew	....	16*	21	27
French	6	6	26	26
Spanish	5	10	22	26
German	16	19	25	25
Russian	76*	41*	3	18
Literature	24	20	26	15
Latin	....	3	7	10

*Comparison involving a group of fewer than 100 students.

or 8 semesters" is probably an artifact arising from the fact that many juniors having more than eight semesters followed some kind of special program, an interpretation supported by the fact that only about 2 percent of juniors were in this category. The corresponding figure for seniors was 7 percent.

Table 4.14 also shows that a majority (55 percent in 1967-68 and 1968-69) of seniors reported "7 or 8 semesters" while a majority (56 percent in 1967-68 and 1968-69) of juniors reported "6 semesters." In interpreting the results for juniors and seniors, it should be kept in mind that although junior candidates are typically tested near the end of the academic year, senior candidates are more likely to be tested near the middle of the academic year.

For Mathematics Level II, only two categories by educational level are used. The advantage for seniors reporting "more than 8 semesters" over those reporting

"7 or 8 semesters" was 43 in 1967-68 and 51 in 1968-69. For juniors, the corresponding figures were 19 and 8. There is no way to evaluate the relative effects of self-selection and training in producing these differences. As would be expected, a larger proportion of seniors than of juniors reported "more than 8 semesters." In fact, about three-tenths (about 30 percent in 1967-68 and 29 percent in 1968-69) of seniors taking Mathematics Level II were in this category.

Examination of Tables 4.12 and 4.14 reveals that in both foreign languages and mathematics, juniors are more like seniors at the next higher level of preparation than they are like seniors at the same level of preparation. In part, this result probably arises from greater self-selection of juniors with respect to academic ability and quality of preparation. Differences in recency of training and detailed differences in amount of preparation must also be considered. Candidates who do not

Table 4.11

*Mean differences in Achievement Test scores earned by
juniors and seniors, 1967-68 and 1968-69*

(Based on data given in Table 4.9)

| | JUNIOR MEAN *minus* SENIOR MEAN | | | |
| | Boys | | Girls | |
Achievement Test	*1967-68*	*1968-69*	*1967-68*	*1968-69*
English Composition	19	19	11	12
Literature	25	5	23	10
American History and Social Studies	25	33	29	34
European History and World Cultures	11	25	24	14
French	50	60	30	40
German	53	38	44	32
Hebrew	38*	31*	9*	20*
Latin	49	52	38	45
Russian	−7*	39*	66*	62*
Spanish	55	49	38	33
Biology	39	20	39	22
Chemistry	27	24	53	44
Physics	41	53	32	47
Mathematics Level I	27	32	29	35
Mathematics Level II	24	29	19	21

*Comparison involving a group of fewer than 100 students.

continue the subject as seniors presumably earn higher scores at the end of the junior year than they would if tested as seniors. Most candidates who study a subject throughout their high school years will have completed about seven semesters when they are tested as seniors and about six semesters when they are tested as juniors. The available results do not permit a definitive evaluation of the relative contributions of these influences.

Trends in candidate performance, 1956-57 to 1968-69 —During the period included in this survey, there were a number of changes in the candidate group. The marked increase in the number of seniors taking the tests has been noted earlier. Also pertinent to the interpretation of test scores are trends and shifts in the percentage of all Achievement Test scores earned on specific tests and on broad groups of tests. In Table 4.16 and in Figure 4.4 the number of scores earned in each of five broad subject-matter categories is expressed as a percentage of the total number of Achievement Test scores earned during the year.

The results presented in Table 4.16 and Figure 4.4, it must be emphasized, describe test choice within the candidate group and do not necessarily reflect patterns of subject-matter preparation in secondary school of College Board Achievement Test candidates. Note should also be taken of the fact that the percentages are based on candidates in the main reporting group and do not include Sunday candidates (except for the Hebrew Test) or the small number of candidates for whom some administrative irregularity caused the removal of their records for special processing.

The general impression produced by these figures is that for most areas, shifts have been fairly small. It is true that the science tests have accounted for a steadily decreasing proportion of Achievement Test scores, from 19.0 percent in 1956-57 to 14.5 percent in 1961-62 and 11.3 percent in 1968-69. Mathematics increased from 23.5 percent in 1956-57 to 28.3 percent in 1961-62 and then remained at about the same general level. The percentage of scores in the foreign languages has been slightly higher (13.2 percent to 14.7 percent) since 1961-62 than during the first five years of the survey, and for the last five years has exceeded the percentage shown for the science tests.

(Continued on page 107)

Table 4.12

Means, standard deviations, and numbers of scores on Achievement Tests in foreign languages, classified by test and by candidate's sex, educational level, and number of semesters of study of the language in secondary school, 1967-68 and 1968-69

Educational level	Semesters of study	Testing year	BOYS			GIRLS			TOTAL		
			Mean	SD	N	Mean	SD	N	Mean	SD	N

French

Educational level	Semesters of study	Testing year	Mean	SD	N	Mean	SD	N	Mean	SD	N
Juniors	3 or 4 semesters	1967-68	474	84	859	487	78	1,998	483	80	2,857
		1968-69	460	80	981	482	79	2,029	475	80	3,010
	5 or 6 semesters	1967-68	545	94	3,719	557	91	8,568	553	92	12,287
		1968-69	545	97	4,311	555	95	9,735	552	96	14,046
	7 or 8 semesters	1967-68	577	90	787	590	87	1,434	586	88	2,221
		1968-69	589	98	751	595	92	1,465	593	94	2,216
	All juniors	1967-68	556	107	9,717	562	100	18,806	560	103	28,523
		1968-69	553	110	10,244	559	104	20,427	557	106	30,671
Seniors	3 or 4 semesters	1967-68	424	61	4,980	440	63	7,517	434	63	12,497
		1968-69	415	57	5,240	428	60	7,442	423	59	12,682
	5 or 6 semesters	1967-68	484	82	6,196	503	79	11,880	497	81	18,076
		1968-69	475	80	6,850	488	77	12,612	483	78	19,462
	7 or 8 semesters	1967-68	568	97	5,827	579	90	16,030	576	92	21,857
		1968-69	550	92	6,299	561	89	17,561	558	90	23,860
	All seniors	1967-68	506	110	22,122	532	105	44,301	523	107	66,423
		1968-69	493	104	23,872	519	102	47,350	510	103	71,222
All grades	3 or 4 semesters	1967-68	433	69	6,110	451	70	9,846	444	70	15,956
		1968-69	423	66	6,479	441	69	9,844	434	68	16,323
	5 or 6 semesters	1967-68	507	91	10,093	525	89	20,719	519	90	30,812
		1968-69	502	93	11,344	517	92	22,612	512	93	33,956
	7 or 8 semesters	1967-68	569	96	6,732	580	90	17,635	577	92	24,367
		1968-69	554	94	7,152	563	90	19,219	561	91	26,371
	All candidates	1967-68	522	112	33,264	541	105	64,889	535	108	98,153
		1968-69	512	111	35,491	531	105	69,549	525	107	105,040

Table 4.12 (continued)

Educational level	Semesters of study	Testing year	BOYS			GIRLS			TOTAL		
			Mean	SD	N	Mean	SD	N	Mean	SD	N
						German					
Juniors	3 or 4 semesters	1967-68	492	83	382	504	80	276	497	82	658
		1968-69	475	87	384	485	78	283	480	84	667
	5 or 6 semesters	1967-68	554	93	840	563	94	547	558	93	1,387
		1968-69	536	87	951	545	83	603	539	86	1,554
	7 or 8 semesters	1967-68	612	93	73	591	89	48	604	92	121
		1968-69	590	86	85	595	74	60	592	81	145
	All juniors	1967-68	557	112	1,777	573	113	1,243	563	113	3,020
		1968-69	538	109	1,966	557	106	1,412	546	108	3,378
Seniors	3 or 4 semesters	1967-68	434	70	2,658	448	69	1,596	439	70	4,254
		1968-69	430	66	2,506	449	69	1,485	437	68	3,991
	5 or 6 semesters	1967-68	505	89	2,899	521	84	1,556	511	88	4,455
		1968-69	501	86	2,788	515	82	1,710	506	85	4,498
	7 or 8 semesters	1967-68	568	88	1,758	581	89	1,309	574	89	3,067
		1968-69	557	87	1,974	569	86	1,511	562	87	3,485
	All seniors	1967-68	504	109	8,834	529	111	5,656	514	110	14,490
		1968-69	500	106	8,884	525	106	5,936	510	107	14,820
All grades	3 or 4 semesters	1967-68	442	75	3,120	458	75	1,921	448	76	5,041
		1968-69	437	72	2,974	454	72	1,801	444	72	4,775
	5 or 6 semesters	1967-68	516	92	3,793	533	89	2,128	522	91	5,921
		1968-69	510	88	3,800	522	83	2,348	515	86	6,148
	7 or 8 semesters	1967-68	570	89	1,852	581	89	1,368	575	89	3,220
		1968-69	558	88	2,081	570	86	1,586	563	87	3,667
	All candidates	1967-68	515	113	10,989	539	114	7,134	524	114	18,123
		1968-69	508	109	11,243	532	108	7,537	518	109	18,780

(*Table 4.12 continued on page 104*)

Table 4.12 (continued)

Educational level	Semesters of study	Testing year	BOYS			GIRLS			TOTAL		
			Mean	SD	N	Mean	SD	N	Mean	SD	N
						Latin					
Juniors	3 or 4 semesters	1967-68	494	86	337	504	76	437	500	81	774
		1968-69	491	78	295	500	78	420	496	79	715
	5 or 6 semesters	1967-68	573	87	1,485	570	85	1,665	571	86	3,150
		1968-69	564	89	1,279	571	84	1,464	568	86	2,743
	7 or 8 semesters	1967-68	597	99	215	600	94	186	598	97	401
		1968-69	606	91	203	590	89	142	599	91	345
	All juniors	1967-68	561	96	2,652	557	92	2,992	559	94	5,644
		1968-69	557	97	2,359	560	93	2,503	558	95	4,862
Seniors	3 or 4 semesters	1967-68	433	70	1,504	441	66	1,577	437	68	3,081
		1968-69	429	64	1,584	443	64	1,490	436	64	3,074
	5 or 6 semesters	1967-68	504	86	1,165	519	83	1,167	511	85	2,332
		1968-69	508	86	1,108	513	81	993	510	84	2,101
	7 or 8 semesters	1967-68	568	91	2,644	579	87	2,183	573	90	4,827
		1968-69	569	94	2,072	579	87	1,795	574	91	3,867
	All seniors	1967-68	512	104	6,128	519	101	5,538	516	103	11,666
		1968-69	505	104	5,442	515	100	4,801	510	102	10,243
All grades	3 or 4 semesters	1967-68	452	80	2,048	459	76	2,205	455	78	4,253
		1968-69	447	77	2,065	458	73	2,088	453	75	4,153
	5 or 6 semesters	1967-68	544	93	2,732	550	88	2,918	547	90	5,650
		1968-69	538	92	2,453	548	87	2,504	543	90	4,957
	7 or 8 semesters	1967-68	570	92	2,903	580	88	2,398	575	91	5,301
		1968-69	572	95	2,297	580	88	1,950	576	92	4,247
	All candidates	1967-68	529	104	9,400	533	100	9,062	531	102	18,462
		1968-69	522	105	8,280	530	100	7,640	526	102	15,920

Table 4.12 (continued)

Educational level	Semesters of study	Testing year	BOYS			GIRLS			TOTAL		
			Mean	SD	N	Mean	SD	N	Mean	SD	N
			Russian								
Juniors	3 or 4 semesters	1967-68	467	58	10	527	98	14	502	89	24
		1968-69	456	48	2	499	38	7	489	44	9
	5 or 6 semesters	1967-68	517	127	38	555	115	8	524	126	46
		1968-69	525	116	38	608	27	9	541	110	47
	7 or 8 semesters	1967-68	582	91	5	564	106	6	572	100	11
		1968-69	532	60	5	769	—	1	572	104	6
	All juniors	1967-68	524	119	61	600	124	43	556	127	104
		1968-69	560	130	65	601	127	28	573	130	93
Seniors	3 or 4 semesters	1967-68	454	88	147	464	89	154	459	88	301
		1968-69	450	106	164	455	102	133	452	104	297
	5 or 6 semesters	1967-68	502	103	215	514	107	125	507	105	340
		1968-69	516	117	175	525	102	135	520	110	310
	7 or 8 semesters	1967-68	583	110	168	562	100	128	574	106	296
		1968-69	551	105	167	558	89	137	554	98	304
	All seniors	1967-68	531	132	707	534	124	549	532	129	1,256
		1968-69	521	136	661	539	126	562	529	132	1,223
All grades	3 or 4 semesters	1967-68	454	86	157	470	91	169	462	89	326
		1968-69	448	105	170	456	100	141	452	103	311
	5 or 6 semesters	1967-68	507	109	256	517	108	133	510	109	389
		1968-69	518	116	216	530	101	146	523	110	362
	7 or 8 semesters	1967-68	583	109	174	562	100	135	574	106	309
		1968-69	551	104	173	560	90	138	555	98	311
	All candidates	1967-68	532	132	783	542	126	603	536	130	1,386
		1968-69	524	137	744	543	128	599	532	133	1,343

(*Table 4.12 continued on page 106*)

Table 4.12 (continued)

Educational level	Semesters of study	Testing year	BOYS			GIRLS			TOTAL		
			Mean	SD	N	Mean	SD	N	Mean	SD	N
						Spanish					
Juniors	3 or 4 semesters	1967-68	456	85	789	478	85	1,058	468	86	1,847
		1968-69	448	86	903	472	81	1,252	462	84	2,155
	5 or 6 semesters	1967-68	530	95	1,809	540	90	2,820	536	92	4,629
		1968-69	530	98	2,192	545	94	3,304	539	96	5,496
	7 or 8 semesters	1967-68	575	90	254	586	94	468	582	93	722
		1968-69	587	95	355	593	89	497	590	92	852
	All juniors	1967-68	543	123	4,446	548	112	6,220	546	117	10,666
		1968-69	538	123	5,201	548	112	7,184	544	117	12,385
Seniors	3 or 4 semesters	1967-68	402	60	4,605	429	68	5,833	417	66	10,438
		1968-69	407	60	5,285	432	66	6,502	421	65	11,787
	5 or 6 semesters	1967-68	471	85	4,369	490	86	5,838	482	86	10,207
		1968-69	472	85	5,012	495	84	6,731	485	85	11,743
	7 or 8 semesters	1967-68	549	98	2,995	561	94	5,939	557	96	8,934
		1968-69	550	98	3,561	568	92	6,897	562	95	10,458
	All seniors	1967-68	488	125	16,178	510	116	22,823	501	120	39,001
		1968-69	489	121	18,581	515	115	25,998	504	118	44,579
All grades	3 or 4 semesters	1967-68	410	68	5,608	437	73	7,076	425	72	12,684
		1968-69	414	68	6,448	439	71	7,989	428	71	14,437
	5 or 6 semesters	1967-68	488	92	6,277	507	91	8,777	499	92	15,054
		1968-69	490	93	7,373	511	91	10,185	502	92	17,558
	7 or 8 semesters	1967-68	550	98	3,306	563	94	6,475	559	96	9,781
		1968-69	554	98	3,974	569	92	7,500	564	95	11,474
	All candidates	1967-68	501	128	21,542	518	117	29,859	511	122	51,401
		1968-69	501	125	24,889	522	115	34,119	513	120	59,008

Table 4.13

*Mean differences in Achievement Test scores in foreign languages
earned by candidates with different amounts of language study, 1967-68 and 1968-69*

(Based on data given in Table 4.12)

| Achievement Test | Testing year | MEAN DIFFERENCES | | | |
| | | "5 or 6 semesters" minus "3 or 4 semesters" | | "7 or 8 semesters" minus "5 or 6 semesters" | |
		Juniors	Seniors	Juniors	Seniors
French	1967-68	70	63	33	79
	1968-69	77	60	41	75
German	1967-68	61	72	46	63
	1968-69	59	69	53	56
Latin	1967-68	71	74	27	62
	1968-69	72	74	31	64
Spanish	1967-68	68	65	46	75
	1968-69	77	64	51	77

Table 4.17 shows the proportion of scores for each Achievement Test. Tests that had a fairly consistent upward trend during the period surveyed included German (from 0.8 percent in 1956-57 to 1.4 percent in 1968-69), Biology (from 3.4 percent in 1956-57 to 4.6 percent in 1968-69), and Intermediate Mathematics (from 14.6 percent in 1956-57 to 20.8 percent in 1963-64, the last year in which it was given). Fairly consistent downward trends occurred for Chemistry (from 8.5 percent in 1956-57 to 6.8 percent in 1961-62 and 4.6 percent in 1968-69) and Physics (from 7.1 percent in 1956-57 to 3.9 percent in 1961-62 and 2.0 percent in 1968-69). Some of the irregular variations are worthy of note. Social Studies declined from 11.8 percent in 1956-57 to 9.8 percent in 1961-62. Its successor test, American History and Social Studies, accounted for 10.4 percent of the scores in its first year, 1962-63 (and the newly introduced European History and World Cultures Test accounted for 0.9 percent of the scores that year). Latin increased from 2.0 percent to 2.4 percent between 1956-57 and 1961-62; since then, however, it has declined to 1.2 percent in 1968-69. French declined from 6.9 percent to 6.2 percent in the first three years and then gradually increased to 7.6 percent in 1968-69.

There has also been a shift in the academic level of students taking Achievement Tests at various administrations. As shown in Table 4.18, candidates attending an Achievement Test administration during their junior year accounted for 19.9 percent of Achievement Test candidate volume in 1956-57 and 26.1 percent in 1968-69. In 1956-57, the March administration accounted for 62.3 percent of the total candidate volume, but in 1968-69, the December and January administrations combined accounted for 50.2 percent of the volume, with March reduced to only 8.5 percent of the total. Clearly, candidates are taking the tests earlier in their academic careers now then they did in 1956-57. A considerable portion of the shift from March to December and January occurred in 1961-62, when Achievement Tests were offered at the regular January administration for the first time since the 1955-56 testing year.

Table 4.19 shows the mean and standard deviations of scores earned by substantially all candidates taking each Achievement Test for each testing year (November to July or August) from 1956-57 to 1968-69. There is a certain amount of year-to-year fluctuation in mean scores. (About half of the year-to-year changes are more than five scaled score points, and about one-seventh are more than 10 scaled score points.) Standard deviations also vary from year to year; about two-fifths of the changes are more than two scaled score points, and about one-seventh are more than four scaled score points. It should be mentioned that in addition to the usual sources of fluctuation—changes in the group choosing the test and random errors arising in score equating—some of the fluctuations in these data result from the fact that Achievement Test scores beginning in December 1964 have been adjusted to take account of current data on SAT performance of candidates taking the various tests, as described in Chapter III. This procedure, which was recommended by Professor S. S. Wilks, is designed to enhance the comparability of scores from one Achievement Test to another.

Some evidence of an upward trend in scores is apparent for Chemistry and Physics. Social Studies scores also

(Continued on page 109)

Table 4.14

Means, standard deviations, and numbers of scores on Achievement Tests in mathematics, classified by test and by candidate's sex, educational level, and number of semesters of study of secondary school mathematics, 1967-68 and 1968-69

Educational level	Semesters of study	Testing year	BOYS			GIRLS			TOTAL*		
			Mean	*SD*	*N*	*Mean*	*SD*	*N*	*Mean*	*SD*	*N*
						Mathematics Level I					
Juniors	Fewer than 6 semesters	1967-68	530	99	7,219	496	90	4,617	517	97	11,836
		1968-69	531	89	7,128	501	81	5,266	518	87	12,394
	6 semesters	1967-68	573	97	26,270	542	88	22,004	559	95	48,274
		1968-69	572	89	27,220	541	81	23,425	558	87	50,646
	7 or 8 semesters	1967-68	635	104	10,519	608	98	6,491	625	103	17,010
		1968-69	630	95	10,582	603	88	6,776	620	93	17,358
	More than 8 semesters	1967-68	585	118	1,398	545	110	575	574	117	1,923
		1968-69	592	107	1,435	543	103	607	578	108	2,042
	All juniors	1967-68	576	106	50,559	545	97	36,222	563	103	86,781
		1968-69	574	97	52,035	543	89	39,034	561	95	91,070
Seniors	Fewer than 6 semesters	1967-68	458	80	11,037	436	68	12,143	447	75	23,180
		1968-69	452	80	11,168	430	68	12,411	441	75	23,579
	6 semesters	1967-68	504	86	25,552	484	74	22,920	495	81	48,473
		1968-69	499	86	26,456	477	73	25,457	489	81	51,913
	7 or 8 semesters	1967-68	571	91	89,047	553	87	41,210	565	90	130,257
		1968-69	563	89	88,949	543	84	43,939	557	88	132,888
	More than 8 semesters	1967-68	616	98	11,512	601	96	4,409	612	97	15,921
		1968-69	607	97	11,736	588	94	4,862	601	96	16,598
	All seniors	1967-68	549	100	150,047	516	95	85,864	537	100	235,913
		1968-69	542	98	149,839	508	92	91,588	529	98	241,427
All grades	Fewer than 6 semesters	1967-68	488	96	19,745	453	80	17,545	471	91	37,290
		1968-69	483	93	19,764	451	79	18,565	468	88	38,329
	6 semesters	1967-68	539	99	53,786	513	87	45,872	527	94	99,659
		1968-69	536	95	55,673	508	84	49,879	523	91	105,553
	7 or 8 semesters	1967-68	577	95	102,631	560	91	48,193	572	94	150,825
		1968-69	570	92	102,454	551	88	51,280	564	91	153,734
	More than 8 semesters	1967-68	613	101	14,306	593	100	5,146	608	101	19,452
		1968-69	605	98	14,517	582	96	5,619	598	98	20,136
	All candidates	1967-68	556	103	210,349	524	97	124,885	544	102	335,238
		1968-69	550	100	211,232	518	93	133,649	538	99	344,883

*Includes candidates who did not indicate sex.

Table 4.14 (continued)

Educational level	Semesters of study	Testing year	BOYS			GIRLS			TOTAL*		
			Mean	SD	N	Mean	SD	N	Mean	SD	N
			Mathematics Level II								
Juniors	7 or 8 semesters	1967-68	717	70	1,912	686	67	634	709	71	2,546
		1968-69	719	77	2,081	686	78	630	712	78	2,711
	More than 8 semesters	1967-68	732	76	227	698	93	29	728	79	256
		1968-69	722	96	258	695	71	27	720	94	285
	All juniors	1967-68	700	86	3,785	673	85	1,071	694	87	4,856
		1968-69	697	95	4,239	668	94	1,055	691	96	5,294
Seniors	7 or 8 semesters	1967-68	670	91	9,798	649	87	2,029	667	91	11,828
		1968-69	660	94	10,889	639	90	2,440	656	93	13,329
	More than 8 semesters	1967-68	713	73	4,956	697	69	1,229	710	72	6,185
		1968-69	711	75	5,259	691	75	1,349	707	76	6,608
	All seniors	1967-68	676	93	16,884	654	95	3,685	672	94	20,571
		1968-69	668	97	18,536	647	96	4,214	664	97	22,750
All grades	7 or 8 semesters	1967-68	677	90	12,142	658	85	2,698	674	89	14,841
		1968-69	668	94	13,396	649	90	3,101	665	93	16,497
	More than 8 semesters	1967-68	712	74	5,500	697	70	1,279	709	73	6,779
		1968-69	709	78	5,813	690	75	1,391	706	77	7,205
	All candidates	1967-68	679	93	21,927	658	94	4,857	675	93	26,786
		1968-69	672	98	24,110	651	96	5,380	668	98	29,491

*Includes candidates who did not indicate sex.

show an upward trend; American History and Social Studies means have tended to decrease. Latin means moved upward until 1962-63; since then, they have shown a decline. German has shown an upward trend over most of the period, with the last four years noticeably higher. Advanced Mathematics showed noticeably higher scores in the last three years that it was offered; in part, this shift arose from a change in the method of relating the score scales on the two mathematics tests to each other.

Summary

Descriptive statistics based on appropriate student groups are useful in intrepreting scores for individual students, in comparing groups, and in observing trends. The latter uses gain in importance from the care with which the tests are developed and the wide scope of the program. The equating of scores on all forms of a particular test facilitates the preparation of statistics. Unfortunately, however, the extensive data obtained in program operations are difficult to interpret because the candidate group is self-selected.

Examination of data on candidates tested during the 13-year period 1956-57 through 1968-69 shows a huge increase in the numbers of candidates along with surprisingly small changes in the means and standard deviations of test scores. Thus, the number of SATs administered was almost six times as great in 1968-69 as in 1956-57, but the mean scores differed by eleven scaled score points for SAT-verbal and five scaled score points for SAT-mathematical for the two years. The Achievement Tests, on the whole, showed a similar pattern: growth in numbers with fairly small changes in mean scores. Even the patterns of choice among the various Achievement Tests, except for some decrease in the proportion of all scores earned on the science tests, were remarkably stable. Presumably, the general stability of the results arises because the various factors that are affecting performance are offsetting each other. It is possible that the tendency toward lower scores that would be expected as the group is broadened is offset by a generally

(Text continued on page 115, Tables and Figures continued on following pages)

Table 4.15

Mean differences in Mathematics Level I Achievement Test scores earned by
candidates with different amounts of mathematics study, 1967-68 and 1968-69

(Based on data given in Table 4.14)

Interval	Testing year	MEAN DIFFERENCES	
		Juniors	Seniors
"6 semesters" minus	1967-68	42	48
"less than 6 semesters"	1968-69	40	48
"7 or 8 semesters" minus	1967-68	66	70
"6 semesters"	1968-69	62	68
"More than 8 semesters" minus	1967-68	—51	47
"7 or 8 semesters"	1968-69	—42	44

Table 4.16

Percentages of Achievement Tests administered in
five subject-matter categories, by year,
1956-57 through 1968-69

Testing year	PERCENT					Total number of tests (base for percents)
	English	History and Social Studies	Foreign Languages	Sciences	Mathematics	
1956-57	33.1	11.8	12.5	19.0	23.5	236,708
1957-58	33.6	11.1	11.9	18.5	24.8	303,254
1958-59	33.9	11.0	11.8	17.9	25.4	373,726
1959-60	34.6	11.2	12.0	16.9	25.3	469,721
1960-61	34.1	10.4	12.5	15.9	27.0	578,679
1961-62	34.2	9.8	13.2	14.5	28.3	708,089
1962-63	33.7	11.3	12.7	14.0	28.2	821,181
1963-64	33.5	11.5	13.1	13.5	28.4	1,023,414
1964-65	34.6	11.9	13.5	12.4	27.6	1,163,240
1965-66	34.6	11.3	13.9	12.5	27.8	1,181,333
1966-67	34.8	11.2	14.0	12.1	28.0	1,229,203
1967-68	35.1	11.3	14.2	12.0	27.4	1,323,643
1968-69	36.1	10.7	14.7	11.3	27.3	1,373,650

Figure 4.4

Percentage of Achievement Tests administered in five subject-matter categories, 1956-57 through 1968-69

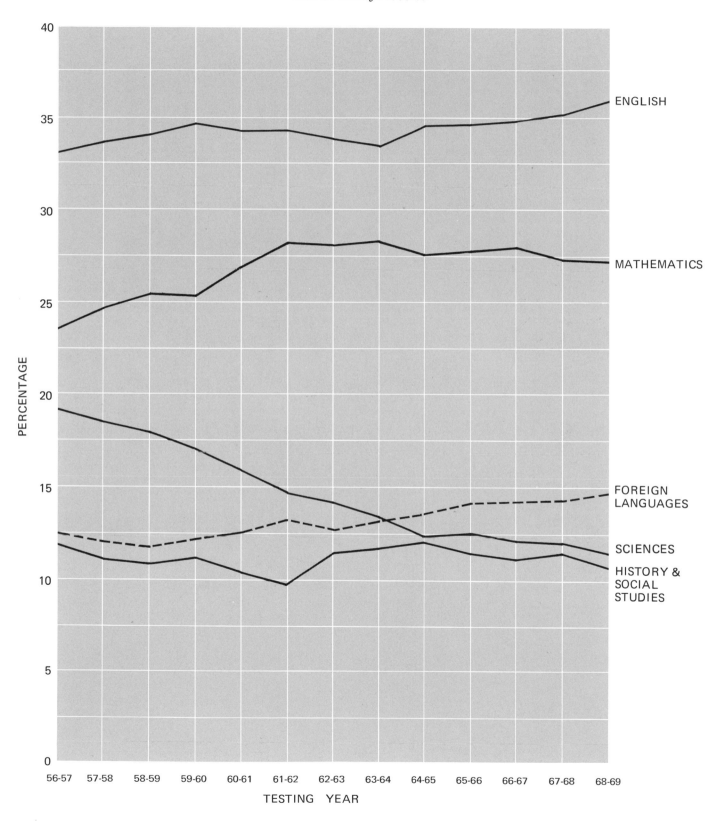

Table 4.17

Volumes for specific Achievement Tests expressed as percentages of
total Achievement Test volumes, by year, 1956-57 through 1968-69

Achievement Test	PERCENT												
	1956-57	1957-58	1958-59	1959-60	1960-61	1961-62	1962-63	1963-64	1964-65	1965-66	1966-67	1967-68	1968-69
English Composition	33.1	33.6	33.9	34.6	34.1	34.2	33.7	33.5	34.6	34.6	34.8	34.4	34.5
Literature	---	---	---	---	---	---	---	---	---	---	---	0.6	1.6
Social Studies	11.8	11.1	11.0	11.2	10.4	9.8	---	---	---	---	---	---	---
American History and Social Studies	---	---	---	---	---	---	10.4	10.6	11.1	10.5	10.3	10.5	9.9
European History and World Cultures	---	---	---	---	---	---	0.9	0.9	0.8	0.8	0.9	0.8	0.8
French	6.9	6.5	6.2	6.2	6.3	6.7	6.5	6.8	7.0	7.3	7.3	7.4	7.6
German	0.8	0.8	0.9	1.0	1.1	1.1	1.0	1.1	1.2	1.3	1.3	1.4	1.4
Hebrew	---	---	---	---	0.1	0.1	0.1	0.1	0.1	0.1	0.1	0.1	0.1
Latin	2.0	2.0	2.1	2.1	2.3	2.4	2.2	2.1	1.9	1.7	1.6	1.4	1.2
Russian	---	---	---	---	0.1	0.1	0.1	0.1	0.1	0.1	0.1	0.1	0.1
Spanish	2.9	2.6	2.5	2.6	2.6	2.8	2.7	2.9	3.2	3.3	3.6	3.9	4.3
Biology	3.4	3.6	3.8	3.7	3.6	3.8	4.0	4.2	4.2	4.4	4.4	4.7	4.6
Chemistry	8.5	8.2	7.9	7.2	7.0	6.8	6.5	6.4	5.7	5.7	5.4	5.2	4.6
Physics	7.1	6.7	5.8	5.5	4.8	3.9	3.3	3.0	2.5	2.4	2.3	2.2	2.0
pssc Physics	---	---	0.4	0.5	0.6	0.1	0.2	---	---	---	---	---	---
Intermediate Mathematics	14.6	16.0	16.8	16.1	18.5	20.9	20.8	20.8	---	---	---	---	---
Advanced Mathematics	8.9	8.8	8.7	9.2	8.6	7.4	7.5	7.6	---	---	---	---	---
Mathematics Level I	---	---	---	---	---	---	---	---	25.9	26.3	26.0	25.3	25.1
Mathematics Level II	---	---	---	---	---	---	---	---	1.6	1.5	1.9	2.0	2.1
Total Number of Tests (base for percents)	236,708	303,254	373,726	469,721	578,679	708,089	821,181	1,023,414	1,163,240	1,181,333	1,229,203	1,323,643	1,373,650

Table 4.18

Attendance at Achievement Test sessions, classified by
candidate's educational level, 1956-57 and 1968-69

Candidate group	1956-57		1968-69	
	Number	Percent	Number	Percent
Juniors	17,708	19.9	157,482	26.1
Seniors tested in:				
December	4,993	5.6	171,085	28.4
January	......	......	131,276	21.8
March	55,308	62.3	51,515	8.5
May	4,406	5.0	43,208	7.2
July	......	......	12,822	2.1
August	1,133	1.3	......	......
(Total seniors)	65,840	74.1	409,906	68.0
All others	5,283	5.9	35,609	5.9
Total Attendance (base for percents)	88,831	......	602,997	......

Table 4.19

Means, standard deviations, and numbers of cases* (in thousands) for all candidates taking
Achievement Tests, by year, 1956-57 through 1968-69

Testing year	ENGLISH COMPOSITION			LITERATURE			SOCIAL STUDIES			AMERICAN HISTORY AND SOCIAL STUDIES			EUROPEAN HISTORY AND WORLD CULTURES		
	Mean	SD	N	Mean	SD	N	Mean	SD	N	Mean	SD	N	Mean	SD	N
1956-57	518	110	78.4	......	......	......	513	108	28.0	......	......	......	......	......	......
1957-58	523	104	102.0	......	......	......	522	112	33.8	......	......	......	......	......	......
1958-59	536	111	126.7	......	......	......	526	110	41.3	......	......	......	......	......	......
1959-60	526	107	162.6	......	......	......	527	108	52.6	......	......	......	......	......	......
1960-61	518	106	197.5	......	......	......	529	109	60.4	......	......	......	......	......	......
1961-62	518	106	242.4	......	......	......	530	109	69.5	......	......	......	......	......	......
1962-63	513	106	276.8	......	......	......	......	......	......	530	110	85.4	532	106	7.8
1963-64	512	105	342.9	......	......	......	......	......	......	522	108	108.8	528	102	8.9
1964-65	521	105	403.0	......	......	......	......	......	......	517	109	128.7	537	105	9.6
1965-66	516	105	408.5	......	......	......	......	......	......	512	110	124.3	539	107	9.1
1966-67	514	104	427.3	......	......	......	......	......	......	500	111	126.2	530	105	11.0
1967-68	514	106	455.9	526	110	8.6	......	......	......	497	107	138.4	534	109	10.7
1968-69	514	106	473.8	522	112	22.2	......	......	......	494	106	135.9	522	109	10.7

*The term "case" is used here to denote the taking of a specific Achievement Test. Thus, if a candidate took the same Achievement Test at two administrations, he is counted as two cases.

(*Table 4.19 continued on page 114*)

Table 4.19 (continued)

Testing year	FRENCH			GERMAN			HEBREW			LATIN			RUSSIAN		
	Mean	SD	N	Mean	SD	N	Mean	SD	N	Mean	SD	N	Mean	SD	N
1956-57	511	113	16.2	493	105	1.8	......	......	....	537	100	4.7	......	......	....
1957-58	499	111	19.8	485	107	2.6	......	......	....	538	96	6.1	......	......	....
1958-59	502	109	23.3	485	103	3.3	......	......	....	536	95	7.8	......	......	....
1959-60	509	111	29.3	489	107	4.6	......	......	....	543	93	10.0	......	......	....
1960-61	499	110	36.5	490	105	6.1	535	105	.6	548	96	13.6	532	126	.4
1961-62	502	110	47.4	492	102	7.9	582	99	.6	544	94	17.1	536	122	.5
1962-63	508	107	53.5	498	104	8.6	579	101	.7	555	94	17.9	532	116	.8
1963-64	502	104	69.7	492	105	11.5	586	92	.8	553	93	21.0	539	120	1.1
1964-65	515	106	81.4	499	111	14.1	588	100	1.0	543	99	22.3	530	122	1.4
1965-66	519	110	86.6	515	112	14.8	581	97	.8	537	100	20.7	545	132	1.3
1966-67	522	109	90.1	519	114	15.9	592	98	1.0	535	100	19.6	538	133	1.2
1967-68	535	108	98.2	524	114	18.1	586	98	1.1	531	102	18.5	536	130	1.4
1968-69	525	107	105.0	518	109	18.8	570	99	1.2	526	102	15.9	532	133	1.3

Testing year	SPANISH			BIOLOGY			CHEMISTRY			PHYSICS			PSSC PHYSICS		
	Mean	SD	N	Mean	SD	N	Mean	SD	N	Mean	SD	N	Mean	SD	N
1956-57	487	119	6.8	493	107	8.1	528	106	20.2	534	98	16.8	......	......	....
1957-58	494	120	7.7	509	111	10.8	534	104	24.8	530	96	20.3	......	......	....
1958-59	501	122	9.5	510	108	14.1	545	104	29.6	543	96	21.6	552	84	1.4
1959-60	497	123	12.3	510	111	17.4	538	107	33.9	546	98	25.9	549	79	2.2
1960-61	510	122	15.1	507	106	20.7	548	104	40.4	536	93	27.6	557	81	3.2
1961-62	512	130	19.8	510	109	26.7	545	104	47.9	542	97	27.3	557	84	.8
1962-63	511	122	22.6	515	109	33.1	546	104	53.7	548	91	26.9	544	76	1.5
1963-64	502	118	29.6	516	110	43.2	541	104	65.1	549	90	30.3	......	......	....
1964-65	499	118	36.8	515	111	48.9	554	102	66.1	567	97	29.5	......	......	....
1965-66	509	123	39.5	520	110	51.7	553	105	67.7	583	99	28.3	......	......	....
1966-67	508	123	44.0	516	110	54.0	564	106	66.7	582	99	28.4	......	......	....
1967-68	511	122	51.4	513	112	62.0	565	105	68.4	579	102	29.1	......	......	....
1968-69	513	120	59.0	514	113	63.6	561	109	63.7	587	106	28.1	......	......	....

Testing year	INTERMEDIATE MATHEMATICS			ADVANCED MATHEMATICS			MATHEMATICS LEVEL I			MATHEMATICS LEVEL II		
	Mean	SD	N	Mean	SD	N	Mean	SD	N	Mean	SD	N
1956-57	524	99	34.5	600	98	21.0	......	......	....	......	......	....
1957-58	526	100	48.7	606	100	26.7	......	......	....	......	......	....
1958-59	532	101	62.6	601	93	32.4	......			......	......	....
1959-60	532	98	75.9	601	97	43.1	......			......	......	....
1960-61	523	97	106.8	603	96	49.6	......			......	......	....
1961-62	526	100	148.1	616	97	52.2	......	......	....	......	......	....
1962-63	519	96	170.7	613	93	61.3	......	......	....	......	......	....
1963-64	517	98	213.0	624	95	77.4	......	......	....	......	......	....
1964-65	......	......	....	......	......	....	536	105	301.4	671	89	19.2
1965-66	......	......	....	......	......	....	540	103	310.3	686	92	17.8
1966-67	......	......	....	......	......	....	542	102	320.1	683	95	23.7
1967-68	......	......	....	......	......	....	544	102	335.2	675	93	26.8
1968-69	......	......	....	......	......	....	538	99	344.9	668	98	29.5

rising level of teaching and academic interest. This interpretation is, however, entirely conjectural; it is possible that the explanation of the observed results is quite different.

A norms and follow-up study of the SAT, initiated in 1960, has provided data that are relatively free of the problems of self-selection by candidates, although only about three-fourths of the schools invited to participate chose to do so. These results show a reasonable progression in the means of SAT scores earned in the last year of high school for students who attained successive educational levels through the end of the first year of college. Comparison of current College Board candidate means with results of the 1960 norms study suggests that the average College Board candidate (in contrast to the average entrant to College Board member colleges) does not differ very much in ability from the average student who entered college in the year after his graduation from high school.

Descriptive statistics on applicants and entrants to specific colleges, provided by many colleges in the various editions of the *Manual of Freshman Class Profiles* and now in *The College Handbook*, constitute an important aid to college guidance and also yield useful information about trends in ability levels of applicants and enrolled students. It may safely be said that during the 1960s there was a perceptible upward trend in these statistics. The shifts were sufficiently great to support the desirability of keeping information about these matters reasonably current.

REFERENCES

Chandler, Marjorie, and Schrader, W. B., *Preliminary Scholastic Aptitude Test: 1960 National Norms.* Statistical Report 66-3. Princeton, N.J.: Educational Testing Service, 1966.

College Entrance Examination Board, *Bulletin of Information for College Board Admissions Tests, 1969-70.* New York: College Extrance Examination Board, 1969.

College Entrance Examination Board, *A Description of the College Board Achievement Tests, 1967-68.* New York: College Entrance Examination Board, 1967.

Flanagan, J. C., and Cooley, W. W., *Project TALENT One-year Follow-up Studies.* Cooperative Research Project Number 2333. Pittsburgh: University of Pittsburgh, 1966.

Hills, J. R., "Diversity and the Effect of Selective Admissions." *Journal of Educational Measurement,* 1966, 3, pp. 235-242.

Levine, R. S., and Angoff, W. H., *The Effects of Practice and Growth on Scores on the Scholastic Aptitude Test.* College Entrance Examination Board Research and Development Report 58-6 and Statistical Report 58-6. Princeton, N.J.: Educational Testing Service, 1958.

Pitcher, Barbara, *Repeater Patterns, College Choices, and SAT Scores of College Board Candidates Tested in 1957-59.* Statistical Report 60-22. Princeton, N.J.: Educational Testing Service, 1960.

Pitcher, Barbara, *Test-taking Patterns of College Board Candidates Tested in 1962-64. Statistical Report 66-72.* Princeton, N.J.: Educational Testing Service, 1966.

Pitcher, Barbara, *Follow-up Study of a National Sample of High School Seniors: Ability Level of Students Who Entered College Directly from High School and Were Graduated from College within Four Years.* College Entrance Examination Board Research and Development Report 68-69, No. 1, and Statistical Report 68-88. Princeton, N.J.: Educational Testing Service, 1968.

Seibel, D. W., *Follow-up Study of a National Sample of High School Seniors: Phase 2—One Year After Graduation.* College Entrance Examination Board Research and Development Report 65-6, No. 1, and Statistical Report 65-62. Princeton, N.J.: Educational Testing Service, 1965. (a)

Seibel, D. W., *A Study of the Academic Ability and Performance of Junior College Students.* EAS Field Studies Report 1. Princeton, N.J.: Educational Testing Service, 1965. (b)

U. S. Department of Health, Education and Welfare, Office of Education, *Digest of Educational Statistics, 1962.* Washington, D.C.: U. S. Department of Health, Education and Welfare, 1962.

U. S. Department of Health, Education and Welfare, Office of Education, *Digest of Educational Statistics, 1965 Edition.* Washington, D.C.: U. S. Department of Health, Education and Welfare, 1965.

Walberg, H. J., and others, *Scholastic Aptitude Stability of Applicants and Freshman Classes in Selected American Colleges.* Research Memorandum 66-24. Princeton, N.J.: Educational Testing Service, 1966.

CHAPTER V

The Predictive Validity of College Board Admissions Tests

W. B. SCHRADER

Introduction

The validation of College Board tests has been an ever-present, driving concern for 43 years as of this writing. An enormous amount of time and energy has gone into conducting studies of this kind, and these efforts have succeeded in establishing validity coefficients which have made it possible for many to use the tests with confidence.

This chapter will cover the role of predictive validity in the development and use of College Board tests, the design of conventional regression studies, the design of validity studies for special purposes, interpreting validity coefficients as a measure of predictive value, and evidence on the predictive validity of the SAT and of the Achievement Tests. Throughout the chapter, emphasis is placed on the use of high school grade-point average or rank-in-class along with the test scores in making predictions.

The role of predictive validity in the development and use of College Board tests*

The first validity studies of the Scholastic Aptitude Test (SAT) were made as soon as the students tested in 1926 earned the necessary college grades. Brigham (1932) describes studies made in 1927 of nine student groups in six colleges. Validity coefficients of the SAT ranged from .14 to .46, with a median of .34. School average (or rank-in-class) had validities ranging from .39 to .61, with a median of .52. Multiple correlation coefficients for SAT in combination with school average or rank ranged from .42 to .65 with a median of .55. The early studies of validity were oriented toward the main goals that have motivated the countless studies that followed: to evaluate the predictive value of the various measures, to find how scores may best be combined with other information to make specific predictions for each student, and to develop empirical evidence concerning the effects on validity of proposed changes in the tests administered in a testing program.

From 1927 to 1964, most validity studies of College Board tests were made by the colleges. A number of studies, however, were made by the College Board, usually to throw light on some decision about the testing program. In the late 1950s, an important stimulus to validity studies was provided by the validity seminars. At these seminars, persons concerned with admission in a number of colleges met together for a few days and each made his own validity study following a standard plan. More recently, summer institutes in admission have included a validity study for each participating college. In 1964, the initiation of the College Board Validity Study Service relieved participating colleges of the tedious task of data analysis and offered aid through the Board's regional offices in planning the studies and interpreting the results.

As evidence accumulated that the tests were almost invariably effective in predicting academic success, primary interest shifted to the question of how different kinds of data about a student could best be combined for predicting subsequent performance. Indeed, regression equations are more important in contributing to effective use of scores by colleges than are the traditional validity coefficients. The coefficients are useful, at present, primarily for comparing and summarizing results for a number of colleges. Fortunately, these coefficients are readily obtainable as a by-product of the regression study. The importance of current information on validity was stressed by Chauncey (1962) in *The Story of the College Board Scholastic Aptitude Test*. He wrote:

> The task of keeping up-to-date on the relationship of the SAT to performance in college is a never-ending one, as the composition of successive classes changes and as the objectives of college instruction are modified.

Two main topics will be discussed in this chapter: (a) the design and interpretation of validity studies, giving primary attention to the so-called routine studies designed to determine the relative contribution of accepted predictors to one or more criteria; and (b) a survey of the main statistical outcomes of a large number of recent studies, including studies from the College Board Validity Study Service during the first two years (1964-66) and from the 1965 and 1966 seminars conducted by the College Board for admissions officers. The sections on

---

*Acknowledgment is due to Dr. Marjorie O. Chandler for extensive assistance in surveying validity study results.

design and interpretation are mainly based upon well-established statistical methods. To a lesser extent, they involve judgments based upon administrative considerations and on the characteristics of colleges. They are developed in this chapter because they have a direct bearing on the interpretation of the empirical findings of current validity studies. (Readers who are familiar with the methodology of validity studies may wish to skip pages 118-122, except perhaps for the discussion of criterion development on pages 118-119.)

Designing conventional regression studies

Designing a validity study of College Board tests requires that a number of choices be made. Decisions are needed with respect to groups of students, predictors, criteria, statistical analysis methods, and ways of presenting and interpreting results. Each decision should be governed by the purposes of the study and should take account of the characteristics of the college making the study, practical considerations of needed precision and scope in relation to cost and effort, and statistical principles affecting the interpretability of the results. Making the necessary decisions can be greatly facilitated by guidelines and rules-of-thumb when, as is often the case, the study is concerned with how best to combine a defined set of predictors in order to predict an accepted criterion of overall academic success. It is with this kind of study that the present discussion will be mainly concerned. Some attention will be given, however, to special problems in designing studies for other purposes.

Choice of criterion — The criterion is the center on which all other aspects of a validity study focus. To the extent that the criterion is judged to differ from the hypothetical "best" measure of success in a college, the value of the results of the validity study will be correspondingly reduced.

The development of the criterion specifically for the validity study could be a profitable, if arduous, venture on the part of a college. Most colleges in the United States, however, take advantage of the fact that their faculty members award grades to each student at the end of each course. These grades play an important part in awarding honors and in determining academic probation and dismissal. Most colleges have some form of average grade, computed according to a definite set of rules established over the years. Since the pattern of courses that enter into the average is also determined within a framework set by college rules affecting a student's choice of courses, the average grade embodies in a realistic way the uniformity and variation of student programs. When a college has an "official" academic average, this number is highly meaningful to administration, faculty, and students, and it is readily available. Psychologists might prefer some other way of combining the basic grade data into a slightly different average, but their procedure would entail a corresponding loss of realism. The virtues of average grades determined by the college's own system, along with the fact that these grades are predictable at a respectable level, have made them an exceedingly popular choice as the criterion for validity studies.

When academic average grade is taken as the criterion, there is the further question of choosing among first-term grades, first-year grades, lower-division cumulative average, four-year cumulative average, and various other possible grade averages. First-term average is opposed on the grounds that too many students perform erratically during the first term. At the other extreme, the four-year average, which has the advantage of being based on the student's entire undergraduate program, is seldom used. Where many students drop out, the four-year group may be a seriously biased sample of entering students. Moreover, the use of four-year criterion data requires a four- or five-year wait before making the study, and thus may delay unduly the introduction of needed changes. Because of the methodological importance of a possible systematic difference in results between four-year averages and averages available earlier, French (1958), and Hills, Bush, and Klock (1964) compared results of four-year with first-year averages, and Olsen and Schrader (1959) compared four-year with two-year averages. Each study included a number of colleges. All agreed that no systematic difference in the level of validity coefficients was discernible. Their findings offer definite support for the practice of using first-year (or two-year) average as the criterion measure.

From the college's viewpoint, the most serious flaw in academic grades as a criterion is the fact that they tend to emphasize the "grade-getting" aspect of a college career to the exclusion of other evidences of a student's success. This fundamental limitation in grades as a criterion strongly reinforces the need to use the calculated predictions *along with other information* about the student in making admissions or guidance decisions. Negative results for a particular predictor must be evaluated in terms of possible limitations of the criterion itself. With respect to this issue three positions may be identified:

1. College grades approximate the "ideal" criterion sufficiently well to justify taking empirical validity results at face value.

2. College grades are too narrow to represent all important aspects of college success. Validity study results and individual predictions based on them must be viewed with appropriate skepticism, and decisions based on them must take account of their limitations.

3. The college needs to develop its own criterion, or criteria, of college success for use in its prediction studies.

A college that adopted the third position would have to face up to a number of difficult problems in defining college success, especially if it tackled the problem of college success in relation to life success. In addition to the broad judgmental and philosophical issues to be resolved, considerable effort would be needed to obtain suitable measures of the qualities considered important.

If the type of multiple regression analysis used in conventional prediction studies is to be used, an overall measure of success could be defined. However, a college could also study different aspects of success separately and obtain separate prediction equations for each criterion. Efforts by a college to clarify its conceptions of college success, whether modest or elaborate, should substantially increase the value of its prediction studies.

An example of a well-conceived effort to develop a broader criterion is the work done by Anastasi, Meade, and Schneiders (1960) for use in the development of a biographical inventory. Evidence about each student was compiled from the following sources:

1. Faculty ratings on six personal characteristics (poise and self-confidence, social adjustment, initiative, maturity, leadership, and emotional control)
2. Reports by faculty advisors
3. Reserve Officer Training Corps records
4. Honors Program records
5. Student Government records of extracurricular activities
6. Extracurricular honor society membership lists
7. Office of Psychological Services records
8. Dean of Men records
9. Academic records

All of these data were drawn from existing college records. Using a carefully worked out set of standards, three groups defined as "positive", "average", and "negative" were identified. Final selection of the 50 students included in each group was made by the Dean of Men, a faculty member, and the Director of the Office of Psychological Services. This study demonstrates the possibility of defining meaningful criterion groups to reflect the broader aims of the college for use in evaluating the effectiveness of possible predictors.

Another significant effort to broaden the criterion is described by Davis (1965). This relatively large-scale study was done with the cooperation of eight well-known colleges.* It began with the identification of characteristics that faculty members regarded as significant and observable. Then faculty members were asked to observe selected students during the final term of the 1961-62 academic year and to rate those students with respect to some 80 characteristics at the end of the term. In all, 407 faculty members rated 398 students. Of the students rated, 305 were upperclassmen. Most students were rated by two faculty members; the total sample of ratings numbered 698. The ability level of the group is indicated by an SAT-verbal mean of 602 and an SAT-mathematical mean of 663.

Davis analyzed his extensive data in a number of ways using factor-analytic techniques. In one particularly interesting study (Davis, 1964a), he identified some 16

---
*Amherst, California Institute of Technology, Cornell (College of Engineering), Dartmouth, Massachusetts Institute of Technology, Rensselaer Polytechnic Institute, Rutgers, and Stanford.

factors within the 80 rating variables. Table 5.1 shows, for 16 rating variables each of which loaded highest on one of the 16 factors, the correlation of the rating with first-year grade-point average and with general desirability. General desirability was an overall evaluation of the extent to which a student was "the kind of student this institution should (or should not) admit." The ratings have been arranged according to the size of their correlations with the general desirability rating. The four ratings that yield the highest correlation coefficients with general desirability also yield relatively high correlations with college grades. The finding that ratings reflecting intellectual quickness, intellectual self-sufficiency and creativity, intellectual interest, and motivation to achieve are assigned a high desirability rating by faculty members in these colleges is not surprising. The fact that these ratings show higher correlation with grades than do the other ratings suggests that the use of college grades as a criterion has merit, although grades may not assign the same relative weight to each intellectual quality that faculty members do when judging general desirability. It may be added that the correlation of first-year grades with general desirability was .31.

Ratings for honesty, open-mindedness, pleasantness, and self-understanding show relatively high correlation coefficients with general desirability but relatively low coefficients with first-year average grades. It may be noted that these four qualities along with altruism have the highest relationship with general desirability when the effect of the rater's estimate of academic performance is removed statistically, as reported by Davis (1964b). The pattern that emerges from the brief summary of a large and complex study is that faculty members who value intellectual qualities highly believe that such qualities as honesty, open-mindedness, pleasantness, self-understanding, and altruism characterize the students whom they rate as high on general desirability. These findings deserve serious consideration in evaluating first-year average grades as a criterion for validity studies.

As admissions have become increasingly selective, the need for a broader approach to criterion development has become correspondingly greater. Clearly, studies that include both intellective and nonintellective measures of college success and both intellective and nonintellective predictors should be especially useful. Yet Fishman and Pasanella (1960) found that of 580 admission-selection studies made in the decade 1949-1959 only three could be classified in this category. The Anastasi and Davis studies show that better criteria can be developed. Much more needs to be done in criterion development, however, if validity studies are to make their full contribution to admission and guidance of college students.

Choice of groups—Choosing the *group* or *groups* to be studied is relatively easy when first-year average grades is the criterion measure. When feasible, it is desirable to divide the total freshman class into groups on the basis of academic program and of sex (e.g., men in liberal arts, women in liberal arts, engineering students). To the extent that the regression equations differ from group to group, the study gains in precision. It may also be useful,

Table 5.1*

Correlation coefficients of selected faculty ratings with
general desirability rating and with first-year grades

Rating	Name of factor	Correlation with general desirability rating	Correlation with first year grades
Originality	Self-sufficiency/Creativity	.57	.30
Intellectual quickness	Intellectual ability	.57	.39
Intellectual interest	Intellectual values	.51	.25
Motivation to achieve	Motivation	.48	.25
Honesty	Ethicality	.46	.13
Open-mindedness	Open-mindedness	.46	.14
Pleasantness	Likableness	.42	.07
Self-understanding	Self-insight	.41	.10
Social maturity	Maturity	.39	.08
Steady work	Dependability	.36	.17
Leadership among peers	Popularity	.33	.12
Concern for others' welfare	Altruism	.30	.01
Freedom from status-centeredness	Status-centeredness	.19	−.03
Extraversion	Extraversion	.09	−.01
Freedom from worry	Anxiety	.06	.02
Conformity	Conformity	−.12	−.11

*Abridged from Tables 3 and 4 of Davis (1964a).

in some colleges, to make further subdivisions of the class (e.g., residents versus commuters, public versus private secondary school graduates, in-state versus out-of-state students). The multiplication of groups, of course, may result in some that are relatively small, so that their regression equations are poorly determined. Consideration of the sampling errors of correlation coefficients suggests that about 100 students should be the minimum number for any validity study and that a proportionately larger sample is needed if many predictors are to be studied.

The proliferation of groups may also produce so many results as to lead to confusion in interpretation. A related question concerns the desirability of pooling data for two or three consecutive years. When conditions with respect to admissions, teaching, and grading are judged to be reasonably stable, the pooling of data enhances the dependability of results by increasing sample size, but it may also produce unexpected effects on the results. In practice, then, the decision as to groups depends mainly upon three considerations: (a) how many groups to study; (b) the size of the resulting groups; and (c) whether to pool data from two or three years. Because of the complications in defining groups, treatment of all students in a particular entering class as the group to be studied is often the most satisfactory decision.

A detailed question arises with respect to the elimina-tion of certain students from the study. Among groups so eliminated might be foreign students or students with a severe physical handicap. On the whole, the elimination of these students from the analysis may be considered justifiable if it is clear that the regression equation would not be used in determining the expected performance of similar students in the future. This kind of "purifying" of the group should be regarded as a possible refinement in technique rather than as an essential feature of good design. Any decision to exclude students should, of course, be made before the criterion data have been examined.

Choice of predictors — Predictors should usually include all measures that are available on substantially all members of the group and that are believed to have possible predictive value. Four special questions need to be considered, however, in planning this aspect of the study. First, it is particularly important to include some measure of high school record as a predictor, since many studies have shown that this measure consistently makes a substantial contribution to predictive effectiveness. (Indeed, high school average grades are usually a better predictor than the test scores.) Second, there is the possibility of administering tests or other instruments at the beginning of the freshman year. Especially where the main orientation of the study is toward guidance rather than admissions, the use of specially administered instruments may well justify the time and cost of broadening the study. Third, there is the possibility of quantifying existing admissions data by a process of rating or some other procedure so that their contribution to prediction may be assessed. Fourth, a difficult practical question sometimes arises when appreciable numbers of students lack data on one or more relevant predictors. Assuming that the usual practice of using only "complete-data" cases is followed, a conflict arises between including the predictors and thereby losing the students who lack data and excluding the predictors. The loss of the students not only reduces the size of the group but may seriously reduce its representativeness. In the College Board Validity Study Service, the rule-of-thumb employed is that not more than 5 percent of the students may lack data on any predictor and that 85 percent of the students must have complete data on all predictors. These rules facilitate decisions with respect to predictors having missing data.

Statistical analysis—In a traditional validity study, the main statistical analysis is the calculation of the multiple regression equations. Multiple regression is a procedure for determining weights for each predictor so that the standard deviation of the errors of prediction will be a minimum for the group studied. Because it has many applications, programs for computing it are widely available for data processing equipment. Multiple regression weights are commonly expressed in two different forms, each of which is useful for a particular purpose. One form (b-weights) gives the actual numbers that would be used in calculating predicted grades from predictor data expressed in their customary units. The other form (beta-weights) gives the weights that would be appropriate if each predictor were expressed in terms of standard scores having a mean of 0 and a standard deviation of 1 for the group studied. The standard-score regression weights, unlike the operational regression weights used in calculating predicted grades, are not affected by differences in the particular units in which the predictors are expressed. They provide, accordingly, a better indication of the weight that each predictor has in determining the predicted grades than do the operational weights, which are often useless for this purpose. The relative sizes of the standard-score regression weights for the various predictors offer useful information about the role that each predictor plays in determining the predicted grades.

Characteristically, regression analyses also yield correlation coefficients between each pair of variables. The coefficients relating each predictor to the criterion, of course, are the familiar single-predictor validity coefficients. Although validity coefficients are difficult to interpret, as will be discussed later in this chapter, they are often useful for evaluating predictors and for comparing results from one study to another.

Reporting the results—The presentation of results of a multiple regression analysis could be limited to the operational regression equation for each group studied. In practice, however, it is customary to provide information on the distribution of scores on each variable studied, the beta-weights and validity coefficients for each predictor, together with results of a significance test of each beta-weight, multiple correlation coefficients for selected combinations of predictors, and the intercorrelations of each variable with each other variable. To facilitate the use of the regression equation, computational aids may be developed so that predictions can be made by looking up predictor scores in a set of tables and simply adding the appropriate values. To aid in interpreting the predictions, an expectancy table showing the probability of equaling or excelling various actual grades for each predicted grade can readily be produced, assuming that errors of prediction are normally distributed. Table 5.2 illustrates one format for an expectancy table. Finally, it is possible, by calculating the predicted grade for each student in the study, to make a scatter diagram relating predicted to actual grades. Table 5.3 is an example of a computer-produced scatter diagram or experience table relating a weighted total of predictor scores to the criterion. The correlation between predicted and obtained grades is .62. All of the outputs listed in this paragraph are currently provided in studies made by the College Board Validity Study Service.

Interpreting the results — The most important consideration in interpretation of results of a multiple regression study is the possible inadequacy of the criterion. By the nature of the analysis, the results can be no better than the criterion measure used. Predictions calculated using the regression equation will tend to embody the limitations of the criterion. If college grades are the criterion data used in developing the equation, the resulting predictions need to be supplemented by other data about the student unless (a) the admissions officer and committee regard grades as a comprehensive measure of admissibility or (b) the college for some reason wishes to use an entirely objective decision procedure. A second consideration in interpreting regression results calls for a scrutiny of the beta-weights. It may turn out that the weights for one or more predictors seem quite unreasonable in the judgment of the college officers. When this happens, additional exploration of the question, including possibly a study based on a new sample, is called for. Occasionally one of the predictors will have a negative regression weight, even though a high score on that variable represents a desirable characteristic. A result of this kind may arise when some ability that is irrelevant to or even detrimental to success contributes to performance on one or more of the valid predictors. The variable that receives a negative weight can then increase predictive effectiveness by reducing the effect of this ability upon the predictions. When predictions are made for use in admissions, however, there is a serious question as to the propriety of allowing a *poor* performance on any predictor to *increase* a candidate's predicted grade. Fortunately, when negative standard-score regression weights do arise in College Board validity studies, they are usually quite small. In this case, the best solution is to recompute the equation, excluding the predictor with the negative regression weight.

A conventional regression study usually yields validity coefficients for each predictor. The interpretation of these coefficients will be discussed in some detail later in this chapter.

Designing validity studies for special purposes

Many validity studies fit readily into the conventional regression analysis design just described. Certain important types of problems, however, require significant additional planning. For example, some of the studies reported in Chapter VI deal with possible changes in the tests themselves. Such studies, in general, must be planned in detail in terms of their specific objectives with special attention to making the design as realistic as possible. Among the many other purposes that might be identified, two will be discussed here. First, how should a validity study be designed to aid in choosing between alternative predictors or sets of predictors? Second, how should tests be validated for use in placement?

Comparison of alternative predictors — A college may wish to compare high school average with high school rank-in-class for admissions use. Or it may wish to compare SAT with a test offered in a different testing program or with a locally administered test (see Duggan, 1962). In studies of this type, of course, the alternatives differ in a number of respects besides validity, so at most the validity findings can be only one factor in the choice that is made. It is nevertheless important that the validity study be well designed. Such a study should use each predictor (or set of predictors) in a separate regression analysis along with the other predictors that are not being compared. Each analysis should involve the same criterion and precisely the same group of students. Interpretation of results is greatly facilitated if the tests being compared have been administered under the same conditions. If the total group can be subdivided meaningfully on the basis of sex and curriculum into smaller groups, the analysis design should be repeated for these groups, provided that this process is not carried so far as to yield groups of less than about 100 students. Each group should be representative of all enrolled students

Table 5.2

Example of expectancy table prepared by the College Board Validity Study Service

EXPECTANCY TABLE

FR GPA AS PREDICTED BY HSRANK, SAT-V, SAT-M

CHANCES IN 100 THAT CANDIDATES WILL EARN
A GRADE EQUAL TO OR HIGHER THAN

PREDICTED GRADE	.50	1.00	1.50	2.00	2.50	3.00	3.50
4.00	99	99	99	99	99	98	86
3.80	99	99	99	99	99	96	74
3.60	99	99	99	99	99	90	58
3.50*	99	99	99	99	98	86	50
3.40	99	99	99	99	97	80	42
3.20	99	99	99	99	93	66	26
3.00*	99	99	99	98	86	50	14
2.80	99	99	99	96	74	34	7
2.60	99	99	99	90	58	20	3
2.50*	99	99	98	86	50	14	2
2.40	99	99	97	80	42	10	1
2.20	99	99	93	66	26	4	1
2.00*	99	98	86	50	14	2	1
1.80	99	96	74	34	7	1	1
1.60	99	90	58	20	3	1	1
1.50*	98	86	50	14	2	1	1
1.40	97	80	42	10	1	1	1
1.20	93	66	26	4	1	1	1
1.00*	86	50	14	2	1	1	1
.80	74	34	7	1	1	1	1
.60	58	20	3	1	1	1	1
.50*	50	14	2	1	1	1	1
.40	42	10	1	1	1	1	1
.20	26	4	1	1	1	1	1
.00	14	2	1	1	1	1	1

*SCALE POINTS SPECIFIED BY THE COLLEGE

belonging to that group. With this design, a comparison of appropriate multiple correlation coefficients should yield useful data to be considered along with other information in choosing between predictors. An alternative procedure that might be used if the tests being compared must be specially administered is to have one random half take one test and the other half take the other test. If this procedure is followed, it is important to take account of the fact that results for the tests being compared are not based on the *same* students. If students are assigned individually at random to the groups, samples of 500 in each group should be adequate for this design. If either of the foregoing designs is used, the effects of sampling fluctuations and of differences between groups are reasonably well controlled. It is possible, therefore, to attribute the differences in validity coefficients mainly to differences in the effectiveness of the predictors being compared.

Placement use — Dyer (1964) has pointed out that "there seems to be some confusion about how one should determine the validity of an Achievement Test to be used in placement. Should it tell the level at which a student may most profitably begin his college work in a given subject? Should it predict the grades he will get at the end of the freshman course?"

The confusion to which Dyer refers may arise in part because the purpose of placement varies from one college to another and from one subject to another. For example, placing a student who has completed four years of high school French into the fifth semester of college French is different from placing the "most promising" English students in a "top" section where they will challenge one another to excellent performance.

Decisions about placement procedures necessarily depend on the rationale of placement as seen by the persons responsible for doing it, the characteristics of the courses or sections into which placement is to be made, and on a number of practical considerations, notably cost, effort, and the time at which the placement data become available. The content validity of the possible measures is obviously important. What, if anything, can empirical studies contribute to the decision?

Perhaps the clearest example of the usefulness of empirical studies is Dyer's (1947) report of a study of performance in French. He administered a test having acceptable content validity to Harvard and Radcliffe students about to complete the fourth term of college French. His analysis of the data yielded a correlation coefficient of .83 between the test scores and the term grades, but more important, it provided empirical evi-

Table 5.3

Example of scatter diagram prepared by the College Board Validity Study Service

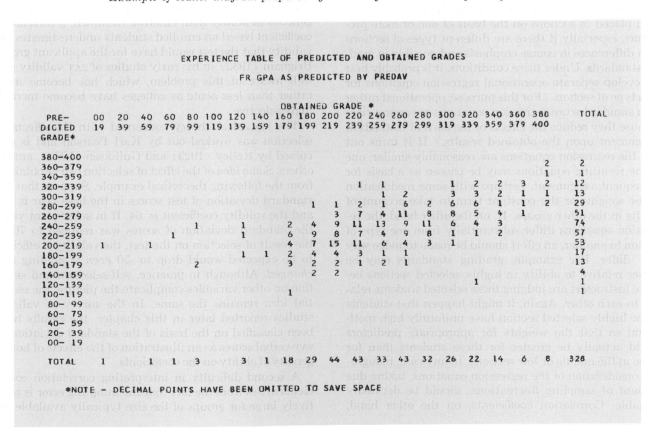

EXPERIENCE TABLE OF PREDICTED AND OBTAINED GRADES

FR GPA AS PREDICTED BY PREDAV

PRE-DICTED GRADE*	OBTAINED GRADE *																			TOTAL
	00 19	20 39	40 59	60 79	80 99	100 119	120 139	140 159	160 179	180 199	200 219	220 239	240 259	260 279	280 299	300 319	320 339	340 359	360 379	380 400	
380-400																			2	2	2
360-379																		1			1
340-359																		1			1
320-339									1	1				1	2	2	3	2			12
300-319												1	2		3	3	2	1	1		13
280-299						1	1	2	1	6	2	6	6	1	1	2					29
260-279							3	7	4	11	8	8	5	4	1						51
240-259			1	1	2	4	9	11	13	9	11	6	4	3							74
220-239		1		1	6	9	8	7	4	9	8	1	1	2							57
200-219	1		1		4	7	15	11	6	4	3	1									53
180-199				1	1	2	4	4	3	1	1										17
160-179			2		3	2	2	1	2	1											13
140-159					2	2															4
120-139												1									1
100-119					1																1
80-99																					
60-79																					
40-59																					
20-39																					
00-19																					
TOTAL	1		1	1	3		3	1	18	29	44	43	33	43	32	26	22	14	6	8	328

*NOTE - DECIMAL POINTS HAVE BEEN OMITTED TO SAVE SPACE

123

dence on which a decision could be made regarding the appropriateness of a given score on the test for meeting the language requirements. The setting of the cutting score requires judgment, because a high cutting score will describe as unqualified some students who earned a satisfactory course grade, while a low cutting score will describe as qualified some students who did not earn a satisfactory course grade. The setting of the cutting score, then, requires a judgment as to the seriousness of the two types of errors in classification. Nevertheless, a study that can help in setting standards as well as in evaluating the test is obviously valuable. An adaptation of this basic design to aid in the use of placement tests administered in the fall for the assignment of students in a two-year course sequence is given in the *College Placement Tests Score Use and Interpretation Manual.* Special test administrations are particularly useful where placement (or exemption from a requirement) is to be based on demonstrated accomplishment.

When a college offers many sections of a large course, students may be assigned to certain sections on the basis of their promise of success in the course. If it is possible to assign students to sections on a random basis for one year, a conventional validity study design should provide an effective and practical basis for placement. A conventional design may also be used when the choice of sections is made by the students. In this case, however, there is a risk that the results of the study may be influenced by the ways in which the students in the validity study sample choose their sections. A much more difficult problem is presented when an attempt is made to improve assignment procedures when students have already been placed in sections on the basis of one or more predictors, especially if there are different types of sections with differences in course emphasis and possibly in grading standards. Under these conditions, it is probably best to develop separate operational regression equations for each type of section. (For this purpose, operational rather than standard-score regression equations are appropriate because they reduce the effects of the current methods of assignment upon the obtained results.) If it turns out that the regression equations are reasonably similar, one of the resulting equations may be chosen as a basis for subsequent assignment, perhaps with some modification of the weights or the constant term to take account of results in the other groups. If, on the other hand, the regression equations differ substantially from one type of section to another, an effort should be made to judge why they differ. For example, grading standards may be higher relative to ability in highly selected sections because instructors are judging these selected students relative to each other. Again, it might happen that students in the highly selected section have uniformly high motivation so that the weights for appropriate predictors would actually be greater for these students than for those in the middle or low sections. In any case, thoughtful consideration of the regression equations, taking due account of sampling fluctuations, should be decidedly valuable. Correlation coefficients, on the other hand,

would have little value under these conditions, because they would be likely to be affected so much by the way in which students had been assigned to sections before the study began.

Interpreting validity coefficients as a measure of predictive value

The correlation coefficient is the customary measure of the predictive effectiveness of a predictor or group of predictors. Since validity coefficients are independent of the units in which the predictor and criterion are expressed, they may be compared from one predictor to another and from one group to another without regard to differences in units. The ease with which these coefficients may be compared is not an unmixed blessing, however. Consideration needs to be given to a number of complications if the comparisons of coefficients are to lead to sound inferences about the merits of a given predictor.

The most significant difficulty in interpreting the correlation coefficient as a measure of predictive effectiveness is that the size of the coefficient is affected by the homogeneity of ability in the group included in the study. Since most College Board validity studies are based on selected groups of students and some studies are based on drastically selected groups, this problem is serious from the viewpoint of interpretation. The same predictor would be expected to yield a lower validity coefficient in a college where students were relatively homogeneous in ability than in one having a wider range of talent. Moreover, if it is assumed that applicants are more heterogeneous in ability than entering freshmen, a correlation coefficient based on enrolled students underestimates the validity that the test would have for the applicant group. Brigham (1932) in his early studies of SAT validity was well aware of this problem, which has become more rather than less acute as colleges have become increasingly selective.

The statistical theory concerned with the effects of selection was worked out by Karl Pearson and is discussed by Kelley (1923) and Gulliksen (1950), among others. Some idea of the effect of selection can be obtained from the following theoretical example. Suppose that the standard deviation of test scores in the base year is 100 and the validity coefficient is .64. If in subsequent years the standard deviation of scores was reduced to 70 as the result of selection on the test, the validity coefficient to be expected would drop to .50 *even if nothing else changed.* Although in practice, self-selection and selection on other variables complicate the picture, the essential idea remains the same. In the survey of validity studies reported later in this chapter, the results have been classified on the basis of the standard deviation of SAT-verbal scores as an illustration of the effects of homogeneity of ability on the coefficients.

A second difficulty in interpreting correlation coefficients arises from the fact that the sampling error is relatively large for groups of the size typically available for validity studies. Although the existence of sampling error is widely recognized, it may be useful to examine the amount of sampling error to be expected for groups of varying sizes. For various correlation coefficients existing in a very large sample, Table 5.4 gives the range that would include 95 percent of the observed coefficients for samples of 50, 100, and 200. (Table 5.4 was calculated using Fisher's z-transformation.) Consideration of Table 5.4 emphasizes the extent to which observed correlations may fluctuate as the result of sampling. For example, it requires a range from .34 to .63 to bracket 95 percent of the observed coefficients when samples of 100 are drawn from a population in which the coefficient is .50.

When validity coefficients are based on the same criterion and the same groups and if the predictors correlate substantially with each other, the sampling error is appreciably smaller than that for the difference in correlation coefficients based on two *different* samples of the same size. An equation for testing the significance of the difference of coefficients obtained under these conditions was developed by Hotelling (1940). Olkin (1967) has recently developed a new equation for this purpose.

The main implication of sampling error for interpretation is to stress the need for reasonably large samples and to discourage overinterpretation of small differences in validity coefficients based upon groups of 100 or 200 students.

A third difficulty in interpreting validity coefficients arises from the fact that to some extent the unreliability of the criterion affects the obtained coefficient. This effect is less serious when the predictors are all correlated with the same criterion, and does not, in general, change the relative weights of the predictors in the regression equation. To an unknown extent, however, the variation of validity coefficients from one college to another is attributable to differences in the reliability of grades. Since it is difficult to obtain a fully satisfactory estimate of the reliability of college grades to serve as an index of their predictability, this problem is particularly vexing.

Table 5.4

*Range of correlation coefficients that would be expected to include 95 percent of observed values for selected population values and sample sizes**

Population value of correlation coefficient	Expected range of observed coefficients when sample size is:		
	50	100	200
.40	.14-.61	.22-.55	.28-.51
.50	.26-.68	.34-.63	.39-.60
.60	.39-.75	.46-.71	.50-.68
.70	.52-.82	.58-.79	.62-.76

*Calculated using Fisher's z-transformation. Tables of z in McNemar (1962) were used.

Finally, there is the difficulty of assigning a directly meaningful interpretation to the coefficient itself. Indeed, certain statistical interpretations of the correlation coefficient, including the coefficient of alienation and the variance interpretation of the coefficient, have led to undue pessimism about the usual validity coefficients, as Taylor and Russell (1939) pointed out over 30 years ago. Cronbach and Gleser (1957) discuss several ways of interpreting validity coefficients when the predictor is to be used for selection, all of them providing a more realistic and more optimistic approach to the interpretation of correlation coefficients. It seems reasonable that an admissions officer, for example, would be especially concerned with the level of performance of the selected group, rather than with the extent to which the predictor "accounted for" the criterion variance.

A careful examination of a scatter diagram (e.g., Table 5.3) relating predictions to observed performance will indicate the extent to which students having low predicted grades tend to do poorly rather than well in their academic work. The probable effects of various admissions standards can be explored with data for the group used in the study. To obtain a quick general view of the kinds of errors in prediction that characterize correlation coefficients of different sizes, Table 5.5 may be useful. This table was constructed by assuming a normal bivariate distribution of two variables and by using the excellent tables developed by the National Bureau of Standards (1959). In the table, each row shows the percentage of students at each of three levels on the predictor who will rank in each of three levels on the criterion for selected correlation coefficients. Thus, with a coefficient of .40 among students in the bottom fifth on the predictor, 38 percent would be expected to stand in the bottom fifth on the criterion. However, 7 percent of these students would be expected to stand in the top fifth on the criterion. Although 7 bad predictions in 100 is much better than the 20 in 100 that would be expected if the coefficient were zero, it is relatively large. With a coefficient of .70, only 1 percent of students in the bottom fifth on the predictor would be expected to stand in the top fifth on the criterion. Table 5.5, then, offers some information on the kind of results to be expected for coefficients of various sizes.

Evidence on the predictive validity of the SAT

The data with respect to SAT validity to be summarized in this chapter are based on a survey of results available from three sources:

1. Studies made during the initial two years of the College Board Validity Study Service (1964-65 and 1965-66)
2. Studies made at the summer institutes in admissions in 1965 and 1966
3. Studies made by French (1963) as part of his work on the testing of high-level aptitude.

The survey is further limited to studies seeking to predict first-term or first-year average grades by using SAT-verbal and SAT-mathematical scores along with some measure of academic success in high school. To avoid duplication, if a college participated in more than one validity study, only the most recent was used, and if, for example, men and women students were studied both separately and as a combined group, the separate groups *only* were included. If a college made separate studies to compare validities of rank-in-class and some other measure of high school record, the results for rank-in-class were used. The choice of rank-in-class was made arbitrarily for the sake of uniformity. The validity of rank-in-class may be higher or lower than other measures of high school performance in any particular study. In the survey of students in liberal arts and general programs, only groups of 85 or more students were included, because 85 was the minimum size used when the Validity Study Service was initiated. Very few of the samples

Table 5.5*

Relation between standing on predictor and standing on criterion for various values of the correlation coefficient

Correlation coefficient	Standing on predictor	Percent of students standing in each criterion group		
		Bottom fifth	*Middle three-fifths*	*Top fifth*
.10	Top fifth	16	60	24
	Middle three-fifths	20	60	20
	Bottom fifth	24	60	16
.20	Top fifth	13	59	28
	Middle three-fifths	20	60	20
	Bottom fifth	28	59	13
.30	Top fifth	10	57	33
	Middle three-fifths	19	62	19
	Bottom fifth	33	57	10
.40	Top fifth	7	55	38
	Middle three-fifths	18	64	18
	Bottom fifth	38	55	7
.50	Top fifth	4	52	44
	Middle three-fifths	17	66	17
	Bottom fifth	44	52	4
.60	Top fifth	2	48	50
	Middle three-fifths	16	68	16
	Bottom fifth	50	48	2
.70	Top fifth	1	43	56
	Middle three-fifths	14	72	14
	Bottom fifth	56	43	1
.80	Top fifth	0.2	35.4	64.4
	Middle three-fifths	11.8	76.4	11.8
	Bottom fifth	64.4	35.4	0.2
.90	Top fifth	(0.002)	25.2	74.8
	Middle three-fifths	8.4	83.2	8.4
	Bottom fifth	74.8	25.2	(0.002)

*Reprinted from Schrader (1965).

were smaller than 100. Within the scope of the survey as defined, all available results were used. In addition to the survey results, brief attention will be given to the usefulness of the SAT for predicting the performance of foreign students attending college in the United States.

The decision to limit this survey to the designated sources was made on the basis of feasibility. The collection and integration of the many published and unpublished validity studies of College Board tests certainly would have enhanced the value of this survey. For example, the extensive and systematic studies summarized by Hills (1964) of studies conducted in the public colleges in Georgia offer much valuable information about the validity of College Board tests. Nevertheless, it was judged that a comprehensive survey of validity studies was beyond the scope of the present report.

Beyond the primary purpose of making conveniently available a substantial amount of data on SAT validity, this survey was concerned with examining the relation between validity and certain characteristics of the groups. In particular, curriculum, sex, level of ability of the group, and homogeneity of ability of the group were considered. These tabulations make it possible for a college to compare its validity coefficients with those of other colleges similar to it in certain respects.

In the discussion of results, main emphasis will be given to average findings for various student groups, although results will be presented in detail for student groups in special fields. There is, certainly, marked variation from one student group to another both in level and pattern of validity coefficient within any classification of groups. Although part of the variations in validity from one student group to another is the result of sampling fluctuations, the observed differences are also attributable in part to specific characteristics of the colleges. Among the probable influences are: selection practices, including self-selection by applicants; differences in preparation for college work in various fields; curricular emphases; relative weight given to various factors in awarding grades; the reliability and dispersion of grades in various fields; sex differences; and differences in interests, motivation, and various non-cognitive variables. In view of the complexity of the problem, it seems unlikely that the development and testing of a theory of the relative contribution of various predictors under various conditions will occur soon. Thus, at least from the viewpoint of the college, the current practice of developing weights for specific curriculum groups within specific colleges, based on reasonably large samples, offers the best solution to the problem of prediction.

Results for students in liberal arts and general programs—For purposes of this survey, a relatively broad definition was used for "liberal arts and general programs." Unless a group was clearly identified as belonging to a specific curriculum or division, it was assigned to this category. For example, when all freshman men were treated as a single group, the study was placed in the "liberal arts and general programs" category even though the college might have several divisions.

A major classification within this category is based on the sex of students. Some coeducational colleges treated men and women as a single group; these colleges constitute a third group. Table 5.6 shows selected percentiles of validity coefficients for the three classifications. The following summary shows the median coefficients for each of the types:

	Men	Women	Combined
SAT-V	.33	.41	.39
SAT-M	.30	.36	.33
High school record	.47	.54	.55
Multiple correlation	.55	.62	.62
Number of groups	116	143	51

Table 5.6

Validity coefficients of SAT and high school record: selected percentiles of validity coefficients based on students in liberal arts and general programs classified by sex

	SAT-V	SAT-M	High school record	Three predictors combined
Men				
Percentile				
90	.48	.47	.62	.68
75	.42	.40	.56	.62
50	.33	.30	.47	.55
25	.24	.24	.39	.48
10	.17	.16	.31	.40
Number of groups	116	116	116	116
Women				
Percentile				
90	.55	.52	.68	.74
75	.48	.45	.61	.68
50	.41	.36	.54	.62
25	.32	.27	.44	.52
10	.23	.21	.35	.43
Number of groups	143	143	143	143
Men and women				
Percentile				
90	.54	.48	.67	.73
75	.48	.41	.62	.68
50	.39	.33	.55	.62
25	.35	.24	.44	.54
10	.26	.20	.33	.46
Number of groups	51	51	51	51

It will be recalled that if a coeducational college studied men and women separately, it would not be included in the combined group. At least for the colleges in this survey, it is clear that validities do run somewhat higher for women and for the combined groups than for the men and that SAT-V has a somewhat higher median validity than SAT-M in all three comparisons.

Over the years, as mean SAT scores have increased dramatically in many colleges, the question of the extent to which the rise in score level is associated with lower validity has often been discussed. The available data make it possible to compare validities for colleges differing appreciably in mean SAT scores. Using SAT-verbal mean as a basis, the various college groups were classified into three levels: (a) SAT-verbal mean less than 500; (b) SAT-verbal mean between 500 and 549; and (c) SAT-verbal mean 550 or higher. Table 5.7 gives selected per-

centiles for men and women separately for the three levels. The median validities for the six categories were as follows:

	SAT-V mean less than 500		SAT-V mean between 500 and 549		SAT-V mean 550 or higher	
	Men	Women	Men	Women	Men	Women
SAT-V	.34	.44	.33	.44	.32	.34
SAT-M	.35	.43	.29	.40	.27	.30
High school record	.50	.55	.50	.57	.44	.49
Multiple correlation	.56	.64	.56	.64	.52	.56
Number of groups	52	45	31	38	33	60

These results support the view that, for the groups having an SAT-verbal mean of 550 or higher, a higher

Table 5.7

Validity coefficients of SAT *and high school record*: selected percentiles of validity coefficients based on students in liberal arts and general programs classified by level of verbal ability and by sex*

	Groups having SAT-verbal mean of less than 500				Groups having SAT-verbal mean of between 500 and 549				Groups having SAT-verbal mean of 550 or higher			
	VALIDITY OF:				VALIDITY OF:				VALIDITY OF:			
	SAT-V	SAT-M	High school record	Three predictors combined	SAT-V	SAT-M	High school record	Three predictors combined	SAT-V	SAT-M	High school record	Three predictors combined
Men												
Percentile												
90	.52	.50	.62	.70	.48	.46	.64	.68	.44	.39	.56	.64
75	.45	.42	.57	.63	.39	.40	.59	.64	.39	.35	.49	.58
50	.34	.35	.50	.56	.33	.29	.50	.56	.32	.27	.44	.52
25	.23	.26	.41	.49	.24	.22	.39	.49	.26	.22	.37	.47
10	.16	.17	.31	.38	.18	.15	.32	.35	.18	.15	.30	.42
Number of groups	52	52	52	52	31	31	31	31	33	33	33	33
Women												
Percentile												
90	.57	.54	.70	.74	.60	.53	.71	.77	.49	.43	.63	.69
75	.52	.49	.62	.70	.50	.48	.64	.72	.44	.36	.58	.64
50	.44	.43	.55	.64	.44	.40	.57	.64	.34	.30	.49	.56
25	.36	.34	.47	.57	.35	.29	.50	.60	.26	.25	.41	.47
10	.29	.26	.41	.49	.30	.23	.36	.46	.16	.17	.32	.41
Number of groups	45	45	45	45	38	38	38	38	60	60	60	60

*Criterion is first-term or first-year grades.

mean score may indeed be associated with somewhat lower validity. The effect is especially noticeable for the women's groups. An alternative hypothesis, that for some reason grades are less predictable in the high-scoring colleges, cannot be eliminated as a possible explanation of the results. In any case, the results indicate that a college having an SAT-verbal mean above 550 might well expect to find lower validities than a college with a lower mean score.

Statistical theory suggests that the reduction in validity associated with a higher mean score comes about because of a reduction in the heterogeneity of ability in the group. Table 5.8 shows the results of classifying the groups using the standard deviation of SAT-V as the indicator of homogeneity in ability. The results obtained show, on the whole, greater differences among the three groups than were obtained using the mean as the basis

of classification. The median validities are as follows:

	Standard deviation of SAT-V 85 or more		Standard deviation of SAT-V between 75 and 85		Standard deviation of SAT-V less than 75	
	Men	Women	Men	Women	Men	Women
SAT-V	.41	.48	.32	.43	.29	.32
SAT-M	.40	.46	.28	.37	.26	.28
High school record	.55	.59	.47	.58	.41	.46
Multiple correlation	.61	.67	.54	.64	.50	.54
Number of groups	43	43	36	42	37	58

An interesting feature of this grouping is that some

Table 5.8

Validity coefficients of SAT and high school record: selected percentiles of validity coefficients based on students in liberal arts and general programs classified by homogeneity of verbal ability and by sex*

	Groups having SAT-verbal SD of 85 or higher				Groups having SAT-verbal SD of from 75 to 84				Groups having SAT-verbal SD of less than 75			
	VALIDITY OF:				VALIDITY OF:				VALIDITY OF:			
	SAT-V	SAT-M	High school record	Three predictors combined	SAT-V	SAT-M	High school record	Three predictors combined	SAT-V	SAT-M	High school record	Three predictors combined
Men												
Percentile												
90	.54	.52	.66	.73	.46	.44	.60	.64	.41	.37	.55	.60
75	.48	.45	.61	.68	.40	.37	.53	.60	.35	.32	.48	.56
50	.41	.40	.55	.61	.32	.28	.47	.54	.29	.26	.41	.50
25	.30	.29	.46	.50	.24	.24	.40	.50	.19	.20	.34	.45
10	.20	.20	.36	.45	.18	.17	.32	.44	.15	.11	.26	.34
Number of groups	43	43	43	43	36	36	36	36	37	37	37	37
Women												
Percentile												
90	.60	.54	.72	.78	.54	.52	.68	.74	.46	.40	.59	.66
75	.55	.51	.67	.73	.49	.45	.64	.69	.39	.34	.54	.61
50	.48	.46	.59	.67	.43	.37	.58	.64	.32	.28	.46	.54
25	.41	.40	.51	.61	.37	.31	.51	.60	.24	.23	.39	.45
10	.33	.30	.41	.48	.31	.25	.41	.52	.16	.16	.31	.40
Number of groups	43	43	43	43	42	42	42	42	58	58	58	58

*Criterion is first-term or first-year grades.

groups with relatively low means may also have relatively small standard deviations. This situation might arise because the college attracts relatively few very able students and is unwilling to accept students who are low in ability. Another feature is that seven of the groups with small standard deviations had mean SAT-verbal scores below 370! (The small standard deviations for these groups may result in part from the fact that reported scores below 200 cannot occur on SAT.) For these groups the SAT-verbal median validity was .45. In one of these groups, the SAT-verbal validity was .00; in the other six, it ranged from .33 to .53. Although seven groups constitute a small basis for generalization, the available results indicate that colleges having an SAT-verbal mean below 370 and an SAT-verbal standard deviation less than 75 may well find that SAT-V has substantial validity. The median multiple correlation was .59 and these coefficients ranged from .53 to .71. It may be noted that five of these seven groups were enrolled in colleges listed by McGrath (1965) as predominantly black institutions. The results obtained are similar to those found by Stanley and Porter (1967) for three low-scoring, low-variability black colleges. Hills and Stanley (1968) found that a form of the School and College Ability Test (SCAT) that was more appropriate in difficulty than the SAT for six low-scoring groups in three predominantly black colleges yielded validity coefficients that were noticeably higher than the corresponding coefficients for the SAT.

Further examination of the data made it possible to identify a "high scoring-homogeneous" set of 18 groups, all having an SAT-verbal mean above 600 and an SAT-verbal standard deviation of 65 or less. For these groups the median and ranges of validities were as follows:

	Median	*Range*
SAT-V	.22	.11-.44
SAT-M	.24	−.01-.46
High school record	.40	.32-.57
Multiple correlation	.46	.35-.61

These results make it clear that the "high-scoring homogeneous" colleges show distinctly lower validity coefficients *for their enrolled students* than do the typical colleges in the survey.

Where predictors play a substantial role in admissions decisions, the applicant group may be appreciably more heterogeneous in ability than the enrolled student group. As noted earlier, statistical methods exist for estimating what the validity would be for the applicant group, provided that appropriate analyses are made of data for all applicants. In a sense, the validity for the applicant group would be a better measure of the predictor's value than would the validity for the enrolled student group. This line of reasoning suggests that it would be useful to analyze data on applicants in validity studies and thus to obtain estimated validity coefficients for applicants. It is fair to add, however, that this additional work would *not* result in any change in the prediction equation for a college. Only the validity coefficient would be changed.

The foregoing results indicate that colleges that have a relatively small SAT-verbal standard deviation have, on the average, lower validity coefficients than colleges that have a relatively standard deviation. There is, nevertheless, a large amount of variation in validity within each of the three groups. Part of this variation is no doubt attributable to the substantial sampling error inherent in correlation coefficients based on samples of moderate size, as shown by Table 5.4. Nevertheless, the wealth of data on validity yielded by the many current studies should permit the development of generalizations about various college characteristics associated with relatively high and relatively low validity. To develop these generalizations efficiently, there is a need for systematic studies designed to obtain data on college characteristics for a substantial number of colleges and to relate these data to validity study results. The atmosphere of the college as perceived by the students, characteristics of the college as described in published data about it, the extent of choice open to students in determining their academic programs, faculty attitudes toward grading, and the extent to which essay or objective tests predominate in classroom testing may serve as illustrations of the kinds of data that might be collected. Studies of this kind would permit a college to judge whether its validity differed appreciably from the level it could reasonably expect after taking account of relevant characteristics.

Table 5.9 shows the distribution of validity coefficients for all 310 groups of students in liberal arts and general programs classified by SAT-verbal standard deviation. This table should be useful to a college for comparing its results with other colleges similar in homogeneity. It is worthy of note that all but one of the 11 SAT-verbal validity coefficients of .60 or above were found in the 113 groups for which the SAT-verbal standard deviation was 85 or higher. Moreover, of 19 multiple coefficients of .75 or higher, 14 were found in the same 113 groups. It is also noteworthy that the median validity coefficient for the most heterogeneous of the three classifications is at or above the 90th percentile of validity coefficients in the most homogeneous of the three *for each of the four predictors.* The homogeneity of the group on SAT-V is only one of many factors that affect validity coefficients. Table 5.9 makes it clear, however, that homogeneity of ability is relevant in interpreting coefficients of the kind summarized here. Study of the relation of homogeneity and level of ability to validity coefficients should certainly be continued as additional data become available for use.

Results for students in special curriculums or divisions —For the separate divisions, Tables 5.10 and 5.11 show results for each study separately. Only those divisions or curriculums studied in at least two colleges are reported. Four classifications — engineering, science, business, and education—had results for 10 or more separate studies.

Table 5.9

Validity coefficients of SAT *and high school record*: frequency distributions and selected percentiles of validity coefficients based on liberal arts and general groups classified by homogeneity in verbal ability*

	Groups having SAT-verbal SD of 85 or higher				Groups having SAT-verbal SD of from 75 to 84				Groups having SAT-verbal SD of less than 75			
	VALIDITY OF:				VALIDITY OF:				VALIDITY OF:			
	SAT-V	SAT-M	High school record	Three predictors combined	SAT-V	SAT-M	High school record	Three predictors combined	SAT-V	SAT-M	High school record	Three predictors combined
Class interval												
.80-.84	....	....	....	2	....	....	....	....	....	....	....	....
.75-.79	....	....	2	12	....	....	....	4	....	....	....	1
.70-.74	....	....	12	17	....	....	3	7	....	....	....	3
.65-.69	1	1	10	29	....	....	7	16	....	....	1	6
.60-.64	8	2	25	17	1	1	15	22	1	....	5	17
.55-.59	10	3	19	11	2	1	13	15	....	....	14	17
.50-.54	16	18	14	8	9	6	17	16	2	1	13	20
.45-.49	21	17	13	10	17	7	11	5	6	3	19	18
.40-.44	19	28	5	2	13	7	12	4	12	4	20	12
.35-.39	16	13	3	3	16	23	5	2	16	14	12	5
.30-.34	8	9	7	2	14	9	5	1	23	19	12	3
.25-.29	7	9	2	....	10	21	3	....	14	27	4	2
.20-.24	2	5	....	....	4	11	1	....	10	16	5	1
.15-.19	4	4	....	....	4	3	....	....	14	9	....	....
.10-.14	1	3	1	....	2	1	....	....	4	5	....	....
.05-.09	....	....	....	....	....	2	....	....	1	5	....	....
.00-.04	....	....	....	....	....	....	....	....	2	....	....	....
(−.01) - (−.15)	....	1	....	....	....	....	....	....	....	2	....	....
Percentiles												
90	.58	.53	.71	.76	.51	.49	.65	.71	.44	.39	.58	.64
75	.52	.48	.64	.70	.46	.39	.60	.66	.38	.33	.52	.60
50	.44	.42	.58	.65	.38	.34	.52	.60	.31	.27	.44	.52
25	.36	.33	.48	.56	.31	.26	.43	.53	.22	.21	.37	.45
10	.28	.23	.37	.47	.24	.21	.35	.47	.16	.13	.30	.39
Number of groups	113				92				105			

*Criterion is first-term or first-year grades.

Some idea of the general pattern of results in these divisions can be obtained from the following median validity coefficients:

	Engineering	Science	Business	Education
SAT-V	.23	.34	.30	.35
SAT-M	.33	.32	.29	.37
High school record	.42	.54	.39	.50
Multiple correlation	.51	.58	.48	.58
Number of groups	23	10	17	13

The results for engineering students show the expected higher validity for SAT-M than for SAT-V. Comparison of validities of SAT-V and SAT-M show mathematical scores more valid in 18 schools, verbal scores more valid in four schools, and one tie. (By the statistical sign test, this difference is significant at the 1 percent level.) A closer study of the five schools in which SAT-V had equal or higher validity than SAT-M would be needed in order to judge whether the atypical results are characteristic of the particular institution or are perhaps attributable to sampling error. This superiority occurs in spite of the fact that students enrolled in engineering are relatively homogeneous with respect to SAT-mathematical scores, with about half the groups having a standard deviation below 70 on these scores. It must be added, however, that the nine groups with a standard deviation below 65 on SAT-M actually showed a median validity for SAT-M slightly greater than the overall median for the 23 groups. Interestingly enough, the seven groups with a standard deviation below 75 on SAT-V *do* tend to have multiple correlations below the overall median. Further exploration of the relation of group homogeneity to validity based on a larger and more representative sample of schools is needed. Finally, the overall results for engineering students may be considered. On the whole, they do not differ very much from those for men in liberal arts and general programs, except that the validity of SAT-V is markedly lower and that of high school record somewhat lower for the engineering students.

The science students, unlike the engineering students, show a slightly higher validity for SAT-V than for SAT-M. In general, their pattern of median validities resembles that of liberal arts and general students. The median coefficients are, in general, somewhat higher than those for men and somewhat lower than those for women. In view of the fact that these results are based on only 10 student groups, the interpretation must be highly tentative.

Results for students in business programs are available for 17 student groups. Compared with the median validities for men in liberal arts, the medians for business students are slightly lower for SAT-V and SAT-M and markedly lower for high school rank and for the multiple correlation coefficients. Detailed examination

of the validities for SAT-V and SAT-M indicates that the validity of SAT-M is higher than that of SAT-V in 10 schools, with SAT-V higher in five schools, and two ties, although SAT-V has a slightly higher median validity. This inconsistency is probably mostly attributable to the instability of statistics based on relatively few observations. It also emphasizes the difficulties in generalizing about the relative merits of verbal and mathematical scores as predictors in a given field.

Except for SAT-M, the results for the 13 education groups are similar to the results for students in liberal arts and general programs, being higher than those for men and lower than those for women. The relatively high validity for SAT-M may simply characterize the relatively small sample of student groups available in the survey.

Finally, the results for students in agriculture, architecture, home economics, and nursing as shown in Tables 5.10 and 5.11 make it clear that the tests are useful in conjunction with high school record in predicting freshman grades in these fields, at least in the colleges represented in this survey. The usefulness of this finding arises from the dearth of previous knowledge about the validity of the SAT for students in these fields.

On the whole, the median coefficients are somewhat higher for students in science and education than for students in engineering and business. Tables 5.10 and 5.11 make it clear that there is much variation from one student group to another in level and pattern of validity coefficients within the same curriculum group. The results should be useful despite their limitations as a rough indication of the kind of validity coefficients currently being obtained.

Validity for foreign students attending college in the United States — Three studies, none of which followed a traditional validity study design, throw some light on the usefulness of the SAT for predicting performance of foreign students. Coffman (1963) located 60 pairs of students in which both members were enrolled in similar curriculums in the same institution. For each pair, he was thus able to determine which member earned higher grades as well as which member had higher test scores. He found no significant relation of SAT-V to grades; SAT-mathematical scores, however, were significantly related to grades at the 5 percent level. Gannon, Oppenheim, and Wohlhueter (1966) and Carlson (1967) studied the relative contribution of the SAT and of Prueba de Aptitud Academica (PAA), a Spanish-language scholastic aptitude test, to the prediction of grades for Spanish-speaking students enrolled in colleges in the United States. These studies, which used an analysis method adapted from one of Tucker's central prediction models, cannot readily be summarized. However, it may be noted that in two separate analyses, SAT-V has an appreciable weight in both studies and SAT-M has a modest weight in one study when used along with PAA scores. It is clear that further studies are needed on this important question.

Table 5.10

Validity coefficients of SAT *and high school record*: results for engineering, science, and architecture groups*

| College group | VALIDITY OF: | | | | SAT-V | | SAT-M | | Number of students |
	SAT-V	SAT-M	High school record	Three predictors combined	Mean	SD	Mean	SD	
Engineering									
A	.43	.47	.61	.69	508	92	616	76	119
B	.42	.39	.52	.64	597	78	692	57	183
C	.34	.41	.52	.60	534	81	653	66	235
D	.24	.34	.54	.60	552	80	636	63	198
E	.27	.31	.53	.57	482	78	588	71	540
F	.20	.39	.47	.56	560	85	643	61	129
G	.34	.31	.52	.56	534	88	635	70	257
H	.13	.35	.48	.55	602	66	692	54	90
I	.30	.38	.44	.53	564	80	653	71	136
J	.34	.41	.33	.52	551	94	619	71	208
K	.24	.39	.37	.52	546	74	643	63	748
L	.21	.29	.46	.51	602	75	707	52	249
M	.26	.41	.28	.50	510	88	610	85	98
N	.19	.33	.47	.50	482	79	588	76	235
O	.21	.27	.42	.47	574	76	672	68	430
P	.11	.32	.31	.47	579	68	665	65	96
Q	.23	.32	.34	.47	625	66	725	48	535
R	.37	.34	.26	.45	327	69	391	80	146
S	.21	.32	.29	.43	494	83	585	71	233
T	.21	.21	.27	.35	501	85	590	78	147
U	.08	.10	.33	.34	648	58	725	45	636
V	.23	.11	.21	.29	532	96	477	90	99
W	.05	.19	.19	.27	666	50	754	31	187
Science									
A	.26	.31	.65	.68	499	69	574	76	152
B	.53	.37	.60	.65	464	86	521	98	190
C	.45	.44	.60	.65	508	89	590	83	157
D	.36	.46	.50	.60	523	82	579	76	227
E	.24	.33	.56	.59	517	76	566	70	115
F	.35	.24	.54	.58	571	88	653	83	87
G	.40	.31	.54	.58	573	85	619	79	150
H	.32	.34	.33	.46	553	81	596	72	216
I	.27	.28	.37	.44	581	78	638	79	139
J	−.08	.15	.37	.42	570	70	621	66	171
Architecture									
A	.10	.31	.38	.46	529	68	579	79	54
B	.23	.09	.33	.39	632	61	675	51	91

*Criterion is first-term or first-year grades.

Table 5.11

Validity coefficients of SAT and high school record*: results for
business, education, and other groups

| | VALIDITY OF: | | | | SAT-V | | SAT-M | | |
College group	SAT-V	SAT-M	High school record	Three predictors combined	Mean	SD	Mean	SD	Number of students
					Business				
A	.37	.40	.60	.70	458	71	501	76	232
B	.45	.48	.45	.63	571	66	643	73	130
C	.29	.36	.56	.62	462	87	510	79	148
D	.33	.27	.53	.58	506	77	537	73	274
E	.36	.36	.43	.56	485	90	527	89	99
F	.34	.29	.47	.52	494	81	536	79	114
G	.18	.27	.46	.52	446	81	526	83	189
H	.28	.32	.35	.49	483	66	499	73	235
I	.31	.31	.37	.48	471	72	524	82	381
J	.34	.31	.32	.47	495	79	541	78	111
K	.02	.17	.42	.46	515	59	553	62	107
L	.30	.26	.28	.44	493	72	507	74	230
M	.31	.22	.28	.43	460	72	507	76	171
N	.15	.22	.35	.42	495	71	545	70	238
O	.14	.18	.39	.41	507	67	560	77	199
P	.11	.31	.22	.38	476	60	502	64	107
Q	.22	.28	.27	.36	455	66	497	82	198
					Education				
A	.58	.29	.66	.75	451	91	484	94	104
B	.43	.53	.65	.73	424	78	440	74	416
C	.31	.45	.63	.68	501	64	504	73	250
D	.54	.38	.55	.66	457	83	465	89	111
E	.36	.30	.57	.59	501	82	505	83	147
F	.46	.38	.46	.59	566	68	573	77	90
G	.33	.39	.51	.58	476	76	471	67	106
H	.32	.38	.50	.56	462	81	459	82	306
I	.35	.37	.44	.56	399	76	456	73	247
J	.34	.34	.48·	.54	452	81	501	89	147
K	.43	.35	.34	.52	421	78	433	66	117
L	.33	.25	.39	.48	482	69	476	76	369
M	.27	.23	.38	.46	503	59	470	73	266
					Agriculture				
A	.27	.24	.42	.46	580	76	638	64	392
B	.25	.12	.40	.45	447	82	490	82	119
					Home Economics				
A	.47	.40	.32	.54	462	79	470	75	149
B	.26	.10	.30	.36	515	77	517	82	149
C	.28	.12	.26	.36	606	60	615	61	190
					Nursing				
A	.54	.49	.52	.69	480	79	485	71	74
B	.46	.35	.58	.66	559	69	536	66	168
C	.23	.27	.43	.50	583	58	582	70	150

*Criterion is first-term or first-year grades.

Evidence on the predictive validity of the Achievement Tests

Over the years, relatively few studies of the predictive validity of the College Board Achievement Tests have been made. There are two main reasons for this state of affairs: First, it is argued that the decisive kind of validity for an achievement test is *content* validity. The judgment and scholarship of the committee members are the essential factor in validity; correlations with more or less appropriate college grades are of doubtful relevance. Second, the fact that most colleges permit students to choose at least two of the tests that they take complicates the validation of the tests against freshman average grades. To test users, using the average score on whatever set of tests a candidate presents may well be less appealing than using the scores subjectively to form a judgment of the candidate's preparation, even though the scaling of the scores as described in Chapter III makes the scores on different tests as comparable as possible. The averaging of scores can be avoided by relating scores on a particular test to grades in an appropriate course. When this is done, however, the matching problem is somewhat laborious and the group having appropriate data may be too small to warrant analysis.

Despite these obstacles, Olsen (1957) and French (1963) obtained a number of validity coefficients for the Achievement Tests in connection with studies concerned mainly with the validation of other tests. In predicting average grades, they used each required Achievement Test as a separate predictor and the average of the other Achievement Test scores as a predictor. A similar design is used in the College Board Validity Study Service and in the summer institutes in admission. These empirical studies offer information on the extent to which Achievement Tests used in the specified way increase the predictive effectiveness over that obtainable from high school record, SAT-V, and SAT-M.

The survey to be reported in this chapter was limited to results from Olsen's (1957) study based on students entering college in 1956, from French's (1963) study based on students entering college in 1960, from summer institutes in admission conducted in 1965 and 1966, and from Validity Study Service studies for the academic years 1964-65 and 1965-66. In surveying the prediction of average grades, only those studies in which at least two Achievement Tests were used are included. All reported coefficients are based on 50 or more students. In surveying the prediction of course grades, only studies involving a specific Achievement Test or logical grouping of Achievement Tests were included.

Prediction of freshman average grade — Tables 5.12, 5.13, and 5.14 present data on the predictive value of high school record alone, of high school record combined with SAT-V and SAT-M, and finally of high school record, SAT-V, SAT-M, and Achievement Test scores. This sequence of coefficients is realistic in that Achievement Tests are almost always used along with the SAT in prediction of college success, while many colleges use the SAT without

Achievement Tests. In these tables, all multiple correlation coefficients have been corrected for shrinkage using the following formula given by McNemar (1962):

$$R' = \sqrt{1 - (1 - R^2)\left(\frac{N-1}{N-n}\right)}.$$

In this equation, R' designates the "shrunken multiple," R is the multiple correlation coefficient, N is the number of students, and n is one more than the number of predictors. The decision to correct for shrinkage was based on the fact that for many groups the number of predictors was fairly large relative to the number of students. For the sake of consistency, all coefficients involved in the comparisons were corrected. Two additional points of procedure may be noted before discussing the results. First, the multiple coefficients from French's study were computed for this survey from the intercorrelation tables given in his report. Second, the designation of colleges is consistent within each major grouping but not across groupings. Thus, College A for Liberal Arts-Men is *not* the same as College A for Liberal Arts-Women.

The results for women students in liberal arts and general programs shown in Table 5.12 make it clear that for many of the groups studied, the use of the Achievement Tests produced a substantial gain in the multiple correlation coefficient. A complication in the interpretation arises from the fact that the earlier studies (Source Codes "F" and "O") tend to produce larger increments than the later studies (Source Codes "I" and "S"). Whether this difference is attributable to greater use of the Achievement Tests in selection, to the fact that the Achievement Tests are now usually taken earlier in a student's career, to differences in the samples studied, or to other factors cannot be determined. In any case, the median increment is .03 for the more recent studies, and the gain is .05 or more in two-fifths of the recent groups (14 out of 35). The fact that the gain is quite small in a number of colleges raises questions about the usefulness of the average of the Achievement Test scores as a predictor of success in these schools. Of course, these studies do not provide any direct information about the usefulness of the Achievement Test scores when they are carefully considered by an admissions officer in relation to the student's academic preparation in forming a judgment about an individual applicant.

In the results for men in liberal arts and general programs shown in Table 5.13, there is little difference between the earlier and more recent studies, on the average. The median gain is .03 whether all 27 studies or only the 17 recent studies are included. Considering the 17 recent studies, five show a gain of .05 or more and five show a gain of .01 or less. For engineering students, there are only eight recent groups. In these eight groups, four show gains of .05 or more, and two show gains of .02 or less. The six older studies showed gains ranging from .04 to .16, with three of the groups showing a gain of .16. All of

(Continued on page 138)

Table 5.12

*Effect on multiple correlation coefficient of using Achievement Test scores
with* SAT *and high school records for predicting first-term or first-year
grades: women in liberal arts and general programs*

| College | VALIDITY OF: | | | Gain | SAT-V | | SAT-M | | Number of students | Source** |
	High school record	High school record and SAT*	High school record, SAT, and Achievement Tests*		Mean	SD	Mean	SD		
	Women in Liberal Arts and General Programs									
A	.41	.49	.63	.14	670	53	652	70	282	I
B	.39	.42	.55	.13	680	50	614	75	154	F
C	.19	.23	.34	.11	520	64	471	73	157	O
D	.32	.40	.49	.09	648	57	623	68	394	S
E	.48	.63	.72	.09	554	75	518	79	135	O
F	.34	.40	.48	.08	698	42	654	68	238	F
G	.41	.50	.58	.08	698	51	649	71	108	F
H	.50	.51	.58	.07	574	77	558	78	279	I
I	.40	.57	.64	.07	477	77	481	75	240	S
J	.52	.57	.64	.07	573	61	555	73	139	S
K	.43	.45	.51	.06	652	56	635	67	379	S
L	.42	.45	.51	.06	588	62	579	72	317	S
D	.35	.45	.51	.06	598	63	539	82	308	O
M	.57	.64	.70	.06	578	76	545	76	171	S
N	.46	.59	.65	.06	608	66	595	83	160	S
O	.41	.48	.54	.06	555	82	499	75	155	O
P	.48	.66	.72	.06	574	81	524	95	130	O
Q	.40	.40	.45	.05	663	52	621	68	357	I
R	.35	.41	.46	.05	599	71	579	81	238	I
S	.34	.51	.56	.05	580	86	580	101	212	S
T	.60	.63	.68	.05	557	73	518	79	204	S
U	.39	.39	.44	.05	639	54	594	82	123	S
V	.42	.47	.51	.04	586	67	563	69	330	S
W	.33	.34	.38	.04	583	70	544	74	285	I
X	.40	.49	.53	.04	523	78	497	80	188	S
Y	.55	.58	.62	.04	521	84	481	86	113	O
O	.47	.53	.56	.03	611	69	589	70	472	S
Z	.34	.44	.47	.03	607	67	613	76	421	S
AA	.41	.48	.51	.03	580	62	551	72	199	S
BB	.64	.68	.70	.02	569	79	564	84	384	S
CC	.34	.34	.36	.02	655	58	643	68	310	S
DD	.56	.62	.64	.02	589	71	580	75	284	I
C	.25	.26	.28	.02	591	58	566	69	255	S
EE	.68	.71	.73	.02	580	75	541	69	231	S
FF	.45	.50	.52	.02	613	52	592	68	223	I
GG	.58	.63	.65	.02	547	72	539	77	191	S
HH	.70	.74	.76	.02	564	83	527	84	165	S
II	.60	.63	.64	.01	560	78	541	82	296	I
JJ	.63	.67	.68	.01	553	84	538	90	215	S
KK	.61	.69	.70	.01	460	96	447	92	170	S
LL	.66	.79	.80	.01	527	80	532	75	136	S
MM	.62	.66	.66	.00	546	69	551	86	208	S
NN	.26	.35	.34	−.01	607	74	611	67	200	I
T	.61	.72	.71	−.01	593	73	545	87	105	S

*All multiple correlation coefficients are corrected for shrinkage.
**Code: F = French; I = Summer Institute; O = Olsen; S = Validity Study Service.

Table 5.13

Effect on multiple correlation coefficient of using Achievement Test scores with SAT and high school record for predicting first-term or first-year grades: men in liberal arts and general programs and engineering students

College	High school record	High school record and SAT*	High school record, SAT, and Achievement Tests*	Gain	SAT-V Mean	SAT-V SD	SAT-M Mean	SAT-M SD	Number of students	Source**
	VALIDITY OF:									
Men in Liberal Arts and General Programs										
A	.46	.57	.68	.11	660	60	690	64	126	F
B	.40	.49	.56	.07	639	61	672	67	762	F
C	.28	.41	.48	.07	567	84	632	85	205	S
D	.40	.45	.51	.06	639	66	665	72	401	F
E	.20	.25	.31	.06	566	67	614	73	216	S
F	.34	.52	.57	.05	654	58	678	66	497	I
G	.38	.50	.55	.05	600	72	663	75	411	S
H	.55	.63	.68	.05	461	86	507	96	115	S
I	.36	.45	.49	.04	662	59	676	73	685	F
J	.53	.64	.68	.04	584	82	605	91	501	O
K	.45	.48	.52	.04	620	69	659	72	122	S
L	.42	.42	.46	.04	486	78	517	87	63	O
M	.38	.40	.43	.03	619	67	657	66	559	S
D	.40	.42	.45	.03	640	63	662	67	461	F
N	.62	.65	.68	.03	547	77	608	86	325	S
O	.32	.37	.40	.03	546	68	619	58	206	S
P	.42	.51	.54	.03	643	63	661	75	107	S
Q	.46	.51	.53	.02	547	83	596	80	271	I
R	.58	.73	.75	.02	640	71	673	70	234	F
S	.51	.60	.62	.02	552	83	593	92	138	O
T	.57	.62	.64	.02	520	82	558	92	114	S
D	.59	.62	.63	.01	603	76	625	88	656	O
U	.39	.49	.50	.01	586	73	634	67	300	I
P	.47	.55	.56	.01	667	59	690	66	219	S
V	.29	.62	.63	.01	565	75	648	59	218	I
W	.52	.60	.60	.00	465	86	521	76	619	S
X	.31	.44	.44	.00	590	71	630	71	391	I
Engineering Students										
A	.28	.39	.55	.16	613	80	698	57	472	O
B	.44	.51	.67	.16	583	74	669	68	180	O
C	.38	.45	.61	.16	454	72	545	69	75	O
A	.33	.34	.43	.09	648	58	725	45	636	F
D	.37	.51	.59	.08	546	74	643	63	748	S
E	.46	.50	.58	.08	602	75	707	52	249	S
F	.19	.24	.31	.07	666	50	754	31	187	F
G	.34	.46	.52	.06	625	66	725	48	535	S
H	.42	.47	.52	.05	574	76	672	68	430	S
I	.29	.42	.46	.04	494	83	585	71	233	I
J	.52	.63	.67	.04	597	78	692	57	183	I
K	.48	.53	.57	.04	602	66	692	54	90	F
L	.28	.47	.49	.02	510	88	610	85	98	S
M	.31	.44	.45	.01	579	68	665	65	96	S

*All multiple correlation coefficients are corrected for shrinkage.

**Code: F = French; I = Summer Institute; O = Olsen; S = Validity Study Service.

the results for various other curriculums, as shown in Table 5.14, come from the more recent studies. In the 21 studies, six show gains of .05 or more and seven show gains of .01 or less. The median gain is .03.

It may be concluded, despite the limitations of the data, that the average of a student's Achievement Test scores makes a modest contribution to predictive effectiveness over and above that provided by high school record and the SAT. It is probable that these scores are more useful in some colleges than in others. Cross-validation studies would be particularly useful in establishing the extent to which systematic differences between colleges do occur. Finally, it should be emphasized that the studies summarized describe the contribution of Achievement Test scores when they are treated according to the formal procedure used in these studies.

Prediction of grades in courses or subjects — Validation of Achievement Tests against grades in particular courses or subjects rather than against freshman average grades has a strong logical appeal. It would seem that validity coefficients would show how closely the educational outcomes measured by the tests correspond to the outcomes reflected in course grades. On closer scrutiny, however, some of this appeal vanishes. Studies based on grades given by a single instructor in a particular course often involve too small a sample to provide stable results. Enlarging the sample by including additional instructors, additional closely related courses, or both, raises questions of consistency of instructional emphasis and grading practices. Course grades are often based to a considerable extent on less carefully prepared tests than those being validated. Despite these limita-

Table 5.14

Effect on multiple correlation coefficient of using Achievement Test scores with SAT *and high school record for predicting first-term or first-year average grades: various student groups*

| College | Group | VALIDITY OF: | | | Gain | SAT-V | | SAT-M | | Number of students | Source** |
		High school record	High school record and SAT*	High school record, SAT, and Achievement Tests*		Mean	SD	Mean	SD		
A	LA: Men & women	.39	.52	.55	.03	513	85	528	81	473	I
B	LA: Men & women	.66	.68	.69	.01	533	78	560	79	290	S
C	LA: Men & women	.26	.33	.33	.00	527	83	517	97	99	S
A	Architecture	.38	.40	.61	.21	529	68	579	79	54	S
A	Agriculture	.40	.42	.45	.03	447	82	490	82	119	I
A	Business	.45	.61	.67	.06	571	66	643	73	130	S
B	Business	.43	.54	.59	.05	485	90	527	89	99	S
C	Business	.42	.43	.46	.03	515	59	553	62	107	I
D	Business	.46	.50	.51	.01	446	81	526	83	189	S
E	Business	.28	.41	.41	.00	460	72	507	76	171	I
A	Education	.46	.57	.62	.05	566	68	573	77	90	S
A	Home Economics	.32	.53	.56	.03	462	79	470	75	149	I
A	Home Economics & Agriculture	.63	.62	.66	.04	468	91	524	78	101	S
A	Journalism	.41	.50	.52	.02	627	67	601	78	103	S
A	Nursing	.43	.48	.54	.06	583	58	582	70	150	I
B	Nursing	.52	.67	.70	.03	480	79	485	71	74	I
A	Pharmacy	.55	.59	.63	.04	473	75	491	83	92	I
A	Science	.37	.41	.48	.07	570	70	621	66	171	I
B	Science	.44	.55	.56	.01	496	89	535	88	185	I
A	Social Science	.46	.47	.47	.00	550	77	556	69	188	I
A	Speech	.27	.41	.42	.01	591	88	560	82	139	S

*All multiple correlation coefficients are corrected for shrinkage.
**Code: I = Summer Institute; S = Validity Study Service.

tions, evidence on the relation of Achievement Test scores to corresponding course grades has some relevance to the utility of the tests for placement. Moreover, if interpreted with due regard to the limitations of grades, these correlations offer some indication of effectiveness of the tests in various fields.

Results for the prediction of English grades are shown in Table 5.15.* In this table, results for specific English courses are given in the upper portion and studies in which the criterion was judged to include several courses are grouped in the lower portion. Considering all groups, the median validity for the English Composition Test is the same as that for SAT-V, being .34 for each predictor. SAT-V has a higher validity in 20 groups, and the English Composition Test has a higher validity in 17 groups. The close similarity in validity against grades is by no means an unexpected finding. Indeed, SAT-V has tended in earlier studies to show a higher validity than the English Composition Test against freshman English grades. When the 29 groups that had data on high school record are considered separately, the median validity coefficient for the English Composition Test and for SAT-V turns out to be .35, and that for high school record is .32. It may be noted that the slight advantage of the tests over the high school record is in contrast to the typical superiority of high school record in predicting overall average grades.

On a priori grounds, the English Composition Test would be expected to be superior to SAT-V in predicting English grades. Godshalk, Swineford, and Coffman (1966), using a specially developed criterion measure based only on writing ability, *did* find that a test of English Composition that included some free writing was considerably more valid than verbal scores on the Preliminary Scholastic Aptitude Test. A plausible reconciliation of these findings with the results of the present survey could be achieved by assuming that grades include other factors than writing ability and that SAT-V is a better predictor of these other factors than is the English Composition Test.

Table 5.16 summarizes validity coefficients against mathematics grades. These coefficients provide substantial evidence of the superiority of the Mathematics Achievement Tests over SAT-M in predicting mathematics grades. In only one group out of 18 did SAT-M have the higher validity. The median validity for the Mathematics Achievement Tests was .47 as compared with .32 for SAT-M. Moreover, in 11 groups for which overall high school record was available, the Mathematics Achievement score was more valid in every instance. However, in one college that had data on average high school mathematics grades, the high school grades had higher validity than the Mathematics Achievement score in two different courses. A complication in interpreting the results for the Mathematics Tests is the fact that beginning in December 1964, the Intermediate and Advanced

Mathematics Tests were replaced by the Mathematics Level I and Mathematics Level II Tests. Although current data on the newer tests will certainly be useful, it is quite probable that the empirical results for these tests will closely resemble those summarized in Table 5.16.

Results for the prediction of grades in science courses, shown in Table 5.17, are considerably more difficult to interpret. It should be noted that all of the studies reported are from French's (1963) study or Olsen's (1957) study and that all of the studies were made in highly selective colleges. Insofar as a pattern can be discerned in the results, it appears that for the courses in chemistry, physics, and physical sciences, the tests in the appropriate sciences and the Mathematics Achievement Tests are usually about equally good as predictors of success. The marked usefulness of the Mathematics Tests as predictors of success in physics and chemistry presumably reflects a strong emphasis on mathematical work in these courses. High school record shows appreciable validity for a number of courses. It is the best predictor for the two laboratory courses, although all validities are relatively low for them. SAT-M, as would be expected, also has appreciable validity and shows higher validity than SAT-V in every group.

Of the 12 studies summarized in Table 5.18, all except that done at College EE are based on Olsen's (1957) study. The Achievement Tests excel SAT-V in all but one of the 12 comparisons; their median validity (.32) is relatively low, however. The limited data available for high school record indicate that it has considerable merit as a possible predictor of language grades. Only in College EE among the four groups for which it was available did high school record have a relatively low validity.

Finally, Olsen (1957) presented results for four groups for the Social Studies Test, as shown in Table 5.19. The small amount of data available shows no clear advantage in predictive effectiveness for the Social Studies Test over SAT-V for the criteria used in her study.

Central prediction: Efforts to improve or facilitate prediction for groups of colleges

Efforts to make high school average grades or rank-in-class more comparable would seem to offer a promising way to improve prediction. Indeed, Brigham (1932) in his early validity studies made such an adjustment. More recently, the research of Bloom and Peters (1961) stimulated a substantial amount of theoretical and empirical work concerned with using data for a number of colleges and a number of high schools to improve prediction. No doubt the rapid advances in computer technology in recent years also contributed to enthusiasm for studies of this kind.

Linn (1966) has published a comprehensive analytical review of work in this field. The present discussion will accordingly be limited to a brief summary of activities directly related to College Board tests. Tucker (1963) developed three theoretical models for central predic-

---

*In Tables 5.15 through 5.19 the letter designating a particular division of a college is consistent through the set of five tables.

Table 5.15

Correlation coefficients of SAT-V, *English Composition Test, and high school record with English grades*

College	Group	Course or subject	VALIDITY OF: English Composition Test	SAT-V	High school record	Number of students
A	LA—Men	English Composition	.35	.40	.29	501
B	LA—Men	English Lit. and Analysis	−.08	.02	.27	333
C	LA—Men	Literature	.29	.39	.14	310
C	LA—Men	Literature	.38	.39	.33	281
D	LA—Women	English Lit. and Comp.	.35	.38	—	251
E	LA—Women*	English	.46	.43	.42	204
E	LA—Women**	English	.30	.46	.27	105
F	LA—Men & women	English	.42	.35	.31	386
G	LA—Men & women	English	.45	.52	.46***	264
G	LA—Men & women	English	.22	.32	.14***	99
B	LA—Men	English grades	.17	.28	.35	656
H	LA—Men	English grades	.38	.54	.43	222
I	LA—Men	English grades	.37	.28	.32	206
B	LA—Men	English grades	.04	−.01	.30	123
J	LA—Men	English grades	.39	.35	.28	120
B	LA—Men	English grades	.25	.03	.06	112
K	LA—Men	English grades	.34	.26	—	101
D	LA—Women	English grades	.27	.36	.15	308
L	LA—Women	English grades	.34	.41	—	281
M	LA—Women	English grades	.42	.43	.43	191
N	LA—Women	English grades	.43	.38	.40	184
O	LA—Women	English grades	.28	.16	—	167
P	LA—Women	English grades	.16	.11	.11	157
Q	LA—Women	English grades	.46	.50	.35	157
R	LA—Women	English grades	.28	.24	.26	153
K	LA—Women	English grades	.44	.34	—	118
J	LA—Women	English grades	.47	.39	.50	97
S	LA—Women	English grades	.25	.35	.29	95
T	LA—Women	English grades	.36	.22	.35	50
U	LA—Men & women	English grades	.56	.49	.42	411
V	LA—Men & women	English grades	.41	.30	—	99
J	LA—Men & women	English grades	.36	.22	.58	90
W	Engineering	English grades	.26	.31	.38***	430
X	Engineering	English grades	.19	.24	.19	187
Y	Engineering	English grades	.12	.23	.32	180
Z	Engineering	English grades	.26	.32	—	98
AA	Architecture	English grades	.03	.12	—	54

*Resident students
**Commuters
***High school English average grade

tion. Two of the models used canonical correlation as the main analytical method; the third, which he designated as the "predictive model," employed multiple regression concepts. Tucker judged that the predictive model was most promising for practical application. Although his primary effort was directed toward formulating an adequate theoretical structure, he performed some empirical studies as well. He strongly emphasized the need for further empirical work, especially on application of the predictive model, and for investigating the stability of parameters estimated from different samples of individuals, schools, and colleges.

Potthoff (1964) examined fully the theoretical issues in applying scaling concepts to the use of test scores and grades to establish appropriate score scales for high school and college grades. This study did not include the analysis of empirical data, and no empirical evaluation of his findings has been made.

Watkins and Levine (1969) conducted studies based on data for groups of College Board colleges. These studies, which used less complex analytical approaches than those offered by Tucker and Potthoff, yielded disappointingly small gains in prediction obtained from grade adjustments. These results, along with disappointing results obtained from studies of other tests, greatly reduced the impetus for undertaking more elaborate studies. No doubt certain other factors, including the serious problem of obtaining reliable parameters for schools sending few students to the colleges in the study and the complex data processing problems arising in any comprehensive approach to central prediction, contributed to the loss of interest in central prediction approaches to grade adjustment.

Possible application of central processing of test scores and grades to facilitate the use of prediction for guidance and admission seems decidedly more promising at the present time. Karas and Kendall (1966) have devised a plan by which a limited number of equations will ade-

Table 5.16

Correlation coefficients of SAT-M, *Mathematics Achievement Tests, and high school record with freshman mathematics grades*

| College | Group | Course or subject | VALIDITY OF: | | | Number of students |
			Mathematics Test	SAT-M	High school record	
BB	Engineering	Calculus	.54*	.34	.19	472
F	LA—Men & women	Calculus	.55**	.42	.28	190
B	LA—Men	Analytic Geometry and Calculus	.52*	.51	.51	168
B	LA—Men	Analytic Geometry and Calculus	.57*	.43	.32	156
G	LA—Men & women	Analytic Geometry and Calculus	.40**	.30	.43†††	149
A	LA—Men	Analytic Geometry and Calculus	.53*	.43	.44	108
G	LA—Men & women	Algebra and Trigonometry	.15**	.02	.36†††	89
CC	Business	Accounting	.35***	.27	—	99
BB	Engineering	Mathematics grades	.34*	.13	.26	636
B	LA—Men	Mathematics grades	.56†	.53	.47	242
A	LA—Men	Mathematics grades	.48†	.39	.41	233
L	LA—Women	Mathematics grades	.30**	.37	—	223
I	LA—Men	Mathematics grades	.43††	.28	—	206
Y	Engineering	Mathematics grades	.59†	.40	.37	180
X	Engineering	Mathematics grades	.25*	.20	.03	147
Z	Engineering	Mathematics grades	.30***	.14	—	98
DD	Engineering	Mathematics grades	.60*	.29	.46	90
AA	Architecture	Mathematics grades	.46***	.23	—	54

*Advanced Mathematics Test
**Mathematics Achievement Test
***Mathematics Level I Test
†Advanced *or* Intermediate Mathematics Test
††Intermediate Mathematics Test
†††High school mathematics average grade

quately represent the great variety of specific prediction equations arising in validity studies involving three predictors (e.g., SAT-V, SAT-M, and high school average grade). They concluded that five primary equations and three reserve equations should be sufficient, provided that negative weights are not permitted. In their work, they regarded a reduction of .01 in validity as acceptable.

Their studies did not, however, include cross-validation. The possibility of producing a limited number of weighted totals of predictors is important because a simple single-predictor study of the appropriate weighted total would replace the more complex multiple regression analysis required for three predictors. Further work along this line is clearly needed.

Table 5.17

Correlation coefficients of SAT, *Science and Mathematics Achievement Tests, and high school record with science grades*

College	Group	Course or subject	VALIDITY OF:							Number of students
			Chemistry Test	Physics Test	Chemistry or Physics Test	Mathematics Test	SAT-V	SAT-M	High school record	
BB	Engineering	Chemistry	----	----	.29*	.18**	.01	.09	.32	636
BB	Engineering	General Chemistry	----	----	.35	.38**	.18	.30	.29	472
X	Engineering	Chemistry	----	----	.30	.22**	−.03	.17	.23	187
BB	Engineering	General Chemistry	.32	----	----	.33**	.22	.27	.29	147
A	LA—Men	General Chemistry	.62	----	----	----	.36	.53	.47	102
DD	Engineering	Chemistry	.13	.32	----	.12**	.12	.26	.20	90
DD	Engineering	Chemistry Laboratory	.01	.17	----	.11**	.00	.04	.19	90
B	LA—Men	Intermediate Chemistry	.51	----	----	----	.31	.44	.40	76
BB	Engineering	Physics	----	----	.29*	.29**	.08	.15	.22	636
BB	Engineering	Physics	----	----	.33	.41**	.17	.21	.21	472
BB	Engineering	Physics	----	.34	----	.41**	.16	.21	.23	331
X	Engineering	Physics	----	----	.31	.27**	.04	.20	.09	187
X	Engineering	Physics Laboratory	----	----	.19	.00**	−.05	.01	.25	187
DD	Engineering	Physics	−.04	.39	----	.38**	.15	.31	.40	90
A	LA—Men	Physical Sciences	----	----	.54	.51***	.30	.47	.48	156
B	LA—Men	Physical Sciences	----	----	.45	.43***	.41	.42	.47	125
Y	Engineering	Physical Sciences	----	----	.40	.42***	.18	.21	.28	116

*Includes biology as well as physics and chemistry
**Advanced Mathematics Test
***Advanced Mathematics Test *or* Intermediate Mathematics Test

Table 5.18

Correlation coefficients of SAT-V, Foreign Language Achievement Tests, and high school record with foreign language grades

College	Group	Course or subject	Achievement Test	VALIDITY OF: Achievement Test	SAT-V	High school record	Number of students
D	LA—Women	French Language and Literature*	French	.29	.31	....	85
D	LA—Women	French Language and Literature*	French	.43	.13	....	61
P		French Language and Literature*	French	.20	.18	....	62
B	LA—Men	French Language and Literature**	French	.52	.08	.51	58
D	LA—Women	French Language and Literature**	French	.26	.05	....	51
D	LA—Women	French grades	French	.40	.22	....	197
B	LA—Men	French grades	French	.14	.12	.45	166
P	LA—Women	French grades	French	.21	.18	....	102
A	LA—Men	French grades	French	.63	.45	.49	58
D	LA—Women	Foreign Language grades	Language Tests	.37	.16	....	307
P	LA—Women	Foreign Language grades	Language Tests	.31	.07	....	149
EE	LA—Men & women	German	Language Tests	.33	.22	.11	131

*Course for students with three or four years of high school French
**Course for students with two years of high school French

Table 5.19

Correlation coefficients of SAT, Social Studies Achievement Test, and high school record with social studies grades

College	Group	Course or subject	VALIDITY OF: Social Studies Test	SAT-V	High school record	Number of students
A	LA—Men	History and Social Sciences	.50	.49	.34	251
D	LA—Women	Historical Development	.40	.45	....	136
D	LA—Women	Social Sciences (excluding History)	.31	.25	....	109
P	LA—Women	History and Social Sciences	.03	.07	....	78

Anastasi, Anne, Meade, Martin J., and Schneiders, Alexander A., *The Validation of a Biographical Inventory as a Predictor of College Success. Part I.* College Entrance Examination Board Research Monograph No. 1. New York: College Entrance Examination Board, 1960. 81 pp.

Bloom, Benjamin S., and Peters, Frank R., *The Use of Academic Prediction Scales for Counseling and Selecting College Entrants.* New York: Free Press of Glencoe, 1961. 145 pp.

Brigham, Carl C. *A Study of Error.* New York: College Entrance Examination Board, 1932. 384 pp.

Carlson, Alfred B., *Further Results on the Validity of the Prueba de Aptitud Academica in United States Colleges and Universities.* Statistical Report 67-67. Princeton, N.J.: Educational Testing Service, 1967. 10 pp.

Chauncey, Henry, *The Story of the College Board Scholastic Aptitude Test.* (Reprinted from the Report of the President, Educational Testing Service Annual Report 1961-62.) Princeton, N.J.: Educational Testing Service, 1962. 46 pp.

Coffman, William E., "Evidence of Cultural Factors in Responses of African Students to Items in an American Test of Scholastic Aptitude." *National Council on Measurement in Education, Twentieth Yearbook,* 1963, pp. 27-37.

Cronbach, Lee J., and Gleser, Goldine C., *Psychological Tests and Personnel Decisions.* Urbana, Illinois: University of Illinois Press, 1957. 165 pp.

Davis, Junius A., *Faculty Perceptions of Students: II. Faculty Definition of Desirable Student Traits.* College Entrance Examination Board Research and Development Report, 63-4, No. 8. Princeton, N.J.: Educational Testing Service, 1964a. 25 pp.

Davis, Junius A., *Faculty Perceptions of Students: IV. Desirability and Perception of Academic Performance.* College Entrance Examination Board Research and Development Report 64-3, No. 10. Princeton, N.J.: Educational Testing Service, 1964b. 11 pp.

Davis, Junius A., "What College Teachers Value in Students." *College Board Review* No. 56, 1965, pp. 15-18.

Duggan, John M., *Recommendations for Evaluating an Experimental Design Comparing the Validities of Two Selection Tests.* New York: College Entrance Examination Board, 1962. (Memorandum, 2 pp.)

Dyer, Henry S., "The College Board Achievement Tests." *College Board Review* No. 54, 1964, pp. 6-10.

Dyer, Henry S., "Validity of the College Board Placement Test in French." *College Board Review* No. 1, 1947, pp. 1, 12-15.

Educational Testing Service, *College Entrance Examination Board College Placement Tests: Score Use and Interpretation Manual, 1966-67.* Princeton, N.J.: Educational Testing Service, 1966. 21 pp.

Fishman, Joshua A., and Pasanella, Ann K., "College Admission-Selection Studies." *Review of Educational Research,* 1960, 30, pp. 298-310.

French, John W., "Validation of New Item-types Against Four-year Academic Criteria." *Journal of Educational Psychology,* 1958, 49, pp. 67-76.

French, John W., *The Validity of New Tests for the Performance of College Students with High-level Aptitude.* Research Bulletin 63-7. Princeton, N.J.: Educational Testing Service, 1963. 32 pp.

Gannon, F. B., Oppenheim, Don, and Wohlhueter, James F., *A Validity Study of a Spanish Language Scholastic Aptitude Test in United States Colleges and Universities.* Statistical Report 66-2. Princeton, N.J.: Educational Testing Service, 1966. 9 pp.

Godshalk, Fred I., Swineford, Frances, and Coffman, William E., *The Measurement of Writing Ability.* College Entrance Examination Board Research Monograph No. 6. New York: College Entrance Examination Board, 1966. 84 pp.

Gulliksen, Harold O., *Theory of Mental Tests.* New York: John Wiley & Sons, Inc., 1950. 486 pp.

Hills, John R., "Prediction of College Grades for All Public Colleges of a State." *Journal of Educational Measurement,* 1964, 1, pp. 155-159.

Hills, John R.; Bush, Marilyn L.; and Klock, Joseph A., "Predicting Grades Beyond the Freshman Year." *College Board Review* No. 54, 1964, pp. 23-25.

Hills, John R., and Stanley, Julian C., "Prediction of Freshman Grades from SAT and from Level 4 of SCAT in Three Predominantly Negro Colleges." *Proceedings, 76th Annual Convention American Psychological Association.* Washington: American Psychological Association, 1968, pp. 241-242.

Hotelling, Harold, "The Selection of Variates for Use in Prediction with Some Comments on the General Problem of Nuisance Parameters." *Annals of Mathematical Statistics,* 1940, 11, pp. 271-283.

Karas, Shawky F., and Kendall, Lorne M., *Development of a Reduced Set of Composite Equations for Three Predictors.* College Entrance Examination Board Research and Development Report 65-6, No. 13. Princeton, N.J.: Educational Testing Service, 1966. 42 pp.

Kelley, Truman L., *Statistical Method.* New York: Macmillan, 1923. 390 pp.

Linn, Robert L., "Grade Adjustments for Prediction of Academic Performance." *Journal of Educational Measurement,* 1966, 3, pp. 319-329.

McGrath, Earl J., *The Predominantly Negro Colleges and Universities in Transition.* New York: Bureau of Publications, Teachers College, Columbia University, 1965.

McNemar, Quinn, *Psychological Statistics.* Third Edition. New York: John Wiley & Sons, Inc., 1962. 451 pp.

National Bureau of Standards, *Table of the Bivariate Normal Distribution Function and Related Functions.* National Bureau of Standards Applied Mathematics Series, No. 50. Washington, D.C.: National Bureau of Standards, 1959.

Olkin, Ingram, "Correlations Revisited," in Stanley, Julian C., ed., *Improving Educational Design and Statistical Analysis.* Chicago: Rand McNally & Co., 1967, pp. 102-128.

Olsen, Marjorie, *Summary of Main Findings on the Validity of the College Board Tests of Developed Ability as Predictors of College Grades.* Statistical Report 57-41. Princeton, N.J.: Educational Testing Service, 1957. 59 pp.

Olsen, Marjorie, and Schrader, W. B., *The Use of Preliminary and Final Scholastic Aptitude Test Scores in Predicting College Grades.* Statistical Report 59-19. Princeton, N.J.: Educational Testing Service, 1959. 25 pp.

Potthoff, Richard F., *The Prediction of College Grades from College Board Scores and High School Grades.* Institute of Statistics Mimeo Series No. 149. Chapel Hill, North Carolina: Department of Statistics, University of North Carolina, 1964. 100 pp.

Schrader, W. B., "A Taxonomy of Expectancy Tables." *Journal of Educational Measurement,* 1965, 2, pp. 29-35.

Stanley, Julian C., and Porter, A.C., "Correlation of Scholastic Aptitude Test Scores With College Grades for Negroes versus Whites." *Journal of Educational Measurement,* 1967, 4, pp. 199-218.

Taylor, H. C., and Russell, J. T., "The Relationship of Validity Coefficients to the Practical Effectiveness of Tests in Selection: Discussion and Tables." *Journal of Applied Psychology,* 1939, 23, pp. 565-578.

Tucker, Ledyard R, *Formal Models for a Central Prediction System,* Psychometric Monograph No. 10. Richmond, Virginia: The William Byrd Press, 1963. 61 pp.

Watkins, Richard W., and Levine, Richard S., *The Usefulness of Adjustment to Secondary School Grades in the Prediction of College Success.* College Entrance Examination Board Research and Development Report 68-99, No. 2. Princeton, N.J.: Educational Testing Service, 1969. 31 pp.

CHAPTER VI

Special Studies

JOHN FREMER and MARJORIE O. CHANDLER*

Introduction

As previous chapters will have made apparent, the College Board has long been committed to research supporting its Admissions Testing Program. This research has required continuing investigation into the nature of tests and of groups taking tests and of the interaction between groups and tests. Additionally, special studies have been conducted into such questions as the relationship between the conditions of administration for a test and performance on that test. The practical orientation of College Board special studies, however, has not prevented such studies from making contributions to basic research. Research on score changes, for example, which were initiated in part to help support test construction and score equating, have helped clarify the issues of stability and change in mental test scores.

This chapter reviews some major areas of College Board special studies. Each section covers a sample of studies within a particular area and relates these studies to the operational questions they were designed to answer. The first three sections—Effects of coaching, Practice and growth, and Fatigue and anxiety—explore different aspects of the relationship between a student's experiences and his performance on a test. The next three sections—Appropriateness of a single SAT, Consideration of new item types for the SAT, and New test content—are concerned with possible changes in the College Board's Scholastic Aptitude Test. The English essay section traces some of the research on the relative merits of essay and objective tests of compositional skill. The two final sections—Special populations, and Curriculum change and diversity—treat different aspects of the problem of preparing tests so that they are appropriate for a variety of student subgroups.

---

*Now with the U. S. Office of Education, Department of Health, Education and Welfare. The initial draft of most of Chapter VI was prepared by Dr. Chandler while she was at Educational Testing Service.

Effects of coaching

The word "coaching" generally means to give instructions or advice. "Coaching" in this sense is equivalent to "teaching"; when done well it results in an increase in ability. There is a specific type of coaching, however, often carried out by coaching schools, that must be distinguished from general teaching.

In the case of the SAT, coaching efforts typically attempt to improve test scores within a time period that is too short for there to be any reasonable expectation of improvement in the underlying ability that the test was designed to measure. This is particularly true for students at college entrance age, with the background they bring to the test. The average student who might consider such coaching has spent 15 to 17 years, including 10 or more school years, developing the skills and abilities measured by the SAT. A coaching course of a few weeks is not likely to have much effect on his ability level at this point in time. One of the principal aims in constructing the SAT is to make it resistant to attempts to increase scores by means of short-term cram courses. Indeed, the usefulness of the SAT as an indicator of a student's potential for college work depends in large measure on the fact that the SAT measures general ability as it has developed over the full range of experiences in a person's life.

The College Board is interested in research on coaching because it is often called upon by students for advice regarding the desirability of being coached and by schools regarding the desirability of including coaching courses in their educational programs. In 1959 the trustees of the Board issued a detailed statement asserting that the general finding of the coaching studies was that increases in SAT scores resulting from coaching are negligible. Their statement ends, "Finally, we worry very little when parents of comfortable means decide that at worst tutoring can do no harm and therefore use their money for coaching toward College Board examinations. We are very concerned when parents purchase coaching they cannot afford or, failing to do so, feel that an unfair advantage has gone to those who have had a few weeks or months of tutoring. But we are concerned most, and have been moved to make this statement, because we see the educational process unwillingly corrupted in some schools to gain ends which we believe to be not only unworthy, but ironically, unattainable." (College Board, 1959, p. 3.)

As noted earlier, another basis for concern about coaching is its implications for test construction. Specifically, if test scores proved responsive to coaching, it would be important to find out precisely what kinds of test materials are most coachable. If some materials were coachable and some were not, studies would then have to be carried out to determine whether a satisfactory test could be produced solely from non-coachable materials. That this long-standing desire of the College Board to avoid coachable test materials has influenced the past development of the SAT can be seen in the following quotation from Coffman's (1963b) review of the SAT: "The double definition item type [calling for the recognition of a correct definition in a context] was particularly subject to criticism as encouraging an undesirable type of coaching in the schools and was dropped after 1941" (p. 10). If research had demonstrated that coaching had a significant effect, further research would have been initiated to find out whether warm-up or practice exercises were needed to put coached and uncoached candidates on an even footing. (Incidentally, there is historical precedent for the notion of practice exercises for the SAT. From 1926 to 1944 candidates were required to present completed practice booklets before they were allowed to take the test.)

Studies of coaching have produced quite consistent results. The score gains directly attributable to coaching generally amount to fewer than 10 points, "a difference of such small magnitude on the SAT score scale of 200 to 800 that it is unreasonable to expect it to affect college admissions decisions." (College Board, 1965a, p. 4.)

In all College Board studies of coaching for the SAT there are some common elements. For example: "First, before each study, the students involved took the SAT. Second, some of the students were then exposed to coaching of some kind, while others received no coaching. Third, a different edition of the SAT was administered to both coached and uncoached students 7 to 10 months after they took the test the first time. Fourth, comparisons were then made to see whether the coached students showed greater improvement than the uncoached students. Beyond these common elements, the studies varied considerably in the coaching materials used, the number of hours of coaching the students had, and the persons who did the coaching . . ." (College Board, 1965a, p. 5.)

These coaching studies also conformed with other principles of design and control. For example, it was clear that if a study compared the subsequent performance of a group of highly motivated coached students with that of an indifferent group of uncoached controls,

the effects of motivation and coaching could be separated. Similarly, it was understood that comparisons of two groups of markedly different ability levels were not always valid; in general, in a total group that takes the same form of any test at the same administration, initially low-scoring students are likely to gain more than initially high-scoring students with or without coaching. It was also clear that score changes attributable to such influences as practice, growth, or errors of measurement would occur regardless of coaching. It is exceedingly difficult to point to a definitive coaching study. Nonetheless, a number of well-done, illuminating studies of coaching are available. Individually they are not decisive, but as a group they provide a sound basis for drawing conclusions.

Because of the availability of the summary of SAT coaching studies (College Board, 1965a), a complete re-summary will not be attempted in this brief treatment. Instead, two contrasting experiments will be described here. One of them, which was included in the College Board summary, is based on highly able students in independent schools. The other, completed after the Board summary was published, is based on black students in Southern public high schools.

Coaching in independent preparatory schools

The first experiment (Dyer, 1953) was carried out during the 1951-52 academic year in cooperation with two independent schools for boys. More than 200 senior boys from each school (the entire senior classes) took part. The two schools were judged quite comparable in the kinds of instruction offered and in student background and ability. Boys at both schools took the SAT in September 1951 and again in March 1952. In the interval between testings, boys in one school received about 10 hours of coaching, 6 hours on verbal sections and 4 hours on mathematical sections. Boys at the other school were not coached in any way. The coaching involved practice on questions similar to those on the regular SAT and also involved discussions of the questions. Near the end of the sessions, a special SAT was given for practice and the questions were discussed. One distinctive feature of the coaching was that the answers were not given for the practice materials; they were identified by agreement and argument, a procedure which hopefully focused on appropriate processes for solving such problems.

A question, of course, arises as to whether the two schools really were comparable. That is, if a difference were found in the final SAT scores, might this difference properly be attributable to the coaching or might other factors be responsible? By means of analysis of covariance, it was possible to control some of these extraneous factors statistically, thus adjusting to some extent for their influence before interpreting the findings. Measures which were controlled statistically were initial SAT scores, length of enrollment in the particular school, and courses in language and mathematics taken during the senior year.

The results of this study showed a very modest advantage for the coached group. On the average, the advantage of the coached group was only about five points on SAT-verbal, a difference which had no statistical significance and certainly no practical significance. On SAT-mathematical, there was an advantage of about 13 points in favor of the coached group, a difference that *was* statistically significant although here, too, probably not of practical significance. Further analysis of data in the mathematical area led to the conclusion that coaching was advantageous only for students who were *not* enrolled in regular mathematics courses. This finding is consistent with the fact that students who take courses in mathematics in their junior year tend to score higher on a senior year SAT-M than they did on a junior year SAT-M, whereas no such gain is registered for students who do not take a junior year mathematics course.

Coaching relatively less able students

In 1965 an especially challenging coaching study was carried out (Roberts and Oppenheim, 1966). This study involved a relatively select group of black eleventh graders in 18 predominantly black high schools in Tennessee. It was estimated that the average SAT score for the study groups was in the vicinity of 300. As the authors point out, "Culturally deprived students might . . . be identified as [individuals who are] in the early stages of learning where gains due to practice are the greatest." (Roberts and Oppenheim, 1966, p. 1.) Since these students presumably had had minimum exposure to tests like the SAT, they might be expected to profit from coaching, if any group could be expected to do so.

In 14 of the schools the sample was made up of volunteers who had indicated that they would like to participate in a program designed to help high school students perform well on the multiple-choice tests that many colleges require for admission and financial assistance. The volunteers were assigned randomly to two groups: an experimental group that received instruction between the first and second testing, and a control group that received no instruction between the first and second testing. (Those in the control group, however, were assured that they would receive coaching after the second testing.) In six of the schools, coaching was limited to verbal materials, and in the other eight, to mathematical materials. The actual coaching involved about 15 half-hour sessions over a four to six week period. To insure at least some uniformity from school to school, programmed instruction materials were used. Instructors were available to answer questions and to supplement the programmed instruction. In addition to the 14 schools where coaching was done, there were four schools in which practice in test taking without coaching was offered; the subjects there were *volunteers*

who had been informed that all they would receive was practice in taking tests.

The PSAT was used in the experiment, primarily because it requires less testing time than the SAT. In view of the similarity between the two tests with respect to both content and scale, there is, of course, no difficulty in referring results of this study to the SAT scale.

In the six schools where the verbal experiment was undertaken, the average gain for the total group of 154 coached students was 0.68 score points on PSAT-verbal (corresponding to 6.8 points on the SAT scale). At the same time, the 111 control students in the same six schools lost an average of 0.76 score points on PSAT-verbal (7.6 SAT points). The difference between the gains (i.e., between $+0.68$ and -0.76) was statistically significant at the 5 percent level, but again, of no practical significance. When the six schools were considered separately, differences between experimental and control group gains were significant in three of the six; in each of these three the gain for the experimental subjects was accompanied by a loss for the controls.

Results of the mathematical experiment showed a gain of only 0.19 score points on PSAT-mathematical (1.9 SAT points) for the total group of 188 experimental subjects in the eight schools. At the same time, the 122 controls lost 0.62 points on PSAT-mathematical (6.2 SAT points). The difference was not statistically significant. Similarly, no individual school showed a significant difference.

The rather curious picture of losses for the non-instructed controls was not observed in the four "practice only" schools. The 113 students in these schools showed a trivial change from the pre- to post-test: an average loss of 0.07 raw score points on the PSAT-verbal and a gain of 0.01 raw score points on PSAT-mathematical.

Interpretation of the results for the control group was rather perplexing. Conceivably, they were disappointed at not receiving instruction immediately after volunteering; perhaps they did not believe the promise of instruction after the second test; perhaps they were determined to show up poorly on the post-tests. On the surface, the study plan seems like one that would go a long way toward avoiding the problem of comparing a motivated experimental group with an indifferent control group. Whether this or some other circumstance is responsible for the poorer performance on retesting—despite presumed effects of practice and growth—cannot be determined from the present data. Despite this problem with the control group, it seems justifiable to conclude from the results with the coached group that coaching of this type and amount yields negligible results.

The two studies described here, one based on highly able students and the other on relatively disadvantaged students, support the view stated earlier: gains from coaching for the SAT are, on the average, very small. Much the same results show up in other quite different studies; for example, coaching with items from the same

SAT form that is taken later (French and Dear, 1959); intensive coaching of small groups of students (French and Dear, 1959); intensive tutoring by a commercial tutoring school in vocabulary, reading, concept mastery, and problem solving (Whitla, 1962); coaching of an unspecified nature for a total of 30 hours in 10 sessions of three hours each in private commercial courses (Frankel, 1960); and participation in a course in accelerated reading (Coffman and Parry, 1967).

Practice and growth

The question of whether special coaching will increase SAT scores is related to the question of whether the simple experience of taking one SAT will result in a higher score on a subsequent SAT, and also to what extent the passage of time and the experiences during the intervening period will have an effect on the abilities measured by the SAT. Just as the College Board has a responsibility to provide well-founded advice to schools and students on the effects of coaching, so it must be able to determine the impact of both practice and growth on subsequent scores. Schools and colleges often wish to compare students tested in their junior year with other students tested in their senior year. Sometimes they wish to estimate from a preliminary "trial run" what the student is likely to do on a later, final testing. Such information has obvious implications for guidance on college plans. In addition, advisers and students may wish to know whether early test taking is desirable for practice or "warm up." Test publishers, in their concern with test development and interpretive materials, need to know how scores respond to growth in the abilities underlying the test and to practice on similar or related materials.

The issues of practice and growth have assumed greater importance as junior year testing has increased. Some of these issues have been discussed in Chapter II, The Scholastic Aptitude Test. During the 1967-68 testing year, some 585,000 juniors took the SAT, as compared with about 146,000 juniors eight years earlier; in addition, the number of juniors taking the PSAT rose from 378,000 to more than 1,000,000 during the same period (Pitcher, 1968). Of perhaps greater relevance than the absolute numbers of junior year candidates are data on the extent of test repeating. Analysis of a 5 percent sample of candidates during the 1962-64 period (Pitcher, 1966) showed that 38 percent of the candidates who took the SAT took it more than once; of the repeaters, the great majority followed a junior year-senior year pattern rather than simply repeating within one testing year. That this figure does not fully express the repeater problem is made clear by Pitcher's findings on PSAT-SAT overlap. She found that about 62 percent of the students who took the SAT only once during the two-year period of their junior and senior years had also taken the PSAT. Although formal detailed studies of test-taking patterns have not been carried out since Pitcher's (1966) report, more students repeated the tests during the 1967-68 period than in previous years.

Problems in the explanation of score changes

The need to provide information on average growth over time poses special problems to the College Board. Students, guidance counselors, institutional researchers, admissions officers—indeed, all who are interested in SAT scores—are also interested in the extent to which these scores may be expected to increase throughout the years a student spends in school. There are substantial differences in the level of sophistication that the various interested parties can bring to the interpretation of any data that are made available. This problem is, of course, the same one that arises in connection with individual test scores. Just as a test score in isolation has no meaning, so an average difference between two test scores in isolation has no meaning. It is possible, for example, to collect and report information on the entire group of students who took the SAT in May of their junior year and again in December of their senior year. Both these measures, however, contain error, some of it attributable to the error of measurement and some (much smaller errors) associated with the score reporting process.

One of the effects of the latter source of error may be to raise slightly the scores of *all* students tested at some administrations and to lower slightly the scores of all students tested at others. Whenever scores earned on the first testing contain a positive equating error and scores earned on the second testing contain a negative equating error, the mean score gain will go down. When the reverse happens, the mean score gain will go up. In addition to this source of score variation there is the problem of changes in the nature of the groups taking the SAT at various administrations. When a number of influences combine to produce a mean score gain that is somewhat lower than "usual," a larger than usual number of schools find an increase in the percentage of students who show a loss on reexamination. A reasoned analysis of this effect is provided by the College Board (see especially Kendrick (1967) and Chapter II of this book), but the schools and students are understandably discomfited. The process of learning to live with error is a part of both formal and informal education, however, and it is hoped that the continuing conscientious efforts by the College Board to carry out research and supply both data and well-founded advice will help in the area of interpreting score gains and losses.

Summaries of score changes

Before reviewing some studies on the relative contribution of practice and growth to score changes on successive testings, it may be well to provide some background on the "average" gain that is observed.

Since 1962 the average gain between various pairs of administrations of the SAT (that is, March-December, May-December) has been computed using the results for all students taking the SAT twice. The average score gains have varied from year to year, as might be expected. A look at one particular pair of administrations will be instructive. The average gains from May of the junior year to December of the senior year from 1962 through 1966 were 24, 16, 21, 19, and 13 for an overall average of 18 for SAT-verbal and 23, 18, 27, 18, and 9 for an overall average of 18 for SAT-mathematical (Kendrick (1967) and Chapter II of this book). These score gains are based on groups ranging from approximately 96,000 students in 1962 to approximately 193,000 in 1966. The score gains noted from May to December during the period 1962-66 are somewhat lower than those reported by Levine and Angoff in 1958 or by Karas *et al.* in 1963. While overall score gains are of limited value in generalizing about the effects of practice and growth because of the number of sources of variation influencing them, they are useful as guidelines for the amount of score change to expect between junior and senior year and for estimating the amount of dispersion in score changes typically observed in the candidate group.

Contribution of practice and growth to score changes

As the preceding discussion has indicated, the issue of score changes on successive editions of the SAT has been under continuous study by the College Board for many years. One of the earlier studies in which an attempt was made to assess the magnitudes of both the postulated growth and the postulated practice effects was that of Pearson in 1948. This study involved the SAT-verbal scores of approximately 7,000 candidates who had repeated the SAT from 1942 through 1945. The experience of having taken the SAT once was estimated to add about 20 points on the average to future SAT-verbal test scores. A growth effect for SAT-verbal of roughly 3½ points per month on the average was found between the junior and senior years of secondary school.

A later major study of the effects of practice and growth involved students tested between May 1955 and March 1957 (Levine and Angoff, 1958). It may be appropriate to begin with a summary of the findings and then to follow with a brief description of the study procedure.

1. The practice effect was estimated to be 10 SAT score points for both SAT-verbal and SAT-mathematical for each of the first two test sessions; the third session does not seem to increase scores appreciably.

2. Growth from May of the junior year to January of the senior year was estimated as 20 points on SAT-verbal for both sexes. On SAT-mathematical, the effect of growth is estimated as 15 points for boys and 5 points for girls.

3. Growth from January to March of senior year was estimated as 10 points on both SAT-verbal and SAT-mathematical for boys. Data on girls were insufficient to permit generalization.

4. On SAT-mathematical, it was found that growth was directly related to amount of mathematics studied during the senior year of secondary school. However, this point could be studied only for a limited sample of boys.

Estimates of practice effect were based on several lines of evidence. One involved students tested in May as preliminary candidates. This group was divided into random halves; four months later (September) only one half of the group was retested; both halves were retested two months later (November). Thus, since one half of the group was tested three times and the other half twice, differences between the two halves of the group on the November test could be used as one estimate of the practice effect, that is, the effect of the September practice. A second line of evidence involved a group that had not been tested as preliminary candidates. This group was also divided into random halves. Only one half was tested in September. Both halves were tested in November, providing a comparison of a random subgroup tested twice with a random subgroup tested only once. Still a third approach involved testing the same students twice within a very short interval of time, so short that the effects of growth could be ruled out. Here, a group of May preliminary candidates was retested two weeks after the regular series. Another group of junior year students who had not been preliminary candidates was tested in special administrations twice in May, also at a two week interval. Evidence from all these groups was taken into account in making the estimate of the effect of practice on test scores.

The same groups used in the practice effect study were involved in the studies of growth. Students who had been tested as preliminary candidates in May were followed up the next January and March after regular College Board testings. Changes from May to January or March, after appropriate adjustments for the effects of practice, were used to estimate growth.

Use of retest scores in prediction

Knowledge of practice and growth, in and of itself, does not indicate which scores to use in predicting academic success. That is, even if he knows that preliminary and final scores differ in fairly systematic ways, the college admissions officer still does not know which to use. A study by Olsen and Schrader (1959) shed some light on this question. This study was done in cooperation with nine College Board colleges in which large numbers of candidates were available, some who had been tested twice and some only once. For students tested twice, preliminary and final scores were about equally accurate as predictors of college performance.

Of course, this finding did not answer the practical question of which score to use, the preliminary or the final score. Perhaps a more reasonable possibility would be to use the higher of the two. Each of these procedures shared the disadvantage that some information would be discarded. Another possibility would be to use a weighted average in which the final score is given double weight. Still another would be for each college to determine optimal weights for prediction at that college. As it turned out, the validity results supported the use of the weighted average with double weight for the final score. For purposes of prediction, this system seemed to be only slightly less accurate than the very cumbersome procedure of developing different weights for each college. In practice, still another question remained to be answered: If some applicants have been tested both as preliminary and final candidates and others only as final candidates, what system yields the best predictive results for the entire group? One possibility would be to use the senior year scores for all, under the assumption that this would put all applicants on an even footing; on this basis, of course, some information on preliminary candidates would be discarded. Another possibility—which actually turned out to be somewhat better from a prediction standpoint—was to use the weighted average for the twice-tested candidates along with the available scores for the final-only candidates.

Although the reliability of SAT score gains is quite low (around .20), it was conceivable that they would have some correlation with success in college. A reanalysis of the Olsen-Schrader data was therefore carried out (Watkins and Schrader, 1963). The validity coefficients of the score differences for the prediction of college grades turned out to be quite close to zero. The weighted average validity was —.03 for SAT-verbal and —.02 for SAT-mathematical, and 11 of the 18 coefficients obtained were negative. These results suggest that the size of an SAT score gain or loss has little to recommend it as a predictor of success in college.

Students view their performance

A questionnaire study of a group of students who experienced large score changes provided some interesting information on students' attitudes toward repeating the SAT (Jacobs, 1966). For purposes of this study, large score changes were defined as increases of 125 points or more or decreases of 75 points or more. Using a sample of schools which were known to have substantial numbers of preliminary candidates, Jacobs identified a group of 120 students for investigation. Sixty of these students were located and interviewed either in person or on the telephone during their freshman year in college. One question in the interview schedule was simply "Why do you think your score changed from your junior to your senior year?" Candidates' explanations were classified into Thorndike's (1951, p. 568) six categories of possible sources of variance in score on a particular test, based on whether the

sources are *lasting* or *temporary*, *general* or *specific*, *systematic* or *chance*.

The sources of variance suggested by the largest number of students (22 of the 60) for their performance on the test fell under the rubric "lasting and general characteristics of the individual." This category included such things as courses taken, subject-matter tutoring, outside reading, and the like. Second, with 16 cases, was the "chance" category. Next (15 students) was "temporary but general characteristics of the individual" such as health, personal problems, subjective state. As the author sees it, the "lasting and general" and "temporary but general" categories would have decidedly different implications for testing and guidance procedures if they indeed proved to be responsible for the score changes. The "lasting and general" category includes influences on test scores (for example, changes in ability level) that would not affect the validity of the test adversely since they would influence performance in college in the same way that they have influenced performance on the test. On the other hand, the "temporary but general" category includes factors that would influence test scores at a particular point in time but would *not* influence later college performance. If temporary factors were indeed responsible for the score changes, it would be desirable to have some mechanism to compensate for such temporary effects; for example, students so affected might be advised to retake the SAT (as students in this study did), and admissions officers might wish to take account of the reason for the difference in scores. Further investigation with appropriate control groups would be necessary before a general statement could be made on this issue.

It may also be of interest to mention certain categories that candidates considered relatively unimportant in their accounts of score changes: "lasting but specific characteristics of the individual" such as knowledge of the sample items, familiarity with the item format, and practice effect; "temporary and specific characteristics of the individual" such as sufficient time to finish, and their set to speed, to omit, or to guess; and "systematic or chance factors affecting the administration of the test or the appraisal of test performance" such as distracting noises.

Fatigue and anxiety

Are candidates who take the SAT and Achievement Tests in a single day at a disadvantage compared with those who are tested on two separate dates? The answer to this question would be useful to the College Board in determining optimal schedules for testing series. The same information would be useful to counselors and students in planning test-taking strategy. To some extent, colleges might also take note of potential effects of fatigue in specifying whether applicants should attend split series or complete series. Similarly, a variety of decisions might rest on knowledge about effects of anxiety on test performance. If, for example, anxiety facilitates test performance, what is the optimal level of anxiety? If the opposite is true, how should practice exercises, reassurances, or other techniques be used to allay anxiety?

In considering fatigue in relation to the College Board Admissions Testing Program, it is pertinent to review the test-taking patterns of students who take the Achievement Tests. Pitcher's 1966 analysis reveals that during the 1962-64 period a little more than a third (37 percent) of Achievement Test candidates *never* took an SAT on the same day as they took the Achievement Tests. Almost two-thirds of Achievement Test candidates did, at some time or another, subject themselves to a complete series; included in the two-thirds were those who at some time may have taken the SAT without Achievement Tests or Achievement Tests without the SAT, but they also took at least one complete series. These figures, of course, tell nothing about student response to the real or presumed effects of fatigue. Furthermore, even if a student knew that he was likely to suffer from fatigue, he might be obliged to be tested on the schedule which his school or prospective college prescribed. At the same time, it is clear that the majority of Achievement Test candidates do not *avoid* a full day of testing.

The effects of fatigue on test performance may be examined from several viewpoints. One possibility is to ask the student for his opinion. How does he feel about so much testing in a single day? Alternatively, school officials may have pertinent observations on the matter. A more analytical approach might be to look into the question, "Do students who take the complete series perform as well on the afternoon tests as students of similar ability levels who take *only* the afternoon tests?" If we think of using data for regular College Board candidates in such research, questions of self-selection enter into the picture. In particular, it is conceivable that students who take a complete series are those who "know" from past experience that six hours of testing will not exhaust them; or perhaps they are exceptionally inspired to "get it over with." At the same time, the less hardy may go out of their way to take a split series. Such decision-making undoubtedly occurs in certain cases; however, it seems unlikely that students have complete freedom of choice, or that they can estimate their susceptibility to fatigue with great accuracy.

Opinions of students and school officials

In the mid 1940s, the College Board looked into the pros and cons of the one-day series versus a two-day series with SAT and Achievement Test programs on different days. Opinions regarding the possible change to a two-day program were obtained from candidates and school headmasters in a questionnaire survey (French, 1947). Replies from some 400 students who took a complete series in December 1946 did not reveal an overwhelming preference one way or the other: 48 percent preferred a one-day program, 40 percent a two-day program, and 12 percent were doubtful. When asked "Did you feel so tired on your last examination this afternoon that you could not do yourself justice as compared to your performance on the first hour of examination that you took today?" a third of the candidates replied that they had been at a serious disadvantage, a little more than a third (37 percent) that they had been at no disadvantage, and the remainder (29 percent) were doubtful. Preference for the two-day schedule was, as might be expected, related to the belief that fatigue produced a score disadvantage. Thus, a large majority of those favoring two days felt that they had been at a disadvantage while a large majority of those favoring one day said that they were *not* at such a disadvantage.

Headmasters seemed to be more favorable than candidates to a two-day session. About 59 percent preferred the hypothetical two-day series, 26 percent preferred the one-day series and 15 percent had no preference. Those favoring the two-day series felt that fatigue had placed their students at a serious disadvantage; as might be expected, the role of fatigue was considered of doubtful or no importance by those favoring the one-day session.

Effect of fatigue on test scores

At about the same time as French's questionnaire survey, Tucker (1948) carried out a study bearing on the relation of Achievement Test scores to fatigue. This study involved a comparison of two subgroups of April 1946 Achievement Test candidates: one made up of students who took only Achievement Tests on that date and the other made up of those who took a complete series. Whether April 1946 Achievement Test only candidates had taken the SAT at some earlier point in their senior year is not reported; it would be reasonable to guess that most of them had. To permit statistical adjustments for ability differences, the study group was limited to candidates who had previously taken the SAT in June 1945 while they were in their junior year. The preliminary June 1945 SAT score was used as the measure of ability (control) in this analysis. Separate analyses were made for subgroups with scores on French, Social Studies, and Chemistry. The question, specifically, was, "How do the two groups, Achievement Test only and complete series, compare on Achievement Test performance *after* appropriate adjustment is made for differences in the abilities measured by the SAT?" Separate analyses were carried out for public and independent school students; because the numbers of boys were very small, the analyses were limited to girls.

Results of the analyses suggested that differences in Achievement Test scores, after controlling for SAT differences, were vanishingly small: candidates who took the complete series did not suffer in their Achievement Test scores. As noted earlier, self-selection may play an unknown role in any such study based on operational testing. Tucker (1948) cites another circumstance that might obscure the results of this study. Assuming that the Achievement Test only subgroup had, in fact, taken the SAT only once (June 1945) whereas the complete-series subgroup took it at least twice (June 1945 and April 1946), one might reason along the following lines: students in the latter subgroup *may* have taken the test twice because their first scores were lower than they or others expected; those who did better than expected would not repeat. If such were the case, the complete-series subgroup would appear to over-achieve on the Achievement Tests in relation to their too-low June SAT's. This point would seem to be important *only* if it were known that the Achievement Test only subgroup had not repeated the SAT earlier in their senior year.

On the whole, it seems unlikely that fatigue from a full day of testing is a major determiner of performance on the Achievement Tests. The fact that about 25 years have elapsed since Tucker's study and that the College Board candidate population has changed considerably since that time might indicate the desirability of a fatigue study at some future date. However, research in this area will probably enjoy low priority on the agenda, at least for the time being, both because of the earlier results and because the main body of research on fatigue in relation to performance on mental tasks supports these results (Wohlhueter, 1966).

Effects of anxiety on test scores

Direct studies of anxiety pose serious problems of design and execution. One of many problems is how to induce anxiety experimentally. Another is how to identify and measure anxiety either in an experimental or an operational setting. Further, even if it is found that anxiety is associated with low test scores, this finding proves nothing about the role of anxiety in bringing about the low scores or vice versa. Despite the many problems involved in the study of the relationship between anxiety and test performance, a substantial number of studies have been carried out, including an extensive series of studies by Sarason and his associates (Sarason *et al.*, 1960).

One approach to studying the effect of anxiety on testing was that followed by French (1962b). In this study, comparisons were made between subtests administered as part of a regular SAT versus the same subtests administered under conditions that were presumably more relaxed. Specifically, each of the candidates from 16 high schools took one of four special half-hour subtests along with his regular January 1960 SAT. The special materials were strictly similar to SAT and were printed as part of the SAT booklet with no indica-

tion that they were experimental; students doubtless assumed they were indeed part of the SAT and were as "anxious" while taking the special sections as they were on the real SAT sections. Two special verbal subtests were involved, so-called Verbal-A and Verbal-B. Students who took Verbal-A with their regular SAT were given Verbal-B at their own school either some days before or some days after the regular College Board series and vice versa. Similarly, two special mathematical subtests were alternated between the regular testing and the special before-or-after testing. In the special testings, students were told that the examination was for research purposes and that the scores would be reported to their school but not to the colleges to which they were applying; it was hoped that these provisions might lead to a relaxed atmosphere while still maintaining some level of motivation. In addition, students responded to questionnaires and to scales believed to provide anxiety measures.

A particularly interesting feature of the analysis was the study of scores earned under anxious or nonanxious conditions in relation to school grades. It turned out that concurrent validities with school grades were about equal for "anxious" scores (earned on the special tests in the regular SAT session), for the "nonanxious" scores (earned in the special school administrations), and for the regular SAT. It seems unlikely, therefore, that there would be differences in the predictive validity of the various scores, that is, their relation to grades subsequently earned in college. Comparison of scores earned under "relaxed" conditions with those earned at the presumably more "anxious" SAT session revealed no significant changes for either boys or girls, for either the verbal or the mathematical test—although for girls there was a significant *difference* between the effect of anxiety on the verbal test and the effect of anxiety on the mathematical test. The girls obtained increased verbal scores and decreased mathematical scores under "relaxed" conditions. French suggests that the reason for this result is that their dislike for mathematics may have led them to give up on the mathematics test in the absence of pressure to persevere, while their preference for verbal material would support good performance on the verbal test. Possible support for this interpretation might come from a further finding of French that the girls who felt most anxious were the ones whose mathematics scores were higher under the "anxious" conditions of a regular SAT administration. On the whole, however, French felt that the effects of anxiety were not sufficiently consistent or reliable to enable him to draw any firm conclusions about them.

French's study explored potential test anxiety as a function of possible exposure to the public view rather than as a function of a threat to one's ego. If, for example, as Sarason argues (Sarason *et al.*, 1960), the test-anxious students have been conditioned from early childhood, then anxiety will be present whether or not the test is given under relaxed or under anxious conditions.

Appropriateness of a single SAT

The Multi-Level Experiment (Angoff and Huddleston, 1958) was designed with particular reference to the question: Is high overall reliability being achieved for the SAT at the expense of accurate measurement at the upper and lower extremes of the range of talent? In the mid-fifties, when the Multi-Level study was initiated, the question of the accuracy of measurement at all points of the score scale assumed substantial importance for a number of reasons. "For one thing, the increases in candidate volume resulting from the population 'bulge' in the college-entrance age group were expected to produce a picture of keener competition for admission to the most selective colleges and presumably a corresponding emphasis on selection at higher ability levels. Secondly, some institutions were expressing an interest in more differentiation among low-scoring candidates. Finally, the growing popularity of scholarship programs made it essential that the limits of accurate measurement be extended, particularly at the upper extreme of the range." (Angoff and Huddleston, 1958, p. 1.)

Two methods for extending the SAT range were selected for experimental investigation:

a. A single *broad-range test* composed of items more heterogeneous in difficulty than the SAT at that time.

b. Two *narrow-range tests* at different but overlapping ranges of talent, each of which was fairly homogeneous in item difficulty. Together, the pair of tests would presumably cover a wider range than the SAT in use at the time.

An advantage was expected for the second plan: two narrow-range tests at different levels, each used with the group for which its difficulty level was more appropriate. What was needed, however, was an estimate of the *size* of the advantage of the narrow-range tests. Clearly, such information would be critical for the construction of future tests. Thus, the study aimed to find out (a) the reliability of each test at different ability levels and (b) the validity of each test in various types of colleges with student groups of varying levels of ability.

It was recognized that decisions on future SATs would not be based solely on statistical characteristics of the tests. In addition, it was clear that formidable administrative and policy problems would be posed by the two-level test system. How, for example, should the candidate be directed to the appropriate test? Should he take a screening test prior to the regular SAT administration? (The PSAT was not introduced until some time after the conclusion of the Multi-Level study, or else it would presumably have been considered as a possible solution.) Should high school officials direct him to the test level they deemed appropriate? Should he be *forced* to take the test considered appropriate? Would it be possible to convince the public that no injustices were being done by the two-level system?

The study itself did not place major emphasis on the experimental evaluation of these routing difficulties. Indeed, if the experiment indicated that the two-level system had no *major* advantage over the broad-range system, there would be no need for an exhaustive analysis of the routing problem. However, the study did incorporate a limited analysis of routing accuracy that will not be covered here. Future explorations of the routing problem will no doubt attempt to make use of computer technology to solve the technical problems of routing.

The study design, as befitted the problem, was a fairly intricate one. Three types of verbal tests were used: a broad-range verbal test, a pair of narrow-range verbal tests (a high-level and a low-level verbal test), and a so-called verbal equating test; the equating test was part of a previously used operational SAT. Similarly, there were three types of mathematical tests. Three categories of colleges were used in the study: colleges with relatively high SAT means (600 and higher), colleges with relatively low SAT means (400 and lower), and colleges with "medium" means (between 425 and 575). The equating tests and the broad-range tests were administered at all three types of colleges. In addition, students at colleges with high means took the high-level narrow-range tests; at colleges with low means, students took the low-level narrow-range tests; and at the middle group of colleges, random subgroups of students took the high- or low-level narrow-range tests.

The reliability analysis began by defining six subgroups on the basis of score level on the verbal equating test. Six reliability coefficients were then determined for the low-level verbal test, one for each subgroup. The reliability coefficient, of course, was based only on students in the subgroup who had actually taken the low-level verbal test. To permit rigorous comparisons, six reliability coefficients were then computed for the broad-range verbal test, based on exactly the same students used in the analysis of the low-level verbal test. Similar procedures were followed for the high-level verbal test. Then, six subgroups were defined on the basis of score level on the mathematics equating test and reliability analyses were repeated for low-level and high-level mathematics tests. In addition to these separate analyses for the six verbal and six mathematics subgroups, analyses were done across the several subgroups for which low-level tests were considered appropriate and then across the several subgroups for which high-level tests were considered appropriate. The overall conclusion of the reliability study was that the narrow-range test had an advantage of about .03 or .04 over the broad-range test for groups that had taken an appropriate test. As might be expected, there were sizable differences in favor of the broad-range tests for groups that had taken the inappropriate narrow-range tests.

On the basis of the reliability differences, it was expected that differences in validity would be very small indeed. This expectation was confirmed in a series of validity studies in which freshman average grade was used as the criterion (Olsen, 1959). Separate validity analyses were carried out for a total of 28 student groups in 21 colleges, involving groups of men and of women, of liberal arts students, and of engineers. Average validities across the 28 groups were exactly the same for the broad-range and the narrow-range verbal tests. For mathematics, the narrow-range tests had an advantage of .01 in average validity.

The problem of accurate measurement at all parts of the score range has recently drawn the attention of a number of researchers who view sequential testing as offering potentially efficient solutions. Several studies have pointed out some of the theoretical advantages of programmed tests wherein performance on initial items determines the selection of subsequent items presented to the individual (Cleary, Linn and Rock, 1968a, 1968b; Rock, Barone and Boldt, 1968). When each individual takes a set of items of an appropriate difficulty level for him, a substantially smaller set of items is sufficient for obtaining a reliable score. Linn, Rock and Cleary (1968, p. 1) indicate that while programmed tests are ". . . not well suited to the present paper-and-pencil technology of the testing industry, [they] are being made more feasible by improved use of computer hardware."

Consideration of new item types for the SAT

The various editions of the SAT that have been prepared since the test was introduced in 1926 have contained a total of 38 different major item types on which reported scores were based. In addition, a considerable number of other item types were used experimentally (Loret, 1960). It is clear that the SAT can best serve its function as a common yardstick of scholastic aptitude if the predictive efficiency of item types in use is periodically compared with other available types of items. Coffman (1963b) has noted that this policy of "continuous evaluation" was provided for in the first form of the SAT and is an enduring characteristic of the test.

The issue of SAT score reliability is often raised when changes in item types are proposed that would have the effect of increasing the heterogeneity of the SAT. It is important to consider in this connection the fact that today's SAT contains considerably fewer items than could conceivably be offered in its present time limit. The 1936 SAT, for example, allowed 115 minutes for 300 vocabulary items, an average of about 2.6 items per minute. Today's SAT allows 75 minutes for 90 verbal items including a significant proportion of reading comprehension items (see Chapter II), an average of 1.2 items per minute. The importance of reading comprehension skills for any definition of potential for college success clearly supports the notion that today's SAT is a more valid measure of scholastic aptitude than it would be if it were made slightly more reliable by the elimination of reading comprehension items in favor of considerably more vocabulary items. Reliability is, of course, a major aim in the development of the SAT, but validity for its function is a higher goal. Ideally, both goals can be served simultaneously. French (1957) notes that score reliability is important from a public relations point of view, as the earlier section on practice and growth points out, but goes on to question the composition of the SAT as follows:

"While there is a commendable variety of verbal item types within the verbal sections and some variety of mathematical item types within the mathematics sections, the urge for reliable scores has resulted in a test that is extraordinarily long for a two-score test. It is theoretically indisputable that replacing parts of the verbal or mathematical sections with diverse test materials would lower the overall reliability of the test. However, the salient question is whether it is possible to raise substantially the validity of the test and to increase flexibility in the use of test scores while reducing reliability only a little." (French, 1957, p. 45.)

Three studies directed toward the possible diversification of the SAT will be summarized here: First, a study begun in 1951 involving the relation of a number of new item types to four-year college performance (French, 1957); second, a study specifically directed toward the evaluation of new item types for highly able students (French, 1964b); and third, a repetition of the second study to check whether materials that looked promising for highly able students would be equally effective across a broader spectrum of ability (Flaugher and Rock, 1966).

New item types for predicting four-year performance

From the standpoint of the present discussion, perhaps the most important feature of the first study was its exploration of the reliability and validity of an SAT having six subscores as compared with the usual SAT (French, 1957). Eleven different item types were chosen for study: 1) Social Studies Reading, 2) Science Reading, 3) Inductive Reasoning, 4) Integration (an artificial language test involving complex directions), 5) Sufficiency of Data, 6) Data Interpretation, 7) Visualization, 8) Best Arguments, 9) Perceptual Speed, 10) Memory, and 11) General Information. General Information involved the type of information that would ordinarily be gained through hobbies or incidental reading rather than the type of information usually acquired in school. There were General Information questions in seven fields (art, literature, and so forth); separate scores on the seven fields were used as predictors in the study. The item types were selected with four main considerations in mind, considerations that also apply to other studies of this nature. First, they should test some function not already in the SAT; second, they should not be coachable; third, they should not depend heavily upon specific school curriculums; and, fourth, they should measure something believed to be important for some phase of college work.

This study was done in cooperation with 10 College Board colleges. Tests were administered to entering freshmen in the fall of 1951; validity studies were undertaken at the end of the first year of college work and again at the end of the fourth year.

Each college administered 4 of the 11 tests. Only one test—General Information—was given at all 10 colleges. Although the practicalities of limited testing time at the colleges necessitated a reduced study design of this sort, nevertheless it hampered rigorous comparision of the usefulness of the different tests.

The analyses of primary interest here—those involving the reliability and validity of a six-part SAT—were done at the three largest colleges only. Results for the seven other colleges were used as a guide in the selection of item types for inclusion. Thus, the three colleges provided cross-validation of a sort.

The six-part SAT included the regular SAT-verbal and -mathematical scores, Literature and Government scores from the General Information Test, and scores on two other item types that were varied across the three colleges.

The hypothetical new test showed up noticeably better than the regular SAT. For the three colleges, the average validity of the six-part test against four-year grades was .64 as compared with .56 for the regular SAT. (These multiple R's were based on correlations adjusted for restriction of range and for test length. The numbers of cases were large, ranging from 449 to 870 for the three colleges. For that reason the author deemed it unnecessary to adjust the correlation values for shrinkage.) The estimated reliability of the six-part test was only .01 lower than that for the regular SAT.

At one of the colleges, high school record was evaluated along with the six-part SAT. In this case the multiple correlation for the six-part SAT was only .048 larger than that for the regular SAT plus high school record, suggesting that at least part of the "new" information in the additional parts was already available in the high school record.

Since the six-part SAT was not uniform across the three colleges, it was not possible to draw firm conclusions about the relative merits of different item types. It did appear that General Information, a score based on only 15 items, was the largest contributor to validity. In commenting on the high validity of this test, French suggests that it "probably reflects the importance to the criterion of width of serious reading outside of school requirements. The validity may be as high as it is because the student who abounds in this kind of information would probably possess not only the kind of aptitude measured by the SAT-V but, in addition, the willingness to spend time in serious extra study that produces a good high school record. While something more complex than breadth of information may be the desirable outcome of a college education, it is, nevertheless, undeniably true that the students who can demonstrate knowledge of facts are often the ones who can think most clearly and are certainly the ones who fill up the academic honor roll." (French, 1957, p. 34.)

The statistical outcome of this study supported the potential usefulness of a General Information type of test within the SAT, yet, for more than one reason, this item type was not introduced into the operational part of the SAT. It was thought, for example, that the introduction of a factual test like General Information might have the effect of encouraging schools to spend time coaching for this type of test rather than on teaching the kinds of material that teachers believe to have the most educational value. Then, too, there were practical reasons, such as the danger of a loss of test security. Information questions, it was felt, are highly visible and would be remembered after the test and transmitted to other students who might take the same form of the test at another time. Finally, information items tend to have current value and become obsolete in relatively short order. Thus they restrict the reuse of test forms, thereby imposing real limitations on the flexibility of the testing program.

Validity of new item types for high-aptitude students

In designing a study of the SAT as a predictor for students with relatively high aptitude, French started with the premise: "The solution to this problem is probably not to give these students more difficult tests of the same kind. It seems contrary to common sense that verbal and mathematical tests should reign so supremely as predictors in the complex domain of college work. The thinking required for success at high-level colleges must be particularly complex. This experiment was set up, therefore, to try out new types of items that would exceed the SAT as a challenge to the student's verbal and quantitative capabilities and also bring a wider range of his capabilities into play." (French, 1964b, p. 185.)

The experiment included the following 15 item types: 1) Spatial Reasoning, 2) Data Sufficiency*, 3) Insightful Reasoning, 4) Logical Reasoning, 5) Alternative Expressions, 6) General Understanding, 7) General Information, 8) Short Item Information, 9) Identification of People, 10) Artificial Language, 11) Induction, 12) Object Sorting, 13) Directed Memory, 14) Verbal Fluency, 15) Reference Reading. A brief description of the four tests that showed up especially well in the analysis appears on page 158. Eleven colleges cooperated by testing their freshmen in the fall of 1960. However, only six of the 15 tests were administered at each college. The analysis also utilized SAT, College Board Achievement Test scores, and high school record as predictors. The ability levels at the participating colleges may be gauged from the fact that the SAT-verbal

---

*The Data Sufficiency item type was introduced into the SAT in 1959. It was included in the study to obtain evidence as to the desirability of increasing the number of such items in SAT-M.

means ranged from 586 to 698 and SAT-mathematical means from 614 to 754.

The average validity against first-year average grades turned out to be .25 for SAT-verbal, .23 for SAT-mathematical, and .35 for high school record. Correction for restriction of range raised the average coefficients to .39, .38, and .43. The Achievement Tests had uncorrected average values of .29 for the English Composition Test and .37 for the average of the other two scores; correction for restriction of range raised these to .40 and .47. French viewed these findings as support for the position that the ". . . effectiveness of the [SAT] is somewhat curtailed at high-level colleges." (French, 1964b p. 191.) The corrected correlation coefficients, however, seem quite consistent with other findings that the SAT is useful even at the upper levels of talent.

When the experimental tests were brought into the picture, validities rose substantially. If the results obtained were confirmed elsewhere, it would appear to be statistically advantageous to substitute General Information or Short Item Information for some of the present SAT-verbal and to substitute Insightful Reasoning and Data Sufficiency (beyond that already used) for SAT-mathematical. Results for the colleges in this study suggested that inclusion of such materials might increase the validity of the SAT by .08 to .15. In any case, it seemed doubtful that the superiority of the hypothetical new test would hold upon cross-validation. Verification of the findings seemed of particular importance in view of the methodological problems stemming from the administration of different tests to different groups.

Finally, it may be appropriate to describe the four item types which showed up especially well in this study:

Data Sufficiency. The same type of item as the Sufficiency of Data item type in the 1957 study, each item consists of a question followed by two statements labeled (1) and (2), in which certain data are given. The task is to decide whether the question can be answered by statement (1) alone, (2) alone, (1) and (2) together, either (1) or (2), or not at all. A number of mathematical areas are covered in various problem settings. Some problems, for example, are like the typical written problem in arithmetic, and other problems involve formal algebraic or geometrical principles.

Insightful Reasoning. The problems in this test involve arithmetic and very simple algebra or geometry. Each one has at least two methods of solution—one laborious and time-consuming and the other insightful and rapid. The directions warn the student that he should look for insightful, short-cut solutions to the problems. In the time allowed, it is not possible to solve many of them by the more conventional, more obvious, but more laborious method.

General Information. The questions here concern world affairs, business, art, and science. They are basically the same type of item used in French's earlier study, requiring knowledge that could be acquired through general reading, hobbies, or school work. They are

relatively unsusceptible to solution through general verbal ability or "common sense." For example:

In contrast to the AFL, the CIO was a federation of

(A) Industrial unions
(B) Craft unions
(C) Company unions
(D) Independent unions
(E) National unions

Short Item Information. The items consist of a word, name, or phrase to be associated with one of the five alternative words, names, or phrases offered. This is essentially a vocabulary test in nonacademic areas. An example might be the following item referring to types of aircraft:

U-2:
(A) Bomber
(B) Interceptor
(C) Reconnaissance
(D) Transport
(E) Cargo

Validity of new item types at various ability levels

Flaugher and Rock (1966) have reported a further study of the tests that French (1964b) identified as promising for high-aptitude students. In the later study, validities were determined for groups at nine colleges thought to be more representative of the range of College Board test users. Mean SAT-verbal scores at the participating colleges ranged from about 400 to the low 600s. Tests were administered early in the freshman year. When end-of-year grades became available, the validity analyses were undertaken.

Experimental item types included in the study were Data Sufficiency, Insightful Reasoning, General Information, Short Item Information, Directed Memory, and Integration. The first four of these are described immediately above. The others may be described briefly as follows:

Directed Memory. This is a test of reading comprehension in which the student is directed to look for certain things in his reading, and where he is unable to refer back to the reading passage in order to search for the answer to the questions. A task of this kind seems close to what a college student must actually perform in carrying out many of his assignments.

Integration. The task here is to follow complex and interconnecting rules in order to solve problems. Tests of integration, often called "following directions," have been constructed with a variety of subject-matter materials. The one used in this study employs a matrix of alphabetic characters through which the test-taker is directed by the instructions, arriving at one letter as the correct answer.

An essential feature of the study was the identification of an optimal four-test battery. For this purpose, test selection procedures (stepwise regression) were applied to the correlation matrix for each subgroup within the nine colleges. Inspection of results across subgroups led to the decision that the four-test battery should include the regular SAT-verbal, General Information, Data Sufficiency, and Insightful Reasoning.

The validity of a best-weighted combination of high school record plus the usual SAT scores was then compared with the validity of a best-weighted combination of high school record plus the four-test battery, after appropriate adjustment for test length. As it turned out, ". . . the improvement achieved by this rather radical alteration (that is, a drastic change in the content of the SAT and the reporting of four scores) is for the most part quite undramatic." (Flaugher and Rock, 1966, p. 25.) Specifically, for only two of the 30 groups was the improvement in validity greater than .05; for another 11 groups, it was .02 to .04. The authors pointed out that the improvement would very likely have been even less if validities had been checked on new groups, since the experimental design involved some capitalization on chance; that is, the validities were obtained on the same groups used in test selection.

On the basis of this analysis, the authors concluded that: (1) SAT-verbal is performing effectively, and any substantial reduction of testing time in order to substitute other measures is likely to impair the overall predictive validity of SAT. (2) The time devoted to conventional mathematics in SAT could be reduced in order to substitute Insightful Reasoning and more Data Sufficiency. (3) Although General Information would add to the predictive power of the test, it should not be included at the expense of SAT-verbal. (As noted earlier, any contemplated operational use of General Information would have had to take into account the practical problems associated with this item type, among them being its high visibility and ease of recall, its apparent susceptibility to coaching, and its tendency toward obsolescence.) (4) There was no indication that the tests were "unfair" to any portion of the population within the limits of the study; that is, separate analyses by sex, aptitude level, and socioeconomic status did not reveal differences in predictive validity.

It is interesting to note that, on the basis of his studies, French suggested a substantial change in the composition of the SAT whereas, on the basis of their study making use of the same tests, Flaugher and Rock suggested only one minor change, a change in the content balance of the mathematical portion of the test. As noted earlier, in the 1957 French study the advantage for the new tests appeared to be decreased when high school record was included in a composite with an operational SAT and in a composite with a hypothetical SAT. In the 1964 French study, high school record was used as a predictor but there were methodological problems including the administration of different tests to different groups. The Flaugher and Rock study used a concurrently obtained SAT that may have helped give a more accurate picture of the relative usefulness of the present test and a possible revised test.

New test content

The item types evaluated in studies discussed in the previous section differed somewhat from traditional SAT materials, but their incorporation into the SAT would probably not alter its basic characteristics drastically. The studies discussed in this section, on the other hand, have evaluated test materials that are decidedly different from those in the present SAT. The only unifying property of the various instruments is that they were developed by ETS staff members in their explorations of individual differences. Each of the instruments has been considered as a possible contributor to the Admissions Testing Program, but as of 1970 none had been incorporated into the operational program. Future educational and social developments will most certainly provide the impetus for continued research directed toward identifying appropriate predictors of academic success. Five tests will be discussed in the following order:

1. Biographical Inventory
2. Tests of Developed Ability
3. Academic Interest Index
4. Myers-Briggs Type Indicator
5. Formulating Hypotheses Test

Biographical Inventory

The work of Anastasi, Meade, and Schneiders (1960) in developing a scoring key for a biographical inventory is of particular interest since the outcomes gave strong encouragement to the use of biographical data in college admissions. Further, the care that went into criterion development should provide a worthy model for other researchers in this area.

The biographical inventory used in the study was a four-page document covering a wide variety of items: objective facts regarding the student's present status and previous history; his reported reactions to past activities, such as preference for school subjects, books, and plays; difficulties he experienced in high school; his plans to fulfill educational and vocational objectives; his intent to participate in college activities; the areas in which he expects to encounter difficulty in college and would like help. The inventory also included items of a more projective nature—for example, incomplete sentences pertaining to college and post-college matters ("Twenty years from now I hope to . . ."). In addition, the student was asked to write an essay on the topic: "How I chose my field of interest in college."

The criterion was defined, rather broadly, as ". . . the extent to which the student fulfills the recognized objectives of the particular college and displays the traits the college has undertaken to foster and develop." (Anastasi et al., 1960, p. 1.) Operationally, of course, such a criterion would vary from college to college; although this study applied only to Fordham College, the authors make the point that Fordham's environment is probably typical of other College Board colleges.

Criterion development involved the identification of three distinct groups of students: a "positive" group who have given repeated evidence of actively advancing the objectives of the college rather than just passively adjusting to the college environment; a "negative" group, made up of students who have clearly failed, for predominantly nonintellectual reasons, to adjust satisfactorily to the particular college environment; and an intermediate "average" group for which concrete evidence was lacking of either personality maladjustment *or* assets.

The breadth of the criterion is indicated by the fact that some nine sources of information were used to identify students for inclusion in the three groups: faculty ratings, faculty adviser reports, ROTC records, data collected in connection with selection for the honors program, student government records, election to the extracurricular honor society, Office of Psychological Services records, Dean of Men records, and the usual academic records. Three judges (the Dean of Men, the Director of the Office of Psychological Services, and an experienced faculty member and adviser) reviewed the records and made final selections for the criterion groups. Positive, negative, and average criterion groups were selected from the class of 1958 and again from the class of 1959.

Scoring keys were determined empirically from responses of criterion groups from the class of 1958; cross-validation was based on the groups from the class of 1959. On cross-validation, the inventory key turned out to be better than SAT-verbal or -mathematical scores for differentiating between criterion groups. It should be noted, however, that the best-weighted combination of SAT-V and SAT-M scores was not used in this study nor was high school record used in connection with SAT-V and SAT-M. Therefore, it is not known to what extent the biographical inventory duplicated the work of these other predictors. Point biserial correlations were computed using these dichotomies: (a) positive versus negative group, (b) positive versus average group, and (c) average versus negative group. Correlations of these dichotomies with inventory scores were .55, .35, and .26 respectively. In each of the three possible comparisons, the two parts of the SAT, taken separately, had lower correlations with the criterion than the biographical inventory. The correlations for SAT-V were .35, .29, and .09 respectively. The correlations for SAT-M were .30, .13, and .19. Since the SAT was used in selection and these correlations were not corrected for restriction of range, it is clear that the parts of the SAT were at a disadvantage when compared with the biographical inventory. It is possible to note, however, that the SAT appeared relatively weak at discriminating between average and negative criterion groups, ". . . a finding consistent with the hypothesis that average and negative groups differ in personality rather than in ability factors." (Anastasi, *et al.*, 1960, p. 33.)

Tests of Developed Ability

As Dyer put it, the Tests of Developed Ability (TDA) represent an attempt to find a common ground on which two sets of grumblers could agree, the subject of the grumbling being the Achievement Tests. "On one side were those who felt that the [Achievement] tests, by putting a heavy premium on factual knowledge, deprived the schools of freedom to organize instruction in the ways they thought best calculated to foster mature thinking. On the other side were those who felt that the content of the tests was not well enough defined to provide the sort of blueprint they thought they needed for preparing college-bound students." (Dyer, 1957, p. 5.) The TDA, by comparison, aimed to place less emphasis on the measurement of specific knowledge and greater emphasis on the measurement of understanding and of the ability to apply knowledge of principles to problems. The new tests were intended to provide a less structured measure of aptitude for college studies than that provided by the traditional Admissions Testing Program.

In 1956, after several years of active committee and staff work, the TDA battery was ready for field tryouts. Tests were available in three broad areas, Social Studies, Humanities, and Science. Within each of these broad areas, the tests yielded two scores designed to measure two somewhat different abilities. All except the Social Studies Essay were of the objective, multiple-choice type. The tests may be described briefly as follows (Coffman, 1957):

Social Studies Ability was designed primarily to measure the ability to apply understanding and information from the student's own background to problems presented in the test. It also contained questions involving recall of basic facts, perception of relationships among facts, terms, concepts, and trends, and ability to draw inferences when factual background was given with questions. *Social Studies Essay* was designed to measure the ability to reveal understanding and impart knowledge in clear and coherent language.

Humanities Reference was intended to reflect primarily the student's breadth of experience in the humanities. (Humanities Reference and Science Glossary described below were not intended to be operational tests; rather, they were included in the experimental battery as comparison tests to throw light on the ability tests and to enable a clearer interpretation of the findings.) *Humanities Abilities* was designed to test ". . . the ability to comprehend—to see form and purpose behind words, paint, stone, and sound and the ability to discriminate—to . . . discern similarities and differences between poems . . . paintings . . . and between musical selections." (Coffman, 1957, p. 8.)

Science Glossary involves understanding the basic forms and concepts in six areas of science. *Science Abilities* aims to measure the ability to apply scientific facts and principles to data such as one might encounter in further study of science. The questions in many cases require the application of quantitative thinking, but there is no mathematics test as such.

One way of evaluating the TDA is to determine their content validity. As Coffman points out, "To a certain extent, any test which involves achievement, whether it involves achievement in the narrow sense of knowledge of particular subject matter or achievement in the broad sense of developed ability, is valid to the extent that competent judges conclude that the test questions require the student to have the desired knowledge or ability in order to make correct responses. A carefully constructed examination, then, becomes its own criterion; it constitutes better evidence of a student's accomplishment than the informal tests and uncontrolled observations which often determine teachers' judgments." (Coffman, 1957, p. 7.) An indication of the content validity of the TDA was provided, first, by the very process of test development: committees of experts agreed on definitions of ability. Second, when committees submitted their statements of objectives and test questions to representative panels of secondary school and college teachers, the panel judgment confirmed the committee judgment (Coffman, 1957).

The validity of the TDA was also evaluated in empirical studies of the prediction of college grades (Olsen, 1957). Eleven College Board colleges cooperated by administering the TDA to all of their freshman in fall 1956. When first-term college grades became available for these students, it was possible to compare the validity of the TDA with the validity of regular College Board tests that students had taken before admission to college.

One validity comparison involved the TDA versus the SAT. The results suggested that the TDA and the SAT were about equally effective for predicting freshman average grades. Comparisons were also made between the TDA and the Achievement Tests. Here, it was assumed that the relevant comparison was the validity of the SAT plus the TDA versus the validity of SAT plus Achievement Test scores. The results suggested that the SAT-Achievement combination had a substantial advantage over the SAT-TDA combination for engineering students; for liberal arts students, there was a rather small advantage in favor of the SAT-Achievement combination. Finally, detailed comparisons were made between the TDA and the individual Achievement Tests for predicting grades in five separate academic areas: English, foreign languages, social studies, mathematics, and science. Within each area, the question was asked: Do appropriate Achievement Tests make a contribution to prediction above and beyond that obtainable from the TDA? Not surprisingly, the Achievement Tests in foreign languages and mathematics appeared to measure abilities not covered by the TDA. The science tests also added to the prediction obtainable from the TDA; however, when the mathematics tests and the TDA were used as the predictive team, the science tests added very little. The Social Studies and English Composition Tests seemed to make only a negligible contribution to prediction

beyond that obtainable from the TDA.

If the TDA had turned out to be as valid or almost as valid as the traditional Admissions Testing Program, it would have been considered as a substitute for the traditional program. In the final analysis, the slightly greater validity for the operational program prevented this drastic change, but many of the approaches first used in developing the TDA were later incorporated into the items in the Achievement Tests.

Academic Interest Index

The Academic Interest Index has a long history, dating back some 30 years to the eight-year Study of the Progressive Education Association (Smith and Tyler, 1942). In recent years, this inventory has been revised with particular reference to the prediction of college grades and satisfaction with major field (French, 1964a). It now consists of 192 activity statements to each of which the examinee must make a like-indifferent-dislike response (for example, would he like to write stories, to model with clay, to repair electrical appliances). The Index does *not* ask the student to make judgments of occupational titles or job duty statements; instead, it focuses on activities that are familiar to students, although it does not include school work as such. The 192 statements include 16 items in each of 12 areas: biology, English, fine arts, mathematics, social sciences, secretarial, physical sciences, foreign languages, music, engineering, home economics, and business (the "executive" scale).

Halpern (1965) administered the revised Index to eleventh grade students on two occasions. Separate analyses were carried out for four subgroups: males and females planning to go to college (N = 577 and N = 593, respectively), and males and females not planning to go to college (N = 362 and N = 499, respectively).

Halpern's study involved analyses of five points which may be summarized briefly as follows: *First*, internal consistency analyses, based on the initial testing, were carried out for each of the 12 scales in each of the four subgroups. The median coefficient was .91. None of the 48 coefficients was under .86. "Reliability" coefficients from self-report inventories such as the Academic Interest Index must be interpreted differently from reliability coefficients for ability tests. Items on the Index have intercorrelations of about .40 as compared with intercorrelations of about .09 for SAT-V items and about .13 for SAT-M items. In interpreting the intercorrelations of the interest items, the possibility of response sets, memory carry-over, or social desirability bias must be kept in mind. *Second*, test-retest reliability was assessed by correlating scores earned on the first administration with those earned three weeks later on a second administration. The median coefficient for the 12 scales in the four subgroups was .86. *Third*, assignment of items to scales was evaluated by checking whether items had higher correlations with scales to which they belonged than with other scales. That is, if an item had a higher correlation with some other scale, it was judged to be misplaced. (In determining correlations, each item was eliminated from the scale of which it was a part.) By this criterion, only 4 of the 768 items examined (192 for four subgroups) were misplaced. An additional 56 items (7 percent of the total) correlated as high with some other scale as with their own. *Fourth*, intercorrelations among the scales were determined to check whether the 12 scores were relatively independent. Of 264 different correlations (intercorrelations of 12 scores for four groups) only 21 were .50 or greater. Where the scales were highly correlated, the relationships seemed to be appropriate. For example, the physical science scale had rather high relationships with the biology and engineering scales. *Fifth*, as a check on the construct validity of the Index, profiles for the four subgroups were compared. It turned out that score patterns were indeed in accord with expectation. For example, females who did not plan to go to college had relatively high scores on secretarial and home economics scales whereas females planning on college were relatively high on the English, fine arts, foreign languages, and music scales.

On the basis of these findings, Halpern concluded: "This study has confirmed the extensive history of developmental research conducted on the *Interest Index*. Looking to the future, we may recall that the item selection carried out in developing this test did more than consider item-scale correlations. Two other criteria were also used. These were item validities for freshman grades and for satisfaction with college major. If the scale property results are any indication, we may expect that this test will perform equally well in additional validity studies." (Halpern, 1965, p. 21.)

Myers-Briggs Type Indicator

The Myers-Briggs Type Indicator is a self-report inventory which is intended to measure variables stemming from the Jungian personality typology. It consists of four scales: Extraversion-Introversion (E-I), Sensation-Intuition (S-N), Thinking-Feeling (T-F), and Judging-Perceiving (J-P). The E-I scale is presumed to measure interest in things and people or concepts and ideas; the S-N scale, tendencies to perceive through the usual sensory processes or indirectly via the unconscious; the T-F scale, tendencies to judge (or evaluate) phenomena rationally and impersonally or subjectively and personally; and the J-P scale, tendencies to reach conclusions about phenomena or to become aware of them.

"These scales were expressly developed to classify people into type categories (e.g., classification as an extravert, an introvert, or, in those cases where the two tendencies are equal, 'indeterminate') which would have real meaning. The cutting (or 'zero') points used in making these classifications were so chosen that those people who are on one side of a scale's cutting point and, hence, in one type category are presumed to be qualitatively different from those who are on the other side of it, and hence, in the opposite type category. In addition to these categorical classifications, continuous scores for each scale can be derived by arbitrarily considering one end of the scale high." (Stricker and Ross, 1963, p. 287.)

The validity of the Myers-Briggs Type Indicator as a predictor of academic performance was studied at two men's colleges (Stricker, Shiffman, and Ross, 1965). One procedure for estimating validity involved treating as a predictor the continuous score on each Type Indicator scale. The correlation of first-year college grades with a best-weighted combination of SAT scores plus high school record was then compared with the correlation of the same grades with a best-weighted combination of SAT scores plus high school record plus the four Type Indicator scores. The combination involving the Type Indicator scores was higher by .05 at one college but had no advantage at the other.

A second procedure utilized as a predicator variable the so-called Four Scale Contingency Prediction based on the Type Inventory. The development of this variable involved classifying students into 81 possible categories (that is, all the combinations possible with three categories on each of four scales). Then, in order to treat this in a standard correlation analysis, it was necessary to assign a numerical value to each category. The value assigned to each category was the average freshman grade for all students in that category. Thus, each student had as his "score" on this predictor the average of grades earned by himself and others in his category. As the authors note, the correlation of these scores with the average grades earned by the same students gives an inflated estimate of validity. As it turned out, the validity of a combination of the SAT plus high school record plus the Four Scale Contingency Prediction was about .09 higher than the validity of the combination of the SAT plus high school record. Taken at face value, the gain would appear to be larger than that found when the continuous scores on the Type Indicator were used as predictors. Whether the gain would hold up on a new group involving an unbiased estimate of the validity of the Four Scale Contingency Prediction cannot be answered from the present results.

Formulating Hypotheses Test

The Formulating Hypotheses Test (Frederiksen, 1959; Cliff and Cliff, 1963) was designed to measure abilities of the sort required of a research scholar as he studies the results of research. The examinee inspects a problem in the form of a graph or table and is asked to write as many hypotheses as he can which might explain the finding shown by the data. He then lists the items of information needed to test his hypotheses. One exercise, for example, asks the subject to suggest explanations for the finding that men entering the Navy in June, July, or August have higher average scores on classification tests than do recruits tested during other months of the year. In preliminary studies, two scores have been obtained for the test, the Hypotheses Score and the Items of Information score. The former is based on the number of possible explanations for the finding; the latter involves a count of the number of acceptable items of information which the examinee has listed as necessary to test his hypotheses. The relevance of the test task of formulating hypotheses to the college task of identifying abstract causes is clear. The fact that the test requires the student to produce responses represents a clear departure from the present dominant approach in testing, that of referring the student to select responses.

Cliff and Cliff (1963) explored (a) the internal structure of the test in terms of selected reference factors (factor study) and (b) the relationship of test scores to measures of academic ability (validity study).

For the factor study, the Formulating Hypotheses Test was administered along with tests in areas corresponding to five previously identified factors: Ideational Fluency, Spontaneous Flexibility, Sensitivity to Problems, Originality, and Induction. Data on academic aptitude tests and grade averages were also available. The authors concluded that the factor analyses indicated minor components of productivity and general knowledge, but that the factors represented were generally not the same as those represented in the marker tests. The authors commented that the test ". . . has considerable appeal as a job sample measure of at least one aspect of scientific creativity." (Cliff and Cliff, 1963, p. 19.)

In the validity study based on the largest group (N=191) grade-point averages showed a significant correlation (in the low .20's) with both the Hypotheses score and the Items of Information score; verbal scores on academic ability tests had a significant correlation (also in the low .20's) with the Hypotheses score. For the other three groups in the validity study, with sample sizes ranging from 16 to 26, correlations did not reach statistical significance.

The authors' overall conclusions were "that (the) two Formulating Hypotheses scores (a) are measuring somewhat the same thing, (b) correlate slightly with measures of academic achievement and potential, and (c) have some relation to the fluency-type measures used here. However, the main part of its reliable variance is not covered by these variables. Insofar as the ability called for is not simply specific to the test, the possibility that it is a measure of what Guilford might call divergent production of semantic implications is suggested." (Cliff and Cliff, 1963, p. 30.) The possibility that the Formulating Hypotheses Test will ever challenge the current SAT item types for general use seems unlikely in view of these findings. It may be that it will demonstrate its usefulness in special science settings.

English essay

"Mankind in a burst of unusual creative activity some day will undoubtedly achieve the perfect English composition test and thereby usher in the millennium. Being a perfect test, the instrument will please nearly everybody: Old Guard English teachers who know beyond the reach of reason that compositional skill can only be measured by essay tests, progressive teachers who respect and use objective English tests, and every shade of opinion in between . . .

"In 60 years of trying, it hardly needs be added, the College Board through its committees of examiners in English has not achieved this testing instrument . . .

"The task of the College Board English Examiners, beyond any question, has been the most complex, most vexing, and most baffling that any College Board test committee has had to face. Certainly no committee has spent more time in sober appraisal and painful reappraisal of its work, and no [other] College Board examination across the years has undergone so many alterations and refinements." (Palmer, 1960, p. 8.)

The full history of research bearing on "alterations and refinements" in the English Composition Test is beyond the scope of this book. Instead, discussion will be limited to a few of the larger studies carried out since April 1947, the date when an objective section was first introduced into the English Composition Test. The following areas will be considered:

1. Opinions of students and teachers on essay testing
2. The first objective English Composition Test exercise
3. The Interlinear exercise
4. Comparison of six item types
5. General Composition Test
6. The Writing Sample
7. The new English Composition Test essay
8. Points of view in essay grading

Opinions of teachers and students on essay testing

Do essay-type tests actually encourage schools to teach and students to work at writing exercises? If so, this fact would be an educationally significant argument in favor of essay-type testing in the College Board program.

According to a survey carried out about 15 years ago, teachers of English do want an essay test in the program (French, 1956a). The fact that they want it is not very surprising. What is somewhat unexpected is that the most frequently checked reason for wanting it was as a measure of competence. On the other hand, only about one teacher in five or six took the view that essay tests served as a goal for students or as a factor in the number of writing assignments made.

The effect of essay testing on student motivation was the subject of another study carried out by French

(1956b). At the outset, both essay and objective tests were given to four groups of students. Two groups were told that their final examination would be of the essay type and two were told that it would be of the objective type. Actually, both types were given to all groups. After the second testing, only a few students (14 percent) said that they had done anything special to prepare themselves for the expected type of test. The "after" scores on a particular test type were not much different for students expecting that type of test than for those not expecting it; further, there was no real advantage on the "after" test for students who said that they had prepared for that particular type of test.

The first objective English Composition Test exercise

Huddleston has reported in detail on the first English Composition Test that contained an objective section, the April 1947 test (Huddleston, 1954). This test was made up of three parts: 1) a free essay, 2) an entirely objective section called Editing (items in which portions are underlined, followed by several suggested ways of rewriting the underlined part), and 3) a section called Paragraph Revision (a paragraph whose imperfections are not identified, which the student is to rewrite as a whole).

English grades and teachers' ratings were used as criteria for assessing the validity of the tests. SAT-verbal was included in the analysis as a predictor. As it turned out, SAT-verbal was better than English Composition total or any of its parts as a predictor of the writing criteria. Among English Composition sections, the objective Editing exercise was more valid than the other two exercises. When the Editing section was used along with SAT-verbal, prediction was improved modestly over that obtainable from SAT-verbal alone (about .03 gain in the validity coefficient). Huddleston concluded that ". . . in the light of present knowledge, measurable ability to write is no more than verbal ability. It has been impossible to demonstrate by the techniques of this study that essay questions, objective questions, or paragraph-revision exercises contain any factor other than verbal; furthermore, these types of questions measure writing ability less well than does a typical verbal test." (Huddleston, 1954, p. 204.)

The Interlinear exercise

After the introduction of objective materials into the English Composition Test, a formidable array of new exercises was developed. (It may be noted that in August 1948 the first wholly objective English test appeared in the College Board program.) One of the new item types was the so-called Interlinear, used for the first time in March 1951. In this exercise, a passage is printed with space between the lines; the examinee makes alterations directly on the test copy. The points

to be corrected—grammatical errors, punctuation errors, awkward constructions—are in no way identified for the candidate. The Interlinear exercises are then graded by a group of readers who have agreed in advance on a set of grading standards.

Evidence on the reliability and validity of the first Interlinear was very favorable indeed (Swineford and Olsen, 1953). It seemed possible to establish a very high level of reader reliability; estimates were in the vicinity of .95. In addition, the test showed up well in a study involving the prediction of freshman English grades at eight College Board colleges. As usual, the best predictor of English grades was SAT-verbal, its average validity before correction for restriction of range was .42 for 12 groups at the eight colleges. What *was* noteworthy was that the English Composition Test closely approached SAT-verbal in validity, with an average correlation of .41. The Interlinear alone had an average validity of .39.

Comparison of six item types

In 1955-56, a comparative study of six English Composition item types was carried out in cooperation with four College Board colleges (Weiss, 1957). This study involved three item types designed to elicit some actual writing from the candidate plus three entirely objective types. They were: 1) Interlinear; 2) Paragraph Interpretation, which requires free answers to questions based on a paragraph of prose; 3) Sentence Revision, which requires the candidate to rewrite entire sentences in clear and acceptable English; 4) Metaphors, involving sentences with a phrase omitted for which the candidate must choose the best of five alternatives; 5) Poetry Groups, poems with a line omitted, followed by four alternatives among which the candidate must decide which is appropriate or inappropriate for various reasons; and 6) Organization, which requires putting a set of sentences into the best order. These six item types occurred in three English Composition forms; students in this study took one form at regular College Board administrations and the other two at special administrations in the fall of their freshman year.

Interlinear turned out to be more valid than the other five item types as a predictor of English grades for freshmen in the four colleges. The other two "writing" tests—Paragraph Interpretation and Sentence Revision—appeared to be the poorest predictors. The three strictly objective types were of intermediate predictive value. In view of the good showing of the Interlinear, the question naturally arose as to whether it might be well to have the entire hour of the English Composition Test devoted to this exercise. As it turned out, a test made up of Interlinear plus other item types seemed superior to an hour of Interlinear alone.

Although the focus of this study was a comparison among English Composition item types, SAT-verbal was also included as a predictor. Once again SAT-verbal turned out to be the best single predictor of college English grades. Use of English Composition plus SAT-verbal had a modest advantage over SAT-verbal alone.

Reliability analyses of tests used in the validity study were very favorable to the Interlinear (Swineford, 1957). Since three item types were repeated in two different test forms, it was possible to investigate their form-to-form reliability as well as their single-form reliability. The form-to-form correlations were .50 for Organization, .48 for Poetry Groups, and .66 for Interlinear. Single-form reliabilities were .45 and .56 for the two Organization exercises, .38 and .58 for the two Poetry Groups, and .85 and .83 for the Interlinears. As Swineford points out, the two subtests by the same name were not strictly similar; for example, one Organization subtest consisted of three sets of items with seven or eight choices each, whereas the other consisted of six sets of items with five to nine choices each. On the whole, it was concluded that reliabilities were reasonably satisfactory for 20-minute tests.

The General Composition Test

In May 1954, after several years of experimentation, a two-hour essay test was introduced into the College Board program. This test—the General Composition Test (GCT)—was intended as a supplement to the English Composition Test, not as a part of it or a substitute for it. It was offered a second time in May 1955 and a third and last time in May 1956.

The General Composition Test had several distinctive features. One was its scoring system; grades were given for five separate qualities of writing: Mechanics, Style, Organization, Reasoning, and Content. Each grade represented the judgment of at least two readers; a third reader was used if the first two disagreed. Another distinctive feature was that the student was not only presented with the topic but also given reading materials for background. However, he was not limited to the material which was presented. Further, he was informed of the qualities that would be judged and given an estimate of the proportion of time that would be most profitably spent on the various elements of the assignment.

The 1954 and 1955 GCTs were the subject of an extensive series of validity studies (Olsen, 1955; Olsen, 1956). The first series was based on eleventh graders in 11 secondary schools and the second on eleventh and twelfth graders in six schools. In these studies, English grades and English teachers' ratings were used as criteria of writing ability against which the GCT was evaluated. The findings of the validity studies were quite clear. The General Composition Test total score was less effective than SAT-verbal or English Composition for measuring writing ability as defined in these studies. Further, SAT-verbal was better than each individual GCT quality score for predicting teachers' ratings on the corresponding quality.

In six of the schools where students had taken both the 1954 and 1955 GCT, the correlation between total GCT scores for the two testings was .46. By comparison, 1954 and 1955 SAT-verbal scores correlated .88 for the same students (Olsen, 1956).

Reading reliability of the GCT was estimated by putting a sample of 200 papers through the entire reading process twice. In each reading, the papers were read by at least two readers with third readings where necessary. The correlation between total GCT scores for the two sets of readings was .70 (Swineford, 1956).

The special subcommittee appointed by the College Board to evaluate the GCT made the following statement in its final report: "We feel that the gap between the concept of the test as good in the sense of being reliable and valid, and the test as being good in the sense of its encouraging and developing skills which are desirable in themselves, even if it lacks precision in terms of scoring, is too wide to be bridged at the present time to the satisfaction of either school of thought." (College Board, 1956, p. 32.)

The Writing Sample

In December 1960, some four years after the GCT was abandoned, the Writing Sample was introduced into the College Board program. Like the GCT, this exercise was a supplement to the English Composition Test, not part of it. The Writing Sample differed from the GCT—and indeed from everything else in the program—in that it was not graded by ETS or the College Board. Instead, copies of the student's essay were simply forwarded to colleges and secondary schools.

Two surveys looked into the colleges' use of the Writing Sample (Ekstrom, 1962; Ekstrom, 1964). In the first survey, a questionnaire was sent to all College Board colleges during the 1960-61 academic year. Altogether, 43 percent of the colleges reported using the Writing Sample in connection with admissions decisions; most often, it was used with borderline or marginal candidates. Reading was most commonly done by an admissions officer or the admissions committee. About a third of the colleges planned to use the Writing Sample for placement; for placement purposes, reading was generally done by a committee from the English Department.

The later survey involved interviews at 23 colleges that did require the Writing Sample (Ekstrom, 1964). Twenty of the 23 colleges used the Writing Sample in their admissions program; 11 reported that they simply read it for a general impression, while nine said that they actually assigned grades. The reading was more commonly done by the admissions office than elsewhere. When asked which qualities they looked for, colleges most often checked: 1) organization, 2) ability to think, 3) spelling, and 4) grammar. In addition, a number of colleges reported using the Writing Sample for placement purposes; in particular, six of the 23 reported using it for assignment to advanced courses, three for assignment to remedial work, four for exemption from composition courses, and one for placement of all students.

Since the Writing Sample was not centrally graded, it was difficult to determine its reliability and validity, or more accurately, the reliability of the grades that were being assigned when grades were indeed assigned and the validity of the grades for the particular uses made of them where they were being used. Ekstrom reported that experimental studies carried out by a few colleges suggested that the Writing Sample had low reliability and validity as it was being used. The responses of colleges to questions about the possibility of a centrally graded essay in the English Composition Test suggested that the Writing Sample would, in general, not be missed if the English Composition Test included an essay. Several colleges expressed the view that they would like to receive the essay itself as well as the grades on it (Ekstrom, 1964).

The introduction after 1963-64 of a 20-minute centrally graded essay into some administrations of the English Composition Test paved the way for the elimination of the Writing Sample from the College Board Admissions Testing Program. In 1967-68, the last year that the Writing Sample was offered, 90 colleges required it or recommended it, or accepted it in lieu of an Achievement Test. Large numbers of candidates were producing samples of their writing even during the last year, but, in general, College Board member colleges did not find the Writing Sample to be a useful component of the Program.

The new English Composition Test essay

A major study of writing ability, leading to the reintroduction of an essay section into the English Composition Test, was published by the College Board (Godshalk, Swineford, and Coffman, 1966). A noteworthy feature of this study was the attention devoted to criterion development. The criterion involved a series of short essays read by a number of different readers. In one phase of the study, the criterion was based on a total of 25 reader judgments, five readers for each of five different essays; in another stage, the criterion was based on 20 judgments. Each reader was asked to make global, or holistic, rather than analytical judgments. Each reader made 30 to 40 judgments per hour, reading rapidly and assigning a single rating on a three-point scale.

The 646 eleventh and twelfth grade students who wrote the essays in this study also took two Interlinears and six 20-minute objective exercises (Paragraph Organization, Sentence Correction, Usage, Prose Groups, Error Recognition, and Construction Shift). In addition the analysis involved the PSAT and one of the short essays as predictors.

With one exception (Paragraph Organization) all of the objective types had fairly high correlations with the

essay criterion (ranging from .57 to .71). Use of objective tests in combinations of three yielded validities consistently over .70. When Interlinear was brought into the picture, combinations including an Interlinear were found to have higher validities than combinations not including one.

Perhaps the most important finding, however, was that a 20-minute essay made a distinctive contribution to prediction above and beyond that obtainable from the other types of test material. Validity coefficients for test combinations that included an essay were consistently higher than those for combinations that did not include one.

Combinations of PSAT-verbal plus any of the one-hour English tests generally showed higher validities than either alone. The PSAT-verbal section alone appeared to be inferior to an English test alone for predicting the essay criterion. Previous studies had demonstrated that SAT-verbal was generally superior to the English Composition Test as a predictor of English grades or of teachers' judgments of writing ability. Presumably, the distinctive results of the present study are attributable to the use of the essay criterion rather than to any distinctive difference between SAT-verbal and PSAT-verbal.

The December 1963 English Composition Test included a 20-minute essay similar to those used in the experiment—the first time an essay had been in English Composition since April 1947. Some 80,000 candidates were tested and their essays were read by 145 readers. Each essay was read by two different readers working independently. A special study was carried out to determine whether the reliability attained in the experimental study would hold up in this major College Board reading (Myers, McConville, and Coffman, 1964). To aid in answering this question, 25 papers were selected for repeated readings. These papers were reproduced by hand so that readers would not recognize an "experimental" paper. On each of five days, each selected paper was given to 25 different readers. The analysis indicated that the reading reliability for a single reader was .41, for two readers, .58, and for four readers, .73; the last figure compares with reliabilities obtained in the experimental study. One disconcerting finding was that reliabilities were noticeably lower on the last day of reading; single reader reliability was .26 for the last day as compared with values as high as .49 for previous days.

Points of view in essay grading

On what basis do readers make their judgments of student essays? Along what dimensions do they differ? In an attempt to answer such questions, French had a group of 300 student essays graded by a rather heterogeneous set of 53 readers: 10 English teachers, 9 social scientists, 8 natural scientists, 10 writers or editors, 9 lawyers, and 7 business executives (French, 1962a). Grading was done without special directives or guidance.

Each reader was simply asked to grade according to his own judgment of what constitutes writing ability. The average correlation between two readers was .31.

To aid in identifying bases on which grades had been assigned, a factor analysis was carried out; the factoring involved a matrix of intercorrelations in which the variables were the 53 sets of readers' grades and the regular College Board scores. One possible outcome was that the factors would simply correspond to readers' occupations. However, this did not prove to be the case. A number of other hypotheses were explored in vain to identify the characteristics shared by the various readers; for example, a check was made to find out whether the factors reflected emphases on different objective characteristics of the essay itself, such as length, proportion of unusual words, or mechanical errors. Finally, comments that readers had written on the essays were reviewed. This analysis did shed some light on the differing emphases of different clusters of readers. It appeared that the five factors might be called: ideas, form, flavor, mechanics, and wording. That is, one group of readers particularly stressed ideas, another particularly stressed form, and so forth.

College Board test scores—SAT-verbal, SAT-mathematical, and the English Composition Test—constituted an essentially separate factor that was not related to the form, flavor, or ideas factors but *was* somewhat related to the mechanics and wording factors. French raises the question: "Isn't this what English teachers have been telling us psychometricians all along—that essay tests of writing ability measure something that objective tests do not measure? They seem to be right. Form, flavor, and particularly ideas are missed by the tests. But, then, of course, they are also pretty much missed by the readers. The low correlations among the readers . . . can only mean that nothing at all is being measured very well by the essays." (French, 1962a, p. 27.) He sees a solution along these lines: "So, if we psychometricians can encourage testing and further clarification of those aspects of writing that objective tests cannot measure, encourage the use of readers who favor grading those particular qualities that are desirable to grade, and see to it that the students are aware of what they are being graded on, we can enlighten rather than merely disparage the polemic art of essay testing." (French, 1962a, p. 28.)

French's negative reaction to the average correlation of .31 between readers can be contrasted to the conclusion of Godshalk, Swineford, and Coffman (1966, p. 41): "For the essays, the first-order validities do not approach the range of validities for other types of questions until the score is based on three readings. On the other hand, when essay scores are combined with objective subtest scores, they produce validity coefficients even higher than those for combinations which include [objective questions and] an interlinear exercise." It is clear that the matter of the usefulness of the essay examination is by no means closed, even within the psychometric community.

Special populations

From time to time, reference is made to *the* College Board test candidate population as though it were a well-defined, unchanging, homogeneous group. Actually the candidate group is made up of boys and girls who come from all parts of the country (increasingly, from all parts of the world), who are applying to a host of different colleges, who represent an increasing diversity of socioeconomic backgrounds, and who cover a sub-substantial range of tested ability. The facts of heterogeneity suggest, first of all, the need for extensive, up-to-date descriptive statistics, including data on the test performance of clearly specified subgroups as well as the manner in which the test is relevant and useful for the different subgroups. The relevance and usefulness of the test for the different subgroups are the general criteria by which one determines the presence or absence of "test bias."

In view of the recent spate of discussions regarding test bias, it might be thought that there exists a single, unequivocal, and generally agreed upon definition of bias. This is not the case. The popular belief that bias is indicated whenever a test yields different mean scores for different groups is clearly an oversimplification. Actually, a difference in means is not only an insufficient indicator of test bias; it is not even a necessary condition for bias to exist.

Bias on a test is a matter of a major concern when the test is used to predict future success. A test may thus be thought of as unbiased in a practical setting if members of two groups differ on the criterion of success (on job performance, on school grades, or on some other measure whose appropriateness as a measure of success is reasonably well accepted) in the same way as they differ on the test. That is to say, a test is biased or unbiased only with respect to an accepted criterion. Moreover, a test may be unbiased for one predictive purpose yet biased for another. In order to explore some of the complexities inherent in considerations of test bias, a monograph "Statistical Aspects of the Problems of Biases in Psychological Tests" by Richard F. Potthoff (Potthoff, 1966) will be reviewed. Pothoff addresses himself to the problems of defining bias, determining whether bias exists, and determining how to eliminate bias if it is discovered. These three problems are considered both for the situation where there exists a criterion variable to be predicted and for the situation where no such criterion exists.

Pothoff defines bias in terms of conditional expectation and observes that ". . . a test is not biased if individuals from different groups who have the same test scores also have the same expected criterion scores." (Potthoff, 1966 p. 7.) He notes the similarity between this definition and the statement by Cardall and Coffman (1964, p. 1): "If the test is used for prediction, the ultimate question is whether or not a common regression equation is appropriate for the several groups to which it is being applied and whether or not the predictions are equally effective for all groups." Potthoff develops equations based on least-squares theory for testing hypotheses of bias under the condition that total test score is being used. He goes on to generalize these equations for the situation where there are multiple tests and where there are multiple criterion variables. Regarding the question of correcting for bias when it is found, Potthoff notes that one solution, the one implicit in the Cardall and Coffman statement, is to use different regression equations for the different groups. The effect of using different regression equations for different groups is to assign a weight to group membership in making the prediction. However, Potthoff goes on to point out that the appropriateness of this solution may be questioned when the group is defined by some characteristic that ought not to be related to success on the criterion—an example being race and success in college. A preferable solution, he suggests, would be to isolate and study the intrinsic characteristics of the groups that are reflected in the relationship between the predictors and the criterion.

Potthoff found it difficult even to arrive at a satisfactory definition of bias in the absence of a criterion. The problem of definition, he observed, can be avoided if there are a priori grounds for believing the groups should be alike with respect to what is measured by each item or by the total test. However, since differences in backgrounds are frequently the basis for distinguishing between groups, it is not reasonable to expect the groups to be alike in their performance.

One approach to a definition of bias in the absence of a criterion is in terms of the interaction between items and groups. This interaction may be shown graphically by plotting the item difficulties for one group versus the item difficulties for the other group. Interaction may be observed when some items are substantially more difficult for one group than for the other *relative to* the remaining items in the test. This definition is unsatisfactory in that it would result in a judgment of no bias when the item-group interaction is nonsignificant, but when a further analysis would demonstrate that the items as a group predicted an outside criterion differently for the two groups.

When a criterion is available and itself unbiased, it is possible to define three main types of bias in the test score by considering the properties of the regression of criterion on test score. The first type of bias is reflected by differences in the errors of estimate in the two (or more) regression lines; the second type of bias is reflected by differences in the slopes; and the third type of bias is reflected in differences in the intercepts.

The first type of bias arises when there are differences in the predictive power of the test score, evidenced by the standard error of estimate, among the various subgroups. If, for example, a test were to be correlated .50 with a criterion for one of two (equally heterogeneous) groups and zero for the other group, the test is clearly biased in the sense that it is not a relevant and useful predictor for the latter group.

The second type of bias arises when the standard errors of estimate for the various subgroups are the same, but the regression lines are not parallel. The two groups may have equal means on both the predictor and criterion or they may have different means on one or both of these measures. The lines for the two groups may actually cross within the usual limits of predictor scores, in which case the test may be considered simultaneously biased against low scorers in one group and against high scorers in the other group. On the other hand, the lines may not cross within the usual range of predictor scores; in this case, the direction of the bias is the same throughout the range, but the test is more seriously biased at one end of the scale than the other.

The third type of bias arises when the standard errors of estimate and the slopes of the regression lines are the same for the various subgroups but the intercepts of the regression lines differ. The difference in intercepts may occur when the groups, even after adjustment for differences in mean test score, show different (adjusted) means on the criterion. When the intercepts are not identical, the test is considered biased in the sense that scores do not have the same meaning for the two groups. That is to say, the test is biased against the group whose regression line is higher, the group that performs better on the criterion *relative to* the predictor score, that is, the group that *tests* lower for the same criterion performance.

A finding of test bias does not, by itself, carry a clear recommendation for action: Is it best to abandon testing altogether in that situation? To seek tests that may be somewhat less biased, and to use them even if they are cumbersome, expensive, or time-consuming (for example, job-sample or training-sample types of tests)? To make allowance in the selection process for score differences? To offer practice, coaching, or training? To find some other alternative? It goes without saying that the optimal course of action is even less clear-cut when bias is suspected but has not been demonstrated empirically. In a statement on the interpretation of SAT scores for the disadvantaged, the College Board (1965b, p. 10) pointed out: "Pending further study now under way, however, schools and colleges can only be cautioned against making the usual interpretation of SAT scores when comparing an educationally disadvantaged student with groups of students who are not similarly disadvantaged." Since the publication of this statement, a number of studies of bias on the SAT have been conducted and reported. Some of these studies are summarized below. The sections that follow will consider a) sex differences on the SAT, b) cultural differences, and c) the appropriateness of the SAT for students with very high or very low scores.

Sex differences

The psychometric literature provides ample documentation of sex differences in mental ability. Attention has generally *not* focused on the question of overall superiority for either sex. Instead, most interest attaches to the determination of differential patterns of ability. This focus seems an appropriate one, since the presence of differences per se is, as was noted earlier, no guarantee of bias.

As a matter of historical interest, findings on sex differences for candidates on the first SAT ever offered—June 1926—will be summarized here. Brigham (1932, p. 334) found that girls were significantly superior to boys on the test as a whole. The sample was a group of 921 boys and 578 girls who had completed nine subtests. The means on the total test were 513 for the girls and 494 for the boys who were tested on that date. (It may be recalled that separate SAT-verbal and SAT-mathematical scores were not reported until 1930.) Analysis of individual subtest scores showed differences in the expected direction. Boys had a significant advantage on Arithmetical Problems and Number Series Completion while girls had an especially large and significant advantage on Artificial Language, Antonyms, and Paragraph Reading. Raw score means and standard deviations are shown below for the nine subtests. All of the differences in means were statistically significant except those on Definitions and on Analogies.

Subtest		Boys (N = 921)	Girls (N = 578)
Definitions	M	16.09	16.48
	SD	4.63	3.77
Arithmetical Problems	M	8.14	6.44
	SD	2.71	2.30
Classification	M	12.98	13.85
	SD	4.32	3.87
Artificial Language	M	18.39	22.35
	SD	5.78	5.53
Antonyms	M	29.80	33.35
	SD	7.57	6.29
Number Series Completion	M	10.70	9.98
	SD	3.43	2.86
Analogies	M	23.84	23.64
	SD	5.79	5.32
Logical Inference	M	24.03	25.16
	SD	6.56	5.35
Paragraph Reading	M	25.20	28.27
	SD	6.99	6.20

On the first form of the SAT on which separate verbal and mathematical scores were reported—June 1930—girls did better than boys on verbal, but boys were superior on mathematical. Verbal means were 518 for the girls tested on that date and 487 for the boys. Mathematical means were 484 and 510, respectively (Brigham, 1932, p. 373).

More recently, it has been found that boys and girls do about equally well on SAT-verbal but that there is a substantial difference in favor of boys on SAT-mathematical. Changes have been made in the content of the SAT-verbal over the years, but no content changes

have been made that would tend to account for the differences between recent findings and those characteristic of earlier years. In a study carried out in the fall of 1966, the SAT means for a random sample of high school seniors in the United States were found to be as follows (College Board, 1968, p. 23):

	Verbal	Mathematical
Senior Boys	390	422
Senior Girls	393	382

It should be stressed that the above figures are estimates for *all* high school seniors, not solely for those who take the SAT. Scholastic Aptitude Test candidates are a select group, and the considerations that determine why some students take the SAT and others do not may not operate identically for boys and girls. It is of some interest therefore to find that candidates show about the same pattern of sex differences as the general group of high school seniors; the candidates, however, do have decidedly higher means. For example, mean scores for all seniors who took the SAT from May 1967 through March 1968 were as follows (College Board, 1968, p. 24):

	Verbal	Mathematical
SAT candidates — Senior boys	463	510
SAT candidates — Senior girls	464	466

The fact that the reported SAT-verbal scores turn out to be equal for boys and girls does not, of course, prove that the boys and girls in this group, or boys and girls in general, are equal in verbal ability. As Coffman points out, "It is well known that women tend to make higher scores than men on tests of verbal aptitude. Therefore, if men and women make comparable scores on a [particular] test of verbal aptitude, one is likely to suspect some bias in the sampling of either men or women or both. On the other hand, consider the possibility that the observed differences in favor of women may be a function of their superiority on *some* of the questions in the test and not on others. If such be the case, and if the test constructor is not aware of *which items* are producing the differences, he might at some point construct a test form which produces essentially equivalent scores for men and women even though there is no bias in the samples of people." (Coffman, 1961, p. 117.) The main task for the test constructor is to develop content specifications that will insure a reasonable sample of relevant tasks. Once such specifications have been developed, the problem for test constructors is not simply to remove the advantage accruing to a particular subgroup. "Rather, the problem is to identify any special sub-categories of items which contribute special weight to such differences as do show up so that specifications may be written which will insure that successive forms of the test are parallel." (Coffman, 1961, p. 117.)

In a study comparing men and women who took the same SAT-verbal test, Coffman found that total scores were virtually identical (Coffman, 1961). He made a distribution of *differences* between item difficulties for the two sexes. Inspection of the items producing the greatest sex differences confirmed test constructors' expectations. Items dealing with "people" favored women: items dealing with science or business—or, more generally, with "things"—favored men. Coffman goes on to suggest that, "In our culture, most of the words related to 'people' are likely to be considered general and thus to be chosen for use in a verbal aptitude test. In contrast, a considerable number of words related to 'things' are likely to be considered specialized and thus to be left out of a verbal aptitude test. If words related to 'people' are easier for women and words related to 'things' are easier for men, is it possible that biases in the sampling of vocabulary may account for the reported superiority of women in verbal aptitude?" (Coffman, 1961, pp. 123-124.)

What should test constructors do on the basis of such information on sex differences? Coffman suggests that "if the differences which appear in response to aptitude test items are relevant for the performance one wishes to predict, then items showing differences should remain in the test; if the differences are not relevant, then items showing differences should be removed from the item pool or controlled at the point of test assembly to insure optimum weighting in the test." (Coffman, 1961, p. 124.) The policy of controlling the weighting of various types of content is basic to the operational procedures used in the construction of College Board tests. Coffman's statement serves to emphasize a point stressed earlier: Bias should be evaluated *not* in terms of score differences or item statistics but in terms of test relevance. By this criterion, a most important consideration is the comparative validity of the test for men and women; or, more precisely, examination of the question "Is the same regression system appropriate for both?"

An early summary of Abelson (1951) is pertinent despite the fact that it involved both the Psychological Examination of the American Council on Education (ACE) and the SAT. Abelson brought together results of seven validity studies in which prediction was compared for boys and girls at the *same* college. (Comparisons of boys at one college with girls at another are likely to be so confounded by intercollege differences associated with factors other than sex that they would shed little light on the question of comparative validity.) Data from the seven studies were reanalyzed to determine whether the standard errors of prediction were identical for boys and girls. Comparisons involved predictions based on the test alone, on high school record alone, and on a best-weighted combination of the test with high school record. Typically, it turned out that the error of prediction was smaller for girls than for boys. Surely any attempt to compare the relative predictability of boys' and girls' grades will have to consider that girls tend to take different courses than boys so that criteria in the two cases are different.

A more recent summary of studies of the relative predictability of boys and girls by Seashore (1962) is entitled simply: "Women are more predictable than men." The conclusion drawn by Seashore is further supported by the work of Stanley (Stanley, 1967; Stanley and Porter, 1967), who found that SAT-V and SAT-M predicted freshman grades at non-black colleges in Georgia significantly better for girls than for boys. No significant differences in predictability were found between boys and girls at black colleges. The following section contains additional reference to the Stanley and Stanley-Porter data.

Cultural differences

There is a great deal of public and professional interest in the question of the appropriateness of standard American tests for subgroups of candidates with backgrounds unlike those of the majority of candidates. Because of the heterogeneity of the College Board test population, it would be possible to identify a large number of subgroups for which the test might be presumed inappropriate. Most research studies, however, have focused on but a few of the possible subgroups—for example black Americans, students from other countries, and students whose native language is not English. The latter two groups are, of course, overlapping.

As noted earlier, comparison of means—however interesting it may be for its own sake—reveals little about the fairness of a test for particular groups. Such comparisons provide some clues as to the appropriateness of the test in terms of difficulty—for example, the mean score for a group may be so near the limits of the range as to preclude effective discrimination among candidates. This aspect of test appropriateness will be treated in the section on extremes of the score range. National surveys of SAT scores for whites versus nonwhites have never been made. The Coleman report (1966) with its extensive SCAT data for twelfth graders is perhaps the closest approximation to such a survey. Nevertheless, comparative data on the SAT are available for selected groups. For example, separate SAT distributions have been published for blacks and whites in the University System of Georgia for a number of years. Results for fall 1963 entrants will serve as an illustration (Hills, Klock, and Bush, 1965, pp. 5, 7):

| | | White | | Black | |
		Male	*Female*	*Male*	*Female*
Number of Students		4,458	2,677	371	528
SAT-verbal	Mean	449	442	268	268
	SD	102	93	52	51
SAT-mathematical	Mean	503	438	310	297
	SD	106	87	52	44

It should be kept in mind that these figures apply only to 1963 entrants in the University System of

Georgia: they are *not* based on all college entrants, on all high school graduates, or on all blacks and whites in Georgia.

Studies of the validity of the SAT have been carried out for each institution within the University System of Georgia (Hills, *et al.*, 1965). Thus, it is possible to compare validities obtained at institutions attended by blacks versus those obtained at institutions attended by whites. Unfortunately, such comparisons are far from decisive in assessing possible bias in the SAT; for example, colleges are likely to differ from each other on a number of characteristics other than the ethnic composition of the student body. At the same time, comparison of validities does provide an indication of the appropriateness and relevance of the SAT for the colleges under consideration. Accordingly, it may be useful to cite a few summary figures based on validity studies of the 1963 entering groups in Georgia. Using data for four-year colleges only, it turns out that a best-weighted combination of SAT-verbal and mathematical has a median validity of .465 at three black colleges based on a total of six student groups, three groups of males and three groups of females. By comparison, the median validity was .50 for 16 student groups at nine colleges attended by whites. These results were obtained despite the fact that the black groups were *considerably* less variable than were the white groups. Female whites were far more "predictable" (that is, female groups showed higher r's) than male whites, male blacks, or female blacks, who differ little from each other. The median of the standard errors of estimate was .50 for black groups and .56 for the white groups. (In interpreting these standard errors, it may be useful to know that criterion grades were on the scale A = 4, B = 3, and so forth.) Even without rigorous statistical tests, it seems reasonable to conclude that the SAT was about equally appropriate for blacks and whites in the University System of Georgia.

Perhaps more decisive in the evaluation of bias are studies comparing white with black groups at the *same* college. As might be expected, College Board colleges with black subgroups sufficiently large for statistical comparison are rare. Cleary (1968) was able to find three colleges for such a study; however, at two of the three, adequate data were available for fewer than 100 blacks. In this study, bias was assessed by comparing the regression system for the black and white groups at each of the three colleges. It turned out that there was no significant difference between the regression systems for the black and the white groups at two of the three colleges. In a predictive sense, a given score meant about the same thing for members of both groups. In the third college, there was a significant difference but opposite in direction from what is often hypothesized: on the average, at this college a black with a particular SAT score actually obtained slightly lower grades than a white student with the same score.

Another approach to the study of bias as it is related to cultural differences involves an analysis at the item level. One method for studying bias at the item level involves graphic procedures. This method has its roots in the work of Thurstone in the middle 1920s. A test is administered to two groups and a difficulty index, converted to a normalized scale (for example, to the "delta" scale; see Chapters I, II, and III), is computed for each of the items in the test. A bivariate plot of these normalized indices is then made, referring one of the two groups to the abscissa and the other to the ordinate. If all items are of equal difficulty for the two groups, then all points lie on the 45° line from the origin. Any item that is easier for one group than for the other is displaced from the 45° line. The degree of similarity of the backgrounds of the two groups will influence the amount of cohesiveness, that is to say, the degree of correlation represented in the plot. For example, the correlation between item difficulties for two randomly different groups is likely to be as high as .98 or even higher. Visual inspection of such plots taken from two culturally different groups sometimes reveals items that deviate markedly from the cluster and give evidence of item-group interaction. These outlying items *might* be considered biased items; yet an absence of such outliers does not exclude the possibility of bias with respect to a criterion external to the test.

Cleary and Hilton (1968) carried out a study of PSAT items based on twelfth grade students classified by race and socioeconomic status. They defined bias thus: "An item of a test is said to be biased for members of a particular group if, on that item, the members of the group obtain an average score which differs from the average score of other groups by more or less than expected from performance on other items of the same test. That is, the biased item produces an uncommon discrepancy between the performance of members of the group and members of other groups. In terms of the analysis of variance, bias is defined as an item x group interaction." (Cleary and Hilton, 1968, p. 61.) Results of their analysis showed that there are few items with an uncommon discrepancy between the performance of black and white students, and most of them are items that are exceptionally difficult for both races, so that scores on them are especially affected by guessing or omissions. Coffman (1964) summarizes a number of studies of bias at the item level and indicates how significant findings lead to changes in the procedures for developing tests.

One group of exploratory studies of non-English-speaking candidates has been directed primarily toward the collection of normative-type information (Howell, 1962; Howell, 1963; Howell, 1964). Such studies are of considerable interest not only because they yield pertinent information about special candidate groups but also because they aid in identifying those candidate groups whose scores should be subjected to further analysis.

A study by Coffman (1963a) evaluated the usefulness of the PSAT as a screening device for African students applying for scholarships at American universities. Large groups of candidates were tested—300 in 1959-60, about 1,000 in 1960-61, and over 3,000 in 1961-62—but only a small number of scholarships were granted—24 the first year, 216 the second year, and 227 in the third year. The fact that the award winners were dispersed among more than 100 colleges hampered an evaluation of the test. It was noted, however, that relatively few students had academic problems. It was possible to locate 60 pairs of students, both members of each pair having entered a similar program at the same college. In the subset of students for whom SAT-verbal scores and grades were available, the higher-scoring student had received higher grades in 28 cases and lower grades in 25—a chance difference. In the subset of students for whom SAT-mathematical scores and grades were available, the higher-scoring student had received higher grades in 33 cases and lower grades in 15 cases. This latter difference was significant at the five percent level indicating that the SAT-mathematical score had predictive validity beyond that used in placement.

In addition to studies like those already carried out, other types of studies are needed—for example, studies aimed at determining how an obtained score should be adjusted before making academic predictions for persons with different language backgrounds who are applying to American colleges.

A somewhat different question in the area of cultural differences concerns the value of the SAT for prediction in institutions in other countries and cultures. (Note that this question does not concern itself with the interpretation of SAT scores for members of different cultures applying to American institutions and competing with American students.) A study of the effectiveness of the SAT in selective secondary schools in England provided some limited evidence on this point (Fremer, Coffman, and Taylor, 1968). Results of this analysis suggested that the SAT did yield reliable measurement for the British groups. Some items were relatively more difficult and others relatively less difficult for the British students than for American candidates; at the same time, it turned out that the British students on the whole performed very well on the SAT. Further, the SAT appeared to be an effective predictor both of rank-in-class and of grades on essay examinations. These results, of course, permit no broad generalizations on the relative performance of British and American students nor do they tell anything about the relevance of the SAT for British students seeking admission to American universities. What they do indicate is that the SAT can have considerable value in quite a different setting from that for which it was devised.

SAT *scores at the extremes of the score range*

Problems of measurement at the extremes of the SAT score scale were considered briefly in this chapter in connection with the summary of the Multi-Level study. There, an experiment involving a two-level test system was described. Such a system, it will be recalled, offered only a negligible advantage from the standpoint of validity or reliability. A number of questions on the subject of testing at the extremes were beyond the scope of the Multi-Level study. This section, therefore, will look at some of these other questions bearing on the effectiveness of the SAT for students with extremely low or extremely high scores.

Extreme lows—The properties of so-called below-chance scores have been the subject of considerable attention. (When formula scoring is used, as with College Board tests, the expected value of a chance score is zero and below-chance scores are taken to be negative.) On theoretical grounds, the interpretation of such scores is somewhat perplexing. For example, Cliff (1958, p. 615) makes the point that the psychologist who must interpret individuals' scores may decide to ignore score differences near the chance level since such differences are frequently due solely to lucky or unlucky guessing or to massive omissions. This point is consistent with Gulliksen's suggestion that one should not interpret a score that is within one or two standard deviations of a chance score as signifying any knowledge of the subject matter of the examination (Gulliksen, 1950, p. 263). On the other hand, Levine and Lord have made the point that "Negative scores are bound to have some discriminating power, if only because an examinee whose true score is +10, say, is less likely to obtain an actual score of −3 than is an examinee whose true score is +1." (Levine and Lord, 1958, p. 7.) Levine and Lord have also pointed out other factors that might lead a student to obtain negative scores. For example, because of careful test construction, distractors may consistently appear to a misinformed student to be more plausible than the correct answer. Also, negative scores may represent a lack of test sophistication rather than unlucky guessing.

Several studies of the discriminating power of negative scores will be cited here. Levine and Lord (1958) carried out a study in which they evaluated a new discrimination index that was designed to measure a test's effectiveness at different score levels. This study involved the administration of two tests to the same group of examinees: the first test was a relatively difficult one on which many examinees obtained negative scores; the second was at about average difficulty for the group. When checked against the second test, the difficult test did show discrimination in the negative score range. In fact, no appreciable difference was found between the discrimination in the negative score range and that for the rest of the score range.

Cliff's study of chance-level scores yielded somewhat less clear-cut results (Cliff, 1958). In this study students were given SCAT and an equating test closely similar to SCAT. On the basis of SCAT scores, the group was divided into chance-level and above-chance-level subgroups, and the regression of the equating test on SCAT was determined for each subgroup. As Cliff points out, "If scores at, or below, the average chance score represented the performance of students with no knowledge of the subject matter, who were merely marking alternative responses at random, one would not expect these scores to relate to anything." (Cliff, 1958, p. 613.) As it happened, results were not consistent for the college-level and high school-level SCAT. On the college-level subtests, the regressions for the chance-level groups were significantly different from zero and did *not* differ significantly from those of the above-chance-level groups. However, for the high school subtests, the regressions for the chance-level groups were not significantly different from zero. In other words, chance scores on the college-level SCAT were predictive of performance on an independent measure, but chance scores on the high school SCAT were not.

Angoff (1964) reanalyzed data from the Multi-Level study in order to examine the properties of chance-level scores. Specifically, the reanalysis involved the regression of the narrow-range low difficulty test on the broad-range test. As it turned out, the regression was less steep at the lower end of the score scale. Interpreted at face value, this finding would suggest that negative scores were not as discriminating as other scores; differences among examinees who score in the "chance" region may be smaller and presumably less dependable than are the differences among examinees who score in the non-chance region. As Angoff makes clear, however, the interpretation of these results is not without complication. One good possibility, for example, is that the findings simply reflect the "floor" effect on the criterion test; that is, the floor on the criterion might be so high that it obscures discrimination among low-scoring examinees. If such were the case, the obtained results would not be considered relevant in demonstrating the validity—or lack of validity—of chance scores.

Boldt (1968) used data from the May 1964 administration of the SAT to carry out his "Study of Linearity and Homoscedasticity of Test Scores in the Chance Range." Pretest data for SAT-V and SAT-M were used to rank the items in these tests for difficulty. Broad-range subtests were defined as those items with odd ranks, yielding a 45-item verbal test and a 30-item mathematics test. Difficult subtests were defined as those even-ranked items with item difficulties lower than .40, yielding a 19-item verbal test and a 16-item mathematics test. The 103,275 answer sheets stored on magnetic tape were then rescored for the broad-range and difficult subtests, using formula scoring (R-W/4) and defining chance scores as negative or zero formula scores. Scatterplots of the scores on the difficult and broad-range tests were prepared for both the verbal and the mathematics tests. The variances of the arrays of broad-range subtest scores for each level of the difficult subtest score were tested for equality, and the hypotheses of homoscedasticity (equal-variance) were rejected. Array variances increased from higher negative to lower negative and low positive scores, then de-

creased toward higher positive scores, indicating more accurate prediction from the very low (high negative) and very high scores on the difficult test and less accurate prediction in the vicinity of zero formula scores.

Despite the statistically significant findings indicating nonlinearity of the regression of the broad-range test on the difficult test, Boldt (1968, p. 7) concludes that ". . . over-all linear relationships can be expected to hold in general except for slight erratic fluctuations and a minor bending at the extremes." This general linearity even in the chance region suggests that the scores in the so-called chance range do not stem from random processes. Each successive score on the difficult test is associated with a higher mean on the broad-range test. This basic linearity definitely does not hold for the regression of the difficult test on the broad-range test, in which case a systematic curve throughout the test range is observed. The part of this curve that lies in the chance score region is quite flat, indicating that chance-level scores on the broad-range test would not have much value for predicting scores on the difficult test. Perhaps this finding can be attributed to the fact that students who score very poorly on a test that contains some reasonably easy items are not able enough to be misled by carefully selected distracters on difficult items.

Hills and Gladney (1968) investigated the usefulness of below-chance SAT scores in predicting college grades. Test and grade data were obtained from 667 students who entered three predominantly Negro public colleges in Georgia in the fall quarter of 1966. These students had means and standard deviations of 274 and 54, respectively, in SAT-verbal and 305 and 53, respectively, in SAT-mathematical. It was possible to determine conveniently for 601 students the formula score corresponding to their College Board scaled score and to define for each test four groups for subsequent analysis:

Group 1. Students scoring below chance level on the test

Group 2. Students scoring immediately above chance level. Group 2 was chosen to be equal in size to Group 1 with the same number of students taken from each of the three colleges

Group 3. Students scoring at the top level of the test. Group 3 was chosen to be equal in size to Groups 1 and 2 and with the same number of students from each of the three colleges

Group 4. All students scoring above chance level on the test

The correlations between test scores and grades were obtained for each of the four groups and adjustments for restriction of range were applied to the correlations to estimate the (already-known) correlations for the total group. The estimates of the correlations between test scores and grades for the total group that were obtained from the below-chance-level and immediately above-chance-level groups were seriously in error, being large and negative in some cases (−.51, −.52, −.81, for example), while the population values were all substantial and positive (+.31 to +.50). The estimates obtained from the high-scoring group and from the total-above-chance group proved to be generally sound ones. The exceedingly small standard deviations of scores for the chance and near-chance groups, relative to those for the total group, led to very large and therefore highly inaccurate adjustments. The authors report that scatterplots of grades and scores were generally linear even in the chance region. They did not show a pattern of flatness in the chance region followed by a rising line above chance, such as one might expect if the chance scores resulted from random test-taking behavior. Tests of the similarity among the standard errors of estimate and among the slopes and intercepts of the regression lines for the various samples showed no significant differences, leading the authors to the conclusion that chance-level test scores are not significantly different in their prediction of college grades from above-chance test scores (Hills and Gladney, 1968). It would appear, then, on the basis of the combined evidence of the various studies summarized here, that chance-level scores do not behave much differently from above-chance-level scores, especially in the prediction of an adequate criterion.

Superior Students—It is sometimes claimed that the very nature of most objective tests is such that the unusually brilliant, imaginative, or perceptive student is disadvantaged by the test and may, in fact, earn lower scores than his less able fellows. If true, this point would raise an overwhelmingly important issue because of the special concern to identify—and most certainly not to overlook—the truly superior student. As Angoff puts it, the obvious question is "Can the SAT, constructed as it is for a diverse and heterogenous population, also do justice to a narrow band of highly able candidates?" (Angoff, 1965, p. 2.)

Summaries of pertinent research on this problem are available in the articles "The College Board SAT and the Superior Student" (Angoff, 1965) and "Are Aptitude Tests Valid for the Highly Able?" (Chauncey and Hilton, 1965.)

One question that has been investigated concerns the relative effectiveness of a narrow-range, high-level test as compared with the broad-range tests now in use. (See discussion of the Multi-Level study on pages 155-156.) It will be recalled that while the narrow-range test did provide somewhat better discrimination, the advantages appeared negligible when viewed in the light of problems inherent in a multi-level testing situation (Angoff and Huddleston, 1958).

Another approach to this question involves analysis at the item level; that is, performance on individual items is investigated to determine whether or not each item may be considered "unfair" to the superior student. An item analysis of this type, based on more than 100,000 candidates, was undertaken for the May 1964 SAT (Lord, 1965). In this analysis, Lord determined for each item the percentage of people at various levels of ability who answered the item correctly; for this analysis, "ability" was defined as total score across all items on the test except the item under consideration. Plots of percent correct versus ability level were then checked for irregularities at the upper end of the scale. For the 90 verbal items and the 60 mathematical items in this analysis, no important irregularity was observed. Thus, the analysis did *not* support the view that the brightest students were disadvantaged as compared with the less able students. Of course, the absence of evidence of irregularities for the items in this one form of the SAT is no guarantee that such irregularities *never* occur. On the other hand, in view of the evidence of parallelism for different forms of the SAT, it seems safe to conclude that such irregularities would occur only rarely.

As Angoff points out, there may be a logical weakness in an item-study design such as Lord's that casts doubt on the meaning of the results. If the total score is indeed biased toward the mediocre student, then the monotonic relationship of the items with total score does little more than demonstrate the internal consistency of the test (Angoff, 1965). To escape from this logical circle, then, it is necessary to know the relationship of the total test score to some valid criterion outside the test, such as academic record. If total test score shows the same degree of relationship to the criterion at the high end of the score scale as at the low end, the test as a whole would presumably not be considered biased against the superior student. Chauncey and Hilton (1965) and Angoff (1965) report on a study by Whitla that bears on this point. Whitla found that the relationship of SAT scores to grades earned at Harvard was no different for the highest levels of ability than for intermediate levels; that is, the relationships between test scores and grades were linear throughout the range. The fact that there is no "dip" at the upper end makes it seem unlikely that the superior student is at a particular disadvantage on total SAT score relative to performance in college. Thus, Whitla's results, which support the validity of the *total* score for superior students, point up the importance of Lord's results on the properties of individual test items.

Curriculum change and diversity

Each year hundreds of thousands of secondary school students take various College Board Achievement Tests. These students represent all parts of the United States and indeed all parts of the world. Some students use quite modern textbooks and study under teachers who are in close contact with the very latest curriculum innovations. Other students use traditional textbooks and study under teachers who have, at most, marginal contact with curricular changes occurring over the past several years. There have always been differences in approach and emphasis within the subject-matter areas, but the post-Sputnik era has been an era of especially widespread and dramatic change. The National Science Foundation, for example, has sponsored new secondary school science and mathematics courses that have had a great impact on schools.

In spite of the diversity of course offerings within subject matter areas, all students of a particular subject usually take a common examination. The question that naturally arises is: How could this one examination be equally appropriate for all students, given the diversity of backgrounds among the group of students taking any one test?

The problem of preparing achievement tests for heterogeneous groups is not a new one, nor is it one that is peculiar to the College Board. It is, moreover, analogous to the problem of developing aptitude tests that are to be used with heterogeneous groups. Efforts to deal with the problem have resulted in a set of standard operational studies that follow certain established procedures. Although these procedures have already been summarized in Chapter III, an additional review is offered here in the context of a discussion of the appropriateness of the Biology, Chemistry, and Physics Achievement Tests for students from various curriculums. A number of comparisons were made between the scores on a given science Achievement Test of two groups of students following two different curriculums who were equally able in terms of science ability as specially defined and measured, and in terms of scholastic aptitude as measured by the College Board SAT. Each analysis employed, as a measure of the particular science ability, a collection of about 25 questions on the relevant test judged by about 10 teachers of relevant courses to be highly appropriate for their students. These questions provide a measure of science ability that could reasonably be assumed to be free of curricular bias.

Scores on the Achievement Test were subjected to an analysis of covariance, using as control variables scores on the SAT and questions in the Achievement Test that were judged appropriate for both groups. The covariance analysis yielded the mean scores on the complete Achievement Test to be expected of two groups of students equal in ability (as defined), but who had studied different courses.

A large number of such analyses were carried out starting in 1962, and plans called for such studies to continue until it was no longer possible to distinguish subgroups with different curricular emphases. The 12 differences in expected mean scores resulting from the analyses of test editions given in 1966 are particularly worthy of note. Four of the differences were statistically significant at the .05 level; eight were not. Six of the differences were positive and hence indicated a bias against students of the more traditional curriculums; six of the differences were negative and hence indicated a bias against students of the newer curriculums. Since the differences were small (11 points or less on the College Board scale), since only a third of the differences were statistically significant, and since the differences

did not consistently favor one type of curriculum over another (half of the differences favored the newer curriculums and half favored the more traditional curriculums), it was concluded that the three 1966 science Achievement Tests as a whole were not markedly biased toward students of the more traditional and against students of the newer curriculums in high school science, or vice versa.

Impact of new physics curriculums

The development of a new physics course by the Physical Science Study Committee had an immediate effect on the College Board's Achievement Testing program. Ferris (1962, p. 113-114) reports that, "Those of us who had been involved in the development of the PSSC course were convinced that its content was so different from that of traditionally taught physics courses at the high school level that students electing to take the College Board Physics Achievement Test would be at a distinct disadvantage because of differences in emphasis and substantive course content." Accordingly the College Board authorized a study of the performance of PSSC students on the Physics Test.

In March 1958 the first group of PSSC students took a conventional College Board Achievement Test in Physics. This group received lower scores than would have been predicted from their scores on the SAT. The inference was made that the conventional College Board Physics Achievement Test was not an adequate measure of achievement in a PSSC physics course. The Board's committee on examinations then authorized the construction of a special PSSC Physics Achievement Test. The PSSC Physics Tests were constructed and offered in March of 1959, 1960, and 1961. Some indication can be obtained from Ferris' (1960) article ,"Testing for Physics Achievement," of the principles and practices employed in the development of a physics test for a Physical Sciences Study Committee Physics course.

The PSSC Physics Tests provided psychometrically adequate measures of achievement in PSSC courses but these tests raised two new problems. One problem was that of the comparability of scores from the PSSC and the conventional physics tests. The other problem was that of confusion, causing students to take the inappropriate examination. In order to eliminate the problems related to the separate test situation, the College Board Committee of Examiners in Physics determined to prepare a single test that would be appropriate for students in both the PSSC and conventional courses.

Fornoff (1962) discusses the steps taken by the Committee of Examiners in Physics in developing a single physics test for both physics courses. The Physics Test had been evolving steadily, before the PSSC curriculum was introduced, in the direction of increased emphasis on ". . . questions which not only asked about important physics concepts but also attempted to evaluate students' mastery of important science abilities: the ability to identify the key question in a problem situation, the ability to screen hypotheses, the ability to select appropriate experimental procedures, and the ability to draw justified conclusions . . ." (Fornoff, 1962, p. 19.) The committee members proceeded to accelerate this evolutionary pattern by writing sets of questions based on some situations involving concepts taught in all physics courses and other situations involving concepts less widely taught. The situations for less familiar concepts contained enough information to allow able physics students to answer the questions. A total of 160 items were tried out in 20 secondary schools, half of them teaching conventional physics and half PSSC courses. An experimental test of 65 items was assembled using the pretest results to obtain questions of about the same difficulty for students in both courses. In order to obtain a large enough group of items, some questions were included that were more difficult for one group, but these were balanced by other items more difficult for the second group.

The 65-item experimental physics test was given in 30 schools shortly after the March 1960 administration of the College Board tests. Half of the schools offered conventional physics courses and the other half PSSC courses. The results from this experimental administration indicated that the single physics test was appropriate in content and difficulty level for both groups of students. Comparisons were made of the scores of students who took the experimental test and either the conventional or the PSSC College Board Physics Test in March 1960. High correlations were obtained between scores on the conventional test and the experimental test and between scores on the PSSC test and the experimental test.

Separate correlations were also obtained for each school between scores on the experimental test or one of the College Board Physics Tests and scores on midterm examinations given by the schools. All three tests proved to be equally effective as predictors of midterm grades, and the coefficients obtained were as high as those reported for other physics tests in current use. These correlations confirmed the committee members' judgments that the experimental test would be as appropriate a measure of the type of achievement they considered important in high school physics as the existing College Board Physics Tests.

In an additional analysis of the experimental physics test, also reported in Fornoff (1962), the experimental physics test was reprinted with a new name, Science Aptitude Test, and administered to a group of 300 chemistry students who had not taken physics. The mean score of 300 physics students from comparable schools was considerably higher than the mean score of the chemistry students, indicating that the experimental test measured something more than general science aptitude.

Different cognitive approaches

Heath (1964) reports on a study of the relationship between physics curriculums and performance on various tests, using data collected during the 1961-62 school year. Thirty randomly selected PSSC teachers and 49 control teachers formed two cluster samples for Heath's study. Each cluster was comprised of students taught by a single teacher. Among the tests that were administered to both the PSSC and the conventional classes were the Cooperative Physics Test, Form Z; the PSSC Special Comprehensive Physics Examination; and Thurstone's Concealed Figures Test (a "cognitive style" test).

A substantial correlation ($r=.55$) was found between scores on the Concealed Figures Test and scores on the PSSC examination for the PSSC group, while no correlation ($r=.01$) was found between scores on these tests for the conventionally taught group. The correlations between the Concealed Figures Test and the Cooperative Physics Test were .60 for the PSSC group and .37 for the conventionally taught group. Although the correlations found by Heath must be interpreted with caution (since they represent the relationship between class means rather than between individual scores), there are, apparently, real differences between the groups in these correlations that may have implications for those who construct and those who use achievement tests in physics. One question that arises is whether a single test like the Cooperative Physics Test, or any test that failed to respond to the objectives of both curriculums, would be appropriate for comparing the performance of these two groups. The continuing attention of the College Board and ETS to the absolute and relative performance of candidates from different curriculums on the College Board Physics Test is witness to the concern that continues in this area and is reflected in the program of continuing studies described in the section on curriculum bias in Chapter III. In addition to regularly conducted analyses of covariance that are based on the test results for students from the various curriculum approaches, separate item analyses are carried out for each new form of each science Achievement Test to provide feedback for the professional test development staff members and ultimately for the committees of content specialists who generate and review test specifications and items.

Achievement in chemistry

A group of chemists organized under the name of the Chemical Bond Approach Project (CBA) worked with teachers of chemistry at the high school and college level in producing a new high school chemistry course which was introduced in 1959. In September 1960 a second new high school chemistry course was introduced, developed by the Chemical Education Material Study (CHEM Study). Ferris (1961) notes that a short

Table 6.1

Relative achievement of the CBA, CHEM, and
control groups on three tests in chemistry

	No. of classes	Mean score on SCAT	Mean score on Cooperative Chemistry Test	Mean score on final test designed for each study
CHEM Study Group	87	37.0	31.9	25.7 (CHEM Study Final)
Control Group A for CHEM	30	37.0	37.7	13.1 (CHEM Study Final)
CBA Group	69	38.0	34.3	25.8 (CBA Final)
Control Group B for CBA	55	37.9	38.1	15.6 (CBA Final)

scholastic aptitude test given to all CHEM Study students before they took their first course achievement test indicated that about three-fourths of the CHEM Study students were above the 75th percentile for the twelfth grade national norms group. The remaining one-fourth of the students ranged down to somewhat below the mean. The CHEM Study group was clearly composed of quite able students. Achievement testing during 1961-62 indicated that both CHEM Study and CBA students were attaining course objectives reasonably well. An answer was sought, however, to the question of the relative performance of students from the new courses on the content of the traditional course. Consequently, in a study conducted by Heath and Stickell (1963) a sample of teachers from the CHEM Study courses, from the CBA courses, and from control (conventional) courses were asked to participate in a research study. All students took SCAT at the beginning of the school year and two specified course examinations near the end of the year. CBA and CHEM Study students took their own course examination and an examination from a conventional course. Students in two control groups took their own course examination and either a CHEM Study or a CBA examination. The results of this testing are summarized in Table 6.1, taken from Heath and Stickell (1963).

Since there was almost no difference between the groups on the SCAT scores, analysis of covariance was not deemed necessary, and direct comparison of unadjusted criterion scores was made. The CBA and CHEM Study groups scored significantly higher on the test designed for their courses and significantly lower on the test designed for traditional courses than corresponding control groups matched on geographic region, community size, and sex of teacher. Heath and Stickell note the clear evidence for a difference in course content

across the three curriculum approaches but point out that their results are only a first approach to assessment of the high school chemistry curriculum.

Culver Military Academy: A case study

A dramatic example of the problem of evaluating achievement test scores earned by groups following new curriculum approaches is available in a report by Stickell (1965) on the performance of Culver Military Academy students on the College Board Chemistry Achievement Test. Culver Military Academy introduced CHEM Study in all chemistry courses in the fall of 1961. At the May 1962 administration of the College Board Chemistry Test the Culver students attained a mean score of 481, which represented a drop of 72 points from the mean score of 553 attained by Culver chemistry students at the previous May administration in 1961. A study, initiated by ETS in cooperation with Culver Academy, involved an examination of the relative performance of Culver Academy students during the period 1960-63 on the verbal and mathematical sections of the SAT, the College Board Chemistry Achievement Test, and the College Board English Composition Test. After adjusting for differences on verbal and mathematical scores, a significant increase in Chemistry Achievement Test scores was found between 1960 and 1961 (both traditional years), and between 1962 and 1963 (both CHEM Study years), while a significant decrease was found between the combined 1960 and 1961 means and the combined 1962 and 1963 means. No changes were observed in the adjusted means for the English Composition Test over the four-year period.

The data for differences among students from different curriculum approaches on the Chemistry Achievement Test showed that the amount of disadvantage for the CHEM Study group was about 40 points at the time (1961-62) the Culver Academy students switched to the new curriculum. As Stickell points out in his report, the decrease in test scores from the time that chemistry was taught conventionally to the time that CHEM Study was introduced could have been due to the inadequate representation of CHEM Study material in the test. On the other hand, it may just as well have been due to the newness of the course and to the fact that it may not have been taught effectively at the outset.

A look ahead

It seems appropriate, during this time when there are major upheavals in educational philosophy and practice, to look to the future when there will be additional developments on the American social and educational scene. Some of these developments will represent minor changes with limited impact. Others will be major ones that will have a wide and lasting influence. In order to keep abreast of these developments and to maintain the role of the College Board tests as a principal instrument of access to higher education, the Board will continue to expand and revise its testing programs in both the aptitude and the achievement areas. The possibility that particular subgroups of students may be disadvantaged by the format and content of College Board tests will always be under consideration. Special studies will continue to be conducted, each designed to answer a question of importance to the educational community and each enlisting the resources of the educational community. The types of studies summarized in this chapter can be considered models for the kinds of studies that will be needed in the future.

REFERENCES

Abelson, R. P., *Sex Differences in Predictability of College Grades.* Research Bulletin 51-8. Princeton, N.J.: Educational Testing Service, 1951.

Anastasi, Anne; Meade, M. J.; and Schneiders, A. A., *The Validation of a Biographical Inventory as a Predictor of College Success.* College Entrance Examination Board Research Monograph No. 1, 1960.

Angoff, W. H., *The Validity of Negative Scores on the Scholastic Aptitude Test.* Princeton, N.J.: Educational Testing Service, 1964. (Multilithed report)

Angoff, W. H., "The College Board SAT and the Superior Student." *The Superior Student,* Vol. 7, No. 2, 1965, pp. 10-15.

Angoff, W. H., and Huddleston, E. M., *The Multi-level Experiment: A Study of a Two-level Test System for the College Board Scholastic Aptitude Test.* College Entrance Examination Board Research and Development Reports, and Statistical Report 58-21. Princeton, N.J.: Educational Testing Service, 1958.

Boldt, R. F., "Study of Linearity and Homoscedasticity of Test Scores in the Chance Range." *Educational and Psychological Measurement,* 1968, 28, pp. 47-60.

Brigham, C. C., *A Study of Error.* New York: College Entrance Examination Board, 1932.

Cardall, Carolyn, and Coffman, W. E., *A Method for Comparing the Performance of Different Groups on the Items in a Test.* College Entrance Examination Board Research and Development Report 64-5, No. 9. Princeton, N.J.: Educational Testing Service, 1964.

Chauncey, H., and Hilton, T. L., "Are Aptitude Tests Valid for the Highly Able?" *Science,* 1965, 148, pp. 1297-1304.

Cleary, T. Anne, "Test Bias: Prediction of Grades of Negro and White Students in Integrated Colleges." *Journal of Educational Measurement,* 1968, 5, pp. 115-124.

Cleary, T. Anne, and Hilton, T. L., "An Investigation of Item Bias." *Educational and Psychological Measurement,* 1968, 28, pp. 61-75.

Cleary, T. Anne; Linn, R. L.: and Rock, D. A., "An Exploratory Study of Programmed Tests." *Educational and Psychological Measurement,* 1968, 38, pp. 345-360. (a)

Cleary, T. Anne; Linn, R. L.; and Rock, D. A., "Reproduction of Total Test Score Through the Use of Sequential Programmed Tests." *Journal of Educational Measurement,* 1968, 5, pp. 183-187. (b)

Cliff, Rosemary, "The Predictive Value of Chance-level Scores." *Educational and Psychological Measurement,* 1958, 18, pp. 607-616.

Cliff, Rosemary, and Cliff, N., *Formulating Hypotheses: Factor Structure and Validity Data.* College Entrance Examination Board Research and Development Report 63-4, No. 2. Princeton, N.J.: Educational Testing Service, 1963.

Coffman, W. E., "The Tests of Developed Abilities—Development of the Tests." *College Board Review* No. 31, 1957, pp. 6-10.

Coffman, W. E., "Sex Differences in Responses to Items in an Aptitude Test." Eighteenth Yearbook, National Council on Measurement in Education, 1961, pp. 117-124.

Coffman, W. E., "Evidence of Cultural Factors in Responses of African Students to Items in an American Test of Scholastic Aptitude." Twentieth Yearbook, National Council on Measurement in Education, 1963, pp. 27-37. (a)

Coffman, W. E., *The Scholastic Aptitude Test—1926-1962.* College Entrance Examination Board Research and Development Reports, and Test Development Report 63-2. Princeton, N.J.: Educational Testing Service, 1963. (b)

Coffman, W. E., "Principles of Developing Tests for the Culturally Different." *Proceedings of the 1964 Invitational*

Conference on Testing Problems. Princeton, N.J.: Educational Testing Service, 1964.

Coffman, W. E., and Parry, Mary Ellen, "Effects of an Accelerated Reading Course on SAT-V Scores." *Personnel and Guidance Journal*, 1967, 46, pp. 292-296.

Coleman, J. S., and others, *Equality of Educational Opportunity.* Washington, D.C.: U.S. Office of Education, 1966.

College Entrance Examination Board, "The GCT Experiment: Final Report." *College Board Review* No. 29, 1956, pp. 31-32.

College Entrance Examination Board, "A Statement by the College Board Trustees on Test Coaching." *College Board Review* No. 38, 1959, p. 3.

College Entrance Examination Board, *Effects of Coaching on Scholastic Aptitude Test Scores.* New York: College Entrance Examination Board, 1965. (a)

College Entrance Examination Board, *Interpreting the SAT Scores of Educationally Disadvantaged Students.* New York: College Entrance Examination Board, 1965. (b)

College Entrance Examination Board, *College Board Score Reports.* New York: College Entrance Examination Board, 1968.

Dyer, H. S., "Does Coaching Help?" *College Board Review* No. 19, 1953, pp. 331-335.

Dyer, H. S., "The Tests of Developed Abilities—The Tests' Background." *College Board Review* No. 31, 1957, pp. 5-6.

Ekstrom, Ruth B., *Use of the College Board Writing Sample.* College Entrance Examination Board Research and Development Reports, and Research Bulletin 62-1. Princeton, N.J.: Educational Testing Service, 1962.

Ekstrom, Ruth B., *Colleges' Use and Evaluation of the College Board Writing Sample.* College Entrance Examination Board Research and Development Report 63-4, No. 5. Princeton, N.J.: Educational Testing Service, 1964.

Ferris, F. L., Jr., "Testing for Physics Achievement." *American Journal of Physics*, 1960, 28, pp. 269-278.

Ferris, F. L., Jr., "The Role of Testing in Evaluation of the CHEM Study." *Chemical Education Material Study Newsletter*, 1961, 1 (2), p. 1.

Ferris, F. L., Jr., "Testing in the New Curriculums: Numerology, 'Tyranny,' or Common Sense?" *School Review*, 1962, 70, pp. 112-131.

Flaugher, R. L., and Rock, D. A., *The Wide Range Validity of Certain New Aptitude Tests.* College Entrance Examination Board Research and Development Report 66-7, No. 8. Princeton, N.J.: Educational Testing Service, 1966.

Fornoff, F. J., "Developing the New Physics Test." *College Board Review* No. 46, 1962, pp. 19-21.

Frankel, E., "Effects of Growth, Practice, and Coaching on Scholastic Aptitude Test Scores." *Personnel and Guidance Journal*, 1960, 38, pp. 713-719.

Frederiksen, N., *Development of the Test "Formulating Hypotheses": A Progress Report.* Princeton, N.J.: Educational Testing Service, 1959.

Fremer, J.; Coffman, W. E.; and Taylor, P. H., "The College Board Scholastic Aptitude Test as a Predictor of Academic Achievement in Secondary Schools in England." *Journal of Educational Measurement*, 1968, 5, pp. 235-241.

French, J. W., *Opinion on the Proposed Change to a Two-day Schedule.* Princeton, N.J.: Educational Testing Service, March 1947. (Multilithed report)

French, J. W., *The Replies of Teachers of English to a Questionnaire on Essay Testing.* Research Bulletin 56-3. Princeton, N.J.: Educational Testing Service, 1956. (a)

French, J. W., *The Effect of Essay Tests on Student Motivation.* Research Bulletin 56-4. Princeton, N.J.: Educational Testing Service, 1956. (b)

French, J. W., *Validation of the SAT and New Item Types Against Four-year Academic Criteria.* Research Bulletin 57-4. Princeton, N.J.: Educational Testing Service, 1957.

French, J. W., "Schools of Thought in Judging Excellence of English Themes." *Proceedings of the 1961 Invitational Conference on Testing Problems.* Princeton, N.J.: Educational Testing Service, 1962, pp. 19-28. (a)

French, J. W., "Effect of Anxiety on Verbal and Mathematical Examination Scores." *Educational and Psychological Measurement*, 1962, 22, pp. 553-564. (b)

French, J. W., *The Revision of the Interest Index.* College Entrance Examination Board Research and Development Report 64-5, No. 5. Princeton, N.J.: Educational Testing Service, 1964. (a)

French, J. W., "New Tests for Predicting the Performance of College Students with High-level Aptitude." *Journal of Educational Psychology*, 1964, 55, pp. 185-194. (b)

French, J. W., and Dear, R. E., "Effect of Coaching on an Aptitude Test." *Educational and Psychological Measurement*, 1959, 19, pp. 319-330.

Godshalk, Frances I.; Swineford, F.; and Coffman, W. E., *The Measurement of Writing Ability.* College Entrance Examination Board Research Monograph No. 6. New York: College Entrance Examination Board, 1966.

Gulliksen, H., *Theory of Mental Tests.* New York: John Wiley & Sons, Inc., 1950.

Halpern, G., *Scale Properties of the Interest Index.* College Entrance Examination Board Research and Development Report 65-6, No. 5. Princeton, N.J.: Educational Testing Service, 1965.

Heath, R. W., "Comparison of Achievement in Two Physics Courses." *Journal of Experimental Education*, 1964, 32, pp. 347-354.

Heath, R. W., and Stickell, D. W., "CHEM and CBA Effects on Achievement in Chemistry." *Science Teacher*, 1963, 30, pp. 45-46.

Hills, J. R.; Klock, J. A.; and Bush, Marilyn L., *Freshman norms for the University System of Georgia, 1963-64.* Atlanta, Ga.: Office of Testing and Guidance, Regents of the University System of Georgia, 1965.

Hills, J. R., and Gladney, Marilyn B., "Predicting Grades from Below Chance Test Scores." *Journal of Educational Measurement*, 1968, 5, pp. 45-53.

Howell, J. J., *An Illustrative Study of Foreign Candidates for College Board Examinations.* Research Memorandum 62-9. Princeton, N.J.: Educational Testing Service, 1962.

Howell, J. J., *Language Background of Candidates for College*

Board Examinations Tested at Foreign Centers. College Entrance Examination Board Research and Development Report 63-4, No. 1. Princeton, N.J.: Educational Testing Service, 1963.

Howell, J. J., College Board Scores of Candidates of Non-English Language Background Tested at Foreign Centers. College Entrance Examination Board Research and Development Report 64-5, No. 2. Princeton, N.J.: Educational Testing Service, 1964.

Huddleston, Edith M., "Measurement of Writing Ability at the College-entrance Level: Objective versus Subjective Testing Techniques." Journal of Experimental Education, 1954, 22, pp. 165-213.

Jacobs, P. I., "Large Score Changes on the Scholastic Aptitude Test." Personnel and Guidance Journal, 1966, 45, pp. 150-156.

Karas, S. F.; Relles, Barbara S.; and Watkins, R. W., Change in Scholastic Aptitude Test Scores of Candidates Tested in the Junior and Senior Years 1960-63. College Entrance Examination Board Research and Development Reports, and Statistical Report 63-27. Princeton, N.J.: Educational Testing Service, 1963.

Kendrick, S. A., "When SAT Scores Go Down." College Board Review No. 64, 1967, pp. 4-11.

Levine, R. S., and Angoff, W. H., The Effects of Practice and Growth on Scores on the Scholastic Aptitude Test. Statistical Report 58-6. Princeton, N.J.: Educational Testing Service, 1958.

Levine, R. S., and Lord, F. M., An Index of the Discriminating Power of a Test at Different Parts of the Score Range. Research Bulletin 58-13. Princeton, N.J.: Educational Testing Service, 1958.

Linn, R. L.; Rock, D. A.; and Cleary, T. Anne, The Development and Evaluation of Several Programmed Testing Methods. Research Bulletin 68-5. Princeton, N.J.: Educational Testing Service, 1968.

Lord, F. M., "An Empirical Study of Item-test Regression." Psychometrika, 1965, 30, pp. 373-376.

Loret, P. G., A History of the Content of the Scholastic Aptitude Test. College Entrance Examination Board Research and Development Reports, and Test Development Memorandum 60-1. Princeton, N.J.: Educational Testing Service, 1960.

Myers, A. E.; McConville, Carolyn B.; and Coffman, W. E., Reliability of Reading of the College Board English Composition Test, December 1963. College Entrance Examination Board Research and Development Report 64-5, No. 3. Princeton, N.J.: Educational Testing Service, 1964.

Olsen, Marjorie, The Validity of the College Board General Composition Test. Statistical Report 55-4. Princeton, N.J.: Educational Testing Service, 1955.

Olsen, Marjorie, Summary of Main Findings on the Validity of the 1955 College Board General Composition Test. Statistical Report 56-9. Princeton, N.J.: Educational Testing Service, 1956.

Olsen, Marjorie, "The Multi-level Experiment: II. Comparative Validities of Broad-range and Narrow-range Tests." American Psychologist, 1959, 14, 401. (Abstract)

Olsen, Marjorie, Summary of Main Findings on the Validity of the College Entrance Examination Board Tests of Developed Ability as Predictors of College Grades. Statistical Report 57-41. Princeton, N.J.: Educational Testing Service, 1957.

Olsen, Marjorie, and Schrader, W. B., The Use of Preliminary and Final Scholastic Aptitude Test Scores in Predicting College Grades. College Entrance Examination Board Research and Development Reports, and Statistical Report 59-19. Princeton, N.J.: Educational Testing Service, 1959.

Palmer, O., "Sixty Years of English Testing." College Board Review No. 42, 1960, pp. 8-14.

Pearson, R., "Effects of Growth and Retesting on SAT Verbal Scores." College Board Review No. 5, 1948, pp. 57, 68-71.

Pitcher, Barbara, Test-taking Patterns of College Board Candidates Tested in 1962-1964 Based on a Five Percent Sample. Statistical Report 66-72. Princeton, N.J.: Educational Testing Service, 1966.

Pitcher, Barbara, College Entrance Examination Board Candidates and Tests, 1967-68. Princeton, N.J.: Educational Testing Service, 1968.

Potthoff, R. F., Statistical Aspects of the Problem of Biases in Psychological Tests. Institute of Statistics Mimeo Series No. 479. Chapel Hill, N.C.: Department of Statistics, University of North Carolina, May 1966.

Roberts, S. O., and Oppenheim, D. B., The Effect of Special Instruction upon Test Performance of High School Students in Tennessee. College Entrance Examination Board Research and Development Report 66-7, No. 1. Princeton, N.J.: Educational Testing Service, 1966.

Rock, D. A.; Barone, J. L.; and Boldt, R. F., A Two-stage Decision Approach to the Selection Problem. Research Bulletin 68-11. Princeton, N.J.: Educational Testing Service, 1968.

Sarason, S. B.; Davidson, K. S.; Lightball, F. F.; Waite, R. R.; and Ruebush, B. K., Anxiety in Elementary School Children. New York: John Wiley & Sons, Inc., 1960.

Seashore, H. G., "Women Are More Predictable Than Men." Journal of Counseling Psychology, 1962, 9, pp. 261-270.

Smith, E. R., and Tyler, R. W., Appraising and Recording Student Progress, Chapter V. New York: Harper & Row, 1942, pp. 313-348.

Stanley, J. C., "Further Evidence via the Analysis of Variance That Women Are More Predictable Academically Than Men." Ontario Journal of Educational Research, 1967, 10 (a), pp. 49-56.

Stanley, J. C., and Porter, A. C., "Correlation of Scholastic Aptitude Test Scores with College Grades for Negroes versus Whites." Journal of Educational Measurement, 1967, 4, pp. 199-218.

Stickell, D. W., Analysis of Culver Military Academy Data Relating to Performance on the College Board Chemistry Test as Affected by Curricular Change. College Entrance Examination Board Research and Development Report. 64-5, No. 17, and Test Development Report 65-3. Princeton, N.J.: Educational Testing Service, 1965.

Stricker, L. J., and Ross, J., "Intercorrelations and Reliability of the Myers-Briggs Type Indicator Scales." Psychological Reports, 1963, 12, pp. 287-293.

Stricker, L. J.; Schiffman, H.; and Ross, J., "Prediction of College Performance with the Myers-Briggs Type Indicator."*Educational and Psychological Measurement*, 1965, 25, pp. 1081-1095.

Swineford, Frances, *College Entrance Examination Board General Composition Test.* Statistical Report 56-3. Princeton, N.J.: Educational Testing Service, 1956.

Swineford, Frances, *College Entrance Examination Board Reliability of the English Composition Test.* Statistical Report 57-8. Princeton, N.J.: Educational Testing Service, 1957.

Swineford, Frances, and Olsen, Marjorie, *Reliability and Validity of an Interlinear Test of Writing Ability.* Research Bulletin 53-9. Princeton, N.J.: Educational Testing Service, 1953.

Thorndike, R. L., "Reliability," in E. F. Lindquist, ed., *Educational Measurement.* Menasha, Wis.: George Banta Publishing, 1951, pp. 560-620.

Thurstone, L. L., "The Calibration of Test Items." *American Psychologist*, 1947, 2, pp. 103-104.

Tucker, L. R, *Memorandum Concerning Study of Effects of Fatigue on Afternoon Achievement Test Scores due to Scholastic Aptitude Test Being Taken in the Morning.* Research Memorandum 48-2. Princeton, N.J.: Educational Testing Service, 1948.

Watkins, R. W., and Schrader, W. B., *The Relation of Differences between Junior and Senior Scholastic Aptitude Test Scores and College Grades.* College Entrance Examination Board Research and Development Reports, and Statistical Report 63-29. Princeton, N.J.: Educational Testing Service, 1963.

Weiss, Eleanor S., *The Interrelationships and Validities of Item Types in the College Board English Composition Test.* Statistical Report 57-25. Princeton, N.J.: Educational Testing Service, 1957.

Whitla, D. K., "Effect of Tutoring on Scholastic Aptitude Test Scores." *Personnel and Guidance Journal*, 1962, 41, pp. 32-37.

Wohlhueter, J. F., "Fatigue in Testing and Other Mental Tasks: A Literature Survey." Research Memorandum 66-6. Princeton, N.J.: Educational Testing Service, 1966.

22006 • T11P12.5 • 251512